Praise for *Class Warfare*

"As an inside account of the Obama administration's moves to fix schools, *Class Warfare* is superb. . . . Brill's access to key players—the famous and the not-so-famous—allows him to give readers privileged glimpses into various meetings that were seldom reported on but had great impact on the thrust of reform."

—*The Washington Post*

"A deeply reported work on the state of the school reform movement in the United States, written in dense bursts that give color to both policy and people."

—*The Daily Beast*

"Brill's approach resembles Bob Woodward's recent volumes on the real wars of the Bush and Obama eras: plenty of inside scoops, vivid quotes, extensive reportage, evocative vignettes and telling examples, lots of short chapters, a fast-paced narrative, and an ample supply of couldn't-invent-'em characters. . . . It's a rollicking romp . . . it works through many issues, conflicts, interests, episodes, and people and comes to a measured set of conclusions that won't please anyone in particular but deserve serious reflection."

—*The Education Gadfly*

"An in-depth, impeccably researched examination of the education-reform movements that have swept America over the last several decades, as well as the obstacles they've faced. . . . The author tackles this beast of a topic admirably, creating a lucid, often riveting history that will be invaluable to the next generation of reformers."

—*Kirkus Reviews*

"Many parents, even those who are educators, may not be aware of the battles that occur daily in the education world. This is a fascinating look at those struggles and at the people who determine how America's children will be educated. . . . Brill's multilayered account of the education dilemma . . . brings hope that change for the better could be on the horizon."

—*Library Journal*

"A superb book . . . Fun to read."

—*CNNMoney.com*

"His writing is crisp, even breathless at times, with the zeal of a recent convert. His insider stories of the politics of education reform are fascinating."

—*Pittsburgh Post-Gazette*

"Brill's book is one of the most in-depth and closely researched looks into the modern workings of the education 'blob' in recent memory."

—CNN.com

"*Class Warfare* is a gripping account of the fierce combat between reformers and their opponents . . . Brill generally does a remarkable job of weaving the lives and experiences of students, teachers, and officials into a coherent story."

—*Foreign Affairs*

"Within the first few pages I was taking the book everywhere—the supermarket checkout line, the dinner table, the movies. It is funny, exciting, surprising and deep."

—Jay Mathews, *The Washington Post*

"Steven Brill's *Class Warfare* is hard-hitting, illuminating, and as fast-paced and gripping as a thriller. His vivid accounts of great teachers at work—and his play-by-play of the battle to remove the obstacles put in front of them by their own union—changed my outlook about the possibilities for American education. A must-read call to action for all thinking Americans, especially parents."

—Amy Chua, John M. Duff Jr. Professor of Law, Yale University, and author of *Battle Hymn of the Tiger Mother* and *Day of Empire*

"*Class Warfare* inspires! This is a unique and critically important story about true heroes in America who against great odds are making a real difference. More than this, Brill's work sheds important light on the educational disparities faced by low-income communities across the country and through his work he trumpets what should be a call to action by all of us."

—Cory A. Booker, Mayor of Newark, NJ

"An extraordinarily well-researched and compelling account of the tectonic shifts in school politics over the past several years. This is a masterpiece, both as history and as a catalyst for continued change. Far from the usual one-sided account the subject typically engenders, Brill's work is balanced, sophisticated—and, amazingly, a real page-turner."

—Chris Christie, Governor of New Jersey

ALSO BY STEVEN BRILL

After: How America Confronted the September 12 Era
The Teamsters

INSIDE THE FIGHT TO FIX AMERICA'S SCHOOLS

Class
Warfare

Steven Brill

Simon & Schuster Paperbacks
NEW YORK · LONDON · TORONTO · SYDNEY · NEW DELHI

Simon & Schuster Paperbacks
A Division of Simon & Schuster
1230 Avenue of the Americas
New York, NY 10020

First Simon & Schuster paperback edition August 2012

SIMON & SCHUSTER PAPERBACKS and colophon are registered trademarks
of Simon & Schuster, Inc.

For information about special discounts for bulk purchases,
please contact Simon & Schuster Special Sales at
1-866-506-1949 or business@simonandschuster.com.

The Simon & Schuster Speakers Bureau can bring authors
to your live event. For more information or to book an event,
contact the Simon & Schuster Speakers Bureau at
1-866-248-3049 or visit our website at www.simonspeakers.com.

Designed by Akasha Archer

Manufactured in the United States of America

1   3   5   7   9   10   8   6   4   2

The Library of Congress has cataloged the hardcover edition as follows:

Brill, Steven, 1950–
Class warfare : inside the fight to fix America's schools / by Steven Brill.
p.   cm.
1. Public schools—United States.   2. School improvement programs—
United States.   3. Education and state—United States.   I. Title.
LA217.2.B77 2011
371.010973—dc22   2011016196
ISBN 978-1-4516-1199-1
ISBN 978-1-4516-1201-1 (pbk)
ISBN 978-1-4516-1202-8 (ebook)

To Emily, Sophie, Sam—and Cynthia

Contents

Class
Warfare

The Race

As he filed into the Oval Office behind the power players who were already household names in Washington—top presidential adviser David Axelrod, chief of staff Rahm Emanuel, and Secretary of Education Arne Duncan—Jon Schnur thought that he had spent years waiting to have this meeting.* Until now he had been jilted. The Democrats he had worked for had always backed away from the education reforms he championed. And they hadn't been elected.

Schnur, then forty-three, got interested in education when, as an editor of his high school newspaper, he read a draft of an article by a student who had transferred from a Milwaukee public school to his school in the city's suburbs. "She was savvier than any of us on the editorial board, but the draft was just so terribly written," he says. "The more I got to know her, the more I became obsessed with why public education hadn't reached people like her."

After he graduated from Princeton, where he had volunteered as a tutor in a nearby high school, Schnur worked in Bill Clinton's presidential campaign, then landed an education policy job in his administration.

That was when Schnur started to distrust his assumptions about why American public education had collapsed to a point where it was an obstacle to the American dream rather than the enabler. As he studied research trickling in by the late 1990s, he began to believe that failure or success in America's schoolrooms, especially in its poorest communities, didn't depend mostly on what kind

---

* Unless otherwise noted, thoughts attributed to anyone in this narrative are based on the author's having talked to that person. A full explanation of sources can be found in the Notes section at the back of this book.

of home a child came from or whether the school had enough resources, which is what most liberals like Schnur had always assumed. Instead, he concluded, it had to do more with the teacher
in front of the class. Truly effective teaching, he came to believe,
could overcome student indifference, parental disengagement, and
poverty—and, in fact, was the key to enabling children to rise above
those circumstances.

However, as the studies and the reports from a new kind of public school called "charter schools" were finding, successful teaching
was grueling work. It required more talent, more preparation, more
daily reevaluation and retooling, more hours in the class day, and
just plain more perseverance than many teachers, and most teachers'
union contracts, were willing or able to provide. In Schnur's view,
the unions and those who ran the nation's increasingly bureaucratic
school systems had settled on low expectations for children, which
allowed them not to be held accountable when the children continued to fail. Change those expectations; put good, determined teachers and principals in there; retrain or, if necessary, remove those
who were not effective; and "demography will no longer be destiny,"
Schnur and his fellow reformers believed. That presented a dilemma
if you were a Democrat, because the Democratic Party had come to
rely on teachers' unions as its strongest base of support.

By 1998, Schnur was Vice President Al Gore's education policy
aide. During his boss's 2000 presidential campaign, he persuaded
Gore to give a speech to the Michigan teachers' union about the
need to pay teachers based on how effective they were in boosting
their students' performance, an idea that struck at the core of union
contracts that mandated lockstep compensation based only on how
many years a teacher had been teaching, or what graduate degrees
the teacher held.

Gore hadn't flinched. He hadn't even tinkered with some of the
language that Schnur had made tougher in anticipation that the
vice president or someone else would water it down.

Right after the speech, the air came out of Schnur's balloon.
Within days, the two national teachers' unions—which donate
three times more money to Democrats than any other union or industry group and whose members account for more than 25 percent of all union members in the country and 10–15 percent of

the delegates to the Democratic Party convention that chooses the presidential nominee—had complained to higher-ups in the Gore campaign. Without anyone's informing Schnur, Gore's education reform positions disappeared from the campaign issues material. Gore never again mentioned teacher quality in his campaign, or any of the other education reforms that Schnur proposed. In the presidential debates between Gore and George W. Bush, the Texas governor talked about how he had pushed to make his state's schools and their teachers accountable for performance by requiring all students to be tested so their progress could be measured. Gore said testing by school systems should be voluntary and called for more federal aid to hire more teachers and pay them all more.

Four years later, Schnur signed on to help John Kerry, who as a senator had taken an interest in education reform. He drafted policy papers and a speech or two. The Kerry 2004 presidential campaign used none of them.

Now, as he took his seat on a sofa near the fireplace in the Oval Office, Schnur recalled how Obama '08 had been completely different. Since coming to the Senate in 2005, Barack Obama had been talking about education in ways that would have alarmed the teachers' unions, if they had cared enough to notice what a junior senator was saying. In 2006, he introduced legislation to provide federal aid to school districts that initiated reforms, such as linking teachers' pay and promotions to how well their students advanced on tests during the school year. The legislation went nowhere. And just two days after he announced his presidential candidacy, on a swing through Iowa to compete in the state's bellwether caucuses, he had answered a question about increasing teachers' salaries by saying that, yes, teachers should be paid more but that "there's also going to have to be accountability," and that students' performance on standardized tests "has to be part of the mix."

"Such candor is refreshing," David Yepsen, the influential political columnist for the *Des Moines Register,* wrote the next day, adding that he had asked Obama after his talk if a "candidate can win if he tells Democratic constituency groups things they don't want to hear."

"We'll see," Obama responded.

Obama's main opponent, Hillary Clinton, enjoyed the longtime support and friendship of American Federation of Teachers president Randi Weingarten. She had been a co-chair of Clinton's first New York senate campaign. Clinton responded to Obama's stance by calling merit pay divisive and insulting to teachers.

A few weeks after Obama's comment in Iowa, Schnur and campaign issues director Heather Higginbottom had presented him with an eight-point education reform platform. Higginbottom, then thirty-eight, had been Senator John Kerry's legislative director and then his issues director in his 2004 presidential run. So she and Schnur were longtime collaborators, and education reform was her favorite issue, too. Perhaps because of the disappointing experience in the Kerry campaign, when education reform had been trumped by the political team's fear of the teachers' unions, they were apprehensive that Obama might cut out or water down one or two of their most union-offending ideas.

Obama signed off on all eight points with little discussion, other than to tell them, "This is what I've been saying for a long time. . . . Just don't poke the unions in the eye with this. No anti-union rhetoric, and keep channels of communication open with them."*

So nothing about this Oval Office session with the new president should have made Schnur nervous. In fact, he was thrilled that eight days into Obama's presidency, amid the fierce economic crisis and other issues that commanded his attention, Obama had reserved a half hour to deal with education. Yet Schnur was nervous anyway, not only because those other Democrats had failed him before, but also because, in terms of its prescriptions for changing K–12 education across the country and how much money it proposed to make that happen, the plan that he, Higginbottom, and Duncan had cooked up was far beyond what any president had ever dared. In a December transition meeting, Obama had signed off more generally on the direction he would follow in education reform. Now it was time for specifics, and the specifics were not conventional.

Schnur had written a three-page memo summarizing how the Obama administration would take the $800 billion economic stim-

* Quotations of conversations are based on the recollections of those who were present. In situations where the recollections are not explicit, quotation marks are not used, and the conversations are paraphrased.

ulus package the president was about to propose and carve out $15 billion as a jackpot to be divided among ten to fifteen states that won a contest related to education reform. It would be a real contest, with no state able to prevail because of size or political influence. The winners would be states that submitted the best, most credible *specific* plans for using data and student-testing systems to evaluate teachers based on student improvement; for creating compensation and tenure systems for principals and teachers that would be based on their effectiveness in boosting their students' proficiency; for taking over and turning around consistently failing schools; and for encouraging alternatives to traditional public schools—such as charter schools.

The proposed contest had a catchy name: Race to the Top.

Schnur had brought thirty pages of backup material that had been attached to the three-pager when it was sent to the president. But Obama, sitting in a chair opposite his desk to the right of Schnur's sofa, said he had read it and didn't need to go over it again. In fact, Schnur and Higginbottom, who was also at this Oval Office meeting, were delighted to see that the president had underlined the part of the memo—and put a big check mark in the margin next to it—that said that not all states would get the money, just those that deserved it on the merits of their reform plans.

The new president asked the others what they thought. Axelrod, sitting on the couch across from Schnur and Duncan, jumped in and said that the unions would erupt in opposition, which could endanger support for the overall stimulus package among the Democrats whom Obama would need to get it through. This was not the way aid bills were done, Axelrod added, a point that was seconded by Obama's just-appointed congressional liaison. It was a direct assault on congressional prerogatives. The members of Congress would insist that, as with most aid programs and certainly ones involving billions of dollars, every state and congressional district should get the money proportionately, rather than have it parceled out to a chosen few by the White House or the education secretary. The unions would fan the flames on that, he added, reminding powerful senators and representatives, who chaired the relevant committees and were the unions' traditional allies and recipients of campaign support, that their states or districts might get nothing.

Schnur and Duncan knew that many of the states that were home to influential Democrats on Capitol Hill, particularly California but also Wisconsin and New York, were unlikely to win any contests related to education reform unless a booby prize was awarded. Duncan, an education reformer who had gotten to know Obama because he had been running Chicago's school system until his appointment to the cabinet, kept that thought to himself. This was a singular opportunity for the president to act on something he cared a lot about, he told Obama.

Schnur—who is deferential and soft-spoken, even when he is the person in the room who knows the most, as he often is—spoke haltingly to the new president. He said he thought they could overcome any opposition on the Hill because this was only $15 billion in an $800 billion package and because there was such goodwill, on the Democratic side, at least, toward the new president.

Although he did not volunteer it, Schnur knew that George Miller, the senior Democrat in the House on education issues, would support the contest. Schnur had already checked with him.

Miller had long been out of sync with the teachers' unions and more traditional Democrats on education reform, in part because of his experience as a volunteer at a hard-pressed school in his California district. "We shouldn't just write checks," Miller had told Schnur. "We should make them do something for it."

As a congressman, Emanuel had co-authored a book the year before on domestic policy, in which he touted education reform of the kind Schnur was now pushing. And as the incoming chief of staff he had on more than one occasion good-naturedly egged on domestic policy aide Higginbottom with whispers of "education reform, education reform" when they passed in the halls at the Chicago transition office. "You don't get any do-overs in education; you get one shot to succeed or fail with a kid, and our schools were mostly failing," Emanuel says, explaining his passion for the issue.

Now Emanuel butted in, saying, "We've got to do this. It's a great plan. . . . This is our great opportunity. And I know we can get a lot of Democrats to support it."

The boss seemed to have made up his mind. "Yes, let's do it," Obama said. "I always say this is supposed to be about the kids, not the adults."

"Just make sure," the president added, repeating what he'd told Schnur and the others in Iowa, "that we don't poke the unions in the eye with this. Just do what we have to do."

With that decision, Obama unleashed a swirl of forces whose ferocity would exceed anything even Schnur expected. Parents would march in Los Angeles and Tallahassee demanding the reforms the contest prescribed. The "Race" and education reform would become defining issues in elections from Florida to Colorado to the District of Columbia. Key laws and regulations would be changed in Michigan, Louisiana, Nevada, Tennessee, and thirty other states.

Indeed, something unusual broke out across America: a substantive policy debate that engaged a broad swath of the citizenry and their elected officials in villages, cities, state capitals, and in Washington—and that actually produced results.

All of that happened because the contest for the stimulus money became a call to arms for a snowballing network of education reformers across the country—an unlikely army of non-traditional urban school chiefs, charter school leaders, researchers at think tanks who were producing data about how teaching counted more than anything else, philanthropists and hedge-fund billionaires who ate up the data, fed-up parents, and a growing corps of unconventional Democratic politicians. Having worked for years in cities and towns across the country, almost unnoticed except among education bureaucrats, they now sprang up and took center stage. Schnur, a behind-the-scenes player, seemed to be at the center of the network. Everyone seemed to know him, even people who didn't know each other.

At the same time, the Race to the Top became a call to the barricades for those who had held back the reformers for years with arguments that their theories were simplistic and untested, and that they glossed over the real obstacles of poverty and racism while scapegoating the one group—educators—who really understood the issues and who really cared.

The leader in making that argument would be Randi Weingarten, who was fifty-one when the Race was launched and who would assume an increasingly high national profile in the two years that followed.

A savvy New Yorker whose mother had been an elementary school teacher for twenty-nine years, Weingarten is a talented leader, able and relentlessly eager to make the case that teachers and her American Federation of Teachers are dedicated enablers of children's success, not self-interested impediments. For years she had teased her mother that she had become a lawyer and her sister an emergency room doctor because neither wanted to work as hard as she had seen her mother work.

Schnur's Race to the Top—because it called for a sweeping overhaul of a system where no one had been held accountable, and because it enlisted the nation's school chiefs, mayors, and governors in a "contest" that caught on in the media—would force Weingarten's side to play defense in political arenas that this side had traditionally dominated. The onslaught would become so heavy in so many places that Weingarten would start confiding to friends that she feared her union was destined to meet the fate of the United Auto Workers, which had been crippled when competing, nonunion carmakers almost put Ford, General Motors, and Chrysler out of business by producing better, cheaper cars.

In Weingarten's world, charter schools were to teachers' unions and conventional public schools what Toyota or Honda had been to the autoworkers' union and the big three Detroit automakers. So it especially alarmed her that encouraging the growth of charter schools would be one of the ways a state could score points in the Race to the Top.

First promoted by the Clinton administration in the 1990s, charter schools are publicly financed and open to any child, but they are run by entities other than the conventional local school district. Typically, they are operated by nonprofit organizations that rely on donations to provide seed money to launch the school but then use the same amount, or less taxpayer money per pupil, as is doled out to the public schools for ongoing operations. Those who run charters are accountable for the school's performance. However, they are free to manage as they wish, which includes the freedom to hire teachers who are not union members. Students are admitted based on a lottery; these are public schools with no admissions requirements or any other filters (other than the lottery when applications outnumber seats).

Charters were a relatively minor factor in the plans the states had to present to win the Race to the Top. However, because Weingarten and her side directed so much vitriol at charters, the role of charter schools in the Race to the Top would get more attention than it deserved. The Obama plan was not about charter schools. Nor is this book about charter schools, except insofar as charters illuminate larger points in the overall battle over public education.

By 2009, out of 95,000 American public schools, fewer than 5,000 were charter schools. So they are unlikely in the short term (or even in the long term) to replace a significant portion of traditional public schools. The larger issues around education reform have to do with how the traditional public schools, run by the government, can be changed. That is why Schnur's Race to the Top would award only a fraction of the points necessary for a state to be one of the winners based on how much or little the state encouraged charters. The most points would go to states that demonstrated commitments to systemic reforms intended to improve their government-run public schools.

Nonetheless, school reformers like Schnur like to point to charters as the experiments that prove the case for those systemic reforms. They argue that the larger significance of charter schools is that the ones that work not only demonstrate that children from the most challenged homes and communities can learn but also suggest how traditional public schools might be changed to make them operate effectively. It can make for an especially compelling argument when a charter school and a traditional urban public school are operating side by side in the same building.

Juicy Words

December 7, 2010, 7:45 a.m., Lenox Avenue
between 117th and 118th Streets, Harlem, New York City

Just before 8:00 on the morning of December 7, 2010, Jessica Reid—a blond, twenty-eight-year-old "leadership resident," the term used for assistant principal at the Harlem Success Academy I charter school—finished supervising breakfast. Wearing an outfit more likely to be seen at a downtown club, Reid circulated the room and complimented several children for having completed reading another book. A small pink notebook in hand, Reid headed off through the silent hallways now filling up with four hundred of Harlem's children, on her way to the first of five observations of the eleven fourth-, fifth-, and sixth-grade classes she oversees. She would observe the other six tomorrow. Reid observes every class at least twice a week, all year, unless she spots particular weaknesses that require her to drop in more often.

In all cases she'll e-mail notes, send text messages, or have quick hallway conversations with the teachers she supervises, going over what she thinks they're doing right or what they need to improve. Today's critiques ranged from the relatively trivial—"You should remember to put the book down when you stop reading out loud in order to make eye contact" and "Stop after each stanza and ask them to make a mental movie of Paul Revere about to ride"—to the more substantive: "Do you think we need to go back over compound fractions?"

Reid interrupted the notes she was taking to prepare these minicritiques and leaned over to tuck one girl's uniform blouse into her skirt, after which she asked her, in a whisper, what had happened to her underwear. She complimented a boy about his shoulders-back posture, then praised another for making "total eye contact" with the teacher throughout the lesson.

At 11:00, Reid headed into a classroom to do some teaching herself. Two weeks before, she had forced out one of her new fifth-grade English teachers. Although the new teacher had come to Harlem Success in August with good credentials, Reid had concluded, having watched her since school had started in August, that she had "pitied the kids rather than pushed them."

It wasn't a hunch. Because Harlem Success monitors each child's progress week by week, Reid had seen that many of this teacher's students weren't completing their assigned reading. Worse, the scores the teacher was giving them on tests were higher than Reid's sense of how they had been doing in class when she looked in on them and their teacher every day or two. Thus her judgment that pity was replacing push.

And then there was the classroom itself, which looked fine to me but to Reid was sloppy and had few of the charts, posters, and other accoutrements that she and the other powers that be at Harlem Success believed were essential.

So the week before Thanksgiving, Reid and the new fifth-grade teacher, who was maybe four years younger than Reid, had agreed that she and Harlem Success were not a good fit.

Now Reid was going to take her place in class for the rest of the year, on top of supervising the ten other third-, fourth-, and fifth-grade classes in the school. It would be exhausting, she knew, and would further upset what had become her increasing effort to achieve some balance in her life, "so I don't get a divorce or end up in a state of total collapse," she told me. Reid had worked her way through UCLA doing personal training for two or three hours before classes and in the evening after class, and working out had always been a cherished ritual. Now she rarely got to the gym except on weekends, and her husband (they were married two years earlier), who worked in the insurance business, was complaining that she was always either working or thinking about work.

The intensified regimen began over Thanksgiving weekend, when Reid had to hang up the "juicy words" in her class. At Harlem Success, these are words that are more expressive than the easier alternatives. Words that improve a child's vocabulary. Words that send the message that these kids can reach higher. *Stout* or *corpulent* instead of *fat*. *Tedious* or *mundane* instead of *boring*. *Emaciated* instead of *thin*.

It had driven Reid crazy that the dismissed teacher had ignored her repeated requests to get this stuff hung up all over the classroom. So the Saturday after Thanksgiving, Reid had come uptown into the building to put up charts she had hand-drawn showing sixteen common words, each with at least four juicy alternatives. She also put up charts spelling out "Writing Expectations" for her fifth graders (depicting various rules of grammar and the basics of a winning topic sentence) and "Idioms We Are Studying" ("going against the grain," "marches to the beat of his or her drum," "on thin ice").

Standing in front of her new class in black stiletto heels, a black and pink crinoline dress, and a black, gold-buttoned jacket not quite covering five different bracelets, Reid called on them, one by one, to line up at the door. Then she marched all twenty-two out into the hall to look at the "Writing Up a Storm" bulletin board. These were displays of personal essays done under the tutelage of the teacher Reid had just replaced.

"Look at it," she said. "What do you notice?"

"It's pretty empty," whispered one tiny girl in glasses.

"Yes, that's right, isn't it," Reid replied. "And think of the irony that it says 'writing up a storm.' Just seven out of forty-six fifth-grade scholars have their essays up there, and some of them have grammatical mistakes and misspellings.

"I sat up last night and realized that the most heartbreaking part," she continued, "was the number of scholars who did not turn in their work, and the number that did whose work was too short or riddled with errors.

"The worst part," she added, "was that last week I said I would edit these for you if you asked, and in the entire grade only two scholars asked for their work to be edited. That tells me you don't even care."

Several of the children shifted nervously on their feet. Most looked embarrassed. "Those of you who know me know that I am the most stubborn person you will ever meet," Reid concluded. "I'll do whatever it takes to make you a good writer, because you'll never get into college if you can't write. So we're going to have extra writing homework every night. . . . You're going to rewrite your paragraphs until they have correct capitalization and punctuation, because when you create a piece of writing that has errors you're sending the message that you're not intelligent. Why would you do that to yourself? I know you're intelligent. Remember, I'm not looking for perfection. I'm really not. I'm just looking for effort, because I know you can succeed."

Reid had them file back into class, where the lesson was about writing a personal essay depicting an important person in their lives. She shifted to an electronic whiteboard to list the bullet points of the person she had chosen to write about—her mother, who is also a teacher, in California. She then put an essay on the whiteboard that she had drafted the night before. It transfixed the children.

Reid's story began by noting that her mother, with "her Swedish face, blue eyes, and blond hair," looks just like herself. Then came a stunning recollection: Her father not only "broke my mother's heart," but because of her parents' divorce, Reid, her mother, and Reid's two siblings had to live on welfare while her mother went back to school to get a teaching degree.

Two weeks later there would be forty-four pieces of nearly flawless writing on the board outside, and Reid had hung 3-D images of clouds from the ceiling above it (accompanied by pencils made to look like raindrops) because, she would tell her students, "You now really are writing up a storm."

Harlem Success Academy I is part of a network of seven Harlem Success charter schools in New York. It is in a forty-three-year-old brick building on Lenox Avenue between 117th and 118th streets that it shares with PS 149, a traditional public school that has 433 students spread through kindergarten to eighth grade. (Harlem Success has 631 in grades K–5.)

The schools are separated only by a fire door in the middle and some staircases. They share a gym and cafeteria. In one wing of the third floor, the schools are separated by only a dividing line down the middle of the hall. On one side, the trim above the classroom doors and along the walls is painted standard city Department of Education black. On the other side, there's the Harlem Success trademark orange and blue.

Across the hall and one floor down from where I watched Reid coach her kids on essays, juicy words, and personal biographies— maybe a fifteen-second walk—I looked in on a goateed teacher in jeans and a sweatshirt sitting back in a chair in front of eighteen fourth graders. His feet parked on the desk, he bellowed: "How many days in a week?" No answer. Half the children had their heads down. Most of the others were chattering away, except for two boys who were wrestling on the floor. The teacher asked again, louder. Still no answer. Then louder still, all the while rocking almost to the point of falling over backward in the chair. Then, "Okay, let's move on to something else."

Outside, some children wandered the halls, while those moving from class to class did so boisterously, as if in the schoolyard. On the first floor, about forty kids were in the auditorium watching what seemed to be an action movie.

The Harlem Success teachers' contract drives home the idea that the school is about the children, not the grown-ups. It is one page, allows them to be fired at will, and defines their responsibilities no more specifically than that they must help the school achieve its mission. Harlem Success teachers are paid about 5 to 10 percent more than union teachers on the other side of the building who have their levels of experience.

The union contract in place on the public school side of the building is 167 pages. Most of it is about job protection and what teachers can and cannot be asked to do during the 6 hours and 57.5 minutes (8:30 to about 3:25, with 50 minutes off for lunch) of their 179-day work year.

Reid and her teachers start work at about 7:45 and finish at 4:30 to 5:00. Their school year begins in August, rather than the day after Labor Day, and often they work at tutorials or other special classes on Saturdays.

Reid's teachers must be available by cell phone (supplied by the school) for parent consultations in the evening, as are Reid and the principal. They are reimbursed for taking a car service home if they stay late into the evening to work with students. PS 149 teachers are not obligated to receive phone calls from students or parents at home; some would and many wouldn't, says the school's principal.

The assumption that every child will succeed is so ingrained at Harlem Success that, as happens at many charter networks across the country, each classroom is labeled with the name of the college attended by its teacher and the year these children are expected to graduate (as in "Yale 2026" for one of the kindergarten classes).

Reid's side of the building spent $18,378 per student in the 2009–2010 school year. This includes actual cash outlays for everything from salaries to the car service, plus what the city says (and the charter school disputes) is the value of services that the city contributes to the charter for utilities, building maintenance, and even "debt service" for its share of the building.

It costs $19,358 per year to educate each student on the public side of the building, or $980 more than on the charter side. That's right. The public school spends more per student than the charter school.

One reason is that instead of the standard matching pension contributions paid to the charter teachers that cost the school $193 per student, the teachers on the PS 149 side have a pension plan that is now costing the city $2,605 per year per pupil.* All fringe benefits, including pensions and health insurance, cost $1,341 per student on Reid's side but $5,316 on the PS 149 side. Union teachers can get up to thirteen paid sick or personal days off a year, an amount that is about the same as, or in some cases less than, what most teachers' union contracts across the country specify. At PS 149, the teachers take most of these days; they averaged eight days absent in the 2009–2010 school year. (The other five days are held over for them in an account that they can use in future years or turn into cash when they retire.) These absences—more than one every five weeks of the school year—not only suspend any progress a class might be making; they also cost the school more than $150 a day for a substitute teacher.

The Harlem Success I teachers were absent an average of 1.1 days.

While the public side spends more, it produces less. PS 149 is rated by the city as doing comparatively well in terms of student achievement, and it has improved since Mayor Michael Bloomberg took over the city's schools in 2002 and appointed Joel Klein as chancellor. Nonetheless, its students are performing significantly behind the charter kids on the other side of the wall. For example,

---

* The annual cost would be multiples more if the city accounted for and funded the actual future cost of these pensions rather than underfunded it, thereby creating an inevitable financial crisis in the next few years.

in the 2009–2010 school year, 29 percent of the students at PS 149 were doing English language arts (reading and writing) at or above grade level, and 34 percent were grade-level proficient in math. In the charter school, 86 percent were at proficiency (or higher) in English, and 94 percent were at proficiency (or higher) in math; and Reid's third graders tied for top-performing school in the state in math—surpassing such high-end public school districts as Scarsdale, the wealthy Westchester County suburb.

Same building in the same community, with similarly qualified, or challenged, students.* (Remember, the charter students are admitted in a lottery, with seven times as many kids entering the lottery in 2010 as could be admitted.) And the classrooms have almost exactly the same number of students. In fact, the charter school averages a student or two more per class, puncturing the myth that, unless there are extreme differences, smaller classes are the key to student learning.

The principal of PS 149 is Kayrol Burgess-Harper, forty. Burgess-Harper is a former stenographer who got an education degree and became a star math teacher after she realized that secretarial work was a dead end in the digital age. She then graduated from the Leadership Academy that Klein created soon after becoming chancellor in 2002 to train a new breed of principals.

Burgess-Harper, who is cheerful yet hard charging, says that making her school a model of excellence is "nonnegotiable." She has made significant improvements at the school since taking over in January 2010 after the last principal was removed for misconduct. However, she is the first to agree that her job of boosting achievement for the kids on her side of the building is far harder than Reid's. When I told her about the teacher upstairs from her office I had seen yelling about the days of the week, she seemed to know exactly whom I was referring to.

Burgess-Harper said that, in fact, at least ten of her forty teachers are not effective and that "their attitude and lack of caring

---

* Union critics of charter schools and their supporters have repeatedly asserted that schools like Harlem Success "skim" from the community's most intelligent students and committed families, or that they teach fewer learning-challenged or impoverished students and fewer students who are English-language learners. None of the actual data supports this.

affects many of the others." She had rated three of them unsatisfactory in the spring of 2010 and said she expected to give the other seven U ratings in 2011. This means that Burgess-Harper has dared to give, or plans to give, 25 percent of her teachers a U rating in a system that gave that rating to 1 or 2 percent of all teachers before Klein arrived.

However, only a fraction of teachers rated U are ever dismissed, although the rare U rating can block new teachers from getting tenure.

Burgess-Harper explained that as a result of her more aggressive posture, her relationship with the union's representative at PS 149 is "really tense." In what no one around her half of the building thinks is unrelated, she has been the target of anonymous calls to a city Department of Education investigator's hotline alleging improper behavior. In fact, her official title on the day we met was still only "acting interim principal," because one of those investigations had not been closed. (She was being questioned about a "conflict of interest" because someone had anonymously reported to the hotline that she had accepted the offer of the daughter of one of her teachers, who is also a friend of hers, to pick up her young daughter at her elementary school across town one day because Burgess-Harper was staying late in the office.) Burgess-Harper's status had been in limbo for more than a year when we met in early 2011, but she said, "I'm not an 'acting' anything. I am doing this job."

"The union does this to principals all the time," says Klein. "If you do anything to piss them off, they put a hit out on you. They call the hotline or they get parents to complain. It's like the mafia."*

"There is a whole new attitude here, since Principal Burgess-Harper took over," says Marie Jones, an assistant principal who began as a reading teacher at PS 149 in 1985. "She wants us out of our offices and into the classrooms." Nonetheless, neither Burgess-Harper nor her assistants can do the kind of daily coaching and quality control that is routine for Jessica Reid. For starters, Burgess-Harper explains, each assistant has a list of twenty-nine separate

* The UFT representative at PS 149, Patrick Walsh, said he was "not aware of any anonymous calls to the DOE concerning Principal Harper, and I highly doubt that any such calls are coming from teachers. I do know that there is considerable unhappiness among parents about various issues regarding the school," he added.

administrative chores for which he or she is responsible. Reid's side of the building, despite keeping to a lower overall cost per student in its operating budget, has a business manager and staff to handle all that. More important, says Burgess-Harper, "If we went into a classroom every day, we'd be charged with harassment."

So while Burgess-Harper has made class observations a priority since she took over, she guesses that at most each teacher is observed three or four times a term, although before she became principal teachers were observed only once or twice a year. "You have to do it informally or casually to avoid trouble," she explains, by which she means those complaints of harassment from the union representative in the building, which can take hours of meetings to resolve, or even anonymous calls alleging wrongdoing to the corruption hotline. Under the contract, only one formal observation per term is allowed to count officially for the annual evaluation, and the union representatives typically insist that the teacher receive advance notice before that observation takes place.

"Give me the ability to hire and fire the ones I want and give me a school day from eight to five like they have on the other side, and I'd have hundreds of little Einsteins running around here, too," Burgess-Harper says.

Burgess-Harper's realization, and frustration, after little more than a year on the job—that she too could produce those little Einsteins, if she could change the rules and the expectations on her side of the building—is something Jessica Reid understands well.

The Epiphanies

Jessica Reid remembers her first day of work at PS 121 in the Bronx on September 7, 2004, as the worst day of her life.

The spring before, Reid, a native of San Francisco about to graduate from UCLA, had applied to Teach For America (TFA), an organization started in 1990 to recruit high-achieving young adults coming out of prestigious colleges to teach for two years at public schools in underprivileged communities. Although her mother and aunt are educators, Reid had never thought about teaching. But she hadn't thought about much of anything else career-wise either. When she did a mock lesson for the TFA recruiters during her interview, she realized that she was pretty good at it—and she enjoyed it.

Her sense that this was going to be a great adventure was reinforced by her experience at the five-week TFA academy she attended at a Bronx middle school that summer. She and the other new TFA corps members got training from TFA veterans and were also paired with experienced New York City public school teachers to teach kids who were attending summer sessions because they fell behind during the year. The whole thing—being in New York for the first time, teaching troubled kids, even the cavernous brick and cinder-block Bronx school—should have been intimidating. She thought it was a breeze from the moment she'd taught her first lesson and her mentor-teacher quickly blurted out, "You're great. You have a real knack for this."

So all was good until that morning the day after Labor Day when Reid walked into her first real class. There were now twenty-five fifth graders and only Reid at the front of the room, rather than the five or ten kids she'd shared with the experienced teacher that summer. Before she could even tell them her name, some were whistling at her, while others laughed about how she looked so young. ("I actually did look about fourteen then," she concedes.)

When one of the fifth graders, who was a half foot taller than Reid's five feet five inches, stood up and started dancing around, none of the tricks she'd been taught at the TFA academy for regaining the class's attention worked. At lunchtime, Reid went to the principal. He had the instigator removed from the classroom and told her not to worry. The kid was back by the end of the afternoon.

During a break, a few of her fellow teachers shrugged when she told them how bad it had been. One said simply, "Welcome to our world."

For the rest of the day, Reid pleaded fruitlessly with her students to pay attention. She found herself looking at the clock, hoping it would move faster. By 3:15 she was on the subway.

By the next morning on the subway ride back to the Bronx, she had decided that she had to take control. She had to be, as she wrote in an e-mail the next night to an old high school teacher she idolized, "a total bitch." She was going to make sure that they knew that their actions had consequences and that she wasn't going to tolerate their not trying to learn.

She did it in baby steps. The second day maybe she was able to connect for a half hour or so, getting them to discuss a book and begin talking about the essays they might write. Then she got traction for two or three periods, then a whole day. All the while, she'd be on the phone at night with her mother and aunt—or with a kindred-spirit, experienced teacher she had befriended on a subway platform one morning—getting encouragement and coaching tips. When her mom came to visit, her first comment after class was, "Jessica, you never sit down."

"That's right," Reid replied. "To do this right you have to be on the entire time." She'd stay coaching some kids until 5:00 or 6:00, often being the only one left in the building. She'd come home, go over a lesson plan, then collapse, her social life so empty that she took to wearing her party clothes to school so she would be in a better mood.

By the spring, Reid was teaching some of her kids Shakespeare. "I can do this," she thought.

Jessica Reid's epiphany would be experienced in one form or another by many of the people who, as we will see, would end up in the middle of a battle to turn around America's public schools.

Michelle Rhee

As Michelle Rhee was nearing graduation from Cornell in 1992, she happened upon a public television documentary about Teach For America. A few days later she noticed a TFA recruiting flyer. Rhee had tutored one summer at a Native American reservation; she remembered this as a "jarring experience, because everyone had written these kids off." Looking for something meaningful to do until she decided what she really wanted to do with her life, Rhee went for a TFA interview. By the fall, she was teaching math in a middle school in Baltimore. She was failing so miserably to control her class, let alone teach anything, that two officials from the school district who came to observe her hinted, with little subtlety, that Rhee should consider another line of work.

Rhee became obsessed with not giving up and with squeezing the most out of her class day. She even tried ten different methods for saving time when her fifth graders had to sharpen their pencils. (Line them up single file in front of the sharpeners? Double file? Hand out sharpeners?) By the winter, she saw that she was breaking through. Her kids were really learning math, and liking it.

"I just made things up—anything that would work," Rhee recalls. "Anything. I had kids all sit in a giant U, except that any kid who misbehaved had to sit in the middle. . . . I used the calendar to teach math and made up something called incredible equations. If it was October 3, I'd create all these ridiculous equations where the answer was three."

When she finished her first year that June, Rhee went home to Ohio. For the first time since before high school, she didn't take a summer job. She had figured out that the best way to get her kids engaged was through charts and posters and, most important, all kinds of physical objects, such as geometric shapes, play money, or Monopoly-like cards for game playing. She spent the summer preparing all of these study aids so that she would have something for every day of class. She plotted out months of lessons, then took over the basement and began making the materials she needed—a trunkful that she would take back to Baltimore. She used the photocopying machine in her father's office, which was attached to the family's home, and she recruited two aunts visiting from Korea to help. "We had a little Asian sweatshop going all summer," she remembers.

Soon after Rhee got back to school that fall, the two supervisors who had observed her the year before returned. They were stunned. They had never seen such a turnaround in a teacher's ability to connect with a class, they told her.

Rhee's success was so startling that the school officials asked her to demonstrate her methods to the other teachers. Her colleagues, Rhee says, reacted "with amusement, like 'isn't that cute.' One even said that what I was doing makes too much noise."

As her second year ended, Rhee was so satisfied with her progress that she decided to stay an extra year in Baltimore, where she pushed her classes to still more improvement. However, she recalls, when she left she was "depressed and even furious that these kids were doomed next year because everyone else had the attitude that they couldn't succeed."

The following year, Rhee enrolled in Harvard's Kennedy School of Government, determined to get a credential that would allow her to do something about that.

Dave Levin

Dave Levin, too, had floundered in his first months teaching for TFA, in his case at a mostly Hispanic school in Houston. He and his roommate and fellow TFA recruit, Mike Feinberg, would stay up all night trying to think of ways to break through in their classrooms.

Levin's moment of realization came one warm spring morning in 1993, when he looked out at his sixth-grade class as the students conferred with each other over essays they had written. He had always had empathy for kids others assumed couldn't learn because he had transferred out of a prestigious Manhattan private school when a learning disability was mistaken for lack of intelligence. He remembers as if it were yesterday the exact moment he watched these children in Houston succeeding—the windows were wide open, the Texas sun was shining in as they edited each other's essays. "Wow," he said to himself. "I'm teaching."

Levin's success was the result, it turns out, not only of his determination to connect with his kids, even if he had to visit them and their parents at home each night, but also of his and Feinberg's eagerness and ability to mimic and expand on the methods being deployed in the classroom across the hall by a veteran Houston teacher, Harriett Ball.

Ball had established, amid a system steeped in failure, an oasis of high expectations and learning, which would forever remind Levin and Feinberg that, whatever the broader failures of public schooling in America, there were thousands of traditional public school teachers—not Ivy League reformers, but young and middle-aged and senior teachers who were members of teachers' unions—who hadn't gotten the memo telling them they were supposed to fail.

Ball took Levin and Feinberg under her wing, showing them how to deploy a tool kit that consisted of lots of songs and rhymes, not the physical objects that Rhee used. Yet in both cases the kit was based on the same mind-set: These children could succeed if you assumed they could, and if you kept trying.

It's a mind-set that Levin and Feinberg were destined to carry with them beyond two classrooms in Houston. Soon they would set out to create the largest and arguably most successful network of charter schools in the country.

Sarah Usdin

After graduating from Colgate in 1991, Sarah Usdin got a prestigious Fulbright Scholarship to teach English in Germany. Her students—in grades five through thirteen (the last precollege grade in Germany) at a rural ski town school designated for pre-Olympians and other athletes—had already passed the country's tests to be on track for university study. So they were a highly motivated, smart group. Teaching them was fun. Because she didn't have a master's degree and a teaching degree, both of which are required in Germany, she was tightly supervised.

A year later, still not sure of a career, Usdin, too, joined Teach For America. That summer, she ended up at the same bare-bones TFA program in South Central Los Angeles where Dave Levin was getting his training. Because she had grown up in Louisville and wanted to return to a Southern river city, she was one of the few TFA recruits to pick Baton Rouge as her first choice for a job.

Usdin's fifth-grade Baton Rouge class was a world away from her experience in Germany. Her school wasn't the hardest of hard-core inner-city schools that Levin or Rhee faced. Most but not all students were entitled to free lunch, and many of the parents were actively involved in the school. However, whether it was replacing the musty posters and other paraphernalia from the teacher who had had the classroom the year before (and had died over the summer), or trying to figure out where her kids were in reading or math, she was, she says, "hopelessly lost, with no support. . . . I had no idea what I was doing or how they were doing."

As Usdin got to know the children, she found that many couldn't even read "sight words"—the simplest, beginning words, like *the* or *and* or *but*. Yet no one in the school had any idea how badly they were doing. The one time a supervisor came to observe Usdin, she slipped Usdin a note with smiley faces all over it, saying the rookie teacher was "fabulous."

The praise only unsettled her more. "I went home every night in the first weeks," Usdin recalls, "and cried."

She was helped by a hurricane that hit Baton Rouge early in the school year. It closed the school and gave her time to regroup and rethink what she was doing.

Usdin discovered her own tricks. She found that if her students listened to taped books while they read along, it helped them learn to read. So she bought taping equipment and read books into it at night, then brought the recorders to class.

By the end of the year, Usdin had been voted "teacher of the year."

"It was more about my hard work and the parents' enthusiasm for me than any measure of what I had accomplished," she says. "Because there were no measures."

That summer she read more than two hundred books into the tape machine. But when she got back to school that fall, she was told that she had been "surplused." Baton Rouge had been forced to lay off teachers, and under the seniority-based rules of last in/first out (LIFO), the most junior teachers were the ones who had to go, "teacher of the year" or not. The students and parents staged a sit-in to keep Usdin from being dismissed. But rules were rules.

Usdin was transferred to a school in a rougher, poorer neighborhood. Yet she thrived there because she quickly put herself under the tutelage of a veteran teacher who was a relentless master of her craft. This teacher, another union member, would have unofficial tutoring sessions before school and drive out into the neighborhood after school and on weekends to pick up students for field trips and study sessions at her house, all on her own time and none of it contemplated in her contract. Usdin followed suit and loved it so much that she stayed an extra year beyond the TFA two-year commitment.

In fact, she never left Louisiana. After that third year she became the executive director of the expanding TFA program in the state. Ten years later, when Hurricane Katrina devastated New Orleans, Usdin would become the point person in replacing the city's failing schools and school system with a portfolio of charter schools and public schools taken over by the state, many of which would be run by other TFA alumni.

Michael Johnston

About five years after Rhee's, Levin's, and Usdin's baptisms, in 1998, a thin, fair-haired Yale soccer player, whose father owned a bar in Vail, Colorado, made the same kind of breakthrough at a violence-riddled high school in Greenville, Mississippi, one of the country's highest-poverty rural areas.

Michael Johnston used chess lessons, intense one-on-one tutorials, constant supplies of popular magazines for his reading classes, and connections that he made coaching track to overcome the mayhem that prevailed during his initial months teaching high school. He refused to go easy on indifferent students whose circumstances he sympathized with or who threatened his physical safety if he gave them failing grades. He ended up tutoring many of them for college admissions exams they had never dreamed of taking.

Johnston had mentored teenagers in a New Haven housing project while at Yale, so joining TFA had not been a spur-of-the-moment decision. He had been thinking about teaching since high school. When Johnston saw he was succeeding but was then brushed off when he suggested changes the high school might make to replicate his success, he decided to go to the Kennedy School at Harvard (and then to Yale Law School) so he could get into politics and try to fix education from the outside.

The epiphany that they could teach that was shared by Jessica Reid, Michelle Rhee, Dave Levin, Sarah Usdin, and Michael Johnston came in three stages. First, they failed in the classroom. But because they weren't used to failure—in fact, typically because they hadn't failed yet at anything in their lives—they kept trying, slogging through one approach after another to connect with their kids. Then one day, the second stage came: They realized that they were succeeding—and that these children could learn and perform.

Whereupon came the third stage and the truly important realization that would propel them and others like them through the narrative that would become the story of today's education reform revolution: What they had achieved in their classrooms wasn't magic and they were not magicians. Yes, they had to have talent. Not everyone could do this. But what was equally important was that they were willing to do whatever it took to connect, because they assumed that they could. They would work extra hours, constantly take stock of what was working, incessantly look for help from other effective teachers, make up word games, buy supplies from Staples that the school didn't have, insist on making eye contact, hold everyone to high grammatical standards even for an offhand classroom comment. As Reid's mother had observed, they would "never sit down."

Yet what was depressing to Reid as she made progress in the Bronx in the 2004–2005 school year, and to Rhee in Baltimore, Levin in Houston, Usdin in Louisiana, and Johnston in Mississippi, was that what they did in their classrooms probably didn't matter in the long run. Sure, Reid had kids in the fifth grade who had come in reading at first- or second-grade level and maybe she was getting them some of the way to where they belonged, or in some cases even all the way. So what? The next year they were going to be thrown back into the same failure factory. For her and the others, that became intolerable.

• • •

That they each saw failure all around was no surprise. American public schools are so consistently failing that on the same day in 2010 that I watched Jessica Reid promise her students she would do anything to get them to write well (while the teacher on the other side of the building bellowed on about the days of the week), a new study was released by the International Organization for Economic Cooperation and Development reporting that American children ranked fifteenth in reading literacy, twenty-fifth in math achievement, and seventeenth in science among the world's developed nations. In an increasingly knowledge-based, global economy, we're not just behind—way behind—countries like China, South Korea, and Japan, whose educated masses our media typically depict as threatening our competitiveness. We're also behind Estonia, Slovenia, Poland, Norway, New Zealand, Canada, and the Netherlands.

Today, more than a quarter of young people who take the low-level baseline language and math test to enlist in our military fail it, and they have to have high school diplomas even to take it. More than a quarter of our children don't graduate from high school, a rate that is worse than and continuing to fall behind that of any other country we think of ourselves as competing with on the global stage.

And our minorities and the poor rank so far below the low national average that they're basically at or near the bottom among the developed countries.

Yet even accounting for inflation, we've more than doubled what we spend on education per student in the last thirty years, in large part to reduce class size by hiring hundreds of thousands more teachers. We are now spending about 50 percent more per student than what other developed nations spend (and about 60 percent more than South Korea, for example), while our children continue to stagnate or fall farther behind.

That's why people like Jon Schnur had come to believe that it's not about more resources. It's about creating school systems where the adults never sit down.

My introduction to the idea that turning around our schools was less about resources and more about not sitting down came on June 5, 2009. That morning I toured a windowless room in a shabby Manhattan office building, as I began work on an article for the

New Yorker about the New York City school system. An unshaven man who looked to be about fifty years old was parked in a folding chair, his head down on a card table in front of him. Next to him was an alarm clock meant "to wake him up when it's 3:15 and time for us to go home," explained a woman sitting next to him. She was knitting.

There were fifteen people in the room. Three others were also asleep, their heads lying on another card table. Three were playing a board game. The rest stood around chatting, although two were arguing over one of the folding chairs.

They were all New York City schoolteachers who had been sent to what was officially called a Department of Education Temporary Reassignment Center but which everyone called the Rubber Room. They were all getting paid their full salaries and accruing increasing pension benefits every day.

These fifteen teachers doing time that day were joined by about six hundred others in six larger Rubber Rooms spread across four of the city's five boroughs. In the largest Rubber Room, in Brooklyn, a poster declared BELIEVE IN YOURSELF as its "mission statement."

All these teachers had been accused either of misconduct, such as hitting or molesting a student, or, in some cases, of incompetence, in a system that rarely called anyone incompetent.

They had been in the Rubber Room for an average of three years, doing the same thing every day—nothing. The fifteen in this Manhattan branch were watched over by two private security guards and two city Department of Education supervisors. They punched in on a time clock for the same hours that they would have kept at school. Like all teachers, they had the summer off. The city's contract with the United Federation of Teachers required that charges against them be heard by an arbitrator, and until the charges were resolved—in a process that typically took three to five years and rarely resulted in dismissals—they continued to draw their salaries and accrue pensions and other benefits.

"You can never appreciate how irrational the system is until you've lived with it," New York City schools chancellor Joel Klein told me later that afternoon. I soon found out that the system Klein had to contend with was not unique. Teacher tenure laws from Los Angeles to Detroit to Chicago to Newark (where it can take five years of hearings and litigation to remove a tenured teacher) all had become so impregnable that teachers across the country charged with this kind of over-the-top incompetence or misconduct were kept on the payroll for years while they reported to designated school offices, stayed home, or were allowed to remain in their classrooms.

That was my introduction not only to this Rubber Room but also to the metaphorical rubber room that had become America's public education system. America's classrooms, too, had largely become places that protect the adults who run them and assume that the children, like those sleeping teachers accused of incompetence, can only be warehoused—that, absent some fairy godfather philanthropy lifting them off to some leafy private school, they were doomed. Nothing and nobody—certainly not any teacher, however energetic—could stand them up.

Except that Jon Schnur, Jessica Reid, Michelle Rhee, Dave Levin, Michael Johnston, Joel Klein, and thousands like them—teachers, policy wonks, idealistic Ivy Leaguers, billionaire philanthropists and hedge-fund operators, a new breed of Democratic politicians (including the newly elected president), and an old breed of Republicans—were too stubborn to accept that. They wouldn't sit down.

As they have gained in numbers and as their efforts snowballed—and as the starter's pistol launched Obama's Race to the Top—a battle erupted that will determine the fate of the children on both sides of that building on Lenox Avenue and in schools across the country.

They're up against the most lavishly funded and entrenched bureaucracies in America (fourteen thousand school districts) supported by an interest group—the teachers' unions—which, the reformers complained, had money and playbooks every bit as effective in thwarting the public interest as Big Oil, the NRA, or Big Tobacco.

But teachers are not cigarette peddlers. Most really want to reach kids as much as Jessica Reid does. And most, according to polls done of teachers and my own interviews, aren't heavily involved in their unions' work. In fact, many have become indifferent to, or even embarrassed by, the positions their unions have come to stand for. The war over our schools arguably has not two but three camps:

the reformers, the unions, and the teachers. And as in any complicated, long-lasting battle, each side is subdivided into all kinds of factions, based on substantive issues or personal rivalries.

Besides, effective teaching is about much more than eliminating union rule. Nor are union leaders always the villains that their hard-line rhetoric and the deadening contracts they have insisted on would suggest.

The story of how our schools became obstacles to the American dream, and today's fierce battle to turn them around, is more complicated than that. It starts with why teachers needed a union in the first place.

"Be Obedient. Be Good. Keep Your Mouth Shut."

The week in January 1953 that Albert Shanker began teaching math at an elementary school in East Harlem, he was ordered by the principal to spend his lunch hour at the supermarket across the street to prevent the children from shoplifting candy.

Shanker, whose father made a living delivering newspapers in Queens, had just dropped out of the PhD program at Columbia University. He had completed all of his course work, yet despite being as intellectually ambitious and accomplished as his pursuit of a philosophy degree (and his gangling, bespectacled appearance) suggested, he had run out of money and patience before finishing his doctoral thesis.

So, at twenty-four, Shanker took a job as a substitute teacher in East Harlem. Philosophy's loss was the labor movement's gain. Shanker would become the galvanizing force behind the unionization of teachers in New York and across the country. By the end of the twentieth century, education reformers would argue that teachers had gained too much control over public education. But through the middle of the century, that pendulum of power was far over on the opposite side. Al Shanker would become the heavy in shoving it the other way.

Shanker joined a workforce whose wages, working conditions, and general stature had never matched the idealized role teachers played in nurturing America's children since free public education had become a core community undertaking, beginning in the 1800s. Shanker was earning $2,600 a year, or $52 a week, in 1953. Men washing cars in parking garages had just won a contract giving them $72. And New York's teacher salaries were higher than those in most other cities.

In the earlier part of the century, teaching had paid comparatively well, especially in the Depression era, when the security and
stability of a teacher's wage were something to be envied. However,
in the period following World War II, as inflation in the postwar
boom hurt the purchasing power of those with relatively stable salaries, teachers began falling behind.

Worse than low pay for people like Shanker was how they were
treated. They didn't think of themselves as factory workers, nor presumably did the parents who entrusted their children to them. Yet
they punched time clocks, left when the last-period class bell rang,
and were expected not to question the bosses or make any other
waves.

It all amounted to a lopsided imbalance of power that expressed
itself in all kinds of rules that seem as hard to believe in retrospect
as the old Jim Crow "white"/"colored" water fountains. In Washington, D.C., teachers were not allowed to contact anyone in Congress
(which controlled the District of Columbia education budget) without getting permission, in writing, from the school board. In Chicago, there was a rule against "teacher-mothers," and teachers were
laid off in waves during the Great Depression while the patronage
jobs of school clerks and custodians were protected.

Until 1937 in New York, ostensibly to avoid having to explain the
birds and the bees to children, female teachers had to take a man-
datory two-year maternity leave as soon as they realized they were
pregnant. In most states even until the 1970s, when the Supreme
Court ruled it illegal in an Iowa case, teachers were forced to stay
home at least a few months before giving birth, usually unpaid.

Earlier in the twentieth century, many school systems prohibited
women from teaching even after they had given birth. "A married
woman's proper sphere is in the home if she has a family," the head
of New York City's Board of Education ruled in 1911, a policy that
was attacked three years later in a commentary by women's rights
activist Margaret Sanger after New York's highest court upheld the
rule.

Communist witch hunts were common through the 1950s. Even
talking about communism in a social studies class could result in
a parent's reporting a teacher, who might then be fired. In Washington, in order to get their paychecks, teachers had to sign what

became known as red rider statements every two weeks; in these statements they declared that they had not discussed communism.

Everywhere, teachers were subject to the whims of principals often as tyrannical as the worst stereotype of an old-time factory boss. They were willing and able to fire or make life miserable for teachers who questioned the curriculum, didn't want to take on an extracurricular assignment, or gave a low grade to the child of a favored parent.

Beginning in 1913, there had been a law in New York State guaranteeing teachers that they could not be dismissed as long as they provided what the law called "competent and efficient service" and "good behavior." These and similar tenure laws in other states—enacted as good government measures to end the firing or hiring of teachers whenever a new mayor or other official overseeing the schools took over—succeeded in eliminating most of that kind of obvious patronage. (The first such law was New Jersey's, in 1909.) However, they were easily circumvented by principals who wanted to get rid of teachers they didn't like, typically under the rubric of charges such as "conduct unbecoming of a teacher." There were no rules attached to these tenure laws to provide an outside, objective judgment about whether the charges were justified, and the local education board typically rubber-stamped the principal's decisions.

As Shanker told his definitive biographer, Richard Kahlenberg (from whom much of this account of his early teaching days is taken), "The message . . . was, 'Be good. Be obedient. Keep your mouth shut. Don't rock the boat. Don't do anything against the administration. Behave.' "

Sexism played a key role in undercutting teachers' status. At least until the 1970s, teaching was among the few professions that were open to women, and it was treated like a women's profession. Taking care of children was seen as a woman's job and something that women who went to college could use their educations for without barging into white-collar offices. The required hours and summers off fit with the idea that women could teach while still taking care of their own children (once those with families were allowed to fill teaching jobs, when schools became so crowded with baby boomers in the postwar period that the rules had to be changed to recruit more teachers).

In short, teachers could be underpaid and treated badly because they were viewed as women likely to be working only until they found a man to marry, or women supplementing the family income provided by their husbands—or because they were men doing a woman's job.

Albert Shanker was determined to change that. He wanted to make teaching a respected, well-paid profession for everyone.

June 11, 1962, New York City Board of Education, Brooklyn

The contract, signed on June 11, 1962, by the Board of Education and the United Federation of Teachers (UFT), where Shanker had by this time become a vice president and lead organizer, had been more than fifty years in the making.

Across the country, public employees had not even been allowed to organize and bargain collectively until a law was passed in 1959 allowing Wisconsin workers to do so.

Through the first half of the century, to the extent that teachers in New York and most other cities had organized unions or guilds at all, they were splintered into innumerable groups: kindergarten and elementary school teachers, high school teachers, shop teachers, teachers who were socialists, or communists, or conservatives who didn't even want to call themselves anything other than a professional association. (Many of these would ultimately become the National Education Association [NEA] which, ironically, would become a much harder-line national union by the end of the century than its rival national group, the American Federation of Teachers, which would be led by Shanker and then Randi Weingarten.)

Beginning in the late 1950s, a group in New York that included Shanker had forged the city's various groups into one United Federation of Teachers. In 1960, they threatened the first citywide teachers' strike, seeking higher wages and limits on class size, plus the right to bargain collectively in the first place—which the city and state had refused them. Shanker and his group picked an in-your-face date for the strike: November 7, the day that John Kennedy faced Richard Nixon in the presidential election.

At the time, New York law dictated that any public employee

who went on strike would be fired. Shanker and his group reasoned that New York, which was run by Democrats, would not risk the embarrassment of the teachers' going out on strike on Election Day. Besides, how could the city's Democratic mayor, Robert Wagner Jr.—whose father had been the senator from New York who wrote the National Labor Relations Act (called the Wagner Act) in 1936—allow himself to be the one to break a union, let alone a union of people who were teaching his city's children?

The crisis was averted at the last hour when Wagner agreed to appoint a commission to study whether the teachers should be allowed to form a union and bargain with the city and, if so, how their grievances might be addressed.

The union's cause was boosted in early 1961, when President Kennedy repaid his union supporters with an executive order allowing federal employees to form unions. However, Wagner's commission delayed acting and didn't even allow the teachers to vote on whether they wanted to bargain as a group until December. When the vote came in overwhelmingly in favor of a union, the Board of Education refused during months of negotiations to agree to the union's demands. The UFT went on strike in April 1962, and within days the board agreed to most of its demands, while also agreeing to ignore the law requiring strikers to be fired.

So in June the first contract was signed, giving teachers a starting salary of $5,300. This was more than double what Shanker had been paid nine years earlier. The contract—which, among other provisions, allowed union dues to be deducted automatically from every teacher's paycheck and paid teachers in charge of sports teams or orchestras $11.75 extra for each session they worked—was thirty-nine pages. Except in special circumstances, the contract guaranteed a duty-free lunch period for every teacher, and added $2 million to the budget to initiate a program to hire school aides in order to relieve teachers of hall patrols and lunchroom supervision "to the extent possible." These were all chores Shanker and his colleagues hated.

This first contract, which was to last for two years, would be replaced by increasingly better, longer ones, as the union gained strength. Three years later, the 1965 contract, now seventy-five pages, boosted starting salaries 30 percent, guaranteed every teacher that duty-free lunch period with no exceptions, and banned hall patrols and lunchroom duties except in special circumstances. Four years after that, the 1969 contract, now 111 pages, absolutely banned those chores, imposed other restrictions on teachers' duties, and stipulated a starting salary of $10,950, more than double the teachers' 1962 pay. The most senior teachers could now make $16,950, up 77 percent from 1962.

By 2007, the contract would be 167 pages and full of restrictions on hours and other working conditions, and the starting salary would be $45,530, or more than eight times 1962's $5,300.

Through the 1960s, Shanker, who became president of the UFT in 1964, pushed his union beyond meat-and-potatoes concerns into a leadership role across a broad range of social justice issues, particularly in the area of civil rights. He led union members to the South to support desegregation sit-ins and marches, often at great personal risk. When liberal Republican John Lindsay took office in 1966, the union overcame a different kind of challenge, which earned it the enmity of many in the civil rights community but dramatically added to its political clout.

Lindsay had responded to the concerns of minority groups about the terrible state of the schools in New York's ghettos by backing the recommendation of an independent group of civic leaders that the city's mammoth school system be decentralized so that minority communities could control their schools. The idea was that more input from local parents into their schools, including who was hired to teach there, would yield better results than what the citywide bureaucracy was producing. But community control was seized as a tool by more militant civil rights leaders, and the decentralization reform idea was catapulted into a call for minorities to replace the mostly white (and mostly Jewish) teachers in Ocean Hill–Brownsville, an impoverished Brooklyn neighborhood that had been picked as the guinea pig for decentralization.

One morning in May 1968, all eighteen white teachers in the Ocean Hill–Brownsville district were summarily fired. Months of near-violent confrontations ensued, including a series of long, bitter strikes, accompanied by anti-Semitic leafleting and newspaper ads from those pushing for community control. The rancor was so bad—and sympathy for those leading the attack on Shanker and the union was so widespread in New York's liberal community—

that, as Shanker's biographer Kahlenberg noted, when Woody Allen produced his 1973 comedy *Sleeper*, he elicited knowing laughs from theatergoers when the lead character woke up after a two-hundred-year sleep to learn that civilization had been destroyed when "a man by the name of Albert Shanker got hold of a nuclear warhead."

Ocean Hill–Brownsville eroded Shanker's and the union's standing in those circles for a decade. Yet the way the fight was settled more than made up for that by strengthening the union's political power and teaching Shanker and his people that they needed always to be poised to use it.

A watered-down version of Mayor Lindsay's push for decentralization was codified by a state law passed as part of a compromise with the union and the civil rights groups. The law established twenty-seven school districts across the city, with district superintendents to be elected by residents in each community. The superintendents would have power over some aspects of school locations, school curricula, teacher placement, and the like, but they would not have the authority to hire or fire teachers or principals, or negotiate contracts. That was left to the Board of Education, some of whose members were appointed by the mayor, while others were appointed by other elected officials. The result was a power vacuum. No one was singly responsible for the performance of the school system or for any school. Everyone could blame everyone else.

Into that vacuum stepped the teachers' union. Shanker's troops were united, disciplined, and ready and able to dispute anything going on at any given school. They were also organized and uniquely motivated to get out the vote in those low-voter-turnout elections for school district leaders, as well as get out the vote for the officials who appointed the education board members.

By 1969, Shanker was calling for a four-day, twenty-class-period teacher workweek (with teacher aides, organized by the union, to be hired to fill in the fifth day) and a class-size limit of twenty students. He didn't get the four days, but he did get limits on class size that began that year at twenty-five in elementary schools and gradually came down in later contracts, which forced education budgets up and severely limited the principals' ability to deploy their staffs.

Shanker—who had learned from Ocean Hill–Brownsville how much politicians could help his cause if he was willing to use the muscle and the money of what was now the state's largest union—also got the state legislature in Albany to address the vague standards around tenure protection that had allowed principals from his teaching days to fire those they didn't like for "conduct unbecoming a teacher." A new law now required not only that "tenured teachers and administrators have the right to retain their positions as long as they exhibit good behavior and competent and efficient service," but also that they "may be discharged or otherwise disciplined" only through a laborious third-party arbitration process where the standard of proof for school systems seeking dismissals would in practice be almost equivalent to that of a criminal trial. Once in the hands of a growing corps of aggressive union-paid lawyers, it would be that law that would metastasize into the Kafkaesque process that produced the Rubber Rooms forty years later, when an aggressive school system chief, Joel Klein, tried to remove incompetent or misbehaving teachers.

Meanwhile, pension benefits were increasing faster than salaries, creating a time bomb of liability that was largely invisible. Who in the press, let alone the public, paid attention to hard-to-fathom payout formulas that wouldn't come due for years? The structure of the pensions also created a perverse set of incentives. They were lavish once paid (typically 40–60 percent of the final year's salary, depending on years of service), but they didn't pay much until a teacher had taught for twenty or twenty-five years. Unlike today's standard 401(k) plans, the money set aside was not portable if a teacher left early in his or her career. With this all-or-nothing structure, even the most burned-out, diffident, or incompetent teachers would stay put once they got close to twenty or twenty-five years—and they could do so with impunity now that the new tenure rules made it almost impossible to remove those simply hanging on.

Across the country, much the same thing was happening. Salaries were increasing rapidly, and, given the low level of compensation for such important work, these increases were hard to argue against. Pensions were increasing even faster, with arcane tweaks piling up to wreak financial havoc decades later. In Missouri, for example, the unions got a law passed in the state legislature that added the value of health insurance to the calculation of what the teacher's final-year "salary" was, against which the lifelong pension was computed.

Work rules, which started as protections against such obvious abuses as teachers' not having a lunch break, were increasingly chipping away a principal's ability to run a good school, a problem exacerbated by proliferating contract clauses requiring elaborate grievance procedures whenever a teacher had a complaint about something a principal was doing that arguably tested the limits of the rules.

As in New York and similarly in the name of reform, management control over most large school systems was being truncated at the same time that the unions were getting stronger. School "reform" typically meant keeping direct responsibility away from elected officials, such as a mayor or county executive. The idea was to prevent patronage or other meddling, while letting the nonpartisan "experts" on a board of education handle things.

Thus, no one politician cared enough (because the voters were unlikely to blame a politician) to cross the one interest group—the teachers—that did care enough to get down in the weeds on work rules or grievance procedures, or push for tweaks in a pension formula. It wasn't really the politicians' school system and it certainly wasn't their money. Why fight too hard and risk a strike?

Moreover, much of the fundamental dynamic in labor-management relations—an adversarial process—was largely absent when it came to politicians negotiating with public employee unions, let alone with the union that was fast becoming the largest, richest, and most politically powerful union in the country. Through the 1970s, teachers were emerging nationally as political kingmakers, especially in Democratic politics. This was particularly true at the local level, where they could staff phones, hand out literature, and volunteer to get out the vote in low-turnout elections or primaries.

In other words, in Democratic strongholds, teachers could pretty much decide the fate on Election Day or Primary Day of the local officials who negotiated their contracts. Whatever else one might say, for example, about management's failure of will in handling labor relations in the auto industry, at least the bosses weren't sitting across the table from the people who might be responsible in large part for hiring or firing them.

The power of the teachers' unions in Democratic politics was accelerated beginning in the 1970s by factors beyond the teachers' escalating success across the country in organizing still more teachers and getting them good contracts—which in turn produced a cascading flow of dues, typically at a rate of 1–2 percent of each teacher's rapidly increasing salary. As the country's manufacturing sector, particularly in industries such as steel and automobiles, declined, overall unionization in the private sector declined, too. In 1960, about 35 percent of all private-sector workers were members of a union. By the turn of the twenty-first century, private-sector unionization had declined to about 7 percent. Union membership in public-sector jobs was about 35 percent.

Thus, the two national teachers' unions—the National Education Association and the American Federation of Teachers—became an increasingly dominant sector of organized labor. In 1960, teachers represented about 3 percent of unionized workers; by 1980, they represented 15 percent, and by 2009, 25 percent. If unions were the base of the Democratic Party, teachers were the base of the base, especially after the country's then-largest union—the Teamsters—defected to the Republicans when Richard Nixon granted clemency and a prison release to corrupt Teamsters leader Jimmy Hoffa in 1971.

In 1973, Shanker moved to reinforce that political power, creating at what by then had become his Washington-based American Federation of Teachers an organization called COPE, for Committee on Political Education. As he had done with a New York COPE organized within his local UFT, the national COPE asked all members to contribute a relatively small sum ($25 at the beginning) that when multiplied by what was then approaching 400,000 members would become a major war chest for campaign contributions. It would quickly become 1.3 million members asked to chip in $45.

Contributions were solicited aggressively, almost as an obligation, by union representatives in every school. They stressed that the money was needed to help elect politicians who supported generous education budgets or union-friendly laws related to pensions, seniority systems, tenure, or even, as with Ocean Hill–Brownsville, laws related to school system governance. More than 90 percent of the members contributed. Regular dues, which in the 1970s were $100 to $200 per teacher and would grow to an average of over $500 per teacher by 2000 (split between the local and the national organization), could be used for lobbying and other political activities, and the COPE war chest would supplement that with campaign contributions in federal, state, and local elections.

By September 1973, the *New York Times*'s legendary labor reporter A. H. Raskin, citing the influence Shanker had gained from the Ocean Hill–Brownsville wars and the power vacuum that he had filled afterward, declared Shanker to be the most politically influential union leader in the country, ahead of such kingmakers as the AFL-CIO's George Meany. The same article quoted a foe of Shanker's from the Ocean Hill–Brownsville fight as saying, "The only honest thing to do would be to designate Shanker as [Schools] Chancellor."

The NEA soon followed suit with its own, larger political war chest.

Thus, by the mid-1970s, teachers, through their unions, had dominant leverage over the growing bureaucracies that controlled public education. This created a dynamic in which the union leaders and the bureaucrats were naturally inclined to find ways to coexist by worrying more about the adults than the children. Combined with other social forces sweeping through the country—not the least of which was the fact that women were now enjoying far broader career opportunities—it was not a recipe for effective, accountable schooling.

Fewer than ten years later, a presidential commission would issue a dismaying report declaring exactly that and spelling out the damage.

"If an Unfriendly Foreign Power Had Attempted . . ."

April 26, 1983, the White House

President Ronald Reagan's National Commission on Excellence in Education was expected to issue one of those long, soon-to-gather-dust reports, the highlights of which would be a call to restore prayer in public schools, to allow for the dismemberment of public education by giving parents government vouchers with which they could pay to send their children to a private school of their choice, and maybe even to dismantle the federal Department of Education, which had been created four years earlier by President Jimmy Carter. At least, that's what President Reagan had hoped.

Instead, the commission, chaired by University of California president David Gardner, presented on April 26, 1983, a thirty-three-page manifesto that deplored the state of public education. "Our Nation is at risk," the report's opening paragraph began, and continued with a warning that sounded like what President Obama would be saying twenty-five years later: "Our once unchallenged preeminence in commerce, industry, science, and technological innovation is being overtaken by competitors throughout the world. . . . We report to the American people that . . . the educational foundations of our society are presently being eroded by a rising tide of mediocrity that threatens our very future as a Nation and a people.

"If an unfriendly power had attempted to impose on America the mediocre educational performance that exists today, we might have viewed it as an act of war," the report continued, using rhetoric that was unheard of for a commission white paper like this, and that some scholars later criticized as hyperbole.

Supplying a horde of disheartening statistics—"average achievement of high school students on most standardized tests is now lower than 26 years ago when Sputnik was launched," and 40 percent of seventeen-year-olds "cannot draw inferences from written material," while "remedial mathematics courses in public 4-year colleges . . . now constitute one-quarter of all mathematics courses taught in those institutions"—the report declared, "We have, in effect, been committing an act of unthinking, unilateral educational disarmament."

The commission recommended a variety of fixes, including more federal aid to schools in impoverished communities, the setting of curricula standards (twelve years of math, three years of science, and one year of computer science), standardized tests to measure student progress, and lengthening the school day and school year. As for teachers, the commission recommended that they be better compensated but that they also be certified for competence in the subject they were teaching and that "salary, promotion, tenure, and retention decisions should be tied to an effective evaluation system that includes peer review so that superior teachers can be rewarded, average ones encouraged, and poor ones either improved or terminated."

The crisis the commission identified had to do with more than how school systems had become leaderless bureaucracies where no one was responsible, or how teachers' union contracts blocked the performance-based evaluations or the longer workdays and school years the commission recommended.

For starters, the building of the interstate highways system in the 1950s and the resulting growth of the suburbs had enabled the haves to separate more easily from the have-nots in the cities, as did the increase in private schools, both of which lessened the political pressure on large school systems to perform.

Worse still for public education was the accelerating end by the 1980s of what had otherwise been a national black eye: job discrimination against women and minorities. Until the 1970s, one of the only professions easily open to women and minorities was public education—not law, medicine, engineering, or much of anything else, all of which pay much more than teaching.

Anyone who went to school in the 1950s or '60s knows this. My best reading teacher at the elementary school I attended in Queens, New York, lived two blocks away with her husband and children (one of whom was in my class). Twenty years later, she could have been a lawyer, like her husband. It's unlikely she instead would have chosen work in what had become a large bureaucracy that featured mind-numbing contracts, thousands of pages of school district rules, and, yes, ironclad job security and a great pension but low pay (for a profession) and incentive-less lockstep compensation based only on seniority or whether she had some kind of extra graduate degree. By 1983, the people more inclined to want that kind of risk-free paycheck were a different talent pool.

"Too many teachers are being drawn from the bottom quarter of graduating high school and college students," the commission found. It was a trend that would continue to accelerate in the three decades following the report, so much so that in 2010 a study by the McKinsey consulting firm would report that just 23 percent of new teachers came from the top third of their college graduating classes (with a large portion of those being Teach For America recruits), while the world's top-performing school systems—those of South Korea, Singapore, and Finland—recruited nearly 100 percent from that upper end.

Klein recalls that when he took over the New York City schools in 2002, he was immediately struck by this generational talent shortfall, which made giving near-total job security, through tenure, to what by then were senior teachers that much more of a problem. "We had," says Klein, "a whole generation of older teachers where some significant portion of them were not what you would call high achievers."

In other words, Randi Weingarten's mother, assuming she was as smart and ambitious as her doctor and lawyer daughters, would have been more likely a generation later to follow one of her daughters' paths. While Weingarten says she thinks of her mother when she thinks of her job defending those 167-page contracts, she is not nearly as likely today to be defending people with her mother's talent and drive. There are still thousands of skilled, highly motivated teachers in America's classrooms, most of whom, polls show, aren't active in their union and don't worry much about how the small print in their contracts protects them. Yet they have been increasingly joined by a different group who approach the 8:00-a.m.-to-3:15-p.m. workday with a civil service mentality. And if, as principal Kayrol Burgess-Harper in Harlem has found in the half of the building she shares with Jessica Reid's school, they make up a fourth or even a third of the teaching corps, they can set back the mission of the entire school. They resist change. They undercut the school's overall environment. And they can reverse the progress a child might have made with an effective teacher the year before.

To be sure, public schools were never the great equalizers in the 1940s and 1950s that they might seem to have been in retrospect. In those days, they assiduously tracked students, steering some into higher education that would give them white-collar jobs but steering more along tracks that would send them out into blue-collar jobs requiring limited academic skills. The problem was that in the post-Sputnik era, as the report *A Nation At Risk* called it, increasingly more jobs required more learning. That trend would accelerate in the last half of the 1990s and into the twenty-first century, when our schools would be challenged to produce "knowledge workers" to compete globally. So the finding that America's children were falling behind in 1983 was destined to become even more of a crisis in the years ahead. The schools would need to do more at the same time that all of these forces were combining to have them produce less.

President Reagan was so disappointed with the commission's alarming report—urging increased federal aid to education and federally encouraged curricula and teaching standards, rather than school prayer, vouchers, and a general retreat from federal involvement in K–12 education—that he almost didn't allow the commissioners to present their paper to him at a planned Rose Garden press conference. However, because the event had already been announced, he let the show go on. And because the report then got so much press attention, he soon began at least talking about the need for a greater federal role in advancing local solutions.

The local solutions that Reagan favored had been ingrained in the tradition of American education since schoolhouses had been opened spontaneously by local churches and civic groups in the early 1800s. It wasn't until the end of that century that even the states became significantly involved in schooling.

By the time of the Reagan press conference, that localized structure had become what education policy wonks liked to refer to as the "50/14,000/130,000" dilemma when it came to moving the nation in any direction education-wise: There were 50 states. There were about 14,000 school districts, most with their own union contracts by then and all resisting state intrusion. And there were about 130,000 K–12 public and private schools, most of which had their own curricula or rules for the classrooms in their buildings.

"You Gonna Put a Horse Head in My Bed?"

December 1984, Washington, D.C.

Brooklyn-born and Harvard Law–educated William Bennett, who is now a prominent conservative talk show host and commentator, had been asked by President Reagan to leave his post as head of the National Endowment for the Arts and become Reagan's second secretary of education. Because *A Nation At Risk* had made Reagan's original goal of dismantling the Education Department untenable in the short term, it seemed time to replace the administration's quiet, caretaker-like first education secretary with someone who would be more of an activist, although in a way that kept faith with conservative values.

Just after he was appointed, Bennett says, he received a visit from a National Education Association delegation. The NEA hadn't much worried about the Reagan administration, which had a hands-off attitude when it came to public education. Bennett, however, had promised to push for reforms in response to *A Nation At Risk*.

"We hope we will have your cooperation," one of the union leaders began after they had exchanged pleasantries. "If not, it will be unfortunate."

"Unfortunate for whom?" Bennett shot back.

"For you. You really don't want to be in a fight with us."

"Are you threatening me? You gonna put a horse head in my bed?" he asked, referring to the classic scene in *The Godfather*. "You guys are the problem," Bennett continued, building up steam, "and I'm coming after you."

I was unable find any of the NEA people who attended that 1984 meeting to corroborate Bennett's account, but it's clear that the new secretary's relationship with the teachers' unions went down-hill from there. He gave countless speeches attacking the unions as a prime cause of the decline of public education, events that were soon accompanied by union-encouraged demonstrations and often heckling.

Bennett also stepped up the publicity his department generated around a wall chart his predecessor, Terrel Bell, had prepared that ranked the states on such measures as high school graduation rates, amounts spent per student on education, and students' performance in the country's annual National Assessment of Education Progress (NAEP) tests. There were enough embarrassing data on the chart to infuriate most states' governors. California, for example, ranked tenth in average teacher salaries yet was third worst when it came to SAT score declines over the prior ten years, while New York ranked second worst in score declines, sixth worst in high school gradua-tion rates, but second highest (behind only Alaska) in spending per pupil. "They hated [the scores]," Bennett says. "What they hated worse was the suggestion that we use the NAEP tests more aggres-sively to independently, and more reliably, evaluate student perfor-mance. State evaluations notoriously vary dramatically," he adds. "It turned out one year, by adding all the state self-evaluations together, that 80 percent of American students scored above the median. Nice work if you can get it."

Meantime, a group of mostly Southern governors—including Bill Clinton of Arkansas, Richard Riley of South Carolina (who would become President Clinton's education secretary), and Tennessee's Lamar Alexander (who would become George H. W. Bush's educa-tion secretary and then be elected to the U.S. Senate)—started to pursue a less confrontational path, seeking reforms that nibbled away at the teachers' prerogatives while not attacking the unions frontally. Clinton, with his wife, Hillary, who headed a state task force on the subject, became a champion of testing teachers for com-petence not only before they began teaching but at regular intervals after. In April 1985, Shanker found himself at an education confer-ence in Chicago debating the young, relatively unknown Arkansas governor on the subject.

In Tennessee, Alexander pushed through a change in the old lockstep seniority system, adding elements of a career ladder that could bring a teacher up to "master teacher" status based on merit. The NEA attacked the plan, declaring, "Everyone is a master teacher."

Shanker and his AFT took a different tack. He became a reformer.

To some, certainly including Bennett, Woody Allen's villain simply saw the handwriting on the wall: Shanker, the shrewd politician, knew that his union had to become more accommodating, or at least act more accommodating. That cynical view sells Shanker short. *A Nation At Risk* had attracted headlines for a while in 1983, but the education reform climate in the 1980s was nothing like what it would become thirty years later. It was largely a talking point for Republicans plus a few Southern Democrats. Rather, as Richard Kahlenberg argues in his biography of Shanker, it's likely that Shanker—who had become a union activist in the first place because he hated the way teachers were not treated as professionals—really believed in reform and was embarrassed by the results public education was producing. He really believed in elevating the profession and thought that doing so would continue to allow teachers to increase their salaries and benefits and maintain their independence in the classroom.

The NEA had immediately attacked *A Nation At Risk* as an assault on teaching and public education. Shanker, who had championed the four-day workweek and resisted any talk of merit or performance pay, would have been expected to do the same. Yet, Kahlenberg wrote, when Shanker finished reading the report, he looked up at his staff and said, "This report is right, and not only that, we should say that."

Soon, Shanker began making a series of speeches and statements in the much-read weekly column his union had purchased for him (the column ran as an ad) in the Sunday *New York Times*, saying that teachers should be open to ideas like merit pay and better evaluation systems. In one column, Shanker wrote about a report in Baltimore that found that many applying for teaching jobs were unable to write a simple letter home to parents without making obvious grammatical and spelling mistakes, yet they were hired anyway. In blunt terms that read like Michelle Rhee's account of her Baltimore experience years later, Shanker said that no other profession would allow "the unqualified to practice," and that, "before we heap blame on Baltimore, we should remember that thousands of other school districts didn't even bother to test their prospective teachers at all."

In another speech, Shanker touted a "peer review" program initiated by the AFT local union in Toledo, Ohio, in which selected senior teachers would observe and evaluate all the teachers in a school and identify those who needed more training and even those who should be dismissed. He used another profession—law—as his analogy, describing how lawyers in local bar associations routinely discipline their own.

For those familiar with lawyer disciplinary systems—which, when not accompanied by some kind of government enforcement mechanism, are notoriously lenient in dealing with client complaints about misbehavior, let alone weeding out lawyers who are not competent—the analogy might have seemed hollow. Moreover, people using lawyers had a choice: They could hire the one they thought most competent and fire any who did not do a good job. Parents sending their children to the local public school had no such choice. Shanker had an answer for that, too. He suggested that parents be able to send their children to schools in their districts other than the closest one. More important, he suggested something called charter schools—alternative schools in local districts that would be given special authorization, or charters, to try different methods of teaching and operating. In Shanker's view, of course, these schools would be unionized. But his embrace of choice for parents—and his overall stance that a teachers' union had to engage in issues beyond those related to work rules, job protection, and wages—was so surprising for a union leader that the press was soon writing about him as a labor statesman.

While the NEA's harder line won support among its members and among many groups of teachers who continued to form new locals across the country, Shanker's stance gained the AFT traction in less traditionally union-friendly places like Texas and Tennessee (where Shanker said that the state's proposed master teacher program "should be open for discussion").

For a while the peer review programs in Toledo (and soon thereafter in Cincinnati and several other cities) did screen out higher percentages of new teachers before they were awarded tenure and even resulted in the removal of more tenured teachers who were not performing. However, as the focus on *A Nation At Risk* faded, these reforms never spread and, in fact, died out. Most locals, even in Shanker's AFT, opposed them or were more focused on continuing to make advances on meat-and-potatoes collective-bargaining issues. In New York, for example, Shanker's designated successor as head of the UFT focused on using her political muscle to win a wage increase of nearly 40 percent in her 1985 three-year contract.

Most of the debate, insofar as the debate continued, was over national curriculum standards or national teacher certification standards. Movement on both issues was stalemated, however, because conservatives on the Republican side rejected almost anything that was nationally imposed, while union supporters in the Democratic Party rejected the idea of standards, despite Shanker's support, because the local unions they depended on still refused to embrace them.

One thing that did change as a result of *A Nation At Risk* was that education budgets across the country increased faster than inflation, fueled mostly by salary increases and the hiring of more teachers to reduce class size. By 1989, although the country was spending approximately two-thirds more per student than in 1983, there had been no improvement in the national student assessment scores. Everyone involved in education policy seemed to understand that American public education was broken—including an idealistic, ambitious student at Princeton.

A "Hopelessly Naïve" Thesis

April 12, 1989, Princeton, New Jersey

Wendy Kopp, a senior at Princeton University, was worried that her gruff taskmaster thesis adviser was going to fail her or send her back for a rewrite. She had handed in her paper two days before, after struggling with it for months. The professor had already called and summoned her to his office. Kopp was a serious student, the kind who immersed herself in do-gooder student activities and heavy public policy courses. As a teenager growing up in a wealthy Dallas suburb, she had always followed her teachers' instructions (though with enough panache to vault her into Princeton). She hadn't followed instructions this time.

The professor had made Kopp promise that her thesis would be an argument for a law requiring two years of national public service. But she'd become so enamored of a different idea that she'd blown that off, producing instead a proposal—which she still called an "argument," hoping it would mollify him—for a *volunteer* national teacher corps that would ease the shortage of teachers across the country.

In fact, Kopp had become so consumed by the idea that she went much farther in the 172-page paper. She included budgets and time lines for launching the program a year later. A term paper had become not just a policy manifesto but also a business plan. And a career plan.

Kopp was going to start big. Recalling how President Kennedy had launched the Peace Corps with a multicountry splash, Kopp wrote that she was going to spend $2.5 million in the first year to deploy five hundred new teachers chosen from thousands of applicants who would be lured in a nationwide recruiting campaign as they graduated from the country's best colleges. She was going to train them at a "summer institute," then send them out to six different school districts spread strategically across the country to achieve maximum national impact.

When Kopp arrived at Professor Marvin Bressler's office at Princeton's Woodrow Wilson School of Public and International Affairs, Bressler didn't want to talk much about the thesis, which he had already graded A. Instead, he demanded to know how she thought she was going to raise $2.5 million. "Do you know how hard it is to raise twenty-five *hundred* dollars?" he asked. Kopp had a quick answer because she'd already thought about that, too: She was sure that Ross Perot, the billionaire from back home in Dallas who had been involved in efforts to improve Texas schools, would love the idea.

It would take a year before Kopp even got a meeting with Perot. But by 2010, Teach For America would be in its twentieth year, a year in which it would raise $216 million in contributions, grants, and other funds. With nine thousand corps members in public school districts or charter schools, TFA would be the largest single employer of students in Princeton's—and Yale's and Harvard's—graduating class, drawing applications from an astounding 15–18 percent of all three schools' seniors.

Kopp's proposal for a "Teacher Corps" argued that as a result of the report *A Nation At Risk* and the persistence of low national test scores, "the American education system has become the preoccupation of the media and of the nation's business and government leaders."

For drama, she quoted a recent *Fortune* magazine article that had one-upped *A Nation At Risk*'s doomsday talk: "It's like Pearl Harbor. The Japanese have invaded and the U.S. has been caught short. Not on guns and tanks and battleships . . . but on mental might. In a high-tech age where nations increasingly compete on brainpower, American schools are producing an army of illiterates."

That kind of press attention, Kopp wrote, combined with polls showing a "new idealism" among American youth or, as she put it, "the yuppie volunteering spirit," and bolstered by "a massive recruitment and publicity effort," would propel her plan to address the shortage of qualified teachers.

"Today's average teacher comes from the bottom rungs of academic achievement," the Princeton senior explained, adding that "children . . . view teaching as a downwardly mobile occupational choice."

Whereupon she cited some of the statistics she had dug up that illustrated how the talent pool had declined following what she described as the opening of "more prestigious, higher-paying occupations to women and minorities": Education majors scored 21 points below the national average on the verbal portion of the SAT and 34 points below the mean on the math portion in 1988. And, "Almost half of students enrolling in teacher education come from non-academic high school programs that are not intended to prepare students for college."

Having disparaged those with whom she envisioned her recruits would be working, Kopp nonetheless wrote that her idea was likely to get the support of, or at least not be opposed by, teachers' unions because "while the unions were not strong supporters of many reform measures, they for the most part refrained from mounting all-out opposition." The reality would be different. The unions would throw all kinds of roadblocks in front of Kopp (even though her corps members would always be required to join the union for their two-year stays if they were in a unionized school). For example, they tried to get school districts to block TFA recruits because they did not have training and degrees from traditional education schools, a position supported, of course, by those education schools. In her paper, Kopp had delved heavily into the fine print of these certification rules in various states and how they allowed for exceptions, but she hadn't explored the political dynamics.

Kopp also wrote (on her first page, in fact) that the TFA rookies would serve under and benefit from "the supervision of experienced teachers." As we know from what happened when Michelle Rhee, Sarah Usdin, Michael Johnston, and Jessica Reid were thrown into their classrooms, that, too, never happened.

However, Kopp got a lot right, including her core idea that despite the relatively low status accorded conventional teachers, she could make her corps a high-status cadre that would, indeed, attract the "best and the brightest."

Nonetheless, her thesis, Kopp recalls, "was hopelessly naïve, in so many ways." That kind of retrospective should be no surprise. Successful entrepreneurs acknowledge that game-changing ideas almost always seem impossible in retrospect, so much so that, as Kopp now says, "if I had had any idea of how ridiculously hard this was going to be, I would never have tried it."

Nor did Kopp's initial idea envision what would be TFA's greatest contribution. In *One Day, All Children . . .* , a book Kopp wrote in 2001 about the founding of TFA, she stated that she had thought from the start that "beyond influencing children's lives directly" for the two years they taught, her recruits would be so sensitized by their experience that "many corps members would decide to stay in . . . education," while others "who would go into other sectors would remain advocates for social change and education reform." That certainly happened, beyond anyone's expectation. Twenty years later, 67 percent of all of TFA's 21,000 alumni would be working in public education. That's more than 14,000 of the "best and the brightest." There would be more than 500 TFA alums working as principals or running school districts or the best charter networks. Thousands more would be teaching or supervising (like Jessica Reid) in charter or public schools (including more than 500 who had been named "teacher of the year"). Others would be working in education-oriented foundations or think tanks. And that doesn't count those who had gone into politics and were focusing on education.

Kopp did emphasize in her thesis that her corps would be recruited only for two-year commitments and then go on to other careers. "The best and the brightest will take a break to serve their nation," is how she put it. However, she didn't mention anything about midwifing this network of education reformers who might leave TFA but stay in the trenches. Nor did she write about, much less espouse, education reforms, such as evaluating and paying teachers based on performance. This is proof perhaps that the best entrepreneurs not only can overcome challenges they were oblivious of at the start but also adapt and even enhance their mission as they go.

From the moment she left the professor's office, TFA became Kopp's full-time work. This was fortunate because the graduating Princetonian had been rejected for jobs at an investment bank, two consulting companies, a food products company, and a commercial real estate venture.

Maybe these would-be employers could tell that Kopp wasn't
the type to throw herself into analyzing spreadsheets and management charts—a diffidence to running an enterprise that would
cause her significant problems in the early years of TFA. Nor was
she the kind of glad-handing Ivy Leaguer who would fake the requisite enthusiasm at these kinds of job interviews. At Princeton
she had immersed herself in policy debates and related student
activities, particularly the Foundation for Student Communication, which she described in her memoir as an organization "designed to bring student leaders and business leaders together to
discuss pressing social issues." One of her classmates, also involved
in campus groups like this, though not this one, was Jon Schnur,
the future Obama education adviser. He and Kopp were casual
friends.

By her senior year, education had become the issue Kopp cared
most about, and her interest had been piqued much the way
Schnur's had been when he had wondered why the smart young
woman who had joined his high school newspaper staff after moving from an inner-city Milwaukee school was so far behind in basic
writing skills. One of Kopp's Princeton roommates, whom Kopp
considered brilliant and creative, had come from a high school in
the South Bronx. Kopp had watched as she struggled to keep up at
Princeton, something that had been no problem for Kopp, who had
been educated at a suburban Dallas school where everyone graduated and 97 percent went on to college (and where, she recalls, there
was a $100,000 scoreboard at the school's $3 million football stadium). As her roommate and others who hadn't gone to good schools
ground through an academic environment that she considered a
cakewalk, Kopp began to delve into issues of education inequality.
By the fall of her senior year, she was so caught up in it that she and
her Foundation for Student Communication organized a conference
in San Francisco of student and business leaders to talk about how
to improve American public education.

Kopp explained in the preface to her thesis that the "action
group" she was part of during the conference soon began "thinking
about the phenomenal amount of interest that the conference par-
ticipants were showing in teaching." And, she continued, because
these students— "nominated by the deans of their universities as
the top students on campus"—were "certainly 'the best and the

brightest' . . . we soon agreed that if given the opportunity, top students would join a 'Teacher Corps.' "

The best and the brightest would fix education for people like her roommate.

When Kopp returned from San Francisco, she still hadn't decided to start the Teacher Corps herself. Instead, she wrote a long letter to President George H. W. Bush suggesting that he start it. (She got a form letter back mistakenly rejecting her application for a job.)

Kopp began thinking of the corps as something she herself could do only when, after she got turned down for those five corporate jobs, she called the New York City Board of Education to find out if she could teach there in the fall while she studied for a teaching degree. She was told that there are often such openings for trainees. However, the board would not be able to tell her anything definitive until about Labor Day of the following year, long after she needed to know that she had a job and where she was going to live. Why so late? Because teaching assignments in New York and most other school systems were doled out based on seniority. Only when all the senior teachers had chosen the spots they wanted if they wanted to transfer, followed by the teachers below them on the food chain making their choices, until the most junior incumbent was placed, would the personnel office know if and where there were openings that fit the subjects Kopp might be able to teach. It was then that Kopp decided that her thesis would be her career plan.

The reasoning behind why her recruits would succeed, she says, was a departure from what she calls "the mythology of superman as the only answer for kids in tough schools." It was a mythology epitomized at the time, Kopp explains, by two popular movies. Both *Stand and Deliver* (1988) and *Lean on Me* (1989) were based on heroic figures who had, through magical powers, tamed classrooms (in the case of Jaime Escalante of *Stand and Deliver* fame in Los Angeles) or an entire school (in the case of *Lean on Me*'s Joe Clark in New Jersey). Twenty years later, Kopp would point out that the school run by Clark (played by Morgan Freeman) might have had quiet children but it had been found to be one of New Jersey's worst-performing schools once student performance data began to be tabulated. And Escalante, portrayed by Edward James Olmos, had been given nearly super powers when, in fact, Escalante's success was attributable to unrelenting hard work and a refusal to assume his students couldn't succeed—a perseverance that echoed Jessica Reid's never-sit-down credo. Kopp was now out to find five hundred of the best and the brightest who would never sit down. They would refuse to fail because they had never failed at anything.

As Kopp was settling into New York to look for money and some like-minded crusaders to help launch TFA, a lavish conference was convened at the University of Virginia in Charlottesville to address the same issue she had now targeted as her life's work. It would be remembered as the most significant thrust ever by the federal government into the traditionally local province of K–12 education.

A Governor and a President
Take Center Stage

September 27–28, 1989, Charlottesville, Virginia

George H. W. Bush was Ronald Reagan's vice president, but Bush (who had said during the 1988 New Hampshire primary campaign that he wanted to be "the education president") believed, unlike Reagan, that Washington needed to be more involved in dealing with the education crisis identified by *A Nation At Risk*. Yes, this was ultimately an issue for the states and their local school districts to deal with, but Washington, which since the days of Lyndon Johnson's Great Society had fed billions of dollars to the states in education aid, ought to do more to push them.

So Bush did something that had been done only by Teddy Roosevelt on the subject of conservation and Franklin Roosevelt when dealing with the Great Depression. He convened a summit of all of the nation's governors to address the education crisis, choosing the University of Virginia and Thomas Jefferson's nearby home, Monticello, as the venues. The purpose was for the governors and the president to agree on a national strategy, with timetables, for improvement of student performance. Since *A Nation At Risk*, there had been a lot of talk about this, particularly among the Southern governors, who saw upgraded public education as a way to bring economic development to their states. So far there had been no action to answer *A Nation At Risk*'s call to arms.

"I wake up at night with a bad dream that the education reform movement will go the way of the Hula Hoop, twist and Edsel," Arkansas's Bill Clinton told the *New York Times* on the eve of the Charlottesville summit. Clinton was the chair of the Democratic Governors Association. Along with his Republican counterpart from South Carolina, Carroll Campbell Jr., he also headed a National Governors Association education study group. The future president would emerge as the leading force among the governors at the summit; photos of the ceremonies during the event typically had him sitting just to the left of the president he would unseat three years later.

Proclaiming that "federal funding is not the major issue" and that "accountability to taxpayers on how education money is spent" was more important, Clinton, who had already boosted his state's school system with increased aid and new teacher certification standards, was among those pushing for specific goals for reducing the disparity in achievement levels among children of different races, reducing high school dropout rates, and increasing the percentage of high school graduates going on to college.

Following a formal dinner at Monticello the first night, on the second day the Democratic and Republican governors and the Republican president emerged with a communiqué—much of it worked out by Clinton and Roger Porter, a fellow Rhodes Scholar who was Bush's chief domestic policy aide—outlining an agreement on a variety of measures. These included the establishment of national education performance goals and then annual reports on how those goals were being met, plus a call for an overhaul of state education systems to ensure, among other things, "an education system that develops first-rate teachers and creates a professional environment that provides rewards for success with students, real consequences for failure, and the tools and flexibility required to get the job done."

The UFT's Shanker, wearing his statesman's hat, praised the conference and said that President Bush's speech there had "defined a vision of public education that was not public relations."

But none of the goals was spelled out, and when they were four months later, they were watered down from what Clinton had wanted. They were more aspirational than programmatic. For example, early childhood education programs would make every preschooler "ready to learn," and American students would become "first in the world in science and math achievement." How and when were not specified. There was no blueprint for necessary funding or for school system reforms, in large part because most of the Democrats, such as New York's Mario Cuomo, thought increased federal funding ought to be the focus, while the Republicans wanted the states to undertake system reforms, not get more funds.

Twenty years later, as Schnur and Obama prepared their Race to the Top, none of the summit's goals would have been met, and in almost all areas there would be no discernible progress toward them.

Nonetheless, Clinton called the meeting a breakthrough. "This is the first time in the history of this country," he said, "that we have ever thought enough of education and ever understood its significance to our economic future to commit ourselves to national performance goals."

On those terms Clinton was right. In fact, in retrospect it could be argued that he had just defined what could be called stage one of the modern education reform movement. Beginning with *A Nation At Risk*—prepared under the auspices of a president who abhorred federal involvement in most domestic affairs, let alone in the traditionally local sphere of public education—the country had at last begun to understand, as Wendy Kopp's thesis had found, that there was a national crisis festering in our schoolrooms. Now, in Charlottesville, six years after *A Nation At Risk*, this first stage had arguably come to a close. A nationally constituted group of responsible public officials had at least rhetorically begun down the path of vowing to fix it. This wasn't enough for Bennett, Reagan's education secretary, who called the summit communiqué "pap." But for the governors and federal officials who went to Charlottesville, and for the press that covered the presidential summit, it was a big deal.

Now would come the second stage: the fight over how to fix it, in which the politicians would soon have to contend with all kinds of players—union leaders, academics, philanthropists, and ultimately Kopp's TFA troops—coming at them from all sides.

But first Wendy Kopp had to struggle with keeping her infant program alive.

Payroll to Payroll

Kopp's budget in her thesis projected that she'd raise $85,000 to get her through September 1989, once she moved to New York and began putting her project together. She got by on a $26,000 grant from Mobil Oil and office space donated by Union Carbide and then Morgan Stanley. At Morgan Stanley and elsewhere, she relied heavily on her Princeton pedigree, typically seeking alums who someone had suggested might be sympathetic.

Almost all these people told Kopp that while they liked her idea, it seemed too speculative. And most wondered aloud how an earnest, wide-eyed, soft-spoken twenty-two-year-old dirty blonde was going to run a far-flung operation like this. (Her answer—that she'd run a sixty-student volunteer group that had organized national conferences—didn't do the trick.) Others thought that the only way to improve education was to improve education graduate schools, not try an end run around them with her best and brightest getting a quick training course, then dropping by for two-year stints in the country's toughest schools before heading off to law school or the investment banks.

Kopp kept at it, becoming a stronger believer in her idea the more she heard herself explaining it to the people who turned her down. Slowly, she picked up other small grants here and there, but nothing like the additional $2.2 million her thesis said she needed from September 1989 through when the first recruits would show up for training the following summer.

It was a hand-to-mouth struggle she would endure for five years, and things were often so bad and so down to the wire that she frequently feared she was not going to meet a payroll that had started with a support staff of two or three, increased to a half dozen (all, like her in the first years, drawing $25,000 salaries), and gradually became dozens of recruiters, trainers, and support people.

Kopp learned that the definition of luck in efforts like this was that after you have twenty calls or meetings in which someone deflates you almost to the breaking point with another rejection, you get "lucky," because the twenty-first meeting is with someone who gets it immediately and agrees to write a check.

Even when she seemed to have made a breakthrough—$300,000 from the Carnegie Foundation and then, following repeated meeting requests to her hometown philanthropist, a $500,000 promise from Ross Perot, conditioned on Kopp's raising a matching $500,000—the money would soon be gone and another cash crisis was looming.

She wasn't wasting money. Her plan to get campus reps to lure thousands of students from colleges all over the country to apply so she could pick the true five hundred best and brightest from among them was expensive. There were plane tickets to buy (Kopp got a friend of a friend to extend $70,000 on his American Express card) and cars to rent for her crew to go campus to campus, enlisting someone on the ground to hand out flyers and hang posters for the new organization and then host initial question-and-answer meetings. Those flyers and other aspects of the "massive publicity campaign" Kopp had envisioned cost money, too, as did the travel expenses to bring in the thousands of collegians whom they had lured into applying for final interviews. And then there was the looming cost of the summer training institute—flying in the five hundred corps members, housing them, feeding them, producing materials for them, paying stipends for their time, paying teachers to train them, and renting a facility where it would all happen.

Early on, Kopp got help from Whitney Tilson, a Harvard classmate of her brother's. Tilson, whose parents had been educators in Africa, was so taken by Kopp's idea that he deferred a job at the Boston Consulting Group to help organize finances and operations. Personable, good-natured, and obsessively numbers oriented, he became the guy who had to tell Kopp every week or two exactly when the money was going to run out. Neither had any idea then of the pivotal role Tilson would play in the education reform movement a decade later, after he had graduated from Harvard Business School with honors and become a successful hedge-fund investor.

Somehow, Tilson, Kopp, and the others in the small band she had gathered kept the money from running out, and by the following summer, in 1990, Teach For America had gathered its first corps of 489 (11 short of the 500 projected in the thesis) for training at the University of Southern California in Los Angeles. (The location would allow the trainees to get exposure to real students because Los Angeles keeps its schools open through the summer on a staggered-semester schedule.)

By all accounts, almost everything about the summer institute was a disaster: insufficient food, misinformation about whether student loans would be forgiven because the recruits had joined TFA (they wouldn't), and, above all, the woefully slapdash training. As Michelle Rhee, Dave Levin, and Sarah Usdin would find, TFA training was not destined to get better for many years. For them and the others it would be sink or swim. One-third of those first 489 recruits would not last through their two-year commitments.

Even by 1994—after lurching from payroll to payroll for four years, and actually shrinking slightly in new recruits—TFA almost wasn't able to open its fourth annual summer training institute because Kopp couldn't come up with a check to pay for the facilities until a few days before it was supposed to begin.

By then, someone on Capitol Hill was taking up the same cause, though from a different angle, and with even more discouraging results.

Lighting Up the Capitol Switchboard

May 4, 1994, U.S. House of Representatives

George Miller, who had represented the Seventh Congressional District in the East Bay area of San Francisco since 1975, thought his proposal was simple common sense. If the federal government was going to give school districts across the country billions in federal aid, why not use the money to try to make schools and their teachers more effective? A lifelong Democrat who had worked as a staffer for Democrats in the state senate before running in 1974 for Congress, Miller had always enjoyed strong union support, including support from the powerful California teachers' unions.

Miller—a modest, avuncular, white-haired, and white-mustached Mark Twain–looking type, who even Republicans say is the classic unheralded real-deal public servant—had been quietly volunteering on weekends at a mostly Hispanic school in his district. As he gradually became more involved in the school's needs and operations, Miller began to think about schoolroom staffing. He kept noticing that the teachers he thought were the best and were filling gaps in the most needed subject areas were repeatedly transferring out to schools with better facilities and more learning-ready pupils. "Why can't we offer them bonuses or some kind of extra pay to stay?" he asked the principal. "It's impossible," the principal responded. "The unions would never allow it."

Miller began focusing on the talent pool from a different angle when he started visiting Indian reservations as part of his congressional duties and ran into some TFA recruits. "I saw what these people were doing—people from all kinds of great schools who were working night and day, and I kept wondering why we couldn't do something with that," he recalls. "All of their friends were going into jobs—like in Silicon Valley or on Wall Street or in the law firms—where they would get paid based on their performance. Why couldn't we do that?"

So in the spring of 1994, Miller began circulating a draft of an amendment to the federal aid to education law that would require states receiving federal aid to certify that their teachers had been qualified for the subject areas they were teaching and that their school systems had provisions in place for awarding merit pay to especially effective teachers. Initially he had lots of supporters. Then, as the time came for a vote, his allies peeled off. By the night of the vote, the teachers' unions back home and across the country had mobilized, as had conservative allies they had recruited with the argument that this was federal intrusion into local schools. The blitz was so effective that the House switchboard was shut down because of an overload of phone calls. The vote was 434–1 against.

On his way to the White House, Bill Clinton, the prime mover of the 1989 Charlottesville summit, had put his education reform zeal in a lockbox. Soon after he won the Democratic nomination in 1992, Clinton had traveled to Pittsburgh for the AFT's annual convention. The governor who had said in Charlottesville that accountability was more important than more funding now promised the cheering teachers that he would expand programs like Head Start, increase funding for vocational education, and push to make sure teachers were paid more. He said nothing about accountability.

However, five months before Miller fruitlessly pushed his teacher certification and merit pay provision, Clinton, now in the White House (where Jon Schnur was working as an education policy aide), had followed up on the Charlottesville summit with a declaration in his January 1994 State of the Union address of something he called "Goals 2000"—a set of education improvement targets to be reached by the year 2000. Clinton's plan was passed by Congress in March. It funded an education standards commission that began developing curriculum standards, although the states would volunteer, not be forced, to adopt them.

Clinton's program doubled down on the Charlottesville summit's vague goals with specifics, at least in terms of time lines. By 2000, early education programs would make all children able to start school "ready to learn." By 2000, the high school graduation rate would increase from about 70 percent to 90 percent. By 2000, American children would "be first in the world in mathematics and science achievement." By 2000, "everyone will attend a safe drug-free school." None of these goals would be reached, yet this would create ammunition for the reformers, who would cite the failures.

In October 1994, five months after Miller was on the wrong end of the 434–1 vote, Clinton pushed through an upgrade in the Great Society federal aid to education act that would stand as one of his major domestic accomplishments. In addition to providing funds for schoolroom technology, bilingual learning, enhanced science and math teaching, and programs aimed at disadvantaged communities, the new law forced states to adopt specific achievement standards for all students. Importantly, the standards had to be the same for all, regardless of race or economic status. And the states would have to report on how they were meeting those standards, based on tests to be given to *all* students. The National Assessment of Education Progress tests, started in the 1970s, had been given only to sample sets of students in each state; now everyone at every school would get some kind of test.

The states could choose their tests and their standards, and they could, and would, otherwise game the rules. Nonetheless, this was a significant step forward. It would force the beginning of data collections across the country that would have huge ramifications into the next decade. It was the beginning of using data—however inaccurate the data might be because the tests were imperfect—to drill down and link students to increasingly more targeted sources of their performance. It started here with the states and school districts. George W. Bush's No Child Left Behind law in 2002 would push it down to individual schools. And Obama's Race to the Top would push for links to individual classrooms and teachers, which is where the real battle would begin.

Moreover, Clinton's 1994 rewrite of the old law provided for federal funding to support charter schools, which at the time were limited to a handful of early experiments in a few states. Clinton declared a goal of vastly expanding the number of charter schools. Six years later, in a May 4, 2000, visit to the City Academy high school in St. Paul, Minnesota, the nation's first charter school, Clinton announced yet another grant program for charter schools. By the end of his term at the beginning of 2001, there would be more than 1,700 charters.

· · ·

The NEA and the UFT fought the testing and charter school initiatives, especially the charter provision, but Clinton won passage after the Democratic leadership, at Miller's urging, relented. "He was the Democrats' new president," Miller says. "So there was a lot of goodwill among people here who would otherwise have toed the union line."

As these tentative pushes for reform from the Democratic side of the aisle became more frequent, and as TFA continued to expand and accumulate positive press coverage, the unions and other forces of the status quo increasingly realized that they had to push back.

The Backlash

Steven Farr was accepted into both Yale Law School and Teach For America on the same day in 1993 as he was about to graduate from the University of Texas. He decided to defer Yale and join TFA. His parents were educators, and he'd caught the bug.

Farr was sent to teach high school English and English as a second language at a mostly Hispanic border school on the Rio Grande in South Texas. Like "all of us in TFA," he says, "I had to go through the experience of experiencing failure that you've never experienced before."

Farr, like Rhee and Levin, had toughed it out and had come, he says, to love coaxing "the potential out of kids who were being lost or squelched on the Texas border."

Now, as he was finishing the final months of his second year, he suffered a different kind of setback: An article had just been published in *Phi Delta Kappan*, the most influential scholarly journal for educators, declaring that what Farr and everyone else in TFA was doing was "bad policy and bad education. It is bad for the recruits because they are ill-prepared . . . and many who might have become good teachers are instead discouraged from staying in the profession. . . . It is bad for the children because they are often poorly taught."

The author was Linda Darling-Hammond, who had been an elementary school teacher in Palo Alto before becoming a highly regarded education professor and scholar at Columbia and Stanford. However, this did not read like the work of a scholar writing for a scholarly journal. It was mostly a write-up of quotes from interviews with TFA recruits who had dropped out because TFA's inadequate training had left them unable to cope when thrown into tough classrooms, or quotes from an article written by one of those dissatisfied recruits. To add flavor, negative quotes were cherry-picked from old newspaper articles covering TFA's start-up struggles. The positive ones—and Kopp had received tons of great press—were left out.

There was no attempt to compare learning achievement by students taught by TFA teachers with those taught by others. In part, that was not Darling-Hammond's fault. There was little if any data at the time anywhere linking student scores to teachers. That kind of data, which would empower the reformers to push for teacher accountability, was years off. Still, Darling-Hammond could have found more anecdotes of the other kind, since by then 82 percent of TFA recruits were sticking it out for the two years, up from 70 percent in the first year's class. (By 2008, the retention rate would be 92 percent.)

Supplementing the accounts from those who had failed were the kinds of broadsides rarely seen in a scholarly journal: Kopp exhibited an "absence of concern for children"; TFA recruits, she quoted one principal as saying, were people who otherwise "could not find jobs"; "Ignorance about teaching, learning and children . . . characterizes TFA's program."

Darling-Hammond's hostility to TFA and Kopp seemed personal. She seemed angry at the young Princeton grad's audacity. She all but conceded as much in one section, where she described Kopp as having come to see her when she was planning the launch of TFA. The older, wiser Darling-Hammond had advised her that programs like this had been tried before and had failed because teachers need much more training and knowledge than Kopp's plan for a summer institute could provide. But Kopp, she wrote, "maintained that she was sure she could do in a few weeks whatever it was that universities took much longer to do."

Darling-Hammond says that she wasn't "angry at anyone." Rather, she wrote the article because "I was hearing so many horror stories from principals, superintendents, and teachers that I felt I had to say something. . . . TFA is a magnificent recruiting enterprise, but so many of these people were falling through the cracks."

Darling-Hammond characterized Kopp's attitude toward her TFA corps this way: "Because of their innate superiority, they don't need—or can't be bothered with—extensive preparation for teaching." That might have been true. Yet it was also true that most TFA recruits had succeeded and many were already starting to make their marks as great contributors to public education. In fact, a large enough majority of the TFA corps had succeeded that principals who had them in their schools were praising them, and other principals all over the country were seeking TFA recruits.

Darling-Hammond's reaction to what she called TFA's "slapdash summer institute" should have been no surprise. She had devoted her professional life to the idea that teachers need more, not less, training. Indeed, at the time she wrote this article she was a professor at the kind of institution (Columbia Teachers College) that Kopp's program sought to sidestep and was serving as the executive director of the National Commission on Teaching and America's Future, a blue-ribbon panel dedicated to raising teacher training and certification standards across the country. Darling-Hammond also espoused reform. Her work as a teacher, as the co-founder of a preschool for disadvantaged children, and as a renowned scholar gave her reform bona fides. But her idea of reform was not to upset the establishment by calling for accountability or advocating for an alternative to traditional education schools. She wanted higher standards and more resources targeted at the same structure. In that sense, Darling-Hammond was one of the education establishment's favorite reformers, so much so that she had collaborated with the NEA and AFT on a variety of professionalization initiatives, such as union-run teacher-training institutes.

Darling-Hammond's article would receive wide play in the education press for years and be something Kopp would have to answer for as she sought money from donors. In the short term, with TFA constantly on the brink of insolvency, Darling-Hammond's attack was almost a death blow.

More generally, it was the beginning of a backlash against education reform. Kopp didn't see herself as being engaged in wholesale reform; she was just placing smart, motivated young teachers in schools that needed them. In fact, she hadn't said a negative word about the unions or any other part of the public education establishment or otherwise joined any of the broader reform debates. She was always careful about that (which would, in later years, be a source of frustration to the education reform network she was helping to create with her TFA corps). But Kopp was doing something that needed to be watched, and checked. She was injecting new people, backed by a new set of supporters and donors, into the old structure. Darling-Hammond's article—its tone, its substance, its author, and its acceptance in the education community's scholarly journal—was a clear sign that Kopp's growing footprint and increasingly good press had stirred the education establishment.

For Steve Farr, who read Darling-Hammond's article one night after he got home from his high school near the Rio Grande, it was, he says, "like a punch in the gut." It jarred him into thinking that maybe what he was doing really didn't make any sense, though not for the reasons Darling-Hammond had outlined. Whatever the truth of the anecdotes she had presented (and he was aware that many of his peers had, indeed, flamed out), he knew that he was connecting with his students. Rather, Farr worried that he and others like him who were succeeding were creating what he called "islands of effectiveness" amid systemic failure. Next year, his students would be thrown back into that system. The system had to be fixed, Farr believed, to find and train good school leaders, to embed a culture of raised expectations, and to create support mechanisms that would attract, train, and continually enhance the performance of good teachers. So Farr, who had decided to reclaim his spot at Yale Law next fall, began thinking about how he might use that Yale credential to get involved in systemic school change.

Then he went back to tinkering with his lesson plan. Whatever Linda Darling-Hammond thought about his work, he knew it mattered. He had kids who were depending on him the next morning.

In the end, the success that people like Farr had in the classroom would also be the best weapon in the reformers' battle, as was about to be demonstrated by one of Farr's TFA colleagues who had a bold plan that stretched from Houston to the Bronx.

Schoolyard Classroom

August 1995, a sidewalk in the Bronx, New York

In August 1995, Dave Levin was on a hot sidewalk on 156th Street in the South Bronx, about ten blocks from Yankee Stadium (and a few blocks from where Tom Wolfe's Master of the Universe has the car accident that unravels his life in *Bonfire of the Vanities*). A tall twenty-six-year-old with wiry dark hair and an easy grin, Levin deftly corralled forty-six African-American and Hispanic fifth graders into a quiet circle. He greeted all of the kids warmly and joked with them before getting down to business. That was the shtick he had perfected two years earlier at TFA in Houston: Always mix fun with the dead seriousness of the mission. Wear loud Sesame Street–like neckties, but always wear a tie.

The pied piper on this Bronx sidewalk was a complicated story. At TFA in Houston, Levin had mixed all-nighters creating lesson plans or word games and obsessive engagement with his kids—phone calls, home visits, whatever it took—with more than his share of beer parties and womanizing. He was the learning-disabled kid who'd been forced out of one prestigious New York private school only to become valedictorian of another before going on to Yale.

The son of a money manager, Levin had grown up on Park Avenue, yet he seemed completely at home here, a few blocks off the seen-better-days Grand Concourse. As I would watch him later in similar settings, it was clear that he felt at home not from some sense of noblesse oblige but because he had a special quality that rendered him clueless to what to others would seem to be the incongruity of it all. He could easily banter with his new students and their parents because to him it really seemed that being here was no big deal, no more out of the ordinary than meeting someone for squash at the Yale Club.

This morning was the first day for the New York version of

the Knowledge Is Power Program (KIPP), which he and Mike Feinberg—Levin's roommate, best friend, and TFA teaching partner in Houston—had started with two KIPP classes the year before in Houston.

Their Houston program had been a great success, overcoming a parade of obstacles skillfully chronicled in *Work Hard. Be Nice*, a book about KIPP by *Washington Post* reporter Jay Mathews. With Levin itching to return home to New York and both wanting to expand their reach, they had decided to branch out. So Levin had spent much of the last twelve months commuting between Houston and New York to get approvals and space for KIPP and then to recruit the students that he and Frank Corcoran, another TFA Houston roommate, would teach.

After lots of false starts targeting one location or another, he talked a district superintendent in the Bronx into giving him space at one of the city's worst schools. This KIPP class was to be a special program for just forty-six fifth graders within PS 156. It would be five years before Levin's program would become a charter school.

Fifteen years later, KIPP schools would be so successful in boosting student performance, and so celebrated for doing so, that getting a seat in a classroom in one of the ninety-nine KIPP schools in twenty states and the District of Columbia would, literally, be the equivalent of winning a lottery. There would typically be seven to ten applications for each KIPP seat, and the winners would have to be chosen by having their numbers picked out of a spinning bowl.

But throughout the spring of 1995, Levin had struggled to fill his first forty-six seats, so much so that, as Mathews reported, he had to sneak into a middle school gymnasium to crash a general student-parent registration event (he had no credentials that the school guard would accept) so he could solicit parents and their children. Parents were skeptical of the tall white guy with the loud pastel sweater (with a KIPP logo) who promised to teach their children from dawn till dusk, and who wanted them to sign a weird KIPP "contract" committing the students to arrive on time, do all their homework, follow the strict dress codes, go on all the field trips, attend the KIPP three-week summer preparation school, and be generally committed to excellence.

This morning was the first day of that KIPP summer school.

Only it wasn't going to be *in* a school. Despite Levin's repeated pleas, the city's Board of Education had refused to allow him to use the building during the summer. When the board relented only as far as letting him come two days before the real school year began, he simply set up shop on the wide sidewalk in front of the school and then moved everyone into the schoolyard adjacent to a larger middle school for the three-week session.

Levin's and Feinberg's plans for KIPP Bronx had been two years in the making. By the end of their first TFA school year in Houston, in June 1993, they had begun having a conversation about the futility of their work that was not unlike the conversations Steve Farr, Jessica Reid, Michelle Rhee, and Michael Johnston would have with themselves: Their kids were succeeding, but now that the year was over they were destined to be thrown back into the same old system, smothered by low expectations and back in the care of adults who thought Levin and Feinberg downright strange for having created so many songs, poems, games, and other tricks to get the kids to learn, for coming to school so early and staying so late to tutor them, and, especially, for visiting their students' parents at home all the time.

Wendy Kopp recalls visiting Levin's Houston TFA class that spring and being overwhelmed with how Levin's sense of urgency— his insistence that nothing get in the way of preparing these kids for college, including a broken air conditioner on the sweltering day she was there—contrasted so strikingly with the culture of the rest of the school.

Four months later, Levin's and Feinberg's frustration had turned into a plan. One night in October, they attended a speech by Rafe Esquith, a legendary teacher visiting from Los Angeles. Esquith was known for having gotten his mostly Hispanic fifth graders to put on Shakespeare plays, tackle algebra, and otherwise crash through those low-expectation barriers.

Levin and Feinberg were mesmerized by Esquith's talk, not because he unveiled some magic that had eluded them, but because he confirmed what they thought this was all about: "It is an honor to have been chosen Disney Teacher of the year," Esquith began (according to Mathews's book about the KIPP founders), before having a group of students he had brought with him do some Shakespeare and a few math puzzles. "But I don't think I am a better teacher than anyone else. I just work really hard at it. We believe there are no shortcuts. That's why my kids come to school from seven o'clock to five o'clock fifty weeks a year." It was also why, he said, he had the kids come back to him for tutoring for the SAT tests years later. Esquith would later write an autobiography with a prologue that began with the lyrics from Paul Simon's "The Boxer" and ended as follows: "All teachers, even the best ones, get knocked down. The difference between the best ones and the others is that the best ones always get up to answer the bell."

It was on that night that Levin and Feinberg decided to start a program that would institutionalize that no-shortcuts mission with its own extended school year schedule, its own rules for parents and students, its own curricula, its own teaching methods and associated paraphernalia (posters, rap songs, field trips), and its own high expectations for the children. The culture might be filled with games and field trips, yet it was also encased in a traditional formality, epitomized in the "SLANT" rules Levin and Feinberg promulgated: "**S**it up straight. **L**ook and listen. **A**sk questions. **N**od your head. **T**rack the speaker." They were determined to take all that beyond their own classroom, first with a two-class Knowledge Is Power Program in Houston in the fall of 1994 and this morning, in August 1995, in that schoolyard in the South Bronx.

April 1997, 110 Livingston Street, Brooklyn, New York

By the spring of 1997, KIPP had four teachers teaching fifth and sixth grade in the Bronx and eight teaching fourth through sixth grades in Houston. The KIPP commitment "contracts" with the students and parents were a page each, but no teacher had a contract or letter of agreement with KIPP; the teachers simply cosigned the commitment contracts that their students and parents signed.

On the other hand, the old headquarters of the New York City Board of Education at 110 Livingston Street in Brooklyn was a paper factory. The union contract now numbered 185 pages, and there was a teachers' manual four times thicker. And then there were the "circulars"—rules issued by a large unit of the chancellor's staff that had the force of law throughout the school system.

On April 3rd, 1997, the chancellor published *Special Circular #6*, which was sixty-seven single-spaced pages. The topic: teacher preparation and training periods, or in Livingston Street speak, the "Provision of Professional Activity Options."

Actually, it was sixty-seven pages devoted to giving teachers an extra period off during the day, a perk they had won in their new contract negotiated a year earlier.

Before the new contract, teachers had been required to attend training sessions, cover homerooms, or do other non-classroom work two periods a day. The two periods had now been reduced to one. That wasn't what took sixty-seven pages. The Board of Education had not wanted this to look like a giveaway to the teachers, so the contract had provided for teachers to use the extra time to engage in their own professional development activities, not those directed by the principal or anyone else. The circular prescribed how the union and administration at each school would work together to create a list of the possible activities the teacher might now engage in. There was even a time line for when these collaborative meetings would take place, along with a process and time line laid out for finding aides to replace teachers for duties they would no longer carry out.

It all seemed pretty business-like and specific, in terms of what the new "professional development" activities would be. Except that buried in a paragraph on page four, the chancellor declared that these "professional activities will be self-directed and do not require a teacher to be in a specific location at a set time." In other words, it was an extra period off—another accommodation between the unions and the bureaucrats that was good for the adults. It was as if taking away that teacher preparation time didn't matter to the kids when, in fact, an expanding circle of academics and other researchers were now finding that quality teacher time was what mattered most.

The Discovery:
"Good Teaching Matters"

June 1998, Washington, D.C.

Kati Haycock has been an affable but persistent advocate for education equity since the 1970s. In 1994, she had left a top position at the Children's Defense Fund, the civil rights group founded by Marian Wright Edelman, to start the Education Trust, a Washington-based foundation whose mission was research and advocacy on issues related to closing the education gap between minorities and the poor and the rest of America's children.

In the June 1998 edition of the trust's research journal, *Thinking K–16*, Haycock published an article, which she wrote herself, that would do more to shake up conventional wisdom about public school teaching and learning and do more to alienate her from the education establishment than anything else the Education Trust had written or said in its four years. This, despite the fact that the article's title seemed obvious and flattering: "Good Teaching Matters: How Well-Qualified Teachers Can Close the Gap."

Haycock and her staff had discovered that although linking student test scores to school districts was just beginning as part of the Clinton administration's education initiatives, there were school systems in Tennessee, Alabama, Massachusetts, and Dallas, Texas, that had been doing that for years and had also taken the further step of making it possible to link the testing data to specific teachers. And, Haycock had found, several academics, led by Stanford's Eric Hanushek, had been crunching the data and finding compelling evidence that the quality of the person in front of the classroom really mattered.

A study in Tennessee had sorted teachers into five levels (lowest, second lowest, middle, second highest, highest) based on the performance gains their students made during the school year in reading and math. When teachers in the lowest group were then compared with the 20 percent of teachers in the highest group in terms of how much they improved student performance in a subsequent year, the differences were dramatic: "Students whose initial achievement levels are comparable have 'vastly different academic outcomes as a result of the sequence of teachers to which they are assigned,' " Haycock wrote, quoting the findings of the University of Tennessee's William Sanders. The differences were also long-lasting: "Differences of this magnitude—50 percentile points—are stunning," Haycock continued. "As all of us know only too well, they can represent the difference between . . . entry into a selective college and a lifetime at McDonald's."

In Dallas, Haycock reported, "the average reading scores of a group of fourth graders who were assigned to three highly effective teachers in a row rose from the 59th percentile in fourth grade to the 76th percentile by the conclusion of sixth grade. A fairly similar (but slightly higher-achieving) group of students was assigned three consecutive ineffective teachers and fell from the 60th percentile in fourth grade to the 42nd percentile by the end of sixth grade. A gap of this magnitude—more than 34 percentile points—for students who started off roughly the same is hugely significant."

Almost from the moment her article was published, Haycock started receiving calls and e-mails from teachers' union officials in Washington demanding to know why she was bashing teachers. The unions and groups like Haycock's, which typically advocated for more resources to be poured into schools in poor or minority communities, had been natural allies. The data threatened to drive a wedge between them.

"The teachers' organizations had been enormously successful in painting all teaches as underpaid, wonderful educators," Haycock recalls. "They immediately attacked, taking the position that anything critical about any teacher is an attack on all teachers, when in fact by then it was clear that a lot of people from the bottom of the college pool were going into education."

The reaction to Haycock's article also exposed fissures between the union and at least some of its members. "We also got e-mails from individual teachers, warm e-mails," Haycock says, "that said, 'We always knew we mattered. How wonderful to see some real data.' "

That summer, Haycock realized that "teachers' organizations have this weird view of their constituency. They want to say they are all in it to change kids' lives. Then, when we present data that say, 'Yes, you can change lives,' and, 'Yes, you really matter,' they say, 'No, we're powerless. It's about race, or poverty, or something else.' "

Haycock's dissemination of that research was the beginning of a flood of similar scholarly work, much of which would be financed by a data-obsessed wonk named Bill Gates. It would reframe the education debate by turning an intuitive notion—shared by anyone who has ever sat in class with a great teacher and a lousy one—into empirical data. The data, in turn, would be ammunition for what was becoming a growing network of reformers.

The Network

After Whitney Tilson had helped Wendy Kopp juggle finances and operations following his graduation from Harvard in June 1989, he had gone back to his plan to work for the Boston Consulting Group. From there he had enrolled at Harvard Business School, then worked with a Harvard professor studying inner-city businesses. In January 1999, using $1 million from his parents, money from relatives, and some of his own money, Tilson launched his own fund, now called T2 Partners. He called it a "value fund," meaning he was a "contrarian" who looked for value in stocks and other investments where others didn't see it.

Tilson was good at it. Within six years he would amass, he says, more than $50 million in his fund from 120 wealthy investors. He was, he says, consistently beating the Standard & Poor's stock index, and was writing a widely followed newsletter called *Value Investor Insight* while running a popular annual conference for investors. At the same time, Tilson got involved in various liberal causes and charities, something he attributes to the fact that his parents were "the original flower children—Peace Corps, educators in Tanzania, the whole thing."

One morning in October 1999, Tilson got a call from a friend who had participated with Tilson in some charity events and fundraisers for Democratic candidates. "Hey, have you ever heard of Teach For America?" the friend asked. "I helped start it ten years ago," Tilson responded.

The friend now wanted Tilson to see Teach For America in action in New York so that he might be encouraged to donate. Tilson agreed, and a few afternoons later they went to a high school in the Bronx, where Tilson was duly impressed watching a few of the TFA corps members performing in front of their classes. Then the friend walked Tilson over to the middle school next door to see something started by a TFA alum, called KIPP.

Hiking up to the fourth floor, Tilson came into a hallway where on one side of an open fire door there was the chaos one might expect in one of the South Bronx's toughest schools. On the other side, as they were greeted by Dave Levin, Tilson saw youngsters in uniforms filing quietly through the halls on their way to class. In fact, what Levin remembers seemed to stun Tilson the most was that the children on the noisy side were running up and down the hall but would come right up to the line where the fire door was and stop, "like it was the DMZ or Checkpoint Charlie."

Tilson's amazement continued as he watched a math class, where the fifth graders were doing complicated algebra, then an English class where they were discussing essays in a way that almost reminded him of a Harvard English class. "It was," he says, "completely electrifying. I just couldn't believe it."

Tilson quickly became involved in raising money for KIPP. More than that, he was so intrigued by what Levin was doing that he began reading up on education reform and e-mailing the articles to Levin.

Soon Tilson's clipping service was so good that Levin suggested he send it to a list of friends who were also involved in education, people such as Mike Feinberg, Levin's KIPP partner in Houston; Sarah Usdin, now working for TFA in Louisiana; and Jon Schnur, who was helping the Gore presidential campaign part-time while enrolled at Harvard's Kennedy School. Within five years, there would be hundreds of people on Tilson's e-mail list, then more than four thousand by 2010. By then, there would be so much activity and controversy related to education reform that Tilson found himself sending two or three clip-filled e-mails a week, which was more often than he e-mailed his network of investors.

"As I'm Sure Mr. Schnur Knows"

October 1999, Kennedy School of Government, Harvard University

Michael Johnston, the Yalie from Colorado who had taught for TFA in the Mississippi Delta for two years, had come to the Kennedy School after having been brushed off by Greenville, Mississippi, school officials when he suggested how they might restructure things to make the school work better. When he got to Cambridge, he cross-enrolled in a Harvard Business School class called Entrepreneurship in the Social Sector. It seemed like a good course for someone who wanted to change the nation's schools.

A few weeks into the class, in October 1999, Johnston's professor had turned to education and education reform, including charter schools. Johnston soon noticed that for this session, the professor began several sentences with, "As Mr. Schnur probably knows . . ." or "As Mr. Schnur could no doubt tell you . . ."

Who was this Mr. Schnur?

After class, Johnston asked around and found that there was a guy named Jon Schnur, also at the Kennedy School and also cross-enrolled in the B-School class, who had worked in the Clinton White House on education issues and was now moonlighting as an education policy adviser to the Gore presidential campaign.

Johnston found Schnur and introduced himself, and the two hit it off immediately. Within a few weeks they and two classmates were working on a paper for the class that would become the business plan for something called New Leaders for New Schools.

Schnur and Johnston quickly realized that they shared a belief that what really mattered in fixing schools was getting better teachers and better principals. And no one and no organization out there was doing anything to improve the talent pool of principals— to find new leaders for new schools who would have two core competencies: the drive and ability to observe, supervise, and improve their teachers' classroom performance, and the management skills to use their school's manpower and money effectively. State principal certification exams didn't screen for that, the two knew.

Their idea was to create a nonprofit organization that would recruit prospective principals from among star teachers and even nonteachers who were interested in making their marks in education. They would train them intensely, place them in charter schools or public school systems looking for new blood, then provide support and training once they were placed. The work would be financed by donations and government grants, as well as placement fees from the charter schools that hired the recruits.

Their plan for NLNS was a finalist in the Business School's business plan contest, although blueprints for nonprofit ventures were not the contest's usual fare. More than that, Schnur actually launched it the following year, while Johnston went off to Yale Law School.

NLNS, which would become Schnur's base for his education reform work, quickly made its mark. Within two years it had raised $5 million and was placing principals in New York and Chicago public schools and in several charter schools. By 2010, the organization would have trained more than seven hundred school leaders.

Tilson, Schnur, and Johnston all thought of themselves as committed Democrats. It was a Republican president who was about to give their movement another push forward.

No Child Left Behind

Al Gore walked away from Jon Schnur's education accountability reform message in the 2000 campaign, but George W. Bush embraced it. Bush had made school accountability a hallmark of his Texas governorship. In Texas and then on the campaign trail, he had decried "the soft bigotry of low expectations" that allowed failing schools simply to continue to fail.

Through the first year of his presidency, Bush had worked with, among others, Democrats Ted Kennedy on the Senate side and George Miller on the House side on a school reform agenda. His new version of the 1960s Great Society's aid to education act—which he called No Child Left Behind, and which he signed in the White House on January 8, 2002—mandated that in return for federal funds, all states had to keep track of the performance of the students in their schools, using the same standards across the state for tests given to all students in different grades. The states also had to measure performance by various categories of race in order to quantify achievement gaps. Moreover, the states were required to develop plans to take over and turn around what were called "persistently failing" schools—schools that were failing to make "adequate yearly progress" toward 100 percent student proficiency by 2014.

For a Republican to assert this much federal intrusion in state and local education was extraordinary, but the bill passed with broad support from both parties. Some in the education establishment, including the unions, feared that NCLB, as No Child Left Behind came to be called, would scapegoat schools whose populations were not destined to make the required yearly progress. They went along because in this post-9/11 bipartisan period there was little chance they could stop the bill, especially with all the extra funding it promised school systems.

In the years following No Child Left Behind, the Bush administration would be criticized for not funding it fully enough, a difficult argument given that federal education funding increased by 40 percent through 2007. It is true, though, that states soon began to game the system by defining their standards of proficiency down.

Those two criticisms ignore what was really the breakthrough forged by NCLB. For the first time, all across the country, student performance was being tied to every school, and demographics were being tied to every measure.

The old National Assessment of Education Progress tests had been administered to only a sample of students in each state and could gauge only a state's overall performance, or perhaps that of a school district if anyone bothered to parse those numbers. Clinton's changes to the law had advanced testing so that every child was tested in every school, but children's year-to-year progress could not be measured, because only one grade in elementary, middle, and high school had to be tested.

Now, with No Child Left Behind, every student would be measured every year in grades three through eight. This meant that teachers could begin to be measured based on how much, for example, a fourth-grade teacher advanced his or her students from their third-grade reading and math levels—if someone wanted to do the measuring.

Eight months after the passage of President Bush's No Child Left Behind, a former member of the Clinton administration would try to use the data it provided to overhaul the country's largest school system.

"Don't Worry, It's Just a Parent"

August 19, 2002, 110 Livingston Street, Brooklyn

August 19, 2002, was Joel Klein's first day on the job as the New York City schools chancellor. Making his way to his office after navigating through the security process at the Board of Education headquarters in Brooklyn (which, after cleaning out two-thirds of the staff, he would soon abandon in favor of a building next to City Hall in Manhattan), Klein saw that a light on his phone console was blinking. "Don't we need to answer that?" he asked his new assistant, a veteran of the office he had just assumed and someone who, he recalls, looked at him as if certain she'd still be there when he, like the chancellors before him, had departed. "Oh, no," she said. "That's just some parent on hold who called complaining about something. If you let it blink long enough, she'll go away."

It was probably that morning that Klein began using a phrase that he would still repeat to friends multiple times a day eight years into his job: "You just can't make this stuff up." To closer friends, and his wife, Nicole Seligman, the general counsel of the Sony Corporation, it was more likely to be, "You just can't make this shit up." Although Klein and his wife now traveled in Manhattan's splashiest business and media circles, Klein had grown up across the 59th Street Bridge in Astoria, Queens, the son of a postal worker. He still spoke more like a kid from Astoria than a Harvard-trained lawyer responsible for educating more children than anyone else in America.

Klein was two months from his fifty-sixth birthday. He was already balding, with tufts of hair sticking over his shirt collar in the back and on the sides, and he still dressed as if he was at his law firm.

He is a workaholic. Subordinates, friends, even parents of New York City schoolkids would soon become accustomed to his habit of BlackBerrying back a response to most e-mails within minutes, even while sitting on the dais at some official event or catching a Yankees game. (He and his wife are manic Yankees fans.)

Klein is one of those Ivy Leaguers with an off-the-charts résumé that suggests that if the best and the brightest can do anything, he can probably do anything even better: Phi Beta Kappa from Columbia College, *Harvard Law Review*, a Supreme Court clerkship, the founder of an elite Washington law firm specializing in high-stakes appeals, deputy White House counsel under Bill Clinton, head of the antitrust division of the Justice Department, where he'd made headlines suing Bill Gates into a settlement. Then, in a daring jump out of law and government, he had taken the top American job at the German media conglomerate Bertelsmann AG, where he was responsible for businesses ranging from Random House books to Sony BMG Music to Grunar + Jahr Magazines.

In the spring of 2002, just after he became New York's mayor, Michael Bloomberg won control of the schools following a battle with the Albany legislature. Bloomberg had not talked about school reform in his 2001 mayoral campaign the way he and Klein later would discuss it—in terms of eliminating union protections. However, along with promising to pay teachers more, he had made seizing control of the schools and turning them around a key campaign promise.

Bloomberg is a billionaire who, having been passed over for promotion at an investment bank, got his revenge by building the fabulously successful financial data and media company that bears his name. As CEO, he was famous in media circles as a tough (but generously paying) boss who insisted on a clear chain of command that stopped at his desk. So Bloomberg had instinctively recognized that the post–Ocean Hill–Brownsville crazy quilt of school districts sharing power with a board of education appointed by multiple elected officials was no way to run anything. Someone—the mayor—needed to be in charge. Albany legislators had ultimately acquiesced in the change, in part because Bloomberg had become the lead financial benefactor of the state's Republican Party, and in part because the Democrats knew the schools were a shambles, making any defense of the status quo untenable.

The United Federation of Teachers at first fought mayoral control but gave in when, as Randi Weingarten later explained to me, "We realized he was likely to win in Albany anyway and we agreed that there was a power vacuum. I also believed Mike [Bloomberg] when he promised me that he would be collaborative with us in filling the vacuum. Besides, who would have dreamed he would appoint someone like Joel?"

The idea of Klein's running the schools actually came from Margaret Carlson, then a *Time* magazine columnist and longtime friend of both Klein and Bloomberg.

When he was twenty-three, Klein had taken a leave of absence from Harvard Law School to spend a year studying education and teaching math to sixth graders in Queens. He had also dabbled in education while in Washington as an informal adviser to the District of Columbia's mayor. That might not have been enough experience for most mayors who had just pushed a plan to seize responsibility for the city's 1,200 public schools by daring voters to vote him out in four years if he didn't improve them. However, Carlson knew that Bloomberg was a big believer in the notion that winners could win on any field. One day, as Bloomberg was talking to her about his need for someone to come in and shake up the school system, Carlson touted her friend Joel.

Bloomberg and Klein met for more than an hour before Memorial Day weekend at Bloomberg's Upper East Side town house. Klein didn't think he had connected with Bloomberg and was surprised when the mayor called in mid-June and invited him for coffee. After about an hour and a half, Bloomberg offered him the job, telling him he should focus on picking a team and making one or two big moves early.

"Jesus Christ wasn't available . . . and I thought Joel was smart and tough as nails for a job that really required that," says Bloomberg.

Klein spent his time off between jobs in June and July reading as much as he could—books on the history of education, books about charter schools, a book about the importance of principals as schoolhouse leaders, articles like Kati Haycock's about teacher effectiveness and the data that could identify it, monographs about the structure of school systems (few of which seemed to agree). He began meeting or calling as many people as he could find who understood school systems and education, traditionalists and reformers. In the beginning he didn't know enough to appreciate the difference, let alone which side all the players were on.

Klein spent a lot of time consulting with Alan Bersin, who was running the San Diego schools. Klein knew Bersin from his Justice Department days because Bersin had been the United States attorney in San Diego before taking the schools job. Like Klein, Bersin is a New Yorker from an outer borough (Brooklyn), an Ivy League lawyer (Yale), and former Supreme Court clerk who had had no background in education.

Bersin had done his own tour of the literature before taking the job and had found, he told Klein, that "while you could play along the edges with structural changes, the core business of education is teaching." However, the people who run school systems, Bersin had concluded, "would rather concentrate on rearranging the deck chairs, because trying to touch teaching was the third rail. . . . Everyone in the system, especially teachers, will fight you. They'll tell you it isn't their fault—that it's all about poverty and demographics. They will attack you and try to get rid of you.

"It didn't even take me ninety days," Bersin told Klein, "before I went from being a Democrat who always thought the unions were the good guys to realizing that unions were not the good guys—that the Democratic Party and the school reform movement had run into a rock because of the transformation of the teachers' union movement from the '60s to the '90s from a progressive force to the most conservative force in the mix."

Bersin—who would ultimately be forced out of San Diego in 2005 when the teachers' union successfully backed new candidates to take over the school board—told Klein that he needed to pick his fights carefully and one at a time. "Don't burn down all the bedrooms in the house at once," he advised. He also warned Klein that he had to start by putting into schools principals whom he could hold accountable. "The word 'principal,' " he told Klein, "comes from 'principal teacher.' It all starts with them." Then, he said, Klein had to make sure the principals could hold their teachers accountable.

Bersin's advice matched how Bloomberg had instructed Klein: Pick the right team that will build a system of accountability at the school level and then at the classroom level.

It should not have been hard to predict that the New York City teachers' union contract—which by 2002 was 206 pages, much of which was devoted to protecting teachers from being judged by management—was about to collide with two executives whose religion was the merit-based accountability that Bersin was preaching. Klein's was the résumé of one of the meritocracy's ultimate winners. Bloomberg's company had been famous in media circles for being the ultimate sink-or-swim shark tank. Not even the top executives had contracts. They could be at their desks one day and gone the next if the boss decided they weren't producing.

Klein knew that the union contract required lockstep seniority compensation and teachers' choice of classroom assignments based on their seniority and that it all but guaranteed them lifetime tenure. However, he didn't read the actual contract until after he had been on the job for a few weeks. Only then did he begin to see that those contract constraints and more were layered over with all kinds of byzantine procedures for teachers to engage in a long, three-stage grievance process, in which they could protest just about anything related to how they were managed by their principals. It was another "You just can't make this stuff up" moment.

Meeting Michelle

August 2002, New York City

Wendy Kopp was exasperated at first that the new mayor would think that "some lawyer" was what the school system needed. Yet when Klein called her right after his appointment, she says, "I could see that he was approaching this from the point of view of changing the whole system. It was clear that he was calling hundreds of people, trying to find out how to overhaul everything." As their conversation shifted to how TFA teachers were placed in New York City schools and how Klein could get more of them, Kopp mentioned that there was another program supplying ambitious young teachers in New York called NYC Teaching Fellows. It was run, she said, under the auspices of something called the New Teacher Project by a young woman named Michelle Rhee—the Baltimore TFA teacher who had used all those shapes and cards and other physical objects to turn her math class around. Like her TFA corps, Kopp explained, recruits from Rhee's NYC Teaching Fellows would have to join the union, but they were not likely to hide behind union contracts when it came to throwing themselves into their work. Call Michelle, Kopp suggested.

In the fall of 1995, Kopp had finally reached an even keel; revenues from donations and government grants were slightly exceeding expenses. One way she had done that had been by shutting down an ambitious offshoot she had established three years earlier called TEACH, which had been intended to fill the gap in TFA's training by becoming a separate unit that would help train TFA recruits and other teachers being recruited through alternative career paths. The plan had been that TEACH would not only solve TFA's training problems but also help financially, because it could raise money separately, plus get grants or fees from those other participating school systems. TEACH had improved TFA training, but the business plan had been a disaster, so Kopp had closed it (while keeping some of its training capacity).

However, Kopp hadn't given up on the idea of a broader organization that could put more of the best and brightest into schoolrooms. So in 1997, with TFA on its feet financially, she had secured a grant to start a separate nonprofit corporation, the New Teacher Project, that would recruit and train a new breed of teachers. To run it, she recruited Rhee, her Baltimore TFA alum, who had just graduated from the Kennedy School with a master's degree in public policy.

Rhee had been immediately tempted by Kopp's offer. But one skill that the Kennedy School had not taught her was how to do a business plan. She went to a bookstore and bought everything she could find about writing business plans. She tried, she says, "about twenty drafts, which kept sucking less and less." In fact, Rhee came up with a solid plan to make the New Teacher Project a consultancy that would draw charitable contributions while also getting fees from the school systems whose teachers it recruited and trained. It had turned out to be a good deal for school districts looking to break the cycle of recruiting teachers only from the traditional graduate schools of education.

By 2002, Rhee's New Teacher Project was supplying teachers in the mold of the TFA recruits to school districts across the country, including 1,300 in the last year to New York City through its NYC Teaching Fellows program.

By now Rhee was used to getting calls from politicians and

school district bosses, like Klein, who would inquire about what
the New Teacher Project did, say how good its Teaching Fellow program sounded, then take months to get back to her, if they did at
all. Injecting new blood into school systems was not for the faint of
heart. So she was amazed not only that when Klein called he spent
more than an hour questioning her, but also that he called back in
about two weeks, after he'd been in office a few days, to ask if she
could double that 1,300 next year.

Klein had big plans on that and other fronts. But first he had to
figure out where all the bodies were buried in the bureaucracy he
had inherited.

Outside Money

October 3, 2002, New York City

In the 1950s, Eli Broad was an accountant who noticed that his
home-building clients seemed to be making a lot more money than
he was. So he and a cousin of his wife, Edythe, started Kaufman
and Broad, a home-building company specializing in houses for
the growing middle class. By 1999, after having diversified into
mortgage banking, Broad sold his Los Angeles–based business for
$18 billion, netting what he says was several billion for his family.
It was then that he expanded a smaller foundation he had started in
the 1970s into the $2 billion Eli and Edythe Broad Foundation.

Broad decided to make public education a priority because, having traveled widely in Asia and Europe, he had seen how far America's schools were falling behind.

"I didn't know anything about curricula and had no idea how to
teach," he says, "so we decided to focus on governance and management of school systems." The effort had begun inauspiciously, with
millions invested in an institute intended to train people elected or
appointed to local school boards. "It didn't work," he says, "because
they'd learn management or finance or human resources and get all
enthusiastic and then go home and fall into the same traps of doing
things the way they were always done, and hiring the same people
they always hired."

Broad had then started a Superintendents Academy, which was more successful. It spread a new breed of school executives across school systems all over the country. He also started supporting Schnur's New Leaders for New Schools with a $1.3 million grant, and Wendy Kopp, beginning with a $800,000 grant to Teach For America to help fund her third year. By 2010, Broad would be one of the largest donors to TFA.

"What we had come to believe," says Broad, "was that our money could work best where we found real change agents to make it work." Thus, except for supporting charter school start-ups (he would ultimately become one of KIPP's largest benefactors), he had shied away from providing support in his hometown of Los Angeles or, despite repeated requests, to school programs in New York City, because, he says, "I knew that the teachers' union was running the show."

Now, thanks to Alan Bersin, who had gotten seed money from Broad for some of his initiatives in San Diego, Broad saw an opening in New York. Bersin told Broad about Klein's background and the conversations they had been having and suggested that Broad reach out to him. Klein seems to be just the kind of change agent that you like to invest in, Bersin told Broad.

So Broad called Mayor Bloomberg, an old friend, and said he'd like to help his new schools chief. Broad and Klein spoke the day after Klein's appointment was announced.

"I've got the money, but I've never gotten the reform," Broad told Klein. "Maybe you can get the reform."

Klein told Broad that he had one immediate problem: "I have all these people—thousands—who work for me but who don't teach and aren't principals. I don't have a clue about what they do and they sure as hell aren't going to tell me what they do."

Broad agreed to help, and also invited Klein to a conference he was convening in a few weeks of education reform people from around the country. It was there that Klein met Schnur. They became fast friends and were soon talking to or e-mailing each other once a week or more, exchanging ideas. "Schnur seemed to know everyone and everything that was happening," Klein recalls.

On October 3, 2002, less than two months after his first conversation with Klein, Broad stood with Klein and the mayor in the ro-

tunda of the elegant old Tweed Courthouse that backed onto City
Hall and that Bloomberg and Klein had converted to the New York
City Department of Education's new headquarters. There Broad announced that he and a close friend, legendary hedge-fund manager
Julian Robertson, had donated $3.75 million for Klein to begin a
top-to-bottom study aimed at completely restructuring the school
system to eliminate bureaucracy and provide better service to the
city's 1.1 million schoolchildren.

Klein told the assembled press that the money would fund the
plans for Children First: A New Agenda for Public Education in
New York City.

"The simple, universally acknowledged fact is that our schools
are not doing the job they must and should do for our kids," Klein
declared. "These circumstances call for dramatic action."

The UFT's Weingarten praised the plan. "The big difference
between what Joel just said today and the normal studies we hear
about," she gushed, "is that this time he talked more about parents
and classrooms and schools and principals and how they interact
and how kids get a better education than he talked about central
bureaucracy."

"I wasn't sure what Randi meant, but I figured, 'What the hell,' "
Klein recalls. "If she's going to go along, fine."

"The Union Won't Allow It"

As Klein pushed to bring in more of Michelle Rhee's NYC teaching fellows, he was told that the UFT was pushing back, saying that the fellows were less effective in the classroom than those who had conventional credentials. Klein's instinct was otherwise. However, he figured, why debate something that was knowable? So he called in a human resources executive and asked, lawyer-like, whether the school had test scores that they could compare from one year to the next for specific students. (Klein knew that even before No Child Left Behind was to take effect, New York did its own testing.)

Yes, we do, the HR specialist said.

So, Klein continued, was there a way, after measuring improvement on those scores for given students over a given year, to link that improvement to the specific teachers who taught those students?

"Well, I guess that would be possible, theoretically."

"So how about we take a sample of, say, one hundred or five hundred kids taught by teaching fellows and compare their progress in a year to one hundred or five hundred kids not taught by the teaching fellows? Could we do that?"

"I guess in theory we could, but we can't."

"Whaddya mean, we could but we can't?"

"The union will never stand for it."

"Does anything in the contract prohibit us from doing that? I mean, we just want to take a sample, so we can have a look and see if these teaching fellows are any good."

There was nothing in the contract, per se, that didn't allow it, the HR person explained, but, he insisted, "I know I will never get anyone here to do it. The union will be furious."

"Well, what if I want you to do it and I tell you to do it?" Klein pressed.

"No, we can't," was the final answer he got. "We just can't."

Klein couldn't let go of the issue. The inmates were running the asylum, he fumed to his staff, most of whom were holdovers who agreed there was nothing Klein could do. Then, in one of his many calls to his new friend Michelle Rhee, he mentioned the problem.

Rhee had a ready answer. Her thesis adviser at Harvard was a professor at the university's Graduate School of Education and was a whiz with education data, she said. "I'll put you in touch with Tom Kane and you can get him to crunch those numbers."

Tom Kane had become interested in the idea of tying teachers to test scores a year earlier, when he'd done a study that found that there seemed to be consistency among student gains and individual teachers.

Using a portion of the Broad-Robertson donation, Klein got Kane and his staff to do a sampling of students taught by teaching fellows and by other teachers. The teaching fellows turned out to have been slightly to significantly more effective, giving Klein the green light to recruit more of them.

The assignment from Klein was the beginning of a new career of sorts for Kane. Working with the professors whose initial research Haycock had used for "Good Teaching Matters," Kane would become the guru of measuring teacher effectiveness.

Principal on a Mission

November 23, 2002, New York City

Klein ultimately wanted the teacher effectiveness data so that he could put this information in the hands of principals and hold them accountable for using it to measure the performance of their teachers. As he was leaving an uneventful first speech to the annual meeting of the New York City principals' union at the Hilton Hotel in Manhattan, in which he talked to them about the new ethic of accountability he intended to create, Klein was accosted by a man who looked more like an overweight middleweight boxer than a school principal. Anthony Lombardi, then forty-four, introduced himself as the principal of a middle school in Queens and declared, "I'm going to help you." Whereupon he started rattling off all the problems Klein needed to address if, as he had just said in his speech, he was really determined to empower principals to improve their schools and reward them or hold them accountable for the results.

"It was a Saturday night and I was holding him at the escalator. He must have thought I was nuts," Lombardi remembers. "But he gave me his card and told me to e-mail him."

"I'd like your help," Klein said before hurrying off.

After wondering if this was really Klein's e-mail address or a bureaucratic dead drop, Lombardi decided to take him up on the offer. He sat down that night and through the weekend and unloaded with an e-mail he sent three days later. It printed out at sixteen single-spaced pages.

"To date," Lombardi began after recounting his twenty-three years' experience in the New York City school system, "there are many poor educational practices that have been established as a result of both collective-bargaining agreements and policies between the union and management. . . . The contracts have diminished accountability and have debilitated effective management at the school level."

Lombardi continued with this snapshot of the job Klein had ahead of him:

> My knowledge of the contract results from the fact that the last three UFT middle schools' vice presidents were elected from IS 61 where I was an assistant principal for six years. The school was extremely union focused and every contractual provision and policy was exercised in the spirit of supporting the letter of the law in contract rather than advancing the educational mission. I have learned that the UFT is as well organized as the Prussian Army and the former Board of Education was not a worthy opponent. They were often outwitted either intentionally or unintentionally. . . . In *The Prince,* Machiavelli contends that when an absence of power exists, it will be filled. This void in management was filled by the UFT.

Lombardi then launched into attacks on a variety of what he deemed to be abuses in the union contract and its implementation—

from granting paid sabbaticals (especially half-year sabbaticals, which, he said, left students "without teachers in the middle of a year") to union representatives being paid as full-time teachers yet teaching as little as one period a day and spending the rest of the time unduly influencing the school districts' selection of principals and other supervisors friendly to the union.

He complained about *Circular 6*, the 1997 contract change that gave teachers an extra free period and that, Lombardi explained, made it "difficult to develop a curriculum committee, report card committee, standards committee, etc. if I, as principal, do not have the authority to assign teachers to a specific location or at an assigned time."

Lombardi also cited a provision, 8-E, inserted into the contract in 1990, allowing the principal no say over the format of a lesson plan. One teacher with whom Lombardi was at odds, Lombardi told Klein, had informed him "she could write her lesson plan on toilet paper," a position, he said, which had been supported by the school's union representative.

Lombardi uncorked his angriest salvo in a section titled "Rating and Dismissal of Poorly Performing Teachers." After detailing all the paperwork involved in rating teachers as unsatisfactory and describing all the grievance hearings such a rating would have to survive, Lombardi concluded, "Pursuing an unsatisfactory rating is like taking on another job." Referring to Klein's upcoming contract negotiations, Lombardi urged Klein to review how long and typically fruitless the hearing process was when the system attempted to dismiss a teacher for incompetence or misbehavior.

Lombardi ended his letter by noting that he and Klein were both from Astoria, Queens. "It's great to have a neighborhood 'guy' rise to the position of Chancellor," he wrote.

The e-mail address was not a dead drop. "I was immediately impressed by this guy," Klein says. "It was so much detail." Klein e-mailed back, thanking Lombardi and suggesting they meet. It was the beginning of eight years of e-mails and occasional meetings, even dinners.

Lombardi is not a typical principal. In fact, although his father had been in the electricians' union, Lombardi didn't even think it right for there to be a principals' union, because "we're supposed to be management."

From his days as an assistant principal contending with those UFT vice presidents he had referred to in his e-mail, Lombardi had made something of an obsession out of working around the union contract to do what he thought he had to do to make a better school.

Soon after he became a principal in 1996, he found a way within the contract to change the school hours a bit, so that the children arrived earlier for tutoring and special classes. The union complained to the district superintendent, the pre-Klein local power in the decentralized era. But it seemed that Lombardi had threaded the needle and there was nothing the union could do contract-wise. So the UFT organized pickets and handed out leaflets. Randi Weingarten even showed up one morning. When that didn't work, Lombardi began receiving visits from members of the Board of Education's disciplinary office. There had been anonymous complaints accusing him of sexual harassment (against a male teacher, with a wife and children, who laughed incredulously when the investigators asked about it) and financial malfeasance. None of the complaints checked out.

Lombardi didn't budge. When he criticized the union in the *Daily News* in 1999 for impeding his school's mission, the union circulated a letter to all Queens teachers saying that Lombardi had not learned the lesson "taught to Al D'Amato"—the recently defeated U.S. senator who had criticized the union—"that an attack on our union was an attack on all teachers."

"It was like they were putting a fatwa out on him," Klein says.

Lombardi had also fashioned an end run around the most onerous union contract restriction, enabling him to get past the tenure and rating system he had complained to Klein about in order to stock his school with teachers committed to his mission and get rid of the rest. Lombardi would target the teachers he thought were laggards and make life miserable for them, constantly observing their classes—which was allowed—but the union would lodge a grievance for it, charging harassment.

Most principals stand down after that kind of push back. Not Lombardi. He'd tell the teachers he was preparing to rate them as unsatisfactory, which was a bit of a bluff because he hated all the paperwork involved that he had described to Klein. And he'd point out that a teacher rated unsatisfactory three years in a row no longer had a unilateral right to transfer to a school of his or her choosing based on seniority. So, he would suggest, why not transfer now to a school where you'll be happier, and you won't have someone like me to deal with? Let's just agree that we're not the right fit.

"When Principal Lombardi came, there was an open rebellion at first," says Mary Shannon, a longtime reading coach and sixth-grade social studies teacher. "There were lunchroom meetings with parents and teachers, who tried to get him fired. . . . But I thought we had lost sight of why we had become teachers, and so did a lot of the others. After a while, as we started to implement a new curriculum [that Lombardi had developed with consultants from Columbia Teachers College], the ones who were uncomfortable left. They had no other option. Within a few years, we had a whole new staff of people who were here for the right reasons."

"I soon found that Lombardi had emptied his whole school of the incompetents," Klein recalls. "He had offloaded them to other schools."

"I told Joel over dinner one night that what I did was good for my team but bad for his league," Lombardi says. Lombardi called it "passing the lemons," a phrase that in a modified version would make its way into a popular documentary about school reform eight years later, *Waiting for Superman.*

It was all necessary, Lombardi told me, "because Randi Weingarten would protect a dead body in a classroom; that's her job."

Randi Weingarten sees Lombardi as a tyrant, not a hero. Her view of labor-management relations, she says, was shaped by three events early in her life. When she was a college student, a close relative was accused wrongly of causing someone's death in what turned out to be an accident. That, she says, made her especially vigilant about due process, which, she argues, is all teacher tenure is really about.

When she was a teenager, her father, an electrical engineer—"a damned good one"—was laid off with no notice and "piddling severance" just before her bat mitzvah. "I remember him leaning over the steering wheel of his Firebird and crying quietly when he got home that night," she says.

A few years later, her mother's teachers' union went on strike for nearly three months in Nyack, New York. "The issues had nothing to do with money," she says, "just with a lack of respect that my mother and her colleagues were getting from a petty, autocratic superintendent."

Although archival news clips from the Nyack teachers' strike reported salaries and benefits as the only issues, and although the other two stories could not be confirmed, there is no doubt that Weingarten, who worked as a union lawyer before becoming a union officer, is a sincere advocate on the union side in what is essentially a labor-management adversarial process. To Weingarten, Lombardi became the archetypal abusive boss. She says that she tried to work with him at first and, in fact, "saved" him from efforts by her UFT people in Queens to force him out of his school early on "because I thought he was sincere"—an account that Lombardi laughs at. But, Weingarten adds, "there are some people like a Lombardi, or like Joel, who you can't work with and can never trust."

Joel Klein would come to detest Weingarten as much as she detested Lombardi and him. To Klein, Weingarten was so smart that she had to know that playing the game of simple advocate was hurting the children she professed to care so much about. "She should be a bigger person than that," Klein told me. Weingarten compounded Klein's frustration by never admitting who her real—and only—clients were. Her counterparts at the rival NEA had no compunction about whom they worked for. But Weingarten's line was always that what was good for teachers was always good for children. There was no daylight between the two, she maintained. And she argued that position tirelessly and eagerly in the press and everywhere else, including to me, with whom she spent more time than any other single source did for this book.

Others just as committed as Klein had a more forgiving attitude. They saw Weingarten as a charming and enjoyable, if tough, adversary. "Randi is at least someone you can do business with," said Eli Broad, whose foundation would lead the way in funding Klein's efforts as well as the charter school networks and education reform political activities that Weingarten opposed. Broad would also fund some of Weingarten's avowed reform initiatives, including a charter school that ended up not performing well. ("Which was probably a good thing," Broad said, "because she realized how hard it is.")

"Randi wants to do the right thing," Broad said, "but she knows she has to go easy because she has members who elect her, and if she does too much she'll be out of a job."

Children First

January 15, 2003, New York City

Working over the past three months with Klein and his new executive team, the consultants paid for by the grant from Broad and Julian Robertson had PowerPointed and flip-charted an elaborate restructuring plan called Children First. In Klein's mind, it was meant to be the opposite of what he thought to be Weingarten's priority: teachers first. On January 15, 2003, Michael Bloomberg unveiled it at a Martin Luther King Day symposium in Harlem.

"If Dr. King were here today," the mayor declared, he would "unflinchingly focus . . . on the yawning gap between the unmatched cultural and academic riches of New York on the one hand and the failure of too many of our schools on the other. Because that gap is the deepest shame of the greatest city in the world."

To the billionaire entrepreneur mayor, eradicating that shame could come only with better management. The Ocean Hill–Brownsville legacy of decentralized school districts that he and Klein had inherited, Bloomberg said, amounted to "forty separate bureaucracies" employing "thousands of people in duplicative and unnecessary positions." Now that he had gotten control of the schools from the old Board of Education, Bloomberg's plan was to eliminate those bureaucracies; this plan, he said, would save tens of millions of dollars and liberate enough space that had been used by the dismissed bureaucrats to create eight thousand new classroom seats, the equivalent of a dozen new schools.

Beginning in September, Bloomberg's new department of education would be divided into instructional or operations units. There would be ten of each to cover the city's 1,200 schools, instead of the old forty.

The instructional units, freed from worrying about operations, would focus only on improving learning and would report directly to Klein's deputy for instruction. Reporting to a second Klein deputy, the operations units would streamline everything having to do with what the schools needed to run efficiently. For example, the education department's antiquated systems for purchasing what now amounted to $3 billion a year in goods and services, such as heating oil, supplies, and textbooks, would be completely overhauled.

The schools would now be "freed from the dead hand of bureaucracy," the mayor declared.

Weingarten told the press she was thrilled by Children First. She called the plan "breathtakingly possible."

It all made sense, and in some cases it helped. But a little more than three years later, another set of consultants would be presenting Klein with another set of PowerPoints outlining a reorganization of this reorganization.

Apart from shuffling these deck chairs, Bloomberg talked about Klein's efforts to make principals more accountable and to bring parents into the mix by hiring a "parent coordinator" at each school to act as a kind of ombudsman.

He didn't say a word about what he was going to ask of the teachers.

It was the elephant in the room that no one talked about. But it was being talked about elsewhere. A lot. The teachers' union contract, negotiated in 2000, was set to expire at the end of May 2003. The two sides were already circling each other. Klein had named his plan Children First to send an unmistakable message.

The Bobble-Head Doll

May 14, 2003, Hilton Hotel, New York City

It took five months for Randi Weingarten to change her tune about Children First. At the annual spring gathering of her UFT members on May 14, 2003, she dubbed it "Control First." With bobble-head dolls swinging overhead, ostensibly to depict the mayor and Klein, and a screen behind her flashing "They Just Don't Get It," Weingarten, standing in the ballroom of the New York Hilton Hotel, ripped into the "CEO mayor" and his "lawyer-chancellor" for ignoring teachers and caring only about exercising top-down control.

Press accounts attributed Weingarten's anger to a variety of moves that Klein had already made. He had laid off over eight hundred school aides (all members of the UFT) as part of his budget streamlining. He had cited emergency budget constraints to justify a decision to reduce the sabbaticals that Lombardi had complained about.

More important, Klein had dealt Weingarten out of her old role of co-running the school system. He never consulted her and refused to have her sitting at the table with his new staff and consultants collaborating in his reform plans. In fact, Klein not only wasn't discussing with Weingarten issues that she pretty much had had a veto on in the past, he was also going around her by writing memos directly to teachers and exchanging e-mails with them, one on one.

There was more. In one of three e-mails Lombardi sent Klein in May, he warned the new chancellor about the changes Weingarten had been publicly demanding for the new contract: teacher input into textbooks and class configuration, more teacher discretion in classroom instruction, teacher input in assessing principals, still more time off from school duties for union reps, and the removal of all derogatory material from personnel files after one year. All of these, Lombardi wrote, were certain to "infringe on managerial and principal prerogatives."

This was one Lombardi e-mail that Klein didn't need to read. He and his staff had already laughed off these demands from the union. They were going in the opposite direction. Among other things, Klein had told Weingarten that he wanted to reform tenure protections, get back that free time period lost in *Circular 6*, end lockstep compensation based on seniority, and streamline the grievance process. He also wanted to change the rules that allowed teachers to transfer to any school, based on their seniority, whether the principal wanted them or not, because otherwise there was no way he could hold principals responsible for their schools.

"No way," Weingarten, who was up for reelection the following year, had told Klein. "Joel, this is just never going to happen."

A month later, in June, as Klein's demands started to leak out, Lombardi cheered him on. He e-mailed that the union, with its constant refrain that it was acting only on behalf of schoolkids, "will use the children as human shields." But if Klein pushed back, he'd find that "Randi is a paper tiger."

Klein intended to push back. However, he was hedging his bets by planning to work around the union contract with experiments, or pilot projects, that could operate outside the conventional school system rules. His major initiative in that regard required not that he confront Weingarten but that he make peace with an adversary from his prior life.

"If Only You Hadn't Sued the Son of a Bitch"

September 17, 2003, Morris High School, the Bronx

In June 2003, America's richest man had to decide whether to hold a grudge against the only man who had ever gone after him and almost brought him down. In the 1990s, Assistant Attorney General Joel Klein had directed a massive antitrust suit against Bill Gates's Microsoft. The suit eventually ended in a settlement after the judge had ruled for Klein. But the long, highly publicized trial—which challenged the propriety of much of what Gates had built and featured a deposition in which Gates had by most accounts been humiliated on cross-examination by Klein's handpicked special counsel, David Boies—had been excruciating for Gates. So much so that to get him to relax during the periods when the trial was adjourned, Gates's wife, Melinda, had had a special pinball machine made for the family's game room in their basement at home in Medina, Washington. It featured figures of Klein's head—bald at the top, tufts on the sides—as the object the pinballs had to hit.

Gates's legal nightmare had ended only eight months earlier, with the final settlement order in November 2002. Now Gates was being asked to give Klein a $50 million gift.

In 1999, Bill and Melinda Gates had consolidated two smaller foundations he had established with some of his Microsoft fortune and added new funds to create the Bill & Melinda Gates Foundation. With more than $17 billion it dwarfed other private charities. Bill and Melinda immediately targeted public education in the

United States as one of the foundation's two key areas of activity. (The other was poverty and disease in underdeveloped nations.)

The foundation's initial efforts were projects that came naturally to the Gateses. Dozens of the earliest grants went for modest pilot programs to train school leaders to use technology. In 2001, the University of Nevada at Reno got $399,000; the Diocese of Yakima, Washington, $1.684 million; and the Kansas Department of Education $1.5 million—all meant to train local principals and superintendents in using computer systems.

By 2003, the Gateses had concluded that few of these investments had yielded much. The vague reports they received from consultants hired to evaluate the programs were especially frustrating to a man famous for devouring hard data. (I read one short report done in 2000 five times and I still have no idea what it says.)

"By about the end of 2002, it had become clear to us that technology wasn't the answer," Melinda Gates says.

"Other than putting computers in school libraries, which was effective, that simply wasn't the right path," adds Bill Gates.

That year, Melinda, who often toured schools looking for answers, visited a high school in San Diego. Alan Bersin, the hard-charging reformer whom Klein had consulted as he prepared to take the New York City job, was the superintendent there. The foundation had allocated $14 million the prior year to support Bersin's reforms, which included splitting large, failing high schools like the one Melinda Gates was visiting into four smaller schools, each run by its own principal and each with its own "theme." For example, one was a school focused on music and the arts, another on careers in technology.

Bersin reported to Melinda Gates that the experiment seemed to be working. The students seemed much more enthusiastic about school, and graduation rates had increased.

Melinda was impressed enough that the Gates Foundation staff began planning to direct more investments at the small-school approach.

Klein also had been impressed by Bersin's experiment. Beginning almost from when he took the job, he had started working with several non-profit education reform groups in New York that had already taken over a few large schools and divided them up this way in the 1990s. He was especially impressed by the work of New Visions for Public Schools, which was run by former lawyer Robert Hughes, chaired by the senior partner at a prominent Wall Street law firm, and largely funded by donations from the financial community.

Schools operated by New Visions were not charter schools. They were public schools supervised by Klein's education department, and the teachers were all union members. But Klein had, like Bersin in San Diego, figured out a way to delegate management of the schools to people like Hughes, allowing them to oversee curriculum and other matters, including hiring. If they took over a large school and split it up, they could "excess" any incumbent teachers they didn't want and interview and hire an entirely new staff—made up of teachers from Rhee's Teaching Fellows, for example—who would be enrolled in the union but would also be dedicated to the smaller school's mission. The catch was that the "excessed" teachers that mini-school operators like Hughes thought were not up to snuff would remain on the city's payroll waiting for a reassignment. But under the union contract rules, they could turn down that reassignment while staying on the payroll until they got one that they liked.

"You can hire, but you can't fire, but that's better than nothing," Klein would explain. "Klein's rule is that it's better to pay them and not have them in front of the kids than to pay them to stay there."

Klein had recruited Caroline Kennedy, the daughter of the president and an obviously well-connected New Yorker, to round up private funds for initiatives like this that would be needed to revamp the schools and pay groups like New Visions to run them. As she, Klein, and Michelle Cahill, a top Klein deputy, had begun to think about how to expand the project dramatically, the Gates Foundation, which, as in San Diego, had already provided grants to New York City for smaller efforts of this kind, became an obvious focus. That raised the equally obvious question: How would Bill Gates feel about helping Joel Klein?

"I figured it was worth a shot, but given our tortured past, it seemed like maybe a long shot," Klein remembers.

Bill Gates also focused on that tortured past. "We were really impressed by what Joel was trying to do, and everyone on the staff wanted to do it," Melinda Gates recalls. "But on the afternoon we presented it to Bill, he hesitated for a minute, which we completely understood. This was hard. Then he said he wanted to sleep on it. Remember, the [antitrust] trial was only several months [in the past] at that point."

The next morning Gates told his wife they should go ahead. Whatever their business differences, he told Melinda, "Klein is a smart, effective person, and he's now doing something important that we should get behind. . . . You always have to be looking forward."

The details were worked out for a grant totaling $51.2 million, to be given to groups like New Visions (which got $29 million of it) to implement Klein's plan to create sixty-seven small, theme-based public high schools out of a dozen large high schools where the graduation rates were typically 50 percent or less.

The announcement on September 17, 2003, featuring Gates, Bloomberg, Klein, and Kennedy, was at Morris High, a huge school in the Bronx built in 1897. Morris had already been split into five small schools. The program went off without a hitch, with Gates shrugging off a question about his history with Klein by saying simply that he was glad they were now on the same team. (About two years later, Klein would attend an education reform dinner convened by Bill and Melinda Gates at their home, and Melinda would take him down to the basement to show him the pinball machine.)

As Klein left, one of the principals at the Morris schools stopped him. "Fifty-one million. That was pretty impressive," he said. Klein thanked him, then turned away. "Imagine how much you would have gotten if you hadn't sued the son of a bitch," the principal added.

"The Idea Wasn't Just to Keep Them from Killing Somebody"

September 2003, Joan Farley Academy, Denver

Mike Johnston had graduated from Yale Law School in May 2003, but he had none of Joel Klein's early interest in being a star lawyer. While he was at Yale he had written a well-received book about his struggles as a TFA teacher in that tough high school in the Mississippi Delta and had stayed involved in New Leaders for New Schools, which was expanding under his friend Jon Schnur's leadership. He had taken a few courses related to education, civil rights, and public policy, and worked in a civil rights law clinic. Yet like many at Yale Law, which prides itself on its eclectic mix of students, he had generally avoided immersing himself in the activities favored by more conventionally oriented future lawyers. He had even shunned the usual prestigious corporate law firm internship between his second and third years in favor of working for a Democrat back home in Colorado making what would be an unsuccessful run for the U.S. Senate.

In fact, well before Johnston graduated, he had targeted what, even for Yale Law grads, was an unconventional career path. If he was going to get involved in education reform, he first was going to take his Kennedy School degree and now his Yale Law degree and become a school principal so that he could test his ideas beyond his experience in one classroom in Mississippi.

The problem was that with those credentials, the best offer he got was to be an assistant principal at a Denver-area school, which itself was a stretch for someone, whatever his Harvard and Yale pedigrees, who didn't have an education degree. But Johnston wanted to run a school. So he leaped at the offer to run what might have been the smallest, most unrunnable school imaginable: In September 2003 he took over the sixty-student Joan Farley Academy, a "therapeutic" center at a Denver juvenile detention facility.

Johnston quickly moved to change the focus from therapeutic to academic. "From my experience in Greenville [Mississippi, where he had been a TFA teacher], I had this relentless belief in kids," he says. "I knew we should run the place as if all kids—even these kids, who were pretty much all learning disabled—are capable of doing good things. Our job should be to make that happen, not just keep them from killing somebody. We picked all kinds of academic areas, then tried to figure out how to interest them." One way was law, something they all had experience with, albeit not pleasant experiences. Johnston taught constitutional law and even arranged to have a federal court of appeals judge hear his students argue a case in front of him.

In the spring of 2004 and then 2005, Johnston would produce more students with high school graduation equivalency diplomas than Farley had seen in its history.

"How Could the Democrats Be Against This?"

January 2004, the Bronx

Like Johnston, Whitney Tilson had an unlikely résumé for a school reformer. The hedge-fund manager's interest in public education, following his pre–Harvard Business School stint helping Wendy Kopp launch TFA, had been rekindled only by chance, when a friend called and asked him to take a look at a KIPP school.

In January 2004, Tilson made what by then was one of his regular visits to Dave Levin at KIPP, which had progressed from a special program within a conventional public school to become one of New York's first full-fledged charter schools.

It hadn't been until 1998 that New York passed a law allowing charters. The new law had survived intense opposition from the city and state teachers' unions, and was passed only because there was a Republican governor, George Pataki. Even then, it got through the Democratic-controlled legislature only because Pataki attached it to a bill giving a pay raise to legislators. Moreover, to placate the teachers' union, the legislators had capped the number of charters to be issued statewide at one hundred.

The key leader of the New York legislature is Assembly Speaker Sheldon Silver, whose district includes the Lower East Side of Manhattan. Like many New York Democrats, Silver has held election-night victory parties at the UFT headquarters. The UFT's website calls Silver "our partner" and quotes him as pledging at a union rally in Albany, "I and my colleagues in the Assembly majority will be your best friends."

By now, the KIPP charter school in New York had twelve classes in three middle school grades, and the students were thriving, out-performing the city's averages on all proficiency scores and blowing completely past the performance of children in similarly challenged communities.

On this January morning that Tilson visited with him, Levin was poring over an application for two more KIPP charters that he was planning to start.

"Well, that certainly can't be much of a problem," Tilson remarked. "Everything is going so well, I assume this is just a formality."

Levin stopped and looked up. "Are you kidding?" he replied. "The better we do, the harder it gets."

Tilson was about to get his first lesson in school reform politics.

Levin patiently explained that although he already had far more applications for the new schools than seats and would have to resort to a lottery, "they are going to try to stop us." Some local politicians in the communities where he wanted to launch, Levin continued, had already come out against KIPP and more were certain to do so. They would be likely to circulate petitions urging the city to block him. Thus, Klein's department of education was making him fill out laborious forms and answer, then clarify, then reclarify, all kinds of absurd questions to make his applications bulletproof. (One asked him to change the punctuation on the name of the proposed school listed on one of the forms to conform to what had been written on another.)

"Who's 'they'?" Tilson asked. "I thought all the politicians around here were Democrats."

"They *are* Democrats," Levin replied. "They're the problem."

Levin explained how the teachers' unions had a stranglehold on local Democrats. How they funded a splinter political party, called the Working Families Party—which Democrats in close races depended on to get an extra line on the ballot—so that the union could use it almost as a subsidiary to do the union's bidding. And how Working Families could deploy its allies in community groups, such as ACORN,* to circulate petitions or deploy troops at charter opposition rallies.

"For me, that was a total revelation," Tilson recalls. "Here I was,

---

* ACORN—Association of Community Organizations for Reform Now—is the activist organization that would be disbanded following scandals in 2010.

a lifelong Democrat whose parents were lifelong Democrats, thinking I was fighting the next great civil rights fight—for equal education in these communities—and Dave Levin is sitting there telling
me that *my* party is what is standing in his way."

Meanwhile, another Democrat, Joel Klein, was looking to a prominent Republican for help. Beginning in 2004, Klein and his staff
began a series of visits and phone conversations with Florida governor Jeb Bush and his staff.

Bush, who had become Florida's governor in 1999, had pushed
through a sweeping law that allowed him to use student testing data (actual scores and improvement in scores) to give every
Florida school a public A–F grade. Parents in schools graded F
were entitled to a voucher from the state equivalent to the cost of a
child's education, which they could use to pay tuition at a private
school. (The voucher provision would later be struck down in the
Florida courts, but Bush was then able to replace it with a modified plan that still allowed tens of thousands of parents to choose
this alternative.)

Klein was so impressed with the Florida data-gathering and
grading effort that he intended to copy it, though it would take
nearly four years (and multiple cost overruns) before he would have
a system in place to grade his 1,200 schools. By then Bush would
have created in Florida some of the themed "schools within schools"
that Klein had expanded, while turning up the pressure with another sweeping Florida reform law. This one tightened curriculum
standards and awarded incentive pay to those willing to teach in the
state's most underserved schools, teach special needs students, or
teach in areas, such as science and math, where there were shortages
of skilled educators.

Bush, whose second term ended in 2006, improved Florida's
public schools dramatically by almost any measure: high school
graduation rates, math or reading proficiency, the achievement gap
among demographic groups, and even the number of students taking advanced college placement exams (because Bush had started
programs to encourage low-income students to reach for these tests).

Klein, a loyal Democrat, came to admire Bush greatly. They became odd-couple partners in school reform and close friends. "Joel

and I hit it off, and then we kind of teamed up," Bush recalls. "He'd
come down to Florida and participate with me in some event, which
gave what we were doing legitimacy, because people were impressed
that someone from New York was using us as a model. And I'd come
to New York and see what he was doing and support him."

Klein's alliance with a prominent Republican was helpful. But
its potential was limited. As Whitney Tilson had now realized, it
would take a turnaround among Democrats to enable the kind of
change the reformers sought.

Seeing George Soros's Apartment

June 7, 2004, Fifth Avenue apartment of
financier George Soros

Whitney Tilson was intrigued by the invitation, which came because he was on some list of Democratic donors. The cocktail party was at the apartment of George Soros, the billionaire investor and philanthropist. It would be fun to see what Soros's place looked like. Plus, the guest of honor was a guy running for the senate in Illinois who was black and had roots in Kenya. Tilson, who had lived much of his childhood in Africa, was intrigued by that, too.

When he got home from the Soros event, Tilson sent an e-mail to his education reform list, which by now was over a thousand people:

> A few years ago, I said that Cory Booker would be our first
> black President. I was wrong—he'll be our 2nd (only because
> of his youth). I met the first tonight: Barack Obama, who is
> running for the Senate in Illinois. He is strikingly similar to
> Cory—young (42 vs. Cory's 35), brilliant, eloquent, visionary
> and able/willing to cut across political lines. For example,
> most Democrats are afraid to take on the teachers' unions and
> support charter schools and school choice, but Obama (like
> Cory) champions this issue.

By now, Tilson, who was thirty-seven, and two other hedge-fund friends—Boykin Curry, thirty-five, and John Petry, thirty-three—had become an informal triumvirate of young, well-off Democrats interested in education issues. Beginning in 1998, they had all become enthusiastic backers of Cory Booker when Booker had won a Newark City Council race in an upset. Curry had even introduced his brother, Marshall, to Booker, which resulted in Marshall making a highly regarded documentary about Booker's unsuccessful 2002 Newark mayoral campaign.

At first look, Ravenel Boykin Curry IV seems the typical preppy socialite. He and his wife have homes in Manhattan (Central Park South), East Hampton, and the Dominican Republic. His father, Ravenel Curry III, also runs a money fund. He and his wife frequently appear in society columns, and she's a well-known high-end interior decorator. He went to Yale and Harvard Business School, and is involved in all the de rigueur charities. But, as with the regular memos on the economy that he sends his investors, Curry's interest in education reform was serious and sophisticated. He was not someone chasing a fad.

After Yale, before going on to Harvard Business School, Curry had worked at the Advisory Board, a consulting company whose specialty was gathering top executives from a given industry and working with them in long sessions to come up with solutions to their common management problems. The meetings were usually held for private-sector executives. However, one week in 1991, a session for superintendents of large school systems was convened. What had stuck in Curry's mind since, he recalls, is "how those executives, unlike any other group, easily agreed that they knew exactly what they had to do to improve their schools. But they all said they were powerless to do it because of all the contracts and rules. I had never seen anything like it."

So when Tilson had pestered Curry to visit KIPP one day after he had discovered it, Curry happily agreed. He was so impressed that he soon got involved with some Yale classmates in forming another charter school, Girls Prep, which would open in the fall of 2005.

"People like us—long-term-value investors—like education reform," Curry explains, "because, first, we're typically geeks who care about numbers, and we can see that the numbers in public education don't add up: more and more money but no better results. Second, it's easy to see that education is a great investment if what you invest in really changes things. It's classic leverage. A relatively small amount of money produces better lives and people who can support our economy instead of having to get handouts from it. . . . Third, it's classic long-term investing, which is what all of us do. Fourth, it's something where we think we can add value, because we can help create good business plans for charters. . . . Fifth, it's exciting and fun for people like us, who usually only work with numbers, to work on something like this. We're nerds who don't get to do exciting stuff in our day jobs. And sixth, because so many of us got interested in this at the same time, you get to work with people who are your friends."

The third in the triumvirate, John Petry, had tutored at an underprivileged school in Philadelphia while attending the University of Pennsylvania's Wharton School of Finance. "I swear I watched a teacher showing kids how to use a calculator to add eighteen plus seven," he remembers. Petry—short, thin, with dark hair and almost always casually dressed—is as modest and unassuming as Tilson is ebullient and Curry is elegant.

By the time Petry came to Wall Street, he was working for Joel Greenblatt, a renowned "value investor" who had in 1985 launched a hedge fund called Gotham Capital. Greenblatt, the author of three popular value-investing books, had already made a fortune and had channeled some of it to various programs aimed at helping schools in New York's poorest communities. But he was increasingly disappointed in the return he thought he was getting on these investments. When a friend introduced him to Joel Klein and he vented his frustration about how his charity wasn't having much of an impact at Klein's schools, Klein had suggested he fund a charter school. By now, Greenblatt and Petry—whom, of course, Tilson had also taken on a KIPP tour—were talking about starting not one charter but a network of charters. They wanted to "scale the model," as Wall Streeters like to put it.

For Tilson, however, the introduction to Obama and the exposure he had had to Booker, combined with what Dave Levin had told him a few months before about the trouble he was having with Democrats, had given a new dimension to his thinking about fixing schools. It seemed that more than smart business models would be necessary. There had to be a political thrust to what they did, he began to think. In fact, putting money into the *politics* of education reform might be the most leveraged investment of all. That soon became the hot topic when he, Curry, and Petry talked.

Through the rest of 2004, Tilson, Petry, and Curry ruminated over how to get involved politically in education beyond simply supporting one-offs like Booker in Newark or Obama in Illinois. One evening, they went to a speech at the Harvard Club given by John Walton, the son of the Wal-Mart founder. The younger Walton had directed much of his philanthropic support to education reform. Walton's speech and others like it at events sponsored by a group called the Alliance for School Choice came at the issue from the old Bill Bennett Republican angle. It wasn't that it was substantively wrong but rather that the tone—more talk about vouchers for private schools than fixing public schools and general attacks on unions—and the Republican pedigree of all the speakers were more likely to repel Democratic politicians than convince them.

By early 2005, Tilson, Petry, and Curry began talking about forming a group called Democrats for Education Reform. Their aim was to make the Democratic argument for education reform and back Democratic politicians who supported it.

But to Jessica Reid, what the Walton family or any of the other reformers, Democrats or Republicans, could do to fix schools first would have been to send over some paper and pencils from Wal-Mart.

New York Realities

"I Have No Maps, Globes, or Even Basic Supplies Like Pencils and Paper"

August 15, 2004, PS 121, the Bronx

Jessica Reid could have told Joel Klein that, despite the consultants' promises, their plan for streamlining how the school system bought supplies, which Mayor Bloomberg had touted eighteen months earlier in his 2003 Martin Luther King Day speech, had failed. When Reid arrived on August 15, 2004, to look at the classroom she would run as a TFA fifth-grade teacher, she was so panicked by the school's lack of supplies that she organized a one-teacher charity drive.

That night, she sent an e-mail to everyone she could think of. She described the thrill of being one of 1,700 college graduates accepted into TFA out of 13,000 applications, then recounted coming to her school to find, "I have no class sets of books so that children can follow along and learn essential reading strategies while I read aloud. I have no maps, globes, or even basic supplies like pencils and paper. Because I recently graduated from college, I alone cannot afford to provide my students with even the most basic necessities for learning," she continued, before asking for "donations of any used books (books on tape are great too) or other supplies (pencils, pens, crayons, markers, composition books, folders, etc.)."

Reid's appeal for charity was only one sign that before Klein turned to the really hard work, such as building data systems to determine how his 100,000 teachers and 1,200 principals were performing and then doing something about it, his effort to make even the most basic management reforms faced significant hurdles.

To be sure, Klein had made some progress. He had established a school safety office that, working with the Police Department, had cut deeply into school violence. He had begun tightening curricula standards and, in a highly controversial move, had set a marker for his and Bloomberg's raised expectations by clamping down on "social promotion," a practice under which children got moved to the next grade at the end of the school year even if it was obvious that they had not advanced nearly enough to be ready. And with $75 million in private money that Caroline Kennedy helped raise, he had created a Leadership Academy, where top educators as well as leaders from the business world, including former General Electric chairman Jack Welch, helped prepare assistant principals and others in the system whom Klein's staff had handpicked to become principals.

Jessica Reid didn't see any of that. All she saw was a school where the principal had visited her once and told her she was doing fine, where most of her colleagues fled at 3:15, where no one seemed to expect much of the children, and where she had to beg friends to send paper clips and pencils.

Nor was Reid impressed with TFA, however much Kopp had done to improve training since the early days. Although TFA was now fourteen years old, Reid says that she got "zero support from them. I was just thrown in. . . . A TFA liaison person came to see me maybe two or three times, and when I complained at the beginning that I was failing, the only thing he said was that I was doing fine and should hang in there."

"Assessments as a Form of Harassment"

February 6, 2005, New York City

Getting substantive feedback of the kind Jessica Reid craved would seem like something any teacher would want. On February 6, 2005, Anthony Lombardi, the Queens middle school principal and Klein's e-mail pal, sent Klein a document that suggested the opposite. It was a protest written by teachers at another middle school and had been passed on to Lombardi by that school's principal. It should have been included in course material at the Leadership Academy.

Apparently, this other principal had, like Lombardi, begun to take Klein's escalating rhetoric about accountability seriously. Now a group of his teachers were circulating this complaint throughout the school and to government officials and the press:

> While teachers are contractually subject to two observation performance assessments per year, [the principal has] implemented perpetual "snapshots"—the practice of doing a never ending series of assessments on teachers. In addition to openly and notoriously violating teachers' labor contractual rights at every turn, [the principal] has long ago degenerated into a rogue principal—an actual depraved knave.

An assistant principal's similar habit of regular classroom observations, the complaint continued, was nothing less than a "sadomasochistic humiliation of teachers . . . a form of union busting and unlawful behavior modification."

"I kept telling Joel that getting control of what is happening in our classrooms is harder than he thinks it is," Lombardi says. "You have to stick at it—unless you can figure out a way, like I did, to encourage the bad ones to go elsewhere."

"Nothing Less Than Total Control"

February 25, 2005

To Randi Weingarten, Klein's and Lombardi's push for control was a red flag. That is why well into 2005 no progress had been made on the teachers' union contract with New York City, which had expired in October 2003.

Under New York law, public employees, such as teachers, can be fined two days' pay for every day they strike. However, if management doesn't reach an agreement with them on a contract before it expires, the contract stays in place and, by tradition, any salary increases ultimately agreed on are made retroactive. So the fact that the contract had expired was not an immediate crisis. But that it was now so long overdue, and that the city was sticking to its guns on the various reforms Klein had told Weingarten he wanted, was becoming a problem for both sides. Weingarten's members had gone without a raise for more than two years, and Bloomberg was facing reelection in the fall with a potential labor confrontation, perhaps even a school strike, looming.

The previous fall, Weingarten and Bloomberg had had a series of talks that seemed to be making headway. They had gotten close, it seemed, on money. But the talks had collapsed when neither side would budge on tenure reform, lockstep seniority-based compensation, or other contract rules.

Weingarten then spent more than $2 million for ads on local television featuring angry teachers demanding a contract, which, they pleaded, was the right thing to do for the city's children.

Then on February 25, Weingarten wrote a letter to all of her members warning of a "prolonged, high-stakes fight. . . . They want nothing less than total control over our members' working lives. Hiring. Firing. Assignments. . . . They want the first, last, and only say."

Two weeks later, Klein volleyed back with a letter to all principals urging them to begin the difficult process of "firing bad teachers" and to speak out against work rules that hamstrung them. Echoing Lombardi's original e-mail, he urged them to stop passing the lemons: "The simple, though unfortunate reality," Klein wrote, "is that many principals pass along their incompetent teachers to others rather than go through the extraordinarily arduous—and often futile—termination process."

The battle would be stalemated for months. During the twelve-month financial-reporting period covering the beginning of the standoff in 2005, Weingarten spared none of the union's considerable resources—$96.7 million in annual dues that year. She spent $3.8 million in fees, including fees for her advertising campaign, to the Glover Park political-consulting firm that was run by skilled Bill Clinton campaign alumni; $343,000 in direct contributions to the state union's COPE (Committee on Political Education) political fund (on top of member biweekly deductions going into COPE); $98,000 for Rubenstein Associates, the city's most politically connected PR firm; more than $400,000 to other policy and communications consultants; $123,000 to pollster Peter Hart Associates; more than $2.5 million in outside legal and lobbying fees; $435,000 in mailings; hundreds of thousands in $10,000 to $15,000 donations to every conceivable political club, civil rights group, and ethnic or civic organization (such as $15,000 to a Latino AIDS support group); $844,000 to cater different meetings and pep rallies (plus $764,000 for the annual UFT spring conference at the Hilton); $415,000 for leaflet printing; even $54,000 to buy seats at the annual dinner of the city's political reporters and $15,000 to hold a two-thousand-teacher rally on July 1 demanding a contract.

All that money didn't help when it came to a young Korean woman Weingarten had never heard of.

Woman with a "Spine of Steel" and the Mayor Who Blinked

June 24, 2005

Contract negotiations between a city and its workers are not the stuff of headlines. It's all done behind closed doors and involves opaque details. But those details are as important to everyday citizens as they are abstruse. A simple piece of legalese can balloon the taxpayers' pension obligations by billions; another clause can render principals impotent when it comes to making teachers prepare good lesson plans. This is why the story of New York City's negotiation with Randi Weingarten in 2005 is so important.

When public employee unions and the city reach an impasse in their negotiations, an arbitration panel is convened to take testimony from both sides and then issue "findings of fact" related to what a fair compromise ought to be. The findings aren't binding, but findings against one side or the other put a strong burden on that side to settle.

In June 2005, the arbitration panel convened to deal with the teachers' union impasse was grinding on. There was a lot of the usual posturing from both sides, all in the form of "testimony." Witnesses at these hearings rarely present new evidence or "facts" as much as they restate their predictable positions, and most of the hearings are only about numbers. The union argues for a higher raise in salary and benefits than the city wants to give, and the arbitrators, looking at comparable agreements with other city unions, recommend a compromise.

However, Klein was determined that this hearing would become much more of a trial about the work rules contained in the contract.

June 25 was the climax of that process. Michelle Rhee, looking younger than her thirty-five years, sat down at the witness table after lunch and provided a trove of original research findings of the kind rarely heard by these arbitrators.

Daniel Weisberg, a Wall Street lawyer recruited by Klein to the new post of chief of labor policy and implementation, had called Rhee several weeks before. He knew that Rhee's New Teacher Project had been studying how union contracts allowing teachers to transfer into a school of their choosing based on their seniority had had a negative effect on school staffing and performance. The city was pushing to change these rules, Weisberg reminded Rhee, and it was going to be a big issue at the fact-finding hearing. Was there any chance that she might want to testify about it?

"Sure," Rhee replied.

"Are you really sure you want to?" Weisberg pressed.

"Why wouldn't I?"

"Because outsiders, especially people involved in education, never testify against the union at hearings like this."

Rhee told Weisberg not to worry. She'd be there.

Rhee took the microphone and began rattling off survey data from school systems across the country demonstrating that when senior teachers were freely allowed to transfer into new schools over the summer it so disrupted the process and so delayed hiring time lines for other, new recruits that a large portion of new talent was discouraged from even applying for the jobs. (This was what had discouraged Wendy Kopp from applying for a New York teaching job in 1989 as she was graduating from Princeton.) Rhee said that this process also deterred better teachers from trying to make a move into schools where they thought their talents might be put to the best use. "School districts were unable to hire highly qualified teachers," she testified. "The most troubling thing we found was that districts lost the candidates with stronger credentials and ended up hiring people with far weaker credentials, specifically that the withdrawers were much more likely to have high GPAs [grade point averages] and content knowledge in the high-need subject areas . . . all qualifications that have been found to be correlated to student achievement."

Rhee put up a slide depicting a study done in New York City that found that 23 percent of all new teachers in the city's schools in the 2004–2005 school year "had been placed in schools [in which the principal] did not have the right to interview or choose them." In just that one school year, such forced placements, she demonstrated in another slide, had been carried out at 79 percent of all schools.

"This is an incredibly important point," Rhee continued. "At a time when principals are being held accountable for school perfor- mance, to have little or no say over this portion of teachers who are assigned to them is problematic."

"I think it's the first time I have ever actually been in a room with Randi [Weingarten]," Rhee recalls. "I saw her sitting to the side of the table glaring at me, as if saying to herself, 'Who the eff is this kid? How dare she?' "

"Michelle was unbelievable," Klein says. "It was then that I real- ized this is a woman with a spine of steel. She didn't give a shit."

The panel was impressed too. On September 5, it issued its re- port, and among its "findings" was that forced placement was detri- mental to the school system and should be eliminated.

Other findings were that *Circular 6*'s grant of that extra free period should be changed, that some kind of merit pay should be considered (perhaps by means of the creation of a "senior" or "lead" teacher position), but that tenure protections should not be modified.

A wave of day-and-night negotiations proceeded through the rest of September. However, Klein and his staff were relegated to second chair. The mayor and his people in the office of labor relations took charge.

In many ways this was not unusual. Labor negotiations in New York or any major city have to be coordinated so that the police, fire- fighters, teachers, or other municipal workers can't engage in trying to one-up each other or demand a me-too clause to catch up to who- ever does the best. This is especially true when the key issues have to do with money. But in Klein's case, everything important had to do with the rules; in fact, the money issues were almost preordained because of other recent municipal wage settlements that had set a pattern for what the teachers' raises would be, percentage-wise.

Nonetheless, Bloomberg insisted on controlling the talks, often conferring with Weingarten himself, and seeking to buy some easing of the work rules with wage increases that went beyond the percentage pattern. "The progress that we made, we bought," the mayor recalls. "It is plain and simple a quid pro quo."

Weisberg and Klein thought paying for the changes that way was a fine idea—it was not their money—but only if they got everything they needed.

As the end of September was approaching, Weingarten had told Bloomberg she would give in on forced placement. Teachers could not force themselves on any school that didn't want them. However, in return, she said, teachers could not be forced to teach in any school they didn't want to teach in. That seemed perfectly symmetrical, but there was one catch: What would happen if a teacher's position was eliminated at a school but the teacher then refused placement at any other school? For example, suppose a school's changing enrollment required one fewer seventh-grade social studies teacher in the new year. Or suppose the school was being broken up into smaller schools and the new management from New Visions didn't want to keep the teacher. Klein wanted the teacher to have to apply for and agree to a new position within a year. If the teacher could not find a principal who wanted him or her, or if the teacher refused to agree to take a new assignment, then the teacher would be taken off the payroll. That way, no teacher could simply refuse to teach but get paid forever.

Weingarten adamantly refused. The deal was to be no forced placement, period. Teachers couldn't force themselves on a principal. And a principal could not force his or her school on a teacher. That would have been fine, but for the fact that these teachers were already on the city's payroll. If either the principal or the teacher did not agree on a placement, then the teacher would stay in limbo for as long as it took (even if it took forever), but remain on the payroll.

Klein capitulated. Bloomberg wanted him to, but it was also consistent with what he had articulated as "Klein's law" when thinking about how best to deal with teachers who were not kept on at those large high schools after they were broken up into smaller, independently managed schools. He knew that principals would "excess," or lay off, only the bad teachers. So, it was better to pay teachers whom no principal wanted, to stay out of the classroom, than to pay them and keep them in the classroom.

Weingarten did offer a compromise on *Circular 6*. In return for some extra pay, she'd add back thirty minutes a day for teachers to work in small groups with students who needed extra help. Klein wanted more substantive sessions—three days a week of fifty minutes each. They compromised, through Bloomberg, on four days of thirty-seven minutes and thirty seconds. Thus, the contract governing teachers in the largest city in America would now spell out the workday down to the second.

Weingarten similarly threw in some of the towel on streamlining the grievance regimen, which was a big win for Klein. Relatively trivial issues would no longer be subject to formal appeals under the grievance process unless and until they escalated. Principals would no longer be caught on a paper-heavy, lawyer-heavy treadmill every time they had something negative to say about a teacher.

Finally, Weingarten held absolutely firm on the big issue: tenure and teacher evaluations. Klein wanted to lower the standard of proof under which an abitrator could dismiss a tenured teacher. The current standard required multiple years of unsatisfactory ratings (all of which could be delayed by the grievance process) and used a "preponderance of the evidence" as the standard of proof to be applied by the arbitrator (which in Klein's view most arbitrators had raised to "beyond a reasonable doubt" in practice). Instead, Klein and Weisberg argued for a system where a teacher rated unsatisfactory at the end of a school year would have several months beginning the following September to improve and could then be removed from class if he or she had not improved, after which the teacher would still be on the payroll and the hearing process would begin. But the hearing would be streamlined and the new standard of proof would be that an unsatisfactory rating, followed by a well-documented failure to "cure" the unsatisfactory performance, would constitute a "presumption" that the teacher should be dismissed. This meant that the teacher's lawyer would then have to succeed in rebutting that presumption in the hearing.

Weisberg and Klein both thought Weingarten would capitulate on this, despite her protests. But Bloomberg argued that they'd never get her to agree, and even if they did, the resulting grievance process put in place to contest the ratings wouldn't be much better than what they had. "We had Randi," says Weisberg. "I really thought we had her back against the wall. . . . But the mayor blinked. He said Randi will never agree—and that even if she did it was a pipe dream that we'd ever succeed in getting arbitrators to dismiss teachers even with the new process. . . . The mayor just gave up."

"We got a whole lot of things," says Bloomberg. "That thirty seven and a half minutes? They count that down to the second and to the penny. . . . We won an awful lot of different things in return for cash."

Throughout the month, Bloomberg had publicly backed Klein, saying to one business group that, despite Weingarten's threats of a strike, the last thing any of them wanted was "for Joel to quit" out of frustration over a bad contract. Yet Klein and Weisberg soon learned that the mayor or his labor chief was on the phone almost daily with Weingarten. Weingarten happily bragged about her pipeline to the mayor, recalls Weisberg, who clashed almost daily with Bloomberg's labor negotiator over this back-channel negotiation.

Fitting a pattern of offhand comments that appear to be unsupported by the facts, Weingarten, in fact, bragged to me in 2010 that she had not even talked to Klein since 2004, a statement which Klein refuted by producing all kinds of calendar entries of meetings with her, as well as e-mail exchanges with Weingarten that referred to conversations they had had. But Klein did not dispute that the mayor and his labor negotiators were ultimately in charge and heavily involved day to day.

Although the gains on *Circular 6* and the grievance process were significant, nothing had been done to address lockstep compensation, tenure, or the teacher evaluation process. "It was tough," says Klein. "A really, really tough time. I thought we got a lot, but not enough and not what we could have gotten. . . . We were under tremendous pressure. Randi was talking about a strike in the fall, around Election Day. The mayor's political people were panicked about that."

Weingarten's union stayed neutral in the election, for the first time in its history not endorsing a Democrat running against a Republican (Bloomberg). In November 2005, Bloomberg won an election that few thought was ever in doubt in a landslide.

The contract provision where Klein had made what seemed like real progress—forced transfers—would come back to bite him, badly. Within five years there would be more than one thousand teachers sitting on a list called the Absent Teacher Reserve. These were the teachers who had been excessed but had not taken positions elsewhere. Some hadn't even gone on job interviews. A teacher corps big enough to fill two-thirds of the classrooms in New Haven, Connecticut, was being paid to do nothing—and, because of seniority rules that dictated that only junior teachers could be dismissed in the event that layoffs were necessary, the prospect loomed that they would continue to be paid even if the city had to dismiss thousands of real teachers because of the budget crunch.

The pension gifts that Bloomberg added in the 2005 contract—including that teachers could now retire with full pensions at age fifty-seven—would be supplemented in a 2007 contract, adding to a cascade of pension liabilities that had quintupled the city's pension costs since 2000.

Placating the powerful union this way was politically convenient because pension costs are invisible. However, that cost and the opaqueness surrounding what it *really* cost when actual returns on the investments were calculated were not entirely Bloomberg's fault. A law passed in Albany had set 8 percent as the expected rate of return to be assumed for all public employee pensions in calculating their liabilities. This meant that in projecting on its books the expected cost of, say, paying a sixty-year-old teacher a $65,000 pension for life, the pension fund accountants would first project how long the teacher would live, then add up what the pension payouts would be, but then assume that all of the money contributed by the city into the pension fund would always earn 8 percent per year, compounded. Always.

Federal law governing private pension funds requires that expected returns be set at far lower rates—typically 3 to 4 percent, or maybe as low as 2 percent—based on actual prior returns. By mandating this assumption of 8 percent, the legislature shielded the real costs of these pensions from the public, delaying the day of reckoning for the city. A realistic return would have required much more be put into the pension funds each year out of current tax funds to pay the coming liabilities.

Based on the pension plan's June 30, 2009, report (the most current one available as of April 2011), since 2000, the average actual annual rate on the city's pension fund has been about 2 percent because of fluctuations in the stock market and bad investments. This includes losses of more $10 billion in 2008 and 2009 at the same time that the assumed gain of 8 percent a year would have resulted in profits of $4 billion. Obviously the funds being put aside to cover the city's liability to its teachers for these generous pensions are not nearly enough. Looked at another way, by 2010, the city would say that it cost approximately $2,600 per pupil to fund teacher pensions. Compared with the $200 to $400 that it might cost to fund a standard shared-contribution 401(k) plan at a charter school, that was a whopping cost disadvantage that has nothing to do with supplying education in a classroom. Substitute real accounting for the guaranteed 8 percent-no-matter-what accounting, and the real cost disadvantage would be somewhere between $5,000 and $8,000 per pupil, which someday would have to come out of future budgets.

All of this pension accounting was the work of a state legislature controlled by Democrats, on whom the teachers' unions had long had a stranglehold. Within some quarters of the party, that was about to change.

"Our Party Has Got to Wake Up on This"

June 3, 2005, Boykin Curry's Manhattan Apartment

It had been ten months since Barack Obama had become a political rock star with his keynote speech at the 2004 Democratic National Convention in Boston. On June 3, 2005, he came to New York ostensibly to do some early fund-raising for what was assumed would be his second Senate campaign. While in town he helped Boykin Curry, John Petry, and Whitney Tilson launch a group they had created called Democrats for Education Reform (DFER). Obama had agreed to be a guest at a party they had put together for people who shared their interest in school reform and wanted to get involved.

Curry, Petry, and Tilson had chipped in a little of their own money, plus some from a few friends, to start DFER. The fourth member of their board was Charles Ledley, another value investor friend. Ledley would become famous in Michael Lewis's 2010 book *The Big Short*. He was one of the unknowns Lewis found who made a fortune betting against the subprime mortgage market.

DFER had hired an executive director, and Obama's appearance was going to be its first effort to build broader support.

The event started with a small, early dinner, at Cafe Gray in the Time Warner Center at Columbus Circle. Curry, Petry, and Tilson were immediately smitten with Obama, who seemed to talk about education reform as if it was no big deal for a Democrat to be doing so. He recalled visiting a successful Chicago school where one teacher had complained to him about what she referred to as the "these kids" syndrome that prevailed at traditional inner-city public schools, which, she explained, "was the willingness of society to accept that 'these kids' can't learn or succeed."

After dinner, the group walked back to Curry's apartment on Central Park South. Curry had hoped for maybe 100 people, but there was such an overflow that some had had to be diverted to a bar in the restaurant downstairs. Curry says that 100 could have fit into his apartment, so there must have been many more than that, maybe 150. "It was the biggest group of education reformers I had ever seen," Curry recalls.

Obama, standing on a chair and speaking extemporaneously, didn't mince words. Curry still remembers one punch line: "If someone can tell me where the Democratic Party stands on education reform, please let me know. Because I can't figure it out. Our party has got to wake up on this!"

When the cheering stopped, Obama went down to the bar and did a reprise for the overflow group.

Obama had spent part of his talk extolling charter schools and what they demonstrated about how all children could learn if they had good teachers in good schools. Joel Klein was about to hatch a plan that would allow charters to proliferate in a vivid way—inside the same building as conventional public schools—that would provide indelible evidence of this.

The Co-location Trap

July 31, 2005, Brooklyn

On July 31, 2005, the New York State Board of Regents approved a new charter elementary school in Brooklyn. The school's charter application wasn't nearly as detailed or ambitious as Levin's KIPP applications, but its intention to "prepare all students to achieve academic and personal excellence" passed muster.

There was something unusual in the new school's plan, beyond even its provision for a standard 8:30-to-3:15 school day. The proposed charter school promised "a collaborative labor-management relationship that respects teachers' voices."

This new school was going to be run by the United Federation of Teachers, with Randi Weingarten as its board chair.

By the time the UFT's charter would come up for renewal in 2010, a state education board's visiting inspection panel would recommend only a provisional three-year (rather than five-year) renewal because the panel found that the school had "an ambiguous or mixed record of educational achievement in meeting its academic Accountability Plan goals." Only 28 percent of the school's students were testing proficient in English and 34 percent in math. Some in the reform movement who had read the initial application and the renewal review report thought the regulators had gone too easy on the UFT in approving the charter in the first place, let alone renewing it for even three years.

But Joel Klein, who was in the middle of his contract battle with Weingarten, was thrilled about the UFT's application and its approval. He loved the idea that Weingarten was in the charter school business.

More than that, her application gave him the chance to implement a plan that would forever shift the ground in the business model for charters and the debate over their effectiveness: Weingarten had needed a place for her new school, and Klein gave her permission to "co-locate" it in a space he made room for in a conventional Brooklyn public school.

Co-location had started with the move to break up the large high schools. The new, smaller ones to be run by groups like New Visions would be co-located in the old, big school. (Arne Duncan, who would become Obama's education secretary, had done much the same thing when he was running the Chicago schools.) Then, Klein had quietly allowed Levin's KIPP and some other charters to share space in the schools where, as with Levin in the Bronx, they had initially launched as a program within the school, not as a full-fledged charter school.

Now Klein had bigger plans. "I got $250 million [of city/state money] put into my capital budget in 2005–2006 for the work necessary to do co-location," Klein recalls. "But nobody noticed because we doubled the capital budget that year to $13 billion, so this was pocket change. And," Klein adds, "Randi wouldn't have cared if she did notice it, because some of it was going for her school. Once Randi's school was co-located, she could never be against co-location in principle. She'd have to oppose the specifics of the co-location plan but not the idea."

Co-location would be the linchpin for the expansion of charters. Suddenly, the $20 million to $30 million up front it might take to buy new buildings and outfit them didn't have to be raised by people who wanted to start charter schools. There was an obvious logic to co-location. If Weingarten's new school was going to seat 138 kids in the first year, as her plan said, or 500 or 700 a few years later as it expanded its grades, then that was that many fewer seats needed in the traditional schools in the same community. Juggling space would turn out to be enormously more complicated than that, but the basic math worked. Klein was facilitating the growth of these alternative schools at the expense of the schools he was in charge of.

"The best thing about Joel Klein," Boykin Curry would tell me five years later, "is that here was a public official deliberately giving up turf. Have you ever seen that?"

Not only was Klein giving up turf, but, as illustrated by the Harlem building where Jessica Reid would end up working, by putting a charter side by side with a public school he also was creating the most vivid argument for school reform and the most effective competition for the schools that he ran. Parents who had kids, or who had neighbors with kids, on both sides of the building didn't need much convincing that all kids could learn if their schools were operated without all the constraints imposed on the public school side.

"Sometimes the tensions of co-location—a door or a line down a hall separating the two sides—are like Israel and Palestine," says Dave Levin. "But when you have visitors and they see the two sides, you really don't have to say much about what this is all about."

However, there was one city with a failing school system where co-location wasn't a necessary instrument of school reform—because beginning on August 29, 2005, there would be no public schools to co-locate with.

Creating a New School
System the Hard Way

Until August 28, 2005, the consensus in education circles was that New Orleans was tied with Washington, D.C., as having the nation's worst urban school system. One high school valedictorian had famously failed the math portion of the high school exit exam five times. In 2004, 96 percent of graduates scored below "basic" on their high school English exit exam and 94 percent scored below basic in math.

There had been a growing movement for school reform in New Orleans, spearheaded by civic leader Lesley Jacobs. Using a law that had been pushed by Jacobs, the state had already taken over five of the city's failing schools and installed new teachers and management. But so far most of the progress had been limited to some improvement at these schools and at a handful of charter schools.

All of that changed when Hurricane Katrina swept through the city on August 29, 2005. The hurricane left almost all of New Orleans's public school buildings unusable. Few of the school system's 66,000 children were around in the short term to attend them anyway. Within thirty days the school system had run out of cash and everyone was laid off, including all teachers.

Wendy Kopp might have started Teach For America with the limited goal of supplying thousands of elite college graduates for two-year stints at public schools, but New Orleans in the days immediately after Katrina became the first place where the network of people she had lured into public education came together and produced sweeping school reform.

A few years before, Sarah Usdin had left her position running TFA in Louisiana to start a state unit of Michelle Rhee's New Teacher Project. The idea was that she would work to supply those new teachers to the schools the state had taken over. Usdin had done so well in both jobs that when the hurricane hit, both TFA and the New Teacher Project had already developed huge footprints in New Orleans and across Louisiana; hundreds of TFA corps members and alums and hundreds more New Teacher recruits were working in Louisiana, teaching or running charters, or trying to improve the traditional schools.

Immediately, a KIPP school run by TFA alum Gary Robichaux that had been opened in New Orleans five days before the hurricane hit was relocated in Houston, where many New Orleans families had fled. That school, called KIPP NOW (New Orleans West), became one of the highest-performing schools in the Houston school district and stayed open through the following year for the New Orleans children who were still evacuated, while KIPP also opened a campus in New Orleans for those who came back to the city.

Meanwhile, Usdin began coordinating a multi-pronged effort put together by local civic groups, the state education department, and several nonprofits—including the Aspen Institute, whose CEO, Walter Isaacson, grew up in New Orleans—to create an entirely new school system. (Isaacson is also the board chair of TFA.) The old school system was mostly abolished. State education department superintendent Cecil Picard, with the support of Democratic governor Kathleen Blanco, took over all but 16 of New Orleans's 118 schools. They were put into a "Recovery School District" that rehired the old teachers who passed muster and, with the New Teacher Project's help, recruited new ones. Neither the new teachers nor the teachers who were hired back had union contracts. These newly staffed old schools (which would be repaired or rebuilt with federal disaster aid) would be supplemented by a rapid expansion of charter schools.

All of it was done under the banner of an organization called New Schools for New Orleans, which Usdin ran. Usdin's new organization solicited TFA or New Teacher Project alums who were now principals or assistant principals at successful schools to apply for charters. She also lured charter operators who had succeeded elsewhere and were typically TFA alums (such as KIPP's Levin and Feinberg) to apply for charters in New Orleans.

At the same time she worked with the New Teacher Project to mount an unprecedented national campaign—"Teach New Orleans"—to lure the best teachers to come to New Orleans and create this new school system, classroom by classroom. Schnur's group, New Leaders for New Schools, joined in, recruiting, training, and placing twenty-four principals in the three years following the storm. Meantime, TFA worked with Usdin to double TFA's recruits there, putting a third of all New Orleans children in front of a TFA teacher.

All of these efforts were pushed enthusiastically by Paul Pastorek, who took over as state superintendent when his predecessor died about eighteen months after Katrina hit and who would quickly build a national reputation in education reform circles. (When Republican Bobby Jindal replaced Governor Blanco in 2008, he would keep Pastorek and continue to back him.)

Pastorek and Usdin's vision was that New Orleans would no longer have a "school system," but instead have a "system of schools," each run independently under standards set by the state and with support from Usdin's umbrella organization in New Orleans and Pastorek in the state capital.

By 2010, successful charter schools would be educating 60 percent of New Orleans's children, and they and most of the other "traditional" schools were performing far beyond the old schools' failure rates, so much so that New Orleans had arguably become one of the nation's best urban school systems. It was certainly at the top of the most-improved list.

While Pastorek and Usdin were making this kind of wholesale progress, Usdin's fellow TFA alum, Michael Johnston, was forging ahead alone in Colorado.

"Colorado Says Half of
You Won't Graduate"

September 2005, Mapleton, Colorado

By 2004, Michael Johnston had been so successful running his first school for juvenile delinquents that they gave him a second one to run. There, too, he boosted graduation rates, so impressing officials in the Mapleton school district, near Boulder, that they offered him the principal's job at a more traditional high school.

Supported by the Gates Foundation's small schools initiative that had aided Klein, Mapleton's two-thousand-student failing high school and middle school had been put in turnaround mode and chopped into four smaller units. Johnston was chosen to be the principal of one of them.

Before he welcomed a mostly Hispanic group of seventh through tenth graders, Johnston's first job was something he relished—choosing his team. The superintendent and the union had agreed that all the teachers had to reapply for their jobs. Those who didn't get hired at any of the four new schools could stay and work at the surviving senior high school, which would still hold the eleventh and twelfth graders and then be phased out when those classes graduated. When that happened, the teachers working there who had still not found jobs would be dismissed.

Johnston's strategy was to hire mostly new teachers, so that he'd be the one to rate them as satisfactory (or not) before they could receive tenure; after that, he would not be able to dismiss them, because they would then be employed under standard union rules. But, he says, "I did hire some tenured teachers, ones I knew were rock stars. One of them was the president of the local union, who was totally terrific and totally committed to our mission."

For Johnston, the silver lining was that this arrangement allowed him to avoid, as he puts it, "having to deal with terrible tenured teachers. I got to bring everyone I wanted into the building, which is something most other principals can't do. The greatest power you can have as a principal," he adds, "is to pick your own team of people who are totally dedicated to the mission."

At one point, a teacher with seniority was force-placed into his school under union rules. Johnston complained to the district but was told nothing could be done. Weeks later he complained more vociferously because the teacher, one of only five teaching ninth grade, was so hostile to the school's culture that the others on the ninth-grade team were distracted and demanded he do something about it. Plus, Johnston says, "It was hard to explain to the kids why one of the adults wasn't on the same page as everyone else."

Ultimately, Johnston pressured the teacher to leave voluntarily. Johnston may be the soft-spoken opposite of Anthony Lombardi, but he was able to pass the lemon Lombardi-style.

On the opening day of Johnston's school in September, he brought all of the new ninth and tenth graders out to a field, gathered them in a circle, and told them how much he was looking forward to working with them over the next three or four years to get all of them into college.

He paused to let that sink in. "The state's statistics say that half of you probably won't graduate and are certainly not going to go to college. At least half of you. Maybe more. I don't believe that. And we intend to prove those statistics wrong. If you can work with us, we know you can do it."

Some of that work went beyond even the tough academic regimen that Johnston had honed at Greenville and at the detention centers. "Some nights some of the teachers or I would be taking calls at eleven from kids who were suicidal or whose fathers had just been deported," Johnston remembers. "This was all about providing them full support."

Johnston and his staff were providing that kind of support mostly on their own. Meanwhile, a bold experiment in "scaling" these efforts, backed by deep pockets from Wall Street and spearheaded by a hardened politician, was taking shape in New York.

The Pol and the Moneymen

At forty-one, Eva Moskowitz—soft-spoken, even demure, and always well dressed—looked like any other well-to-do Manhattan mother. Yet almost everyone who knew her, even those who liked and admired her, seemed to settle on the same assessment: "Eva can be a real pain in the ass."

This mostly had to do with her quiet stubbornness, her inability to accept what she believed to be unacceptable, and her willingness to hammer away at it, with both her own hard work and her constant pestering of anyone who got in her way. She never raises her voice, but her sullen face bespeaks a kind of seething determination that seems never to let up.

Much of what Moskowitz thought was unacceptable had to do with public education in New York, where she had lived all her life except when she attended the University of Pennsylvania as an undergraduate, then got her PhD in history at Johns Hopkins and taught briefly at Vanderbilt.

As a teenager, Moskowitz had won a seat at Manhattan's Stuyvesant High School, where admission is based solely on a hotly competitive citywide test. Those who think of Moskowitz as a chronic complainer would not be surprised to know that she even complained about Stuyvesant.

Stuyvesant is New York's star high school, from which an outsize portion of students, like Moskowitz, cruise into the Ivy League. But to Moskowitz, many, if not most, of the teachers were anything but stars. She thought half of the teachers were incompetent and vividly remembers math and science classes where "the students, who were all gifted, literally carried the class. The teachers were cruising on the students' talent," she says. "I remember one of the kids taught the rest of us physics, while the teacher sat there drunk. . . . It was easy to be a teacher there."

By the time she was a Stuyvesant senior, Moskowitz had figured out why there was such a gap between the abilities of her classmates and the teachers: The seniority system allowed senior teachers to transfer out of schools where it was hard to teach and into Stuyvesant, where the students could teach themselves.

Moskowitz's preoccupation with how Stuyvesant worked, or didn't work, came naturally. She had, she says, "been obsessed about education since I was a kid. All my friends played house. I played schoolhouse."

None of this would have mattered much to Randi Weingarten— who would come to regard Moskowitz with a loathing that she had reserved only for Joel Klein—had Moskowitz not decided after a year at Vanderbilt that the academic PhD world was not for her. With her fiancé back in New York, she came home in 1996, and while thinking about what to do next, volunteered in a local City Council campaign. By 1999, she had been elected to the council from a district that included Manhattan's Upper East Side and also encompassed parts of Harlem, which is where she actually lived.

By 2002, she was the chair of the council's education committee and had begun being a "pain in the ass" not only to Weingarten but to Bloomberg and Klein as well. She criticized them for not moving fast enough, pushed Klein to implement co-location in charter schools two years before he actually began to do it, and complained that he had not delivered on his promises that the schools' basic operations would be managed efficiently. At one point she even held a hearing to gripe about toilet paper not being available in the children's bathrooms. On another occasion, she publicly attacked Bloomberg for being too friendly with Weingarten after the mayor took the union leader to a Yankees game. She urged the mayor to stay tough, telling the *New York Daily News* that "some fights are worth having, and this is one of them."

Moskowitz had turned her guns most memorably on Weingarten in a weeklong council hearing in November 2003. Chairs of committees can decide which hearings to convene, taking testimony on everything from car alarms to streetlights to food store inspections. Yet every one of her Democratic colleagues on the mostly Democratic fifty-one-member council begged Moskowitz not to hold this hearing about the education of New York's children. She had declared that she was going to spend a week delving into the union contracts, particularly the custodians' and teachers' contracts, that, she said, prevented the schools from delivering for the children. Moskowitz had studied the contracts to the point where she could recite major provisions.

A public discussion of some of these provisions—such as one freeing custodians from cleaning certain kinds of floors, another requiring two people to change certain kinds of lightbulbs, or those that protected teachers from dismissals and gave them free periods—would not have been welcome at any time. But for Weingarten, with her contract having expired five months earlier, in May, and Klein demanding reform of exactly the provisions Moskowitz was zeroing in on, the hearings could not have come at a worse time. Some City Council Democrats attacked Moskowitz for interfering in the collective-bargaining process, as if a public airing of provisions in contracts the public was paying for was somehow improper. Others said that if anything was wrong with the contracts, it was the fault of the Republican Bloomberg administration. Moskowitz hit back, charging that union leaders were trying to "sabotage" her hearings by pressuring and threatening her colleagues.

Klein and Daniel Weisberg, his labor chief, testified that the contracts were impediments that they were working to change, with Weisberg zeroing in on tenure protections, saying that the process for firing teachers is "unusually long, expensive, cumbersome and complex. . . . We have principals who say, 'I have handcuffs on.' "

Weingarten attacked the hearings as a Star Chamber and said that the problem with the city's schools had nothing to with union work rules and everything to do with Klein's bad management. In her testimony she ducked when asked about any specific contract provisions, steering all questions about the impact of the work rules on classrooms back to Klein's bad management. "You have a very good way of twisting words," Moskowitz said at one point.

"Eva had a clear political agenda," Weingarten says of the 2003 hearings. "She was going to use this to run for higher office."

Perhaps. But it was unprecedented and ultimately suicidal for any New York Democrat with a political agenda to run against the

UFT. Moskowitz claims that two weeks before the hearings, Weingarten took her aside at a local political event and whispered to her that if she went ahead with the hearings, "We will destroy you politically in New York. You will be over."

Weingarten denies the threat, but there is no denying that when Moskowitz ran in the Democratic primary for Manhattan borough president less than two years after the 2003 hearings, the UFT paid for phone banks and media for her opponent, Scott Stringer. The union also funded radio ads and leaflets attacking Moskowitz that were sponsored by the Working Families Party, the splinter group that derived much of its financial support from the UFT. One leaflet, headlined "It's Hard Enough for Working Families to Get By and Eva Moskowitz Is Just Making It Harder," declared, inaccurately, that Moskowitz had been against anti-sweatshop laws. Another attacked her for "interfering in negotiations for a new teachers' contract." Moskowitz lost badly to Stringer.

About three months later, on a December morning in 2005, she found herself at Gotham Capital on Madison Avenue meeting with Gotham founder Joel Greenblatt and his young partner, John Petry. Boykin Curry had been involved with Moskowitz's husband, Eric Grannis, in starting the Girls Prep charter school. With Petry and Greenblatt now thinking of going beyond that and starting a network of New York charter schools, they set up a meeting through Curry with Moskowitz to get advice.

Greenblatt and Petry laid out their idea and financial model. Because charter schools got the same money per pupil from the state and city to cover costs as the public schools did, they had calculated that once each school, which would start with one or two grades, had expanded to three grades, they would be breaking even on operating costs because there would be enough per student stipends coming from the government. Because teachers would have a standard 401(k) pension plan and good but not platinum health insurance instead of the lavish benefits provided for in the union contracts, and because other costs embedded in the city schools bureaucracy could be trimmed, more of that per pupil stipend could be spent on education—equipment, books, teacher bonuses, field trips.

Other support costs—such as the salary of the CEO to run the network, extra training, financial and operations staffing, and recruiting new students and planning new schools—would be financed by the network's umbrella organization. That would take some up-front investment from people like Greenblatt, but even that network operation would ultimately be self-supporting once there were thirteen schools, each with at least seven grades, paying some portion of their stipends into a network support fund. "You see, it scales," said Petry, showing her the spreadsheet.

Better yet, Klein's co-location initiative had eliminated most of the up-front cost of buying, building, or renting property. Co-located space would have to be refabricated, but the cost of that was nothing compared with what it took to procure real estate in New York.

Once they proved the business model—thirteen schools and the network would be self-sustaining—Greenblatt, Petry, and others would be ready to raise start-up money for another network. This was the way to scale; it's what KIPP was also doing.

Moskowitz listened, correcting them on certain points and peppering them with issues they hadn't thought of. For example, even though the per pupil formula for paying charters was supposed to be the same as the public schools formula, it was actually less because of some wording slipped into a budget bill in Albany by the teachers' union. She also made the case that this would be more complicated than it looked: The unions would fight them wherever they could—from Albany, where there was a one-hundred-school cap on charters, to the neighborhoods where the charters were to be co-located. Moreover, calling something a charter school didn't guarantee success. Lots of charters were lousy. It all depended on talent and the details of the operational support provided to the talent.

Nonetheless, Moskowitz thought that this was an exciting idea and said she'd be glad to think about whom she might suggest to help them get it off the ground. Then she left.

"John and I looked at each other for a few seconds," says Greenblatt; "then we both got up and chased her to the elevator. We brought her back in, sat her back down, and asked her to run it."

Bruised by nearly ten years in public service jobs, Moskowitz had been thinking about how to make some decent money in this new phase of her life. "I told them they couldn't afford me." She obviously hadn't checked Gotham Capital's returns lately.

"She gave us a salary number"—$250,000, which would become $367,000 by 2010—"that was actually just slightly lower than what we had budgeted for the person to run this," says Greenblatt.

Moskowitz made two other demands that Greenblatt and Petry agreed to: Although many charter schools were almost totally focused on math and reading, especially in the early grades, she wanted to teach science in every grade. She also insisted that the schools have a chess program. Her young son, she explained, had a learning disability, and the way chess had forced him to think strategically had enabled him to advance academically while gaining self-confidence.

A month later, in January 2006, Moskowitz would be sitting in a Starbucks in Harlem with Jenny Sedlis, who had worked on her borough president campaign, drafting leaflets aimed at getting parents interested in having their children attend Harlem Success Academy I in the fall—the school where Jessica Reid, having put her terrible Bronx TFA experience behind her, would end up hanging her "juicy words" and making her fifth graders "write up a storm."

While Moskowitz prepared to establish this beachhead of reform outside the school system, Joel Klein was still struggling to make progress inside.

Foxes in the Henhouse

*March 10, 2006, conference room at Manhattan law firm
of Skadden, Arps, Slate, Meagher & Flom*

Almost three years into his tenure, in 2005, Klein had still not gotten hold of his school system. So he made two major though unlikely additions to his management team. Once again looking for smart people rather than veteran school administrators, he hired Columbia Law professor James Liebman to design a data system that would grade all his schools based on performance the way Jeb Bush now did in Florida.*

Klein also brought on Christopher Cerf, another lawyer who had been at Klein's law firm. Cerf was assigned to redo the reorganization of the department of education that had been announced in January 2002, with a focus now on managing human resources, including teachers and principals.

Unlike Liebman, or Klein, for that matter, Cerf had experience running public schools, though with a unique twist: He had been the president of Edison Schools, the country's first corporate for-profit public school management organization.

On March 10, 2006, Cerf got Klein and the senior staff to come to a conference room at a Manhattan law firm. He wanted them away from the office—at a kind of mini-retreat—so he could pitch his reorganization uninterrupted. He used a thirty-four-page PowerPoint that he and a team of consultants (paid for with private contributions, including, again, funds from the Broad Foundation) had labored over. One consultant was Sir Michael Barber, a partner at McKinsey & Company who had been British prime minister Tony Blair's top education aide.

Klein and Cerf had concluded that a school system the size of

---

* The system would be built and publicly report the first school grades in 2008, for the 2007–2008 school year.

New York's could not be managed centrally. "I always knew that getting rid of the old forty districts that were run by a combination of local politics and the UFT would restore some order, standardize things like curricula, and maybe turn a horrible system into one that was adequate or almost adequate, but it was never meant to be the final answer," Klein told me. This seemed to be his way of walking back from the first plan, to centralize, without admitting what now seemed an obvious mistake. Centralization didn't make sense if the idea of empowering principals trained in the new Leadership Academy was to have any meaning.

Thus, the core of Cerf's plan was "portfolio management." As with the initiative to break up the high schools into smaller units, and the push for more charter schools, the entire school system would become a "portfolio" of individually managed schools, with the central office empowering principals as long as they produced satisfactory results. Principals were now picked by Klein, often after going through the Leadership Academy, and they could be more easily fired if they did not produce results, because union rules governing principals had been renegotiated. Under Cerf's plan, they would now be given more leeway in spending and budgeting. They would have to pay union wages, of course, and adhere to the union contract, and cover their share of central costs, such as heating or maintenance. Beyond that, people like Lombardi could, for example, decide to eliminate one assistant principal in exchange for a literacy coach and a part-time orchestra leader.

One of Cerf's slides declared that while they had made some progress since 2002, teacher "hostility" to the idea of accountability had created "a fox in the henhouse structure," "human capital/talent systems remain primitive," and principals had been "put in charge, but not in control." Cerf was adamant that this, more than anything else, had to change. They had to be given real control. To do this, Cerf's slides continued, they had to come up with a battle plan that would "aim high," "identify structural origins of existing system failures and solve for them," and "candidly acknowledge 'failure points' in new design and plan around them." If the consulting industry ever establishes, as it should, a Museum of the Obvious, this slide could be hung at the entrance.

Cerf then listed those "failure points"—the reasons his new idea might fail. They included "practical realities make 'autonomy' fatally weak" and "politics preclude real accountability for failure."

The way to address that, the slide reiterated, was that principals "have to be given the power to build their staff—eg, GB."

"GB" meant Great Britain, which was a nice thought, although Sir Michael Barber didn't present a slide outlining how to deal with Sir Sheldon Silver, the Democrat and union loyalist who controlled the state assembly, and Dame Randi Weingarten. Another potential failure point was "capacity," by which Cerf meant the ability to produce enough real leaders to become effective principals and assistant principals. One of Cerf's solutions referred to the company that had been led by Jack Welch, who was now helping at the Leadership Academy: "Ask, 'How would GE do it?' " GE, of course, would not do it with a 167-page union contract, backed by union-sponsored state laws forbidding changes in tenure and lockstep compensation.

Finally, there was Cerf's solution to the general proposition, as expressed in another slide, that the political cost of confronting the union was so high that the administration "had to be utterly unapologetic and willing to take the hit." This, of course, was what Bloomberg had not been willing to do in the 2005 contract negotiation.

What Cerf's slides didn't show was that an avalanche of data was being gathered by the academics that proved even more convincingly how critical being "willing to take the hit" was.

Mounting Evidence

April 5, 2006, Washington, D.C.

In education research circles, Harvard's Thomas Kane—Michelle Rhee's thesis adviser who had helped Klein crunch some sample teacher effectiveness numbers in 2003—and Dartmouth economics professor Douglas Staiger had, says Kane, become known as the "volatility guys." It sounds exciting, but it meant only that when they began using the data now being created by President George W. Bush's 2002 No Child Left Behind law, they found that if student advancement on test scores was linked to the students' schools, the overall score for the school was "volatile" from year to year. One year a school would look as if it was performing a lot better than it would the next year. Looked at over a three- or four-year period, the numbers jumped around so much that it was hard to tell which schools were actually doing better or worse over the long term (though as a general matter most schools were not improving student proficiency in any way close enough to meet the Bush law's requirements).

Kane and Staiger had assumed that this volatility, which they thought might have to do with the unreliability of the tests, would be even more pronounced when looked at in still smaller sample units—the year-to-year performance in improving student scores of the *teachers* within a school. However, as they dived into those numbers they were stunned to find exactly the opposite. Teachers who did well one year typically did well every year, and those who did poorly kept doing poorly. It seemed that the teachers were the key variable.

This should not have been a surprise, given the results reported in the 1998 article that Kati Haycock of the Education Trust had written using data from the few school systems that had long since started linking scores to schools and teachers. Yet because Kane and

Staiger were now able to look at data from school systems across the country, the impact of what they had found was more compelling.

"All these new data—the test scores—were a divining rod pointing to a new energy source, a new point of leverage: teachers," Kane explains.

The divining rod would soon become a lightning rod. Kane would become increasingly frustrated that opponents of his focus on teacher effectiveness confused it with an obsession with testing. Kane knew that the two could not be synonymous—that tests weren't perfect, and that tests couldn't be used to measure the effectiveness of teachers who taught subjects like social studies or history, for which there were not yet standardized tests, let alone subjects like music, drama, or art, for which there might never be good tests. Rather, his point was that for the subjects where there *were* tests, the tests showed remarkable consistency among teachers: Individual teachers' performance in advancing or not advancing their students' proficiency was remarkably consistent. This obviously suggested that the key to student advancement was the person in front of the class—not that tests could always be used to gauge all teachers. There would have to be many tools used to measure teachers: peer observations, maybe video reviews of classroom performance, perhaps even student assessments. The point was that teachers needed to be the focus, not that tests needed to be the all-important or only tool.

By 2005, Kane and Staiger had put together much of that research, while also culling through similar studies by other education academics, and had written a paper detailing it. Peter Orszag—a protégé of former treasury secretary Robert Rubin—had heard about it, and he and Rubin decided it would make a good paper for their new Hamilton Project to publish as part of its launch. The Hamilton Project had been conceived by Rubin as a think tank focusing on financial and economic competitiveness issues, and was to be housed within the most establishment center-left think tank in Washington, the Brookings Institution.

Because he wanted to provide a policy context, Orszag recruited Robert Gordon, who was working at the Center for American Progress, to become the third author. Gordon, then thirty-four, had graduated from Yale Law School and clerked at the Supreme Court before becoming the domestic issues director for the 2004 presidential campaign of South Carolina Democratic senator John Edwards. When Edwards dropped out, Gordon had become issues director for John Kerry, and in that capacity he had befriended Jon Schnur. Like Schnur, Gordon had been frustrated by the Democrats' avoidance of education reform, so much so that in 2005 he had written a controversial article in the *New Republic* titled "What Democrats Need to Say About Education."

Gordon's article urged Democrats "to stop their unprincipled attacks" on Bush's No Child Left Behind and laid out the array of reforms that they should support, even if it meant confronting the teachers' unions. He also charged that his party had abandoned principle in order to stay true to the unions' mantra that lack of money was the problem in education:

> To get the politics right, progressives need to act on a policy principle that Americans understand: Money ain't everything. The United States has tripled education funding per student since the 1960s, and we now outspend all but a few countries. . . . Strengthening teaching requires changes to the pay system and school culture that abet mediocrity. Standing alone, the usual liberal solution—across-the-board pay hikes—perpetuates the maldistribution of good teachers and reinforces the irrelevance of achievement. High-poverty schools need to attract more teachers with bonuses, and all schools need to attract better teachers with the promise of higher earnings for better results.

With Gordon now having joined Kane and Staiger, on April 5, 2006, the Hamilton Project released "Identifying Effective Teachers Using Performance on the Job."

The paper attacked the two core assumptions about teachers that had become conventional wisdom and were the bedrock of public education's we-can't-do-much approach to human resource management: First, that "paper qualifications required for certification," such as having the requisite graduate degree in education or passing a standardized teacher test, are strongly related to a teacher's effectiveness. Second, that school districts can learn nothing more about a teacher's effectiveness after the initial hire; this was why almost all teachers initially received satisfactory ratings and then got tenure.

The authors began dismantling those assumptions by laying out the evidence from data that Staiger and Kane had crunched in Los Angeles, whose school system had a habit of hiring lots of noncertified teachers because of shortages of those with certification. Linking certified and noncertified teachers to student scores, they found "not much difference" between the two groups.

However—and this is where the second premise, that teachers couldn't be measured once hired, was demolished—there were huge differences *among* those in each of the two groups. The difference in student performance between teachers ranked in the top quarter in terms of effectiveness (based on test score improvements among their students) and those ranked in the middle in effectiveness was, they wrote, "roughly five times as large as the difference between the average certified teacher and the average uncertified teacher."

Moreover, the differences, teacher by teacher, remained relatively stable, meaning a teacher shown to be effective one year was typically shown to be effective the next year, too, while those who performed badly one year kept performing badly. This was the lack of volatility that had so surprised Kane.

Over three years, they wrote, the difference in a child's learning progress between being assigned to a bottom-quartile teacher versus being assigned to a top-quartile teacher was "massive."

After piling on reams of additional data from other school districts, Gordon, Kane, and Steiger turned to the policy implications. They recommended that the barriers for entry into teaching for those not having traditional certification be removed and that data of the kind they had used related to teacher effectiveness should become the key factor in screening new teachers for three or more years before granting them tenure. "We thought," says Gordon, "that if we emphasized using the data for making tenure decisions, rather than using it to fire teachers who already had tenure, we could defuse the political issues around tenure. But the unions and most Democrats rejected this, too."

One Democrat who did not ignore or reject the paper was Barack

Obama. The junior senator from Illinois came to the Brookings press event that launched the Hamilton Project and praised it.

In fact, a month earlier, Obama, who had barely completed his first year in Washington, had introduced what he called an "education innovation" bill that proposed something else the Hamilton authors had recommended: Give federal grants to school systems that, among other initiatives, used data measuring student progress to evaluate the effectiveness of teachers. Like the Hamilton paper, Obama's bill was ignored, despite the fact that a Democrat was challenging his party's most important base. However, some in the budding education reform movement noticed, including Schnur, who had started telling friends that he thought Obama "could be a great education president—in 2017."

As for the present, despite the mounting evidence being gathered and promoted by the researchers and their think tanks, Schnur and those in his network who were trying to turn the Democrats around continued to struggle.

"This Just Seemed So Obvious"

July 2006, office of Greenlight Capital, Manhattan

In the summer of 2006, Democrats for Education Reform was floundering. Tilson, Petry, Curry, and their fourth co-founder, Charles Ledley (all of whom were not yet the heavy hitters they would become), had put a total of about $75,000 into the group. The executive director they had hired, Amy Wilkins, lived in Washington and had a young family; this, she and the DFER co-founders recall, was not the ideal setup for someone who needed to be in Albany, Tallahassee, Providence, or Sacramento more than on Capitol Hill. Besides, Wilkins, a politically savvy former press aide in the Clinton White House, didn't hit it off with three New Yorkers and one Californian who had what Tilson calls "short attention spans and habits of sending e-mails or texts at two in the morning."

"These guys had watched too many movies or read too many bad political novels," Wilkins recalls. "They figured money in, product out."

In any event, they were getting no traction. They needed more money just to keep their small payroll going and then expand it and to find a person better suited to lead the charge. They wanted DFER to be a big public organization and a powerful political action committee capable of funding candidates across the country, not a group of moderately wealthy friends with good intentions and one employee. Just when they thought they might have to shut down, David Einhorn came through—with a check for $250,000 in July 2006.

Einhorn, who runs a hedge fund called Greenlight Capital, is best known today as the short seller who sounded the alarm in 2009 about Lehman Brothers' assets being underwater.* Even in 2006, at

---

* In May 2011, Einhorn also made headlines as a likely minority investor in the New York Mets.

age thirty-eight, he was already one of Wall Street's most successful short sellers.

Einhorn had, he says, always been interested in education. "I happen to have a mixed marriage," he explains. "My wife is a Republican, and when we debated issues, I had to admit that I usually thought she was right on this one topic."

Einhorn resented the idea that education was only about money. He also didn't think it took Tom Kane and all his research to prove the point. "This just seemed so obvious. Anyone who had any experience in any school as a kid knows that it isn't about money; it's about teachers," he says, offering as an example his sixth-grade math teacher in the suburbs of Milwaukee: "The only thing he taught me was how to loop my twos. I never forgot that guy."

Einhorn wrote the $250,000 check from his charitable trust to DFER after Petry, Tilson, and Curry came to see him, because, he explains, "To me this was a Nixon-goes-to-China kind of thing. Democrats taking this position have a better chance because they have traditionally been on the other side."

For the next several months, Petry, Tilson, and Curry scoured the country looking for someone to run the group and build on the new foundation Einhorn had supplied. It wouldn't be until early 2007 that they decided to offer the job to Joe Williams, an education reporter for the *New York Daily News*, and even then it was only because they couldn't find anyone else.

Williams's reporting on the fights between Klein, Bloomberg, and the unions had been straight down the middle, as had his coverage of Moskowitz's jousts with the two camps. However, he says, "I knew that teaching was what really counted. . . . As a reporter, I could go to a school and ask the third-grade teachers who the good and bad second-grade teachers were, and they would always know, because they had to deal the next year with the results. And my own kids went to schools in Brooklyn, and I can tell you that a good or bad teacher made a huge difference. A shitty teacher affected our entire household."

Williams might have been the moneymen's default choice, but once he got over his initial hesitations and learned to swallow hard and ask people for money, he would turn out to be "the luckiest thing that ever happened to us," says Tilson.

Like Wilkins, Williams struggled with the founders' short attention spans, their impulsive decisions, and, more important, their initial political naïveté. But he'd soon succeed in turning DFER into the transformational force its founders had envisioned—with help from Barack Obama.

The gains were small at first—a state senator embracing them here or there, then maybe a mayor or a congressman. Williams kept at it, slowly building support wherever he could find even the slightest opening. He put together small fund-raising receptions for candidates for a school board in California or Ohio; for mayor in Providence, Hartford, or Sacramento; for state legislatures in Colorado or Michigan. He would enlist stars of the reform movement who he knew were strong Democrats—particularly Alan Bersin in San Diego and Klein in New York—to show up at these events and help him find others to join the cause. DFER's website began naming an Education Reformer of the Month, for whom special contributions were solicited. Williams began posting a blog that steadily picked up traffic.

Curry looked at their progress as a long-term investor: "I began to see it like compound interest. You plant a few seeds here, and it has a small yield, which keeps compounding, until you get to the point where your influence starts to grow rapidly. That's the beauty of making steady investments in an instrument with compound interest."

At the same time the city of New York, which under Mayor Bloomberg and Chancellor Klein was supposedly in the vanguard of reform, was accruing interest of another kind—in costs for a new, expensive but reform-free union contract.

More Money, No Hassles

November 8, 2006, New York City

In the summer of 2006, New York City and the UFT began negotiating what Klein calls "a quickie, nothing contract." Bloomberg had told Klein that he wanted to get any possibility of labor unrest put aside well in advance of the election in 2009. The mayor was already contemplating a run for a third term, something that would be difficult. It wasn't only that his overall approval ratings in various polls were down. To run again, Bloomberg would have to do a complete flip-flop on his long-held support for a recent law limiting city officeholders to two terms. The law had been passed in a public referendum. Now, Bloomberg would have to get the City Council to override the referendum. Having Weingarten as an ally, or at least not an enemy, was a necessity.

So, on Bloomberg's instruction, Klein and Dan Weisberg, his labor relations chief, didn't push again on issues such as tenure. They did try to get a provision cutting off the salaries of any of those excessed "Absent Teacher Reserve" teachers who had not found a new job in another school within twelve months. This group of paid-to-do-nothing teachers was now pushing one thousand. They argued that Chicago—where then-superintendent Arne Duncan had also used the reorganization accompanying the splitting of large schools into smaller, themed schools to remove teachers—had a ten-month cutoff. But Weingarten refused, and Bloomberg's team told Klein and Weisberg to stand down.

The only ostensible reform was a fig leaf, added later to the agreement, that seemed as though the union had conceded on allowing merit pay but amounted to no concession at all. A pilot project would be tried at a few schools. If the schools performed well, they would be allotted bonuses, to be contributed by Eli Broad's foundation. However, those bonuses would be spread among the entire staff, not awarded to individual teachers based on performance. "A waste of money," Broad would later say. "Nobody got anything based on their own performance. . . . Even the union rep or the clerical help got some of the money." The program never spread beyond a few schools and was all but abandoned by 2010.

The new agreement, which was announced in November 8, 2006, but took effect in October 2007, was anything but a "nothing" contract for New York's taxpayers. It piled on still higher salaries and benefits, including the ability of teachers to retire with full pensions at age fifty-five instead of what had been fifty-seven in the 2005 contract and had been sixty in prior contracts.

With this 2007 contract in place through 2009, the cost to the city for the average teacher in 2009 would be $110,551 compared with $63,022 in 2002, the last year before the contracts Bloomberg negotiated took effect—a 75 percent increase. The key drivers were the raises in average salary, from $48,200 to $70,876, as well as pension costs. The bill for pensions skyrocketed from $4,820 per teacher pre-Bloomberg to $22,680—a 370 percent increase. And if the pension fund accountants had kept the books in a manner consistent with the real world (rather than project an 8 percent return forever, as mandated by Albany), the actual amount needed to be reserved for those pensions would have been as much as double that.

To the reformers, none of that was as costly to the next generation of New Yorkers as the mayor's unwillingness to do anything about teacher evaluations, tenure, or lockstep seniority compensation. "Bloomberg did not do his civic duty," Moskowitz told me.

On November 7, 2006, Klein was scheduled to have dinner with Lombardi. At the last minute, the chancellor canceled. The next morning, Lombardi realized why: The new contract was announced, with the headlines featuring the teachers' outsize raises in salaries and pension benefits and no changes in the work rules. "Joel was too embarrassed, I think," Lombardi says, an account Klein does not dispute.

"The plan," says Klein, "was to make some progress in the 2005 contract—which we did, though not enough—and then go in for the kill in 2007. Mike deciding to run for a third term completely killed that."

"We fought as hard as we could and got whatever we could," says

Bloomberg. As for whether an eagerness to avoid labor unrest on the eve of his quest for a third term played any role, Bloomberg said, "People who know me would say that that's just preposterous."

It was one thing for Klein to have complained indignantly about the restrictions in his own contract with the union in front of Moskowitz's City Council committee in 2003. At the time, he was working off a contract negotiated by the previous administration. And although he and the city hadn't gotten anything close to what Klein would have wanted in the 2005 negotiation—including an end to tenure protection—they had still made progress, and, says Klein, "we expected to really break through in 2007." But that was before Bloomberg decided to seek a third term. Instead, with this contract, they got nothing and hadn't even tried. For the rest of his tenure Klein would be the rabid school reformer whose most eloquent arguments would be about union protections that remained embedded in the contract he had just signed.

Weingarten stayed neutral again in the 2009 mayoral race, which Bloomberg won by a far closer margin than in 2005.

On another front, however, Moskowitz would be the first to agree that by unabashedly supporting charter schools—and pushing for them to be co-located—Bloomberg and Klein were certainly doing their "civic duty."

Building Harlem Success

"Eva Decided to Show Me How to Do It"

*November 20, 2006, Harlem Success Academy,
118th Street and Lenox Avenue, Manhattan*

When it was announced that Eva Moskowitz was going to run the Harlem Success Academy being financed by Joel Greenblatt and John Petry, Joel Klein decided to do a smaller version of Bill Gates turning the other cheek. Moskowitz had been his tormentor on the City Council. Nothing he did had been good enough for her, from how erratically he got toilet paper into school bathrooms to how aggressively he took on the union. Nonetheless, Klein favored charter schools, thought the Greenblatt/Petry plan was sound and well financed, and knew that Moskowitz was smart and laser focused on school operations. So he did everything he could to support her—including arranging for Harlem Success to be co-located in the PS 149 building on Lenox Avenue.

That last part had not been easy. Through the spring and summer of 2006, parents, accompanied by Working Families Party and ACORN troops deployed by the UFT, protested and scared Klein's space-planning bureaucracy into scrapping plans for various colocation sites. Harlem Success bounced from one announced location to another, a school without a building. Moskowitz had spent the summer fighting these brushfires, while making final hiring decisions and getting her incoming kindergartners and first graders to read at least six books per week for ten weeks with their parents before school started.

In a drama that would be repeated as Moskowitz opened new schools, she and the parents hadn't been given the final location decision until the first week in August. Amazingly, Moskowitz—who began what would be years of incessant e-mails pestering Joel Klein about issues like this—got word of the location from a district UFT person, who told her a week before Klein's department of education did that she was being moved from PS 154 to PS 149, a school that had not even been on the department's list of schools with available space. "That should give you some idea of who was running the bureaucracy," Moskowitz says.

This sudden, final switch gave her three weeks to get her side of the building painted, wired for computers, and otherwise ready to create what she envisioned as a completely new environment.

By November 20, things had settled in enough that Moskowitz held a belated opening ceremony for the parents and the community in the auditorium she shared with PS 149. Klein was the lead speaker, offering his congratulations. He reminded the group that Moskowitz had been among those who had been most critical of him and most eager to offer advice from the sidelines about how to run the schools. "But Eva fooled me," he said. "She decided to show me how to do it. She's got skin in the game now, and she's doing the hard work of transforming education."

Yes, it was hard work. In a long e-mail update to Harlem Success co-founders and financiers Petry and Greenblatt just after midnight about three weeks later, Moskowitz covered everything from her progress in writing grant requests, to her trouble squeezing twenty-four hours of sports into the sixteen hours of gym space she had been allotted, to her urgent need to rewrite the science and social studies lesson plans because the students were learning faster than the plans, to the art of writing a recruiting brochure to attract parents for the spring admissions season, to scheduling the painting and wiring of expansion space next summer "to avoid another summer like last," to the new budget spreadsheets she had created, to how the science curriculum "on teeth" had been a huge success, to how she had to stop writing in order to prep for a *Billy Goats Gruff* lesson she was teaching the following morning.

"Three Teachers Cried . . . Make That Four"

Friday night, January 26, 2007, Harlem Success Academy

Not being constrained by a union contract doesn't mean that managing talent becomes easy. If anything, it opens the door to all the challenges inherent in treating people individually rather than as interchangeable assembly-line workers. On Friday night, January 26, 2007, barely five months into her career as a school principal, Eva Moskowitz shared her frustration with Petry and Greenblatt in another e-mail:

> Three teachers cried: they are not used to their work product being scrutinized. They are not used to anyone saying this is good but here's how to make it better. We are dealing with teachers who have taught for 3 years and never got feedback. We are also dealing with a teaching culture that has not internalized shooting high. It requires a culture shift. We'll get there but requires lots of kleenex and therapeutic skills. . . . Make that 4 teachers: Friday at 7p.m. We lost another to tears. All is fine. There are days I wish I could send them to a law firm for a few months so they knew what tedious review of work product looked like. Anyway, they are not used to being told that they need to improve.*

In other words, Moskowitz was worried more about the children than the adults. That always sounds right whenever the reformers say it, but what if the adults feel so abused that they quit on the children? During the course of my reporting, beginning in 2009, I found four Harlem Success teachers who told vivid stories of being subjected to so much criticism, or so pressured by Moskowitz (in two cases) or her staff (in all four cases), or who felt so under the gun to prepare students for standardized tests, that two of them said they had quit and the other two seemed as of this writing to

---

* Where e-mails are quoted verbatim, the text is changed in limited instances to correct typographical errors or spell out abbreviations and other shorthand that might not be clear.

be on the verge of doing so at the end of the 2010–2011 school year. Because they said they were afraid of reprisals from Moskowitz (or their new employer in the case of the two who said they had quit), I was unable to check their accounts with Moskowitz. Two others said that while they appreciate all of the feedback they get, they are often told to implement changes in their teaching immediately, with no priority suggested for which changes should come first. All six of these teachers also said they believed that Harlem Success over-emphasized test preparation at the expense of learning. On the other hand, I found twice as many Harlem Success teachers who told me they were happy working there and totally committed to Moskowitz's mission.

"Yes, it's hard work," Moskowitz told me when I asked about some of her staff's complaints. "But it's also hard work to be a great lawyer or a great doctor."

Moskowitz's same e-mail, however, went on to report how all this pressure on the teachers was producing good results for the children, who, because this was the school's first year, were all kindergartners and first graders:

Literacy: children are making amazing progress. . . . I am literally going to get through 5th grade so that we don't run out and have lag times. But in general it is impressive to see how much our kids learn every day/week.

Math: we have high levels of mastery and have very specific sense of where we fall short—which is itself very unusual. So, for example, we know that all of our kids have trouble with greater than or less than. To be precise only 65 percent of our kids get it. Again we have all-out campaign and plan in place to get that to 100 percent. In kindergarten the curriculum is way too easy. . . . We are supplementing like mad.

Art: our teacher is very talented, though we are working to connect more closely to our social studies. We are also working on exhibiting the kids' work at a gallery.

Chess: we are teaching parents chess in 2 weeks and preparing for an internal all-day tournament in march.

Basketball: just started. Kids love!!!!!!

Operations: I sent you a few e-mails about pencils. I did so because thought it was a good example of how small things can get in the way of instruction. Our kids didn't have pencils and teachers were running out and not good about replenishing and we were losing instructional time. So we are taking over this function. And teachers love it. So we deal with instruction and teacher morale at same time.

Greenblatt, who was Petry's senior partner at Gotham Capital, recalls how impressed he was with Moskowitz's determination and her willingness to get down into the weeds on everything. But he was worried about one aspect of her grit. Was she being too tough on the kids by sending them home, for example, if one aspect of their uniform was out of place more than a day or two in a row, or by threatening to hold them back if they didn't do their heavy volume of assigned reading consistently? "I told Eva, 'Isn't that a bit harsh for these kids? I have kids, too, and I think maybe you need to cut them some slack.' "

" 'Your kids have you,' Eva said. 'These kids don't. They need a lot more from a school than your kids do.' "

Albany Attack

March 31, 2007, Albany

Two months later, in March 2007, Petry, Greenblatt, and Moskowitz watched in panic as the Albany legislature tried to strangle their business plan in its crib.

In 1998, the legislature had yielded to pressure and gifts (a salary increase for them in the same bill) from the Republican governor, George Pataki, and passed the law allowing charter schools. However, the legislators had insisted on a limit of one hundred charters statewide. The ostensible reason was that the lawmakers ought to be able to take a look at whether charters were working before allowing them to proliferate, though this also provided a way for the teachers' unions that had demanded the cap to contain the charters if they were working.

By the beginning of 2007, it was clear not only that charters, such as Levin's three KIPP schools, were succeeding, but also that there were about to be more promising applications for new schools than the cap could accommodate. So a proposal to double the cap to two hundred did not seem controversial, except insofar as charter proponents argued for no cap at all because the granting of charters was already regulated by the state in a careful process. (Careful to the point of anal, in the view of people like Dave Levin.)

As often happens in Albany, the most mischief is done at night. In this case, Democratic speaker Sheldon Silver's staff inserted a rider into a budget bill late on the night of Sunday, March 11, 2007, that lifted the cap by only fifty schools. Moreover, it shifted the authority to grant charters from Klein and the State University of New York to the Board of Regents (which is appointed by Silver, the union's best friend in Albany). It also required the consent of a majority of the parents in a community before any charter could be co-located in a public school, and it reduced the per pupil stipend given to charters by 10 percent.

Worst of all, the proposed law would require that all teachers in charter schools with more than 250 students in their first two years (a threshold Moskowitz was about to cross) be members of the UFT. The original law had had this unionization requirement for charters starting in their *first* year with more than 250 students, something that Moskowitz had resented but that had not affected her or most other charters, which started with small enrollments in the first year. Now it would be the first two years, which would wipe out Harlem Success by forcing it to unionize or force the school to throw out some students. This would put a monkey wrench in Petry's economic model; fewer students meant the schools he had modeled could not achieve economies of scale when they were expected to.

Greenblatt remembers that this was the first time he "ever really knew who Shelly Silver was." But he and Moskowitz knew who then-governor Eliot Spitzer was, and they called him to say that this would kill off Harlem Success.

By Friday, March 30, following a round of furious lobbying led by Klein and New York City's lobbyists, as well as Moskowitz and other charter operators, Silver had been beaten back. The cap would be lifted from one hundred to two hundred and all the other restrictions were deleted. But there was one exception: the union membership requirement. More calls went out to Spitzer, and by the following morning the charters' and the city's lobbyists were able to get another provision added. It still imposed the union requirement on charters that had more than 250 students in their first two years, but it exempted any already existing charters from that rule.

Moskowitz's Harlem Success, which was expanding in its second year beyond 250, now would be exempt. However, she was against taking the deal because allowing the student count to be extended from one to two years could set a precedent for its extension to three years the next time the cap had to be lifted. "It's a bone that the politicians can keep throwing to the unions," she warned. Her allies accepted the compromise as the best they could do. As a result, New York charter schools would forever have legislatively mandated, contorted business plans forcing them to stay relatively small in their first two years and then scale up more quickly in the third year in order to achieve economies of scale.

The cut in per student funding also remained. Now and in future years, charter schools would receive less in city and state funds to educate each student than the traditional schools did. "Well, these charter school people always brag that they can do more with less because they don't have the unions," Silver would later explain to me. "So we'll let them prove it."

"There are three ways the union and their Albany puppets try to get us," says Moskowitz. "They can underfund us. They can cap us. And they can regulate us to death."

Nonetheless, Moskowitz was relieved to have dodged all the other bullets. "That was way too close a call," she e-mailed Petry and Greenblatt. "If it was a year ago, I think we would have been screwed. But I think we are starting to get better at this." She then went back to her real job—planning a final leafleting and ad campaign to attract parents to enter the March 28, 2007, lottery for her new first grade in September, for which there would end up being 600 applicants for 107 seats.

"Bypassing Dysfunctionality"

June 2, 2007, Harlem

In addition to planning for the lottery, Eva Moskowitz had a lot on her plate beyond Albany's political intrigues. On June 2, 2007, she sent a long e-mail to Petry and Greenblatt that included the following updates:

> Every day and week there are significant hurdles. . . . We have one of our dv [in a domestic violence shelter] families whose son needs real help. We have about ten kids who have non-trivial psychiatric problems. Then we have another 15 who teachers think have problems.
>
> Can't remember if I told you about our 2000 light bulbs. Unintentionally engaged in union busting. Our lights go out constantly, even when power is not shutting down.
>
> There are 2 parts to lights in nyc school system, the ballasts and bulbs. Custodians only change bulbs and not ballasts. Ballasts go out even more frequently than bulbs. Kids and teachers get screwed on a regular basis because the electrical workers union and custodian unions have agreed to split the work. Electrical workers do jobs every 3 years and do 100 schools so all ballasts get fixed at once—union's version of economies of scale!!!!!
>
> Anyway, we don't have that problem because despite the deal, I make my custodian change ballasts. But the bulbs too need constant changing and the guys require constant harassing to get fixed.
>
> I have sent more emails about bulbs and ballasts than any other subject. So I asked Tom to investigate what kind of weird defective bulbs is the Department of Education purchasing that they go out constantly? Sure enough the department did massive contract with bulb company that, by the way, only sells bulbs to schools.
>
> They're both expensive and last a short time. But they provide a lot of overtime. Handymen change bulbs at 29/hr a cou-

ple hours a week after 7 pm. Truth be told I discovered this after I purchased bulbs that last 30,000 hours as opposed to 5000 hours. Custodian explained I was taking away jobs!!!!! Welcome to public education. But for about 7k our kids and teachers will have lights and we can bypass dysfunctionality.

Of course, in the reformers' view the overriding dysfunctionality was political, and it had to do with the Democratic Party, which Harlem Success cofounder Petry was trying to address with his Democrats for Education Reform.

"This Is Not a
Self-Esteem Movement"

June 3, 2007, Boykin Curry's apartment

Two years after the founders of Democrats for Education Reform hosted the cocktail party featuring Senator Barack Obama, their now formally incorporated political action committee, led by Joe Williams, hosted a kickoff at the same venue: Boykin Curry's Central Park South apartment.

The day before, Williams sent a pre-party e-mail to Curry, Petry, and Tilson. He listed the "themes for the evening":

a. This is a national movement to fundamentally change public education for the better.
b. This is not a self-esteem movement or a social network. It is about pushing a political revolution.
c. Some people (including many people present like Bob Hughes from New Visions [which ran those themed mini–high schools for Klein with Gates Foundation money] are going to be very uncomfortable with what we are saying and doing—and that's the f__king point. There is too much comfort felt by those with power and too much discomfort felt by the little guys.

Williams went on to note that among other plans, they had arranged to give special "Warrior" awards to two politicians who were attending: Indianapolis mayor Bart Peterson, who was in a tight reelection race; and New York state senator Malcolm Smith, who had promised the group his support.

Peterson would end up losing his race, and Smith would disappoint DFER during a crucial fight over charter schools in 2010.

Despite those false starts, Williams was acquiring some real insider political chops. Four days after the party, he sent his board this tale of intrigue involving Green Dot, a well-regarded charter network in California. Apparently a quiet deal was being worked out with Joel Klein, philanthropist Eli Broad, and, in the background, Randi Weingarten, to bring Green Dot to New York:

> After being approached repeatedly by Joel Klein to come to NYC, Green Dot is, indeed, going to submit a charter application to open a high school in the Hunts Point section of the Bronx in 2008. . . .
>
> It will use the Green Dot model and the Green Dot teachers' contract [a much-modified and abbreviated contract worked out between Green Dot chief Steven Barr and the Los Angeles teachers' union]. As part of the deal with Randi, she will support the application and will serve as a board member, and teachers will pay dues to the UFT, but the "just cause" process for firing [meaning teachers could be fired much more easily] will be in effect, and the Green Dot contract will rule. Teachers, for example, will be expected to work however many hours it takes, rather than the rigid school hours. There will be no prohibitions against doing lunch duty, etc.
>
> Eli Broad will provide the start-up costs, as he is close with both Steve Barr and Randi, and he believes Barr's argument that charter schools are only good models for the reform of a unionized system if the charters also are unionized.

Williams also reported that the Green Dot group wanted him to agree to serve on its board to provide independent credibility. He ended up declining to do so, but within two years Green Dot's Bronx high school—with a thin, twenty-nine-page union contract offering teachers 14 percent higher base salaries but none of the usual tenure protections, and with Randi Weingarten on its board—would be welcoming its first classes. In fact, the UFT would even end up loaning Green Dot $373,000 to get started.

"If I could count on principals like Steve Barr instead of Anthony Lombardi," Weingarten would later explain to me, "I would do that everywhere. But you can't have a contract like this with people like Klein supporting people like Lombardi."

"It's great for the kids in that school that Randi agrees to things like Green Dot," Klein would later tell me. "But for her it's a fig leaf. She gives a little here to look reasonable, while resisting to the end any kind of sweeping change."

As Klein's cynicism about Weingarten suggests, the reformers were dividing into two camps—those, like Jon Schnur or Eli Broad, who were persistent but also willing to compromise to get half a loaf, and those who were more confrontational. Klein was in the second camp. He was about to engineer a surprise move that would result in his being joined there by another chancellor of another big-city school system: Michelle Rhee.

"You Really Don't Want to Hire Me"

In early May 2007, Michelle Rhee received TFA's annual alumnus of the year award at a dinner in the ballroom at New York's Waldorf-Astoria hotel. Joel Klein sat with her at the head table. As Klein chatted with Rhee, then heard the tributes given to her for her work in Baltimore, as well as for the national impact she had achieved with the New Teacher Project, he began to think about conversations he had been having with Adrian Fenty, who had taken office in January as the new mayor of Washington, D.C.

Fenty had made fixing Washington's public schools a major campaign issue. Then again, so had lots of mayors before him. But as five district superintendents came to and left the nation's capital over the last ten years, the schools had only gotten worse.

Although the law had recently been changed to abolish the D.C. Board of Education and give the mayor control over the schools, Fenty had not gotten off to a good start. He had still not found a chancellor, and a much-heralded "blueprint" for fixing the schools prepared for him by advisers and outside consultants had recently been panned by a panel at the Council of the Great City Schools—a Washington-based consortium of urban school districts—as vague, impractical, and unlikely to produce measurable results, in part because it included no plan to track student achievement.

As he sat at the TFA dinner at the Waldorf, Klein got what he thought was a crazy but maybe not so crazy idea: What about Michelle?

Like Klein, Rhee had never run a school, let alone a school system. Worse, unlike Klein, she would be a young (thirty-seven) Asian-American woman in a mostly African-American city and school system previously run mostly by African-American men. Still, she certainly knew everything there was to know about what was needed to make schools work. And, as Klein recalled from her testimony in front of Weingarten at that arbitration hearing, she "had a spine of steel."

Klein leaned over and asked Rhee about it. With no hesitation, she told Klein it was a bad idea. The last thing she wanted to do was run a school district, she said. And she'd be terrible at it because she would "piss off everyone."

"I was not being coy," Rhee recalls. "I thought it was a stupid idea."

The next day Klein called Rhee and asked if he could at least suggest to Fenty that he meet with her. Rhee again said no, then said she'd meet with the new mayor but only because she wanted to get him enthusiastic about the New Teacher Project and how it could fit into his plans. So she agreed to go to Washington for what she was determined would not be a job interview.

"I told him hiring me would be the worst thing he could do," Rhee remembers. "I said that I would be run out of town and he would probably be run out of town with me."

Fenty was taken by Rhee, especially by the fact that she seemed not to care if she got the job and was saying she'd make life miserable for her prospective boss.

Fenty put on a full-court press, promising repeatedly that if she took the job he would back her all the way. She wouldn't have to worry about politics.

"A lot of politicians say that," says Rhee. "And he said it well enough that I kind of believed him, but not completely. I figured at some point the shit would hit the fan and I would be run out of town. But the totally amazing thing is that Fenty actually did it. He never, ever wavered. I know from Joel that Randi could always call Bloomberg and undercut Joel. . . . Randi never even got Fenty to return her calls. It drove her nuts."

On June 13, 2007, Michelle Rhee was announced as Fenty's choice to overhaul the D.C. schools. To most of the Washington press corps and local politicians, she might as well have landed from another planet.

But one journalist, longtime *Washington Post* education reporter Jay Mathews, quickly saw an angle to the Rhee appointment that I happened on nearly three years later as I was writing a story for the

New York Times Magazine about the education reform network quietly proliferating across the country: the TFA alumni affect.

Mathews's June 18, 2007, article was headlined, "Maverick Teachers' Key D.C. Moment, Program Behind Fenty's School Pick Finds Fame, Clout." Mathews described what "might be called the Teach For America insurgency." Rhee and other TFA veterans were now "pushing into educational leadership and policymaking roles," he reported.

Mathews's list of the troops in this network included Rhee; "one in 10 principals in the D.C. public school system"; top aides whom Rhee was bringing to D.C. with her, including top deputy Kaya Henderson; KIPP founders Feinberg and Levin, whose sister, Mathews wrote, was "a leading researcher" at Rhee's New Teacher Project; the CEO of the KIPP Foundation, Richard Barth, who was married to TFA founder Wendy Kopp; and Chris Barbic, the head of the YES charter network, who was married to the head of the TFA office in Houston. Had Mathews had more space, he could have pointed almost anywhere else in the country—from Florida to Louisiana to Colorado to New York—and found hundreds more examples. The far-flung presence of this network would have a national coming-out party when Obama launched his Race to the Top two years later. TFA alumni would have a hand in shaping almost all of the reform plans created by the forty-six states that would compete in the contest.

But that didn't mean the battle in Washington or anywhere else was over. The teachers' union had its own network.

"Pulling the Rug Out"

August 16, 2007, Capitol Hill

In 2005, California congressman George Miller, the senior Democrat on the House Education and Labor Committee, had again taken a shot at putting the federal treasury to work encouraging states to measure and reward their most effective teachers. With Ted Kennedy as his senate cosponsor, he introduced the Teacher Excellence for All Children—or TEACH—Act. It would amend President Bush's No Child Left Behind by giving states money to give merit pay to the best teachers, pay extra for teachers to work in the hardest-to-staff schools (which were typically in the most impoverished communities), and create advanced career ladders for the best teachers. It would also provide funds to recruit and train principals.

Given his failure at earlier efforts, Miller had been surprised when he and his staff were able to persuade the two national teachers' unions—the American Federation of Teachers and the United Federation of Teachers—to support it. He was even able to include, along with statements from the usual suspects when it came to education reform (Jon Schnur, Wendy Kopp, Kati Haycock), one from then NEA president Reg Weaver, who praised the bill's "commonsense incentives for teachers."

But, with the Senate showing little interest in passing TEACH, Miller's 2005 efforts in the House had petered out.

Two years later, Miller (now the committee chairman, because the Democrats had recaptured the House) began to pick up momentum. He held new hearings on the bill in March 2007 and got the NEA's Weaver to testify in support of it again. Things were looking better on the Senate side, too. So in May, Miller and Kennedy formally reintroduced the TEACH Act—with an accompanying list of twenty-three education, civil rights, business, and research groups, plus the teachers' unions, that backed it, supplemented by an updated letter from Weaver extolling it. Staffers on Capitol Hill now thought it was going to pass, as did Miller. "I really thought we had it," he recalls.

A vote was scheduled for early September.

On August 15, Miller and his staff came to the office in the morning and were alarmed by an item in *Congress Daily*, a Capitol Hill newsletter, reporting that "the nation's two largest teachers' unions have weighed in heavily against House Education and Labor Chairman George Miller's plan to include performance pay for teachers in his upcoming No Child Left Behind reauthorization." That storm signal was followed the next day by a letter to the entire Education and Labor Committee from the NEA (but from its chief lobbyist, not president Weaver) stating that the NEA would not support any bill that "includes pay-for-performance" language.

"What happened," says Miller, "is either that they were playing along and not opposing this so they wouldn't look bad, because they never thought the bill would pass, or that they got a revolt from their locals, who were angry that their people in Washington were caving in on this. They never explained why they flipped. The NEA never explains anything to anyone. They don't think they have to. They just pulled the rug out from under us and made it clear to all of the Democrats they support that they had to oppose this. The phone calls and the letters piled in."

Miller's TEACH Act never came up for a vote.

From 1989 through 2010, the NEA and the AFT together contributed $60.7 million to candidates for federal office, far more than any other union, business, or interest group. With 95 percent of it going to Democrats, their impact on the party was in a class by itself. In 2008, $3.5 million was split among nearly all House Democrats and $575,000 was split among nearly all Senate Democrats.

The Democrats may have been willing to bow to their teachers' union patrons, but a billionaire who didn't have to worry about campaigns, let alone campaign contributions, was about to begin a learning process that would make him determined to use his checkbook to get the unions to budge on accountability.

Money Meets Data

October 20, 2007, Pierre Hotel, New York City

In August 2007, Bill and Melinda Gates hired Vicki Phillips to run their foundation's education division. They were not satisfied with the results of their investments so far, including even the small schools initiative that had broken up and reconstituted failing high schools. "It wasn't that they didn't succeed, as much as that we moved the goal line as we started to learn more," Bill Gates says. "Yes, we did improve attendance, and even graduation rates, but when we started looking at what they were actually learning to graduate and whether they were prepared for four-year college, it was disappointing." *

The Gateses had also gotten heavily involved in funding charter networks such as KIPP, which had inspired them to aim higher. Their goal, they had decided, was, in Bill Gates's words, to "get more schools to do for kids what KIPP does."

Phillips, who had been running the Portland, Oregon, school system and before that had been Pennsylvania's state education superintendent, was a generation ahead of the TFA network in school reform battles. "In every job I had," Phillips says, "I knew if I didn't have relentless focus on teaching, I was not going to make progress."

Her first assignment at the Gates Foundation, she says, was "to take a year completely reexamining what education projects the foundation should build on, which ones to stop, and which ones to add." Within a month, she was focused on what she had read in the Hamilton Project paper written by public policy guru Robert

---

* Actually, Klein's results in New York with the New Visions schools had been much better than that, as had Michael Johnston's in Mapleton, but that was because, unlike most of the mini–high schools that Gates funded, these schools were allowed to dismiss the old staff and hire back only the teachers they wanted.

Gordon and Professors Kane and Staiger. She gave it to Bill and Melinda Gates.

On October 20, she organized a meeting for Bill Gates, while he was in New York, with Gordon and Kane.

What Kane remembers most about walking into Gates's suite at the Pierre Hotel that day was that "the richest man in the world was holding a dog-eared copy of our paper that was filled, completely filled, with comments and questions scribbled into the margins."

"I remember being really impressed with their data about the differences between good and bad teachers," says Gates. "But I was also dumbfounded that they had nothing in there about what makes a teacher good. Nothing."

Gordon and Kane explained that there were not any data on that because until now no one had even had data proving that there *was* a difference in teacher effectiveness. To prove that, there needed to be data tabulated according to individual teachers over multiyear spans and across hundreds of their students, but such statistics had never been collected.

As Kane and Gordon had stressed in their Hamilton Project paper, they told Gates that they were not arguing that test scores alone could measure teacher performance, let alone measure it for teachers who taught hard-to-test subjects like the arts. Rather, their research had found that students' advancement, as measured in test scores when linked back to teachers, provided consistent enough results that there was now clear, empirical evidence of the intuitively obvious reality—the reality that anyone who had ever been in a schoolroom appreciated—that some teachers are better than others. And this, they and Gates agreed, was a reality that needed to be acted on.

"In other industries you came in at the entry level and then got promoted based on someone's perception of how good you were," Kane told Gates. "If you were a great talent, you'd go from the mailroom to junior management to middle management and then maybe to the executive suite." But schools didn't work that way, Gordon added. Teachers got promoted based only on how long they stayed on the job or if they got some advanced degree or other new credential.

"How can you have an organization where no one cares about talent?" Gates asked. Gordon responded that the traditional argument was that it was hard to judge talent because of other factors, like the students' socioeconomic backgrounds, so everyone had just agreed simply not to try.

It wasn't that poverty or other factors didn't affect student performance, Gordon continued. Rather, it was that teacher effectiveness could overcome those disadvantages.

Every industry has problems measuring productivity, Gates answered. But that doesn't mean you don't do it. How can a school system have a hundred or a thousand or, as in New York, a hundred thousand teachers and have no measurements for who's producing, let alone why and how, so that the system can take the methods of the producers and try to teach them to the non-producers or remove the non-producers if that doesn't work?

The conversation continued for about two hours, with Gates getting increasingly frustrated—and eager to do something about it.

For America's richest man, with no personal agenda other than improving education, these solutions may have seemed obvious. But as Gates, Kane, and Gordon met, a fierce political battle was being waged for the Democratic presidential nomination. For Democrats whose personal agendas included the White House, none of this was obvious or without peril.

Hillary for Teachers,
Teachers for Hillary

November 15, 2007, Las Vegas •

With the crucial Iowa caucus and New Hampshire primary fast approaching, seven candidates for the Democratic presidential nomination assembled on November 15, 2007, at the Las Vegas Convention Center for a debate sponsored by CNN. The headline coming out of the face-off would be Hillary Clinton's seemingly confused answer on the question of whether illegal immigrants should be given driver's licenses. All but overlooked was this exchange she had with co-moderator Wolf Blitzer:

BLITZER. I want Senator Clinton to weigh in on the issue of merit pay. If there's a teacher out there who's doing a great job, should that teacher get merit—get a bonus for doing a great job, that individual teacher who works really hard, does a great job educating young people?

CLINTON. Well, I support school-based merit pay for a lot of the reasons. . . . We need to get more teachers to go into hard-to-serve areas. We've got to get them into underserved urban areas, underserved rural areas.

But the school is a team, and I think it's important that we reward that collaboration. You know, a child who moves from kindergarten to sixth grade, say, in the same school, every one of those teachers is going to affect that child.*

BLITZER. But what if there's an excellent teacher in that team and

---

* This "team-based" merit pay concept was the plan Weingarten had negotiated in New York in 2007 as a way of rejecting individual merit pay. Under the plan, if a school performed well, everyone at the school would get a bonus, including non-classroom personnel. By 2010, the program, which had been limited from the beginning, had been judged ineffective and had mostly been scrapped.

a crummy teacher in that team, a teacher who's simply riding along and not really working very hard, not really educating those young kids?

Do you give just everybody the merit pay, or do you give it to individual teachers?

CLINTON. Well, you need to weed out the teachers who are not doing a good job. I mean, that's the bottom line. They should not be teaching our children. [*Applause.*] I mean, what I believe so strongly is that our education system has served this country very well. But we're in the twenty-first century. We do need to reimagine it. We've got to get everybody to talk about it.

But what I object to with the Bush administration is it's always talking down. We need to have a collegial collaboration. And the teachers need to be at the table . . .

BLITZER. All right.

CLINTON. . . . helping us figure out what the best way is to achieve our goals.

With the stage filled with candidates, Obama was not asked to answer that question, but then-Senator Joseph Biden was put on the spot. Obama's future vice president also punted, saying that teachers should be paid based on merit but that merit should be based only on the advanced degrees a teacher had.

As he had nine months before in Iowa, Obama had by now regularly made his union-unfriendly positions known on the campaign trail. During a town hall meeting in Iowa a few weeks before this debate, when a teacher stood up to attack Obama, his answer— that while we should be fair to teachers and pay them well, we also needed to start "worrying more about the children than the adults"—had been so effective that campaign issues deputy director Higginbottom had it made into a video to be given to Iowa field organizers.

It was no surprise, then, that about five weeks before this Las Vegas debate, on October 7, 2007, Randi Weingarten had held a press conference endorsing Clinton, whose Senate campaign committee she had co-chaired. And on December 5, Clinton got the endorsement of the New Hampshire chapter of the National Education Association, although the Manchester unit endorsed John Edwards.

In the ensuing battle, first with Edwards and Clinton, then just with Clinton, Obama would contend with telephone banks organized by the teachers' unions getting out the vote for his opponent.

"We sort of felt liberated," remembers one top Obama campaign aide, "because we knew we had no chance of their support in the primaries. Obama's record was clear to anyone who looked at it. So we couldn't have tailored our positions even if we wanted to. And all of the Republicans were far more absolutely hostile to the unions than we were, so we thought we'd be okay with the unions in the fall, if we got there."

The Obama '08 troops may have been liberated, but their candidate was not completely unshackled. Later in the campaign, Obama would have to walk back from some support he had offered for school vouchers during an interview. Vouchers are the ultimate extension of school choice. They allow parents to take a government check meant to cover the cost of their children's education in public schools and use it to pay for any private school of their choice. Many school reformers who support charters—public schools open to all children without entrance requirements, except for winning a lottery where applications outstrip seats—do not support vouchers, because vouchers could allow public funds to pay for religious or politically affiliated schools, and because the whole idea of the government paying for private schools undermines the idea that K–12 education is a core government service.

Other reformers, like Rhee, support vouchers, as do most Republican school reform advocates. In fact, after Obama was elected, Rhee criticized his decision to withdraw support from a voucher program that presented extra competition for her District of Columbia school system. "If he can send his kids to Sidwell," she told me, referring to the Obama children's prestigious private school, "why can't the parents of other black kids who live here make the same decision?"

Democrats for Education Reform was in a tricky position through 2007. Tilson, Curry, Petry, and now Joe Williams, their new executive director, loved Obama. "But like everyone else we figured Hillary was going to win, and our first goal was not making an enemy of a Democrat in the White House," says Williams. "We didn't endorse anyone and kept lines open to all of them, including Hillary. . . . I remember we met with her at some event, and when we told her what we did, she blurted out, 'Oh, I love KIPP.' "

Another Democrat who loved KIPP was Eli Broad, one of the charter network's biggest donors. But unlike Hillary Clinton, Broad continued to look beyond even the most successful charter networks, trying to back the kind of systemic reforms that Clinton had shied away from in the debates and that Joel Klein personified.

Forward, Backward in New York

Prizewinner

September 17, 2007, Washington, D.C.

Since first funding Klein's initial reorganization consultant study in 2002, Eli Broad's foundation had continued to support Klein's work and a variety of other projects that Broad thought were getting traction. He had become a major benefactor of both KIPP and TFA, and was supporting a number of other charter schools and networks, as well as the New Teacher Project and Jon Schnur's New Leaders for New Schools.

Another favorite investment was the Broad Prize—$1 million given every year since 2002 to the "Nation's Most Improved Urban School District." The prize was awarded by a multilayered committee of independent reviewers and judges hired by Broad's foundation. So it is unlikely that any kind of fix was in when on November 17 Broad's old friend, Mike Bloomberg, and Broad's new partner in education reform, Joel Klein, accepted the Broad Prize at a Washington press conference.

According to the award proclamation, New York City was given the 2006 prize for:

- Outperforming other districts in New York State serving students with similar income levels in reading and math at all grade levels
- Progress in closing the achievement gaps for Hispanic and African-American students
- Raising participation rates for Hispanic and African-American students taking college entrance exams

The award, not to mention the $1 million to be used for college scholarships, was nice. And New York's schools were inching ahead.

Principals from the Leadership Academy were starting to make their mark. The mini–high schools were producing higher graduation rates and proliferating to the point where schools run by New Visions and similar groups would be serving more than 100,000 New York City students by 2010. Those were 100,000 lives being changed for the better. But New York has about 1,100,000 public school students, and these achievements and the bullet points cited in the Broad Prize represented only the beginnings of the turnaround that Klein and Bloomberg had promised. Klein knew that, except for his success in encouraging the mini-schools and more good charters and co-locating them, he was still chipping away at the margins. "On an individual level," he told me, "you can circumvent the union in some areas, but if you want real improvements systemwide, you can't just do these kinds of workarounds."

The Gotcha Squad

November 26, 2007, the steps of City Hall, New York

That didn't mean that Klein wouldn't keep trying. He may have had to capitulate to Randi Weingarten on the contract, but he was not giving up on solving the tenure problem. With what would come to be known as the city's Rubber Rooms filling up with teachers whom Klein wanted to dismiss, he, his labor relations deputy Daniel Weisberg, and Deputy Chancellor Chris Cerf—all Ivy League lawyers—had decided that they'd fix things by sending a SWAT team of best-and-brightest lawyers into the fray.

Weingarten had agreed in the 2005 contract to streamline the grievance process so that every negative comment placed in a teacher's personnel file could no longer trigger a separate grievance, which would then trigger a long three-step hearing process. Klein and his deputies now decided to take advantage of that change by recruiting the squad of lawyers to help principals paper their files so flawlessly and so completely that dismissing teachers for incompetence or misbehavior would be easier; they would have bulletproof dossiers to offer as evidence to the arbitrator hearing the dismissal case. The same lawyers would then argue the cases before the arbitrator.

On November 26, 2007, after word got out of the establishment of the six-lawyer Teacher Performance Unit, the UFT called a "candlelight vigil" at City Hall to protest what Weingarten dubbed the "Gotcha Squad."

"You would think candlelight vigils would be reserved for Gandhi or something like that, but you could hear this rally all the way over the Brooklyn Bridge," Cerf remembers.

Randi Weingarten was unapologetic, even two years later. "We believed that the way this Gotcha Squad was portrayed in the press by the city unfairly maligned all the teachers in the system," she told me in 2009, long after it had become clear that her union's less-pedigreed counsel had been able to tie the Gotcha Squad in such procedural knots at these hearings that the typical stint in the Rubber Rooms exceeded three years.

The real solution, of course, rested with the New York State legislature, which at the unions' behest had written the tenure law with all of the "due process" guarantees that protected the Rubber Roomers. Albany had repeatedly resisted efforts to repeal or amend the law. The Gotcha Squad was an attempt at a legal fix to a political problem, one that Democrats for Education Reform was continuing to chip away at.

$45,000 Well Spent

December 3, 2007, New York City

Joe Williams and Democrats for Education Reform continued to pick up steam following their June 2007 party in Boykin Curry's apartment. They had been regularly invited to meetings on Capitol Hill with Congressman George Miller and the small band of Democrats pushing the TEACH Act, and had made inroads beyond that, holding a series of meetings with Democratic majority leader Steny Hoyer, Majority Whip James Clyburn, and their staffs. These more traditional Democrats weren't ready to sign on fully to their platform, but they were learning that in the Democratic Party, there was now a view other than the unions' view.

In a December 3, 2007, note to his board, Williams celebrated the success of one breakthrough event—a fund-raiser they had held in New York, with Klein's help, for Clyburn of South Carolina, who is also the most influential member of the Congressional Black Caucus. "It was a great event," Williams began. "But the aftermath has been even greater. We ended up raising about $45,000 (short of our $50,000 goal) for the congressman, but the impact has been pretty dramatic. I anticipated the impact that Clyburn's public statements would have within the Congressional Black Caucus, but I was not prepared for the ripples his visit would have within the state legislature in South Carolina. . . . His involvement is helping restart negotiations in the statehouse over a school choice bill. . . . Clyburn not only came out in favor of charters but a tuition tax credit as well."

On the afternoon of the fund-raiser, Klein and Williams had accompanied Clyburn on his first visit to a charter school—Eva Moskowitz's Harlem Success Academy I.

In January, Williams would report to his DFER board that

Clyburn had celebrated his one-year anniversary as House whip by visiting a South Carolina charter school—his new pet cause.

As DFER was gathering steam on Capitol Hill, another reform drama was beginning to play out elsewhere in Washington. Michelle Rhee was starting to break some china.

"Faceless Bureaucracy"

December 7, 2007, Washington, D.C.

On August 7, 2007, just weeks after taking over the D.C. schools, Rhee made her first splash, telling the *Washington Times* that the city's school system was a "faceless bureaucracy. . . . We have thousands of people [in school administration] right now who don't know what their jobs are and who are not being effective in the positions they have."

Rhee had quite an orientation period. She had found an all-but-forgotten warehouse holding thousands of textbooks at the same time that she had discovered that her schools routinely suffered from severe textbook shortages. Yet she had been told by parents who had wanted to transfer books themselves from a middle school that was moving its ninth graders into a high school that they had been told that the books first had to be sent back to the black-hole warehouse.

Constantly reading and answering e-mails from parents and disgruntled teachers (twelve thousand e-mails by the middle of September, according to one *Washington Post* report), Rhee had uncovered a parade of other abuses and problems. Meantime, the overseer of the district's charter schools had just pleaded guilty to hundreds of thousands of dollars' worth of fraud related to dummy companies she had set up so she could give herself a no-bid contract.

Rhee had started the school year in September with unannounced visits to her schools. Always holding her BlackBerry so she could fire off an e-mail as soon as she saw something that needed attention, she would often confront principals who had never seen a superintendent (now called the chancellor), had no idea who this attractive young woman in the tight skirt and high heels was, and were shocked when she stopped to take complaints from teachers and even from the children. She found air-conditioning that had stopped working years ago, leaking roofs, and paint peeling onto desks, and immediately summoned repair help with her BlackBerry or cell phone.

In one visit, documented by Richard Whitmire in his 2011 biography of Rhee, her staff saw and later told her about a sign, posted low enough so that the children could read it, that summarized the attitude of the old order: "There is nothing a teacher can do to overcome what a parent and a student will not do"—meaning, Rhee concluded, "It's not our fault if you fail."

On December 7, 2007, Rhee and Mayor Fenty announced that they were going to ask the City Council to approve a measure that would have been unthinkable in the old days. Rhee was going to quadruple the old one-person textbook supply staff, but she wanted to be allowed to fill a budget gap of $81 million by firing hundreds of those "faceless bureaucrats" in the district's central office. In a city where so many of the voters were government workers who cherished their secure jobs and did not think of themselves as bureaucrats, she was going to blow her building up. Protest rallies were quickly organized, but Fenty and Rhee held firm. "This is the first step in getting [the school system] on sound financial footing to create a system that works for students and families," Fenty said. Fenty had passed his first test in backing Rhee.

Although one member of the City Council in this civil service–friendly city said he feared the city was "throwing out civil service rules that shielded government workers from arbitrary terminations," the council's vote was 10–3 for Rhee and Fenty.

Rhee's return to school following her TFA stint was paralleled in New York, though with none of the fanfare, by Jessica Reid's return to class.

Back in the Classroom

March 2008, Harlem Success Academy, New York City

After her second TFA year in the Bronx had ended in June 2006, Jessica Reid had, she says, "retired from the classroom because it was too depressing." But she liked New York and had stayed in town, talking her way into a variety of jobs. For a while she worked in the KIPP development office, providing support for Levin's money-raising efforts. But she says she found KIPP "not a good fit; it was too formal, and I didn't like raising money." Next had come a stint at an education software company, helping sell software for teachers to use on mobile devices. That hadn't worked out either. Reid had then decided she wanted to earn some serious money and persuaded a hedge fund to let her get her foot in the door. But the fund put her in its tax department, where she worked on structuring offshore tax entities and, she says, did "boring paralegal-type work."

By 2007 she was feeling that she wanted to be back in a classroom. Her work for the education company and for KIPP had exposed her to charter schools, where, she says, "It seemed like the whole building had the attitude I had had in my classroom in the Bronx. I wouldn't be alone."

Reid had soon focused on Achievement First, another New York charter network, and on Harlem Success.

In March 2008, she arrived for an interview at Harlem Success I, where Moskowitz was recruiting teachers who in September would join her next school in the planned network, Harlem Success II. Reid's interview went well, and she was asked to come back and do a demonstration lesson for Moskowitz (who was then spending most of her time recruiting teachers and running a massive leafleting and local advertising campaign to recruit parents to try to enroll their children in Harlem Success II).

"I was rusty, but I got right back into it," Reid recalls. "And while I was waiting to do it, I was sitting in the main office and I noticed that everyone was so polite to the parents and kids, and seemed so happy. I decided I had to have this job. So I knocked the demo lesson out of the park."

The only catch was that she was offered a spot teaching first graders, although her experience had been teaching fifth grade in the Bronx. (Moskowitz had to start with only two grades, kindergarten and first, in part because of the rule requiring unionization for any school that had more than 250 students in its first two years.) "I figured that was okay," say Reid. "I'll just treat them like fifth graders—raise them to that level."

Another aspect of the support Reid would get at Harlem Success— at least, she thought of it as support—was the constant stream of data on her students' progress. To her this was essential—"I wanted to know how I was doing," she says—and it was something she had never had during her TFA tenure in the Bronx. Joel Klein was about to try to change that.

Quarantine the Data

On January 21, 2008, the *New York Times* reported that for several months Klein had been embarked on "an ambitious experiment, yet to be announced" that would link students' progress on test scores to 2,500 of their teachers in schools where principals had quietly been recruited to conduct the experiment. "While officials say it is too early to determine how they will use the data, which is already being collected," the *Times* reported, "they say it could eventually be used to help make decisions on teacher tenure or as a significant element in performance evaluations and bonuses."

The pilot project was being run by Harvard's Tom Kane, with financing from the Gates Foundation.

"If the only thing we do is make this data available to every person in the city—every teacher, every parent, every principal, and say do with it what you will—that will have been a powerful step forward," Klein's deputy Chris Cerf told the *Times*. "If you know as a parent what's the deal, I think that whole aspect will change behavior."

Weingarten was quoted as saying that she had "grave reservations" about the project and would "fight if the city tried to use the information for tenure or formal evaluations or even publicized it." If that were permitted, she said, "It would be one of the worst decisions of my professional life."

Weingarten added that the data system was not needed, because "any real educator can know within five minutes of walking into a classroom if a teacher is effective." She was not asked to explain why, if that were so, principals were not able to dismiss teachers after observing them.

"It seems hard to know who is going to be effective in the classroom until they are actually in the classroom," Kane told the

Times, picking up on the theme of his Hamilton Project paper. "But most school districts spend very little time trying to assess how good teachers are in their first couple of years, when it is most important"—and, he could have added, after which they are almost all routinely granted tenure simply for not leaving.

For Weingarten and her teachers, the *Times* article was a wake-up call. Cerf and Kane had clearly signaled their plan.

So on April 5, once again at night, Weingarten convinced Assembly Speaker Sheldon Silver to insert into an unrelated budget bill a provision that prohibited Klein from using student test data to evaluate teachers for tenure. A similar data "firewall provision" had been passed in California in 2005, also as a rider to an unrelated bill and also pushed by the union.

"Test scores should be used only in a thoughtful and reflective way," Weingarten told me in 2009. "We acted in Albany because no one trusted that Joel Klein would use them to measure performance in a fair way."

Climbing the Ladder

May 14, 2008, Mapleton, Colorado

Michael Johnston was so serious about making sure his students shared his mission to get them into college that he created his own accountability system aimed at that goal. Soon after they had returned to school in September 2006, he had assembled the forty-four eleventh graders (the new and growing school still had no twelfth graders) to launch the College Admission Commitment Board.

Michelle Rhee had used board games to teach math. Johnston was going to use one to build career paths. First, he had all forty-four students sign the College Commitment Board, a thin piece of wood about 11 by 14 inches he had mocked up to look like a contract. After they all signed, he hung it in the hall outside their class. It committed them to do everything necessary to apply and get accepted to college.

Then he showed them his Climb to College map, a 4-by-4-foot laminated chart that had each of their names on a separate note-card. Two-sided tape affixed to each card allowed them to place their names in various boxes based on where they were on the "climb." The cards that morning were all pasted at the bottom left corner of the map, which was called "base camp." Moving up the map and "east," to the right, were myriad stopping off points, beginning with the places they could advance to in the eleventh grade, such as preparing for the college entrance tests, taking a sample test, making a list of possible colleges, or getting admissions materials. At the top right was College Admission, where Johnston intended to be hanging all forty-four index cards within eighteen to twenty months, in 2008.

With each admission to college, the student would sign an Acceptance Board, another laminated wood plaque that Johnston had fashioned and hung in the auditorium.

Johnston was also keeping his hand in politics. He was the education adviser in what would be the successful 2006 gubernatorial campaign of Colorado Democrat Bill Ritter. And he and Schnur were regularly in touch, not only because he remained on the board of Schnur's New Leaders for New Schools, which the two had launched from their Harvard thesis, but also because they were constantly gossiping in 2006 about the prospect that Obama might leapfrog what Schnur had thought might be a 2017 White House timetable and run in 2008. Then, they had both become involved in the Obama campaign, once it started, as education advisers.

Beginning in the spring of 2008, each time one of Johnston's students, who were now seniors, was able to hang his or her card in that final square on the Climb to College board and then sign the Acceptance Board, there was a ceremony—actually more like a ritual—attended by all forty-four, plus students from one of the lower grades whom Johnston wanted to inspire.

As a prop, Johnston had hunted around for what he describes as "the most rickety, awful, broken-down ladder I could find." The ladder, he told his students, represented "the rickety ladder that each of you were dealt in life, but you were still able to climb it."

The newly admitted college student would choose four people from among friends or family members to hold each side of the ladder, because, Johnston explained, "You've had some important people in your life help you climb this ladder."

As the student proceeded up the ladder to sign the Acceptance Board, his or her new college's theme song (or that of the Denver Broncos if the college didn't have one) would blare through a loudspeaker. Classmates, the students invited from the other class, and other guests would erupt in cheers.

On the morning of May 14, 2008, the forty-fourth student was about to climb the ladder. This was the biggest ceremony of all, the final act, and it attracted a brief story and photo in the *Denver Post* celebrating the class's accomplishment.

A few days later, Johnston got a call from a member of a Barack Obama Colorado campaign advance team, who was responsible for planning a Denver-area campaign stop for the now presumptive Democratic nominee. Someone in the campaign had seen the inspiring *Denver Post* article, he explained. And Senator Obama was a big believer in education innovation. Could we bring Senator Obama to your school, the staffer asked.

Johnston chuckled and replied that he was actually one of the campaign's education advisers—a fact the advance worker had had no way of knowing. "That's even better," the advance man said.

Johnston called Schnur to make sure this coincidence wouldn't be seen in the press as some sort of conflict. Schnur checked and reported back that everyone thought the connection to the campaign was a plus. Then Schnur and Johnston helped prepare Obama's remarks.

"It was such a great day," Johnston recalls. "It actually was our graduation day, so we had all forty-four kids there with their families and Obama. Then he had a town hall meeting with them and lots of invited guests."

"I'm here to hold up this school and these students as an example of what's possible in education if we're willing to try new ideas and new reforms based not on ideology but on what works to give our children the best possible chance in life," Obama declared.

Obama, like Johnston and Schnur, was an instinctive collaborator, more prone to try to win people over than to run them over. Michelle Rhee was about to take a different approach with Randi Weingarten.

Rhee's Choice:
Your Union or $130,000

July 2008, Washington, D.C.

If Michelle Rhee had made nothing else clear with her blunt public assessments of what she was up against, or by showing up unannounced at Washington's failing schools and angrily acting as if failure wasn't a given, it was, as she told me the first time we met, that "I don't believe in the warm and fuzzy stuff. I don't believe in collaboration, because it hasn't worked. I don't care about hurting the adults' feelings. I care about getting kids the education they deserve. This is an emergency. It is not a time to be polite."

That didn't mean Rhee wasn't capable of strategic subtlety. After insisting that she would take charge of negotiating with the Washington Teachers' Union (a local affiliate of Weingarten's AFT), in July 2008 Rhee unveiled a proposal that was unprecedented. Her goal was to drive a wedge between the unions' leaders and what she believed to be the majority of Washington teachers who *were* competent, who *did* care, and who didn't think they needed the union to protect their careers.

As a general matter, union leaders depend on the union contract being the most important thing in their members' work lives. Treating all teachers the same, regardless of performance, as if they were workers on an assembly line, gives union leaders exactly that lead role. Letting teachers determine their own fates based on their performance would give each teacher—or management, if you believed management was capricious or unfair—the lead role. Rhee believed that given the choice, most teachers would take the chance of determining their own fates.

So in July 2008 she offered exactly that choice. She gave the union a proposal that promised unheard-of rewards for teachers willing to take that chance on their own performance. And she infuriated

Weingarten and the local union leaders by making the proposal public so that their members would immediately know about it.

Rhee offered huge salary increases, pushing top pay over $130,000, with the money coming in part from a private fund she had set up with support from Eli Broad's foundation, the Walton Foundation, and others (but not Gates*). The increases would be available to those teachers who were willing to give up lifetime tenure guarantees and lockstep compensation. They would agree to have their performance linked to an evaluation system that would include intensive in-class observations and student test score improvements. Especially good performance could bring bonuses on top of those high salaries. The cleverest part of the proposal was the seemingly irresistible choice Rhee offered: Teachers who did not want to volunteer for performance-based compensation could keep their current pay scales and tenure-protected job security. In other words, Rhee was not trying to take away the old system from those teachers who wanted to keep it, but she was making the choice theirs, not their union's. No one had to give up those protections, but anyone could choose to. Who could be against letting consenting adults make that kind of choice?

Rhee soon had polls taken of teachers, indicating that most liked the deal. For nearly two years, Weingarten would refuse even to allow the proposal to be put up for a vote.**

Although Weingarten was no more willing to collaborate with Michelle Rhee than Rhee was with her, Weingarten would soon find a partner with whom she could work: Bill Gates.

---

* In the education reform network, there were several muted intrafamily divisions. One involved Rhee and the Gates Foundation. They simply never hit it off. She thought the foundation was too tentative and bureaucratic. The Gates people thought she was too much of a bomb thrower.

** Weingarten disputes the characterization that she did not let the offer be put up for a vote as unfair. She says that it is standard in labor-management negotiations that a union does not send a contract to its members for a vote unless the union's leaders endorse the proposal.

Turning Around the USS *Gates*

July 17, 2008, Seattle

When Eli Broad compares his own $2 billion foundation with what by 2009 had become the $33 billion Gates Foundation, he thinks of his as a nimble speedboat looking for problems and investing in solutions and Gates as a battleship that takes a long time to turn around. Others in the education community are less kind, likening Gates to a huge bureaucracy of grant application readers—which it is, but which it probably has to be, given its size and ambition.

The battleship analogy explains why it took until July 17, 2008, for Bill and Melinda Gates to decide formally what they and their staff had actually decided soon after Gates's intense October 2007 session with Tom Kane and Robert Gordon in New York. Ten months after Bill Gates had been riveted by his discussion with Kane and Gordon, and following what Kane estimates were hundreds of conversations and multiple trips to the Gates Foundation's Seattle headquarters (where Kane had become a part-time consultant), Bill and Melinda Gates and the foundation's senior education staffers, led by Vicki Phillips, met in Seattle to sign off on turning most of its education effort and money toward effective teaching.

Bill Gates says that despite the evidence he had seen that focusing on teaching was the key to improving public education, the decision was "the riskiest thing we have ever done." He cites two reasons. First, while there were now data that could show which teachers were most or least effective, there was still nothing that gave the information-obsessed Gates the assurance that they could identify what made teachers effective and then train other teachers to do it. Second, there was the political risk rarely associated with this type of foundation work: Getting the data, not to mention having school systems do something about the information, meant changing the political dynamic in the nation's public schools.

"We knew we couldn't avoid those union issues," Gates recalls.

"We went forward," Melinda Gates says, "because we knew that if we really wanted to have an impact on public education, we had to get into this."

The strategy they settled on was not to use the money to gather still more data (though more data would certainly be a result of what they did) but rather to hold the money out as a lure to get school systems to compete in a contest to come up with the best plans to measure and improve teacher effectiveness.

Although he was back in Washington working at the liberal-leaning Center for American Progress, Kane's co-author, Robert Gordon, who was more the policy thinker than the data cruncher, had consulted with the foundation on this contest strategy. In fact, it mirrored the government grant incentive program that he had written into the Hamilton Project paper as a key policy recommendation. Now Gordon and Kane would have use of the Gates checkbook to try the idea. The plan that the Gateses signed off on was elaborate, expensive, and meant to give school systems and their teachers a tough choice: They could compete for what would ultimately be four or five huge grants that would have a game-changing impact on their school budgets, including what could be paid to teachers. But to do so they would have to join in the drive to measure teacher effectiveness and do something about the results after it was measured.

Earlier in 2008, the Gates staff drafted a plan for up to $350 million to be allotted to four or five winning school districts that would compete for the money based on the plans they submitted to initiate teacher effectiveness programs. Phillips and the foundation targeted twenty school districts that they thought would be most amenable to the program. By April they had narrowed the districts down to ten after initial discussions with the twenty. The ten competitors were chosen and given formal invitations to compete, in part because they were not super-huge districts and, therefore, would be places where the prospect of getting a $75 million or $100 million check from Bill and Melinda Gates would get their competitive juices flowing.

Pittsburgh was one of the cities that got an invitation in April 2008.

"We immediately went to work," says Mark Roosevelt, who had recently taken over as superintendent of the Pittsburgh public schools. "For us it came at exactly the right time. It was a matter of civic pride; we wanted Pittsburgh to be back on the map. And because we are a relatively small urban school system [66 schools and 26,000 students] with a high African-American population but not much of an English-language-learner group, you could see where the Gates people thought they could get a good bang from their buck."

Roosevelt, who is a great-grandson of Theodore Roosevelt, is in many respects the archetypal new breed school leader and Democratic education reformer. After chairing the education committee in the Massachusetts statehouse and sponsoring the state's successful Education Reform Act, which tightened curricula standards, he ran for governor and lost, badly. He then ran a biomedical venture fund and was managing director of the Massachusetts Business Alliance for Education when he heard about Eli Broad's Superintendents Academy. He applied and was accepted in 2005. Five months later, he was appointed to run the Pittsburgh schools after having negotiated—at his suggestion—an "accountability contract" with the city's education board that set specific goals he had to meet, including balancing the budget, improving student performance, and improving teacher evaluation systems.

When Roosevelt had negotiated his first contract with the union a few months after he took the job, "We really didn't have a chance to get to any of these issues," he says. "Now the lure of the Gates money, coming as it did as we began negotiating again, forced the issues.

"One of my big arguments with the union folks," Roosevelt adds, "was that I'm a nice guy and a reasonable guy and they might as well negotiate with me. Sitting at the table with me is a lot better than having someone like Michelle Rhee come in here and do it herself. Michelle has one kind of style," Roosevelt explains, "and I have another, though I guess you could say that the specter of someone like Michelle or a Joel Klein helped a lot of the rest of us."

"I have a pretty good idea of how I'd respond to a Michelle Rhee," says Pittsburgh Federation of Teachers president John Tarka. "Mark took an entirely different approach, and so did I."

By now Rhee's style was well known, especially in teacher circles. A few months after Roosevelt began negotiating with his Pittsburgh union, in late November 2008, Rhee's picture would appear on the cover of *Time* magazine headlining an article on how she was shaking up the D.C. schools with her take-no-prisoners approach. She was holding a broom in front of a blackboard and glowering into the camera. Union leaders across the country didn't need to read *Time*; they had all heard about Rhee. Many thought she traveled on that broom.

If Roosevelt's more collaborative style was facilitated by people like Klein and Rhee, people like Roosevelt also offered Weingarten a way to backpedal in selected circumstances from her hard line but with a rationale that made her posture seem consistent and principled. "Randi told me she wanted to find a place where she could support cutting-edge work in a different environment," Roosevelt says.

Thus, instead of looking as though she was simply throwing bread crumbs of reform in a few places to offer examples of how reasonable her union could be—which was Klein's, Rhee's, and Moskowitz's view—Weingarten could offer up places like Pittsburgh as evidence that she was always willing to do reforms that "were good for children" but, as she often told me, she "could only do so where there was an environment of mutual trust, which is impossible with people like Joel and Michelle." If these collaborative reform efforts didn't get the same publicity as her fights, she said, that was only because "reporters like you like conflict, not collaboration." Of course, the converse could also have been true: She might have singled out people like Roosevelt simply to make tougher opponents in larger school districts, such as Rhee and Klein, look bad.

Whatever the players' motives, everyone involved agreed that the lure of the Gates money made good things happen in Pittsburgh, once Roosevelt and his team sat down to hammer out a new contract with Tarka that would be part of the proposal they submitted to Gates.

"At first, it was really hard," Roosevelt says. "There was all of this posturing. 'We will never do this.' 'We have to do this.' 'That won't work.' But then we decided to clear all the lawyers out and agree to stop all the rhetoric. . . . We took each issue, one by one, and put it up on a whiteboard and didn't leave the room until we solved it. We all wanted Pittsburgh to win."

"It was not exactly a love fest," recalls Tarka. "But we were determined to get it done."

The result was a contract that laid out all the parameters of a Kane- and Gordon-friendly teacher effectiveness strategy. All teachers would be measured with a combination of classroom observations and testing data. Even music and art teachers—where standardized tests are not available—would be measured based on a rubric of goals and assessments that a committee would devise. There would be multiple career ladders, provisions for merit pay, and bonuses paid to teachers who were chosen (based on their effectiveness) and agreed to work extra hours tutoring or working through what would become an extended school day and school year.

These scattered efforts, generated by the Gates money, mostly happened under the radar. Much more visible was the political confrontation shaping up in the Democratic Party.

The New Democrats

August 24, 2008, Denver Art Museum

Whitney Tilson would tell me in 2010 that getting an education reformer elected president in 2008 had been the core of the original strategy of Democrats for Education Reform. If that were really true, he would have been better off starting Republicans for Education Reform. Well after DFER started gathering support in 2005 and 2006 at small and then not-so-small events around the country, anyone contemplating the notion of a DFER disciple in the White House would have had to put it more in the category of dream than plan. After all, there was little reform sympathy among the eight Democratic presidential candidates. The odds were high that Randi Weingarten's friend Hillary Clinton would come out on top of that pack, and the odds looked impossible for the one Democrat—Obama—who really believed in DFER's mission.

By August 24, 2008, all that had changed. On the eve of the convention in Denver that was to nominate Obama, DFER staged an event offering dramatic evidence that the actual, more modest plan that Williams, Petry, Curry, and Tilson had put together more than eighteen months before was on track, and then some. The plan had always been to build slowly, gradually making it safe, or at least not instant suicide, for increasingly more Democrats to support school reform. DFER would provide the campaign cash that might counterbalance the unions' largesse, while offering safety in numbers by growing as large a group as possible.

The DFER Denver event, funded by contributions from the Broad and Gates foundations, featured enough prominent national Democrats that it almost could have been a rally for abortion rights, increasing the minimum wage, or some other traditional party cause. Present on the stage were not only Democrats who were educators, like Klein and Rhee, but also Mayor Adrian Fenty of Washington, Mayor Cory Booker of Newark, former Denver mayor and Clinton transportation secretary Federico Peña, Sacramento mayoral candidate (and former basketball star) Kevin Johnson, and former Colorado governor and Democratic National Committee chair Roy Romer, as well as Colorado's lieutenant governor and state senate president and several civil rights leaders, including Al Sharpton.

DFER executive director Williams opened the session by introducing Peña, who was also a national co-chair of the Obama campaign. Peña introduced Michael Johnston, who introduced his buddy Jon Schnur, who said he felt like he was "at a family wedding and giving the tenth toast." (In fact, the meeting was not only another in what was now becoming a proliferating series of education reform gatherings that felt like family reunions, it would also become the genesis of a planned wedding: Rhee's encounter with Johnson, the future Sacramento mayor, resulted in their getting engaged less than a year later.)

What was striking about the speakers' remarks was not only the urgency they conveyed but also their exuberance that the gathering had drawn so many prominent Democrats and such a large audience of supporters. It was as if all of these Democrats had harbored a secret sin—a view of education that offended the party's teachers' union base—that they were now willing to talk about publicly in a large group.

"I was tarred and feathered when I started talking about school choice ten years ago," Cory Booker told the group. "Four years ago I tried to put something in the [Democratic] platform and couldn't do it. This group is my wildest dream."

Perhaps, but there was nothing substantive in this year's platform either about education reform. And 12 percent of the convention delegates were members of the teachers' unions. The DFER group was growing, yet it was still a splinter group.

"It's time to face the fact that the Democrats have been wrong on education," Booker continued.

Joel Klein echoed Booker's call for those gathered to face the facts about their party, saying that it was "almost unimaginable" that the party that stood for civil rights was fighting on the wrong side of *the* civil rights issue of this generation—guaranteeing every child the right to a decent education. He then shared his disgust that because of opposition from the Democrat-controlled legislature, it had taken more than a year to lift the cap in New York State on charter schools that were providing real choice for parents in places like Harlem.

Yet despite those continuing challenges, there was a great sense of anticipation. Everyone in the room seemed to agree that the progress that Williams and DFER had made was now likely to be propelled forward by the almost-too-good-to-be-true prospect that one of their own was about to become their party's presidential nominee and was probably going to make it to the White House.

However, advancing the agenda was a bit more complicated than that. The Obama people had an election to win, whereas Joe Williams had a single-issue interest group to run. The two goals were not wholly consistent, as illustrated by the concern that developed within the Obama camp over civil rights leader Al Sharpton's involvement in the Denver meeting.

Sharpton has a mixed reputation, even in Harlem. Some of it has to do with issues related to his finances (no wrongdoing has ever been proved, though he has settled some civil tax claims). There is also still some hangover from a controversy in the 1980s, when he helped publicize a young woman's rape accusations against upstate New York law enforcement authorities, which a grand jury ruled were fraudulent.

Nonetheless, from Williams's standpoint, winning Sharpton over to the reform cause, which Klein and others in New York had worked hard to achieve in 2007, had been a breakthrough. With the exception of New Orleans and possibly Washington, D.C., Harlem was fast becoming the American community with the largest concentration of charter schools. Thus, it had also become ground zero in the UFT's fight to use its allies—ACORN and the Working Families Party—to recruit parents to protest any new charters or expansions. Such protests had been especially vehement when co-locations accompanied the charters, as they usually did. In those situations, the parents would be told, wrongly, that the charters were being run by "outsiders" who were grabbing space that was needed and occupied by children going to "real" public schools. Getting Sharpton on the reform side had helped undermine that opposition and increasingly put pressure on local Democratic politicians in Harlem and other minority communities, who almost always were steadfast teachers' union allies.

Williams, his DFER board, and Klein were so convinced of Sharpton's commitment and the credibility he would bring to their cause that they had decided to form a new group—the Education Equality Project, funded by Broad, Mayor Bloomberg (through his private foundation), and other DFER allies—that would emphasize education reform as a civil rights issue and initially be co-chaired by Klein and Sharpton. (They were not, however, so eager to recruit Sharpton that they were willing to accede to his initial request that he be paid $50,000 a month for his participation; he later agreed to work without pay.)

Whatever Sharpton's value to DFER, his visibility in Denver was not welcomed by the Obama campaign. Jon Schnur, who was the campaign's chief education adviser and ambassador to the reformers, was in charge of dealing with the problem.

"Jon [Schnur] was basically assigned to babysit us in Denver because of Sharpton," says Williams, an account that Schnur does not deny. With Schnur's encouragement, Williams began to whittle down Sharpton's profile so that by the time the forum was staged on August 24, he was relegated to the last panel, by which time most people had left. Williams and Schnur recall that Sharpton was furious.*

Nonetheless, DFER continued to benefit from Sharpton's support in places like Harlem, where Eva Moskowitz's Harlem Success was about to grow from a school into a network.

---

* Sharpton did not respond to repeated phone calls to his office and calls and e-mails to his spokesperson explicitly asking him to comment on his initial request for a $50,000 monthly fee, or whether he had felt slighted by the role he was given at the Denver forum.

Two Returns to the Classroom

Jessica Reid

August 25, 2008

On August 25, 2008, Eva Moskowitz opened Harlem Success Academy II, III, and IV. As with the launch of Harlem Success I, II's co-location site had been settled on only a few weeks before, after the school had been bounced into and out of two other school buildings in June and July.

Standing out on the sidewalk at Harlem Success II, greeting the first graders, was Jessica Reid, now twenty-six.

It had been nearly three years since Reid had finished her second TFA year in the Bronx, and she was glad to be getting back into a classroom. But she was concerned that she was rusty. Also, she worried that teaching first graders instead of the fifth graders she had had in the Bronx would be an extra challenge. "I was terrible at talking down to kids," she recalls. "I hate it and had refused to do it in the Bronx. These were first graders. Would I be too tough on them?"

However, Moskowitz had assured her that part of HSA's culture of high expectations was that no child was to be talked to the way some adults talk to children. She was sure Reid would handle it well. In fact, Moskowitz thought Reid would be a star, even if she was skeptical of Reid's glib vow to get her kids into Shakespeare as she had done with the fifth graders.

"I may be the only one who has higher expectations for these kids and for myself than Eva," Reid would tell me two years later.

Reid quickly fell in love with everything about Harlem Success. "There was calm, there was structure," she recalls. "Suddenly I was not alone. There was support. Everyone was doing the same thing, on the same mission. There were resources, supplies, books. The kids were in uniform. This was heaven."

However, she faced a new kind of challenge. Now simply never sitting down was not enough. "Before," she says, "everything I was able to do looked great compared to what was going on around me. Now I had to meet all these high expectations. It was the hardest job of my life. It's like you're up in front of the class spinning plates, and then you just keep adding plates, and you wonder every day if you are going to keep being able to do it."

Reid spent most nights planning how she would keep the plates in the air the next morning.

New York State has no standardized tests for first graders, but Harlem Success had adopted its own. When Reid's students would be tested the following June, all would be performing above grade level, though almost all had started the year (following kindergarten in a conventional Harlem school) well behind.

Patricia Adams

September 4, 2008

Sometime in 2007, the UFT, apparently reasoning that the best defense is a good offense, had started a section on its website featuring stories of teachers who had been wrongly removed from the classroom on charges of poor performance or misbehavior. The teachers were now being sent to the special reassignment centers, dubbed Rubber Rooms, that Klein and his deputy, Dan Weisberg, had set up.

It was part of the effort (which also included that new lawyer squad, the Teacher Performance Unit) to push these teachers off the payroll. Previously, those removed from classrooms pending their often endless arbitration hearings were assigned, one by one, to report each day to some school district office, where they might be asked to do make-work clerical chores or simply be sent home. Some, in fact, had been required to report in only weekly.

By establishing the Rubber Rooms, where the accused teachers had to sit all day doing nothing, except read or chat with each

other, Klein and Weisberg were trying to make life more unpleasant for them, hoping they would quit (as some did) rather than
milk the long hearing process. The union called it harassment.
Weisberg called it a fair business decision. He argued that there
was nothing unreasonable about making the Rubber Rooms boring or otherwise unpleasant. These teachers were in there, he told
me, "because they have an entitlement to stay on the payroll. It's an
economic decision on their part. That's okay. But don't complain
about it."

On September 4, 2008, Patricia Adams* was allowed by the city
to return to the classroom from the Rubber Room. Soon an account
of her case was added to the UFT website as an example of a teacher
and a union that had overcome the injustice Klein was perpetrating
on the city's teachers.

Headlined "Bravo!" the report quoted a speech that Adams had
made to union delegates soon after her September return to class.
According to the union website, she received a standing ovation as
she declared, "My case should never have been brought to a hearing." The website account continued, in its own words, not Adams's:
"though she believes she was the victim of an effort to move senior
teachers out of the system, the due process tenure system worked in
her case."

In fact, as I would later learn when I included this case in the
article I wrote for the *New Yorker* on the Rubber Rooms, on November 23, 2005, according to a report prepared by the education
department's special commissioner of investigation, Adams had
been found "in an unconscious state" in her classroom at Stuyvesant High School, the gifted students' school that Moskowitz had
attended.

"There were 34 students present in [Adams's] classroom," the
report said. When the principal "attempted to awaken [Adams] he
was unable to." When a teacher "stood next to [Adams], he detected
a smell of alcohol emanating from her."

Adams's return to teaching, more than two years later, in 2008,
had come about only because she and the department of educa-

---

* This is not her real name; she requested that given the circumstances described below she
be allowed to use a pseudonym.

tion had signed a sealed agreement. Rather than litigate whether the city might have violated federal protections for people with disabilities—in her case, alcoholism—the two sides agreed that Adams would be allowed to teach for one more semester, then be assigned to non-teaching duties in a school office. (In other words, she'd become one of those teachers with no assignment who stayed on the payroll.)

The agreement also required that she "submit to random alcohol testing" and be fired if she again tested positive.

In February 2009, Adams would be found passed out in the office where she had to report every day. A drug-and-alcohol-testing-services technician called to the scene would write in his report that she was unable even to "blow into breathalyzer," and that her water bottle contained alcohol. As the stipulation had required, she was fired. Yet the story of her being a victim of Klein's effort to push out senior teachers remained up on the UFT website through the summer of 2009.

When I found Adams to ask her about all of this for the *New Yorker* article, she was mortified about the account by the union that she had been targeted by the city because she was a senior teacher. She told me she had first seen that spin in a 2008 UFT newsletter and had called the union to complain about it. Thus, she had never assumed the same story would be published on the UFT website, much less be there more than a year later.

"My case had nothing to do with seniority; I was a drunk," she told me. "It was about a medical issue, and I sabotaged the whole thing by relapsing. . . . The union has its own agenda."*

The day the *New Yorker* article appeared (in which Weingarten acknowledged that the union website should have been "updated" following Adams's relapse), Weingarten personally called Adams to apologize.

There is no doubt that some teachers sent to the Rubber Room were put there unfairly; I met two or three who I suspect fall into that category. Nor is there any doubt that in a school system with

---

* Adams has since gotten alcohol addiction treatment and says she is sober. She is no longer teaching.

1,200 principals, some are, to use Weingarten's word, "tyrants." To Weingarten this was why due process was so necessary.

It was an argument that drove Klein and his people crazy. To them, it turned a school system's priorities upside down. Sure, teachers shouldn't be thrown out on a whim or based on some bias, and guarding against that might require some kind of hearing before a neutral third party. However, they believed it should not be a gauntlet of legal hurdles.

After the three to five years that it typically took for those in the Rubber Room to have their cases resolved by the arbitrators, the arbitrators rarely dismissed anyone. Klein and his people thought that this was in large part because the contracts for the arbitrators' $1,400 per day assignments (which contained no cap on how many days they could allow the process to drag on) came up for renewal every year, and each arbitrator then had to be reapproved by the UFT.

To Klein and his team, the system was all about protecting the adults, not about protecting the children by getting bad teachers out of their classrooms and by not wasting school budgets to pay idle teachers and as-long-as-it-takes arbitrators.

Klein's deputy chancellor, Chris Cerf, expressed his frustration this way: "We all agree with the idea that it is better that ten guilty men go free than that one innocent person be imprisoned. But by laying that onto a process of disciplining teachers, you put the risk on the kids versus putting it on an occasional innocent teacher losing a job. For the union, it's better to protect one thousand teachers than to wrongly accuse one."

Asked if she thought due process should mean that a thousand bad teachers stay put so that one innocent teacher is protected, Weingarten responded, "That's not a question we should be answering in education. Teachers who are treated fairly are better teachers. You can't have a situation that is fear based. . . . That is why we press for due process."

Whereupon she recounted a story related to the criminal process, of a close family friend who was wrongly accused of negligent homicide.

Weingarten, of course, is a loyal Democrat. Her loyalty was being tested in this presidential election season by the nomination of

Obama, who supported the kind of reform agenda that would not tolerate Rubber Rooms and who had defeated Weingarten's friend Hillary Clinton. Her devotion to the party was about to be tested still more when Obama aligned himself on national television with none other than Michelle Rhee.

"Wake Up, Obama Just Talked About You"

*October 15, 2008, final McCain-Obama
presidential debate, Hempstead, New York*

Like Weingarten, Michelle Rhee is a Democrat. However, when it came to the presidential election, she was not a Democrat for Education Reform. People like David Einhorn, the short seller who had written that early $250,000 check to DFER, might argue that DFER would be effective because its thrust was akin to Nixon's going to China, but Rhee was so put off by Obama's opposition to school vouchers and so appreciated John McCain's rhetorical blasts against the teachers' unions that she had told her boyfriend, Kevin Johnson, that she was going to vote for McCain. Johnson, the Sacramento Democratic mayoral candidate whom Rhee had met at the DFER event in Denver, was appalled. "You can't cast a vote on this one issue," he insisted.

As the last presidential debate began on the night of October 15 in Hempstead, Long Island, Rhee curled up on her bed in Washington. Soon, she fell asleep—only to be woken up by a blast of phone calls and beeps on her BlackBerry.

The first call was from Johnson, in Sacramento. "Obama just said great things about you. What do you think of him now?"

In the last question of the debate, moderator Bob Schieffer of CBS had asked what the two candidates proposed to do about the fact that the United States spent much more than any other country per capita on education but produced such bad results.

Obama scarcely and only vaguely talked about accountability, stressing instead his plan to pour more funds into pre-kindergarten education, better training for teachers, and college tuition tax credits. It was McCain who echoed what probably half of the DFER speakers had said at the Denver event that preceded Obama's nomination—that this was "the civil rights issue of our generation." McCain extolled charter schools as offering parents better choices. Only then did Obama counter that he, too, supported charters and that he favored getting bad teachers out of the classroom. McCain hit back at Obama's vulnerability—vouchers—saying that only he supported continuation of a voucher program in Washington, D.C., which was true, because Obama had backtracked on the issue.

It was then that Obama, in the candidates' last exchange on the issue, weakly parried the D.C. voucher issue:

OBAMA. I'll just make a quick comment about vouchers in D.C. Senator McCain's absolutely right: The D.C. school system is in terrible shape, and it has been for a very long time. And we've got a wonderful new superintendent there who's working very hard with the young mayor there to try . . .
McCAIN. Who supports vouchers.
OBAMA. . . . who initiated—actually, supports—charters.
McCAIN. She supports vouchers, also.

Other friends e-mailed and called Rhee. "How bad can Obama be if he thinks that about you?" one kidded her. Rhee told them that she was sticking to her guns.

DFER co-founder Tilson e-mailed his list of education reform pen pals, saying he wished Obama had supported vouchers and not criticized President Bush's No Child Left Behind law. However, he rationalized, "There's no upside for him right now to ruffle any feathers when it looks like he's coasting to a landslide(!). It was good to see him agree with McCain on supporting charter schools and removing bad teachers."

A month earlier, Tilson had sent his troops a full version of his own Nixon-to-China argument:

Even if you like McCain's education reform proposals better, you still want Obama to be President because only a Democrat can bring about the needed reforms. It's like only Nixon could have gone to China and only Clinton could have reformed welfare. It's the whole idea behind Democrats for Education Reform: it has to be an inside job! As long as it's Republicans

pushing for reform, the unions can continue to make this a
Republican vs. Democrat issue (rather than a what's-best-for-
children vs. what's-best-for-adults issue) and gridlock will continue. Think of it this way: would you rather have a President
with 90% of what you want, but only a 20% chance of making
it happen, or a President with 70% of what you want, but a 60%
change of making it happen?

Rhee ended up voting for Obama. "Kevin convinced me," she
says.

Now the question was whether, if Obama was elected, he really
would be the president who, as Tilson had put it, could deliver 60
percent of what the reformers wanted. Weingarten and her allies
would be at the ready to make sure that didn't happen. But Democrats for Education Reform was gearing up too.

"Inside Baseball"

October 26–November 7, 2008, Washington, D.C.

With just over a week to go before Election Day, veteran Capitol Hill staffer Charles Barone was working with his new boss, Joe Williams of DFER, to put the final touches on a document that Williams excitedly told his board and dozens of supporters in an e-mail on the night of October 26 would be a game changer in "one of the greatest inside baseball battles in edu-history." A copy of the latest draft was attached for them to review.

During the summer, Williams had used funds provided by Broad and a few other DFER supporters to hire Barone, who had worked for George Miller, the reform-minded California congressman. His job was to craft an encyclopedic education transition memo that would give the education reformers an inside track during the changeover in presidential administrations, presumably to a new Obama administration.

"The idea was to have the best, most complete, most detailed document in the hands of the right people on day one," Williams says. Williams had gotten the idea from Geraldine Ferraro, the former congresswoman and 1988 Democratic vice presidential nominee. Ferraro had been pitching Williams to hire her consulting firm. "We didn't hire her, but I liked her suggestion that we crash a memo. She said the oil industry, the unions, and everyone else does it, so why not us?"

The draft that Williams circulated on October 26 was divided into two sections. The first was nine pages of Beltway-ese. It purported to "pose education policy questions, a possible message, and broad legislative ideas for the post-election transition that . . . are politically viable, both vis-à-vis the party and the general public." Different ideas for legislation were outlined. None were surprising. None reflected the more drastic accountability agenda that people like Williams and Tilson were really all about. None would end up being a significant part of the incoming administration's first-year agenda. The purpose of this section was to be moderate, not scare off readers before they got to the second section.

It was the twenty-six-page second section that packed the punch: It named names, lots of names, who would be qualified to fill all of the dozens of federal policy jobs related to education—from secretary of the department to assistant secretaries to Education Department spokespeople and legislative affairs aides to White House domestic policy aides.

Williams's strategy, he had reminded his board in an e-mail earlier in October, was to "flood the White House domestic policy office, the Department of Education, etc., with reform-minded folks to help us continue moving the needle for reform." Schnur, who helped vet drafts of the memo, later explained to me that he had learned from his days working in the Clinton White House "that it's so important who is at all these staff meetings. Beyond who the president is, people you never heard of can really make a difference. Big business is great at understanding that and getting its people inside."

Williams had another goal. Just the intrigue surrounding a Beltway memo that picked people for various jobs (and did not pick others) would elevate DFER's influence. He wanted the network to keep the memo secret yet not keep secret that it was being written.

"I want to have people gossiping about who is—and isn't—in our pile, and observing that we are connected to a lot of interesting people around the country," he wrote his board. "If we can create the right mystique behind this project, we will get credit for having influenced the transition team even before anyone gets tapped for a job."

Except for Williams and Barone themselves, the memo slotted heroes and worker bees of the growing reform network into different spots, with their résumés and the rationale for why they were a good fit provided in detail. If someone had great experience in this or that area and was also a member of a minority group, that information was helpfully, though subtly, included.

Robert Gordon, the Hamilton paper co-author, was recommended for the key associate director position at the Office of Management and Budget overseeing education, or to be the assistant secretary for planning. Congressman Miller's top education policy aide, Alice Cain, was also suggested for that spot, while Ted Kennedy's top education people were suggested for two others. Michael Bennet, a former businessman who had taken over the Denver school system, was suggested for assistant secretary for elementary and secondary education.

"The goal was to be there first and fill the information vacuum," Williams says. "Whoever was going to run the transition could not possibly know what all these dozens of positions were, let alone have a list of possible people to fill them, with detailed résumés. We provided all that, along with a full, annotated org chart."

The October 26 draft, which was circulated by Williams to about two dozen DFER insiders, stopped short of making a firm recommendation for the most important job, education secretary. Schnur was listed as a possible secretary, as were Duncan (who ran the Chicago schools), Bersin (from San Diego), and former North Carolina governor Mike Easley. Eli Broad, who was heavily behind this effort, urged Williams and Barone to add former secretary of state Colin Powell, but they didn't.

On election night, the reformers were, of course, euphoric. However, by the next afternoon, word whipped around their network about whom president-elect Obama had just chosen to head his education transition team. This was the person for whom their memo was ostensibly being written, the one they had expected would be so grateful to receive it. The shocking choice was Linda Darling-Hammond—Wendy Kopp's nemesis who had been attacking TFA since that first article she had written in 1995, and who was the unions' favorite "reform" advocate because she favored more funding of current school system structures and tougher teacher certification rules. Darling-Hammond had consistently been the most media-handy academic critic of the agenda being pushed by DFER.

Wendy Kopp was "speechless" about Obama's choice, she says. "It took my breath away. Had we all been misled by this guy?" By now a large portion of Kopp's budget to recruit and train a corps that was going to be more than 7,500 teachers in 2009 (compared with the original group of fewer than 500) was dependent on federal grants.

Johnston phoned in from Colorado to ask if what he had heard was some kind of prank.

"When I heard about Linda, I told Kevin [Johnson, her fiancé] and some of the others, 'I told you so,'" Rhee recalls. "I couldn't help it."

Tilson was ready to hit Send on another blog post (which by now went as an e-mail to more than 2,500 people, including most of the education press) attacking Darling-Hammond even more harshly than he had done a year before when Obama had named her one of his education policy advisers to the campaign. (She had had little input in the campaign, though she had acted as an ambassador of sorts to the NEA and AFT.) DFER's Wilson begged Tilson to hold off. Then he, Klein, Broad, and others spoke with Schnur, who swore that Darling-Hammond's appointment meant nothing.

Schnur was always trying to calm the troops; he was like a den mother. Besides, Obama was his candidate, so he could be expected to put the best face on this.

Schnur told Wilson and the others that he had already spoken to Melody Barnes, the campaign issues director, and to her deputy, Heather Higginbottom, both of whom were clearly slated to have major White House staff positions. Both had assured Schnur in so many words that these titular transition appointees, like Darling-Hammond, were mostly people who were being rewarded with the posts because they were not likely to get administration jobs. Their work would be limited to doing organization charts and an issues memo to be given to the incoming cabinet secretary of whatever agency they were working on. Darling-Hammond had gotten her title, they told Schnur, because she was close to Christopher Edley Jr., the dean of the Berkeley law school and a former professor of Obama's at Harvard Law School. Edley is a longtime friend of Obama's, and he had provided issues input to the campaign, but he was only on the periphery, Schnur had been told. In fact, it was only at Edley's behest that Darling-Hammond had been named a campaign education adviser in 2007, and Schnur and Higginbottom had had little to do with her, Schnur reminded his friends.

Darling-Hammond was just going to write a transition memo for the incoming secretary, who was *not* likely to be Linda Darling-Hammond, Schnur assured them. Besides, he said, the head of the overall transition was John Podesta, the former Clinton chief of staff who ran the Center for American Progress think tank. That's where Robert Gordon—co-author of the pivotal Hamilton Project paper on teacher effectiveness—was the associate director for economic policy. Read all these tea leaves, Schnur was telling his friends, asking them to play a traditional Washington game. There is far less here than meets the eye.

Schnur was pretty sure he was telling them the truth. At least he hoped he was. But he wondered, too. He had been jilted before.

Williams wasn't taking any chances. He and the three DFER founders—Tilson, Curry, and Petry—with help from Barone (the memo's key drafter) settled on a nuanced strategy. They would not engage in a direct attack on Darling-Hammond; in fact, they would not talk about her at all. There would be no Tilson e-mail blast. Schnur told them that was the right approach.

Tilson, who seems to draw breath from sharing his enthusiasms with as many people as possible, was a hard sell. By now he had three different blogs and e-mail lists: One covered education reform, a second his investment activities, and a third Africa, including accounts of the trips he took there with his wife and three daughters. He thought his readers would be expecting to hear from him on something this surprising and troubling.

In that sense, Tilson was the opposite of Schnur, a classic inside player. Schnur always tried to stay out of the limelight yet showed up, Zelig-like, whenever anything important was going on in education reform.

"We decided to tiptoe around Linda," is how Williams puts it, "so as not to create a fight in the press that might force the administration to defend her." (Her original article about TFA notwithstanding, Darling-Hammond, in fact, is not the kind of hard-edged person who would fail to garner sympathy if attacked frontally. She's not only a respected academic but a likable one.) The strategy mostly worked, except that *New York Times* reporter Sam Dillon got hold of Tilson's 2007 blog post attacking Darling-Hammond when she was named only one of many campaign education advisers. Tilson had written then that she was "as bad as it gets in terms of education reform." Now Dillon wrote an article focusing on the choice of Darling-Hammond as transition head and reporting on the ten-

sions in what seemed to be two Obama education policy camps—
basically the Darling-Hammond camp versus everyone else. The
story had limited impact because no one from DFER or the reform
network commented, except for the irrepressible Tilson, whose old
blog post was cited and who was now quoted acknowledging the
split, but in muted terms.

Although the DFER people tried not to engage Darling-
Hammond by name, they decided to reframe their memo to attack
the *idea* that someone like her could get a seat at the table in the
Obama administration. At the same time, they rewrote the still un-
distributed memo to double down on a recommendation that the
top job go to the reformer they figured had the best chance of edg-
ing out Darling-Hammond: Obama's Chicago friend, Arne Duncan.

Thus, just before one in the morning on November 5, two days
after the election, Williams circulated another draft of the transition memo in which Duncan was touted as the absolute number one
recommendation for secretary. Hoping they might lure Darling-
Hammond into reprising her contempt for TFA, which Obama had
repeatedly praised on the campaign trail, Wendy Kopp was added
as the second recommendation for secretary behind Duncan, if
Duncan was "unable/unwilling" to serve. Kopp had "created an entire army ready to fight to save and improve public education," the
DFER memo said, daring Darling-Hammond to respond because
she so disdained that army.

Listed as a possible alternative for secretary behind Kopp was
Schnur, who, the memo said, "has epitomized the incoming administration's optimistic, entrepreneurial spirit on the education reform
front." That was meant to remind Obama of who in the campaign
had really done the education work, and in which camp, based on
his campaign positions, Obama really belonged.

Then the memo confronted the reformers' biggest fear by adding
a pregnant paragraph that had not appeared in any of the earlier
drafts:

> A "team of rivals" approach, or one in which the administra-
> tion seeks to placate/mollify all of the various education inter-
> ests by giving everyone a seat at the table, will do very little to
> advance any sort of agenda which could possibly be considered

"change" absent strong leadership at the top. Likewise, promoting individuals who are incapable of publicly backing the entirety of the president's agenda will squander our opportunity as Democrats to make the most of our return from 8-year exile. Put plainly, we are advocating for a strong team, comprised of savvy, trustworthy team players.

Another paragraph was added, this one throwing two of DFER's heroes under the bus:

It has been no secret that Democrats for Education Reform has been a strong backer of school leaders like New York City Chancellor Joel Klein and Washington, DC Chancellor Michelle Rhee. We believe that their intensity and urgency is necessary at the local level considering the severity of the nation's K–12 education problems. We acknowledge, however, that the need for them to occasionally break some china in order to affect much-needed change puts them (and other hard-charging reformers like them) in an unlikely spot to be selected for a role like Secretary of Education (a role for which either would be well-suited). We believe that there are, nonetheless, several strong reform-minded candidates who represent a closer alignment with President Obama's bold policy agenda and his less-confrontational style.

When Klein's deputy Chris Cerf heard what the memo said about his boss, he e-mailed this message to Williams and Tilson: "In my humble view, this is pretty craven. What has the world come to when you could seriously propose Jon Schnur or suggest that people who are likely to actually change things should be disqualified in favor of the usual porridge?"

"We were really scared about Linda," says Williams, "and we knew that if Obama was trying to please her, the last thing he was going to do was appoint Joel or Michelle anyway. So we doubled down on Arne."

Cerf, who would become New Jersey governor Chris Christie's superintendent of education in 2011, was also offended that the memo had proposed him for a "communications and outreach" job.

"I think of myself as more of a policy guy, who has actually done something in this space, than a communication flack," he wrote to Williams and Tilson.

Cerf had found out about the memo because Williams had decided that he needed some outside help for this "inside baseball" game. Beginning the weekend after the election, he began leaking the final version of the memo (dated November 7)—which was now ostensibly supposed to go to Linda Darling-Hammond—to education reporters. Meanwhile, Williams, through Schnur, made sure that Rahm Emanuel, slated to be White House chief of staff, and others in the incoming administration got copies, while Broad and a group of what Williams described in another board e-mail as "other billionaires" carried it to their contacts in the new administration.

By the end of the second week of November, Williams felt they were making progress in beating back the Darling-Hammond threat. Schnur was becoming increasingly confident that his assurances had been real. Emanuel had been widely quoted in transition circles as responding, "Are you kidding?" when he had been asked in a transition staff meeting if Darling-Hammond might be appointed the education secretary.

Better yet, by the following week, Schnur and Michael Johnston (although he was still in Colorado) had been asked to join Higginbottom and Barnes in what would be an informal yet real education transition team, charged with mapping the new administration's reform strategy. And word was seeping out that Peter Orszag, who had helped orchestrate the Hamilton Project's white paper on teacher effectiveness, was in line to run Obama's Office of Management and Budget.

"What Do You Guys Think You Could Do with a Hundred Billion?"

November 15, 2008, Washington, D.C.

Joe Williams and other outsiders, however well connected, didn't know it, but within ten days of the November 3 election, Schnur and Higginbottom had become all but sure that the Darling-Hammond fire drill was over. Duncan was being talked about as the almost certain secretary, with Klein getting the second most mentions. On the afternoon of November 15, they got a call at their makeshift transition office in Washington. (Higginbottom would soon move to the larger Chicago transition office.) A transition aide working on stemming the fall 2008 financial meltdown with a giant economic stimulus package that the president-elect was preparing to propose to Congress immediately following Inauguration Day had a question: "If you guys got, say, $100 billion for education as part of the package, could you use some of it to move Obama's reform ideas?"

Was he kidding?

In fact, Schnur told the transition aide, this is exactly what Obama had proposed as a junior senator: dangle aid to the states that promised to undertake real reform.

Most of the money would have to go to provide the instant economic jolt that the stimulus package was going to be all about, Schnur was reminded, such as funding to keep teachers on the payroll who might otherwise be laid off as local tax revenues dried up in the Great Recession. But there was so much—a hard-to-fathom $100 billion for the education pot—that Emanuel and the president-elect were thinking that maybe they could use, say, 15 percent of it to get some reform projects going. Fifteen percent would be $15 billion conditioned on reform, which amounted to almost half the federal aid given to all of the country's K–12 schools for any purpose in any single year. Think about how you might do that, Schnur and Higginbottom were told.

Later that day, Schnur and Higginbottom got more news that explained the dream assignment they had been given and gave them confidence it wasn't a dream. They heard that Robert Gordon—the Hamilton project co-author and advocate for using federal aid to encourage accountability reform—was likely to become associate director of the Office of Management and Budget, with responsibility for, among other areas, education spending. This was exactly the position the Democrats for Education Reform transition memo had recommended Gordon get.

Meantime, Gordon had been working on an eerily similar project. He'd been helping with the Gates Foundation's teacher effectiveness contest, which was about to point the way for much of what Schnur was being asked to come up with using the federal purse.

The Chosen Four

November 19, 2008, Seattle

On November 19, 2008, Jean Clements and Hillsborough County officially entered Bill Gates's orbit, when the Gates Foundation announced that the Hillsborough school system, which is in and around Tampa, had won an "intensive partnership" grant—for $100 million.

Jean Clements's story seems familiar. As a sophomore at the University of Oregon in 1975, she had no idea what she wanted to do with her life. She was toying with majoring in anthropology, philosophy, or maybe even music. (She had been a star bassoon player growing up in Tampa, Florida.) One day, as she was shooting the breeze with some college friends, somehow a heady discussion about the differences among the species morphed into a discussion of programs designed to teach people who had different learning capacities and methods. Someone mentioned that their university had a terrific graduate program in special education.

Before long, Clements had become a special education major and then enrolled in the graduate school. Her focus, as she puts it, "was on kids in regular classrooms who didn't connect the dots the way everyone else does. . . . It's not that they are not intelligent." (She could have been referring to KIPP founder Dave Levin, who'd been pushed out of the private school in Manhattan for exactly that reason only to become valedictorian at the equally elite private school where he ended up.) Clements's passion, she says, "was doing something about a system that simply let these kids go, that refused to accept responsibility for helping them learn, that set low expectations and met them."

Because of a romantic entanglement, Clements ended up going home to Tampa after getting her master's degree and becoming a special education teacher in the Hillsborough County school system. "I figured I would do it one or two years, before doing something like law school," she recalls. "I never expected to stay in education." But she did—because, she says, "Teaching was a blast every day I was in the classroom, and I was compelled by the challenge of teaching kids who were seen as unteachable."

Clements fits the model of a TFA alum/school reformer: gets into teaching almost by accident as a placeholder for a "real" career; likes it and realizes she can do it, but is frustrated by public education's low expectations for kids who are disadvantaged; decides to stay in the field and try to change those expectations. Yet Jean Clements is different. She never was in TFA—and is now the head of the Hillsborough County teachers' union, one of the largest locals in the country.

In 1983, Clements heard that the school district's special education unit was looking for a new director. Although she was young and had only four years' experience in the classroom, she did have a master's degree, and after some friends urged her on, she applied. "I figured," she recalls, "that since I was still thinking about doing something else, applying for the job—doing a résumé and having interviews—would be good practice." She got the job.

Before long, Clements and her special education colleagues, who were still earning teachers' salaries and were members of the union with a union contract, got wind of a plan by the district to reorganize their work in a way that they thought did not make sense. They sought their union's help and ended up forming a union committee within their special education office to meet with the school district officials. They also took the opportunity to complain that although they were paid for the seven-hour-and-twenty-minute union workday, the need to travel from school to school in the sprawling Florida county, plus the demands of the work, typically meant they worked ten hours a day. They got no relief on the hours, though they did get the district to alter the reorganization plan. Then, after Clements got disgusted with termite infestation and other conditions in the condemned school that the district used to house ancillary service units like special education, she organized every union member in the building to lodge a complaint. She was designated lead complainer.

Meanwhile, she and the other special education teachers, who all seemed to share Clements's determination to upend the self-fulfilling prophecy of low expectations, became close friends. "We were all teacher snobs," she says. "We all believed there were good teachers and bad ones, that it mattered how you taught. That your pedagogy and attitude really counted."

As the overall union contract came up for renegotiation in the mid-'90s, she put together a set of proposals for the special education unit. "That did not go over well with the others in the bargaining unit," Clements says. "Here we were asking for something extra."

What struck Clements most, she recalls, was that "these teachers would tell me how lucky I was to have escaped the classroom. I resented that. It made me sad. I thought being in the classroom was a joy, the best thing anyone could do. . . . But," she adds, "I gradually came to see that what they were saying, or at least what the good teachers were saying, was that being in the classroom is really, really hard. And they're right."

By 2002, after having served in various union posts, Clements was elected president of the union in a three-person race. To the extent that the candidates had differences, Clements stood out for wanting to professionalize her profession and being willing to embrace the Jeb Bush reforms rather than take a hard line against them. Her stance was not terribly out of line in Hillsborough, because the union there had always been less confrontational and more collaborative than most other teachers' locals in Florida. Florida is also a so-called right-to-work state, meaning that employees cannot be required to pay dues to a union that has won the right to represent workers at their workplace. This makes the unions weaker there than in places like New York or California.* Clements gets dues from only about half of the twelve thousand teachers in the Hillsborough County school system, even though they all get to vote on their contract.

In February 2008, someone at the AFT in Washington tipped Clements off that the Gates Foundation, aware of her union's his-

---

* Not forcing teachers to pay dues to their union and not having dues payments automatically deducted from paychecks were two of the changes that newly elected Republican governors of Ohio and Wisconsin would push through their legislatures in early 2011. The new laws also stripped public employee unions of the ability to bargain collectively over most issues, except salaries.

tory of collaboration with the school district, was exploring the possibility of including Hillsborough County in some kind of grant. (Clements's union—the Hillsborough Classroom Teachers Association—is part of the Florida Educational Association, which is the product of a merger in Florida between locals affiliated with the NEA and the AFT.) She hadn't heard anything more about the contest until April, when district superintendent MaryEllen Elia, who has a close working relationship with Clements, called to say that the Gates Foundation was considering them and forty or fifty other districts around the country as possible recipients of competitive grants. Elia told Clements that a firm condition of competing was that the union leader had to be on board. Clements immediately said she would work with Elia on a plan.

That planning had begun in earnest after the July 2008 meeting in which Bill and Melinda Gates signed off on the contest. With the school's office building closed on summer Fridays, they often met at Elia's home so that they would have an air-conditioned place in which to draft the plan.

At times, they were at loggerheads. Clements was, she says, adamant that test results could not count for more than 40 percent of the three-pronged evaluation, which also included the principal's classroom evaluation and an elaborate process of peer reviewers' evaluations. Elia originally wanted tests to count for 50 percent but settled on 40 percent.

And, after lots of discussion, they agreed that current teachers could opt out of the new career-ladder-based compensation plan, because the evaluations would still go forward for them and they could be removed, even if they had tenure, after two straight years of unsatisfactory evaluations emanating from the new, more rigorous system.

Clements and Elia were sure they had done a good job, but they were worried about Palm Beach County, which was also a contestant. With Florida's reputation as a reform leader, they figured the state would get at least one Gates grant. But that two might go to Florida, out of the four or five they anticipated the foundation awarding, seemed unlikely.

This made the foundation's announcement on November 19, 2008, that Hillsborough had won a $100 million grant that much more satisfying. (Palm Beach did not win.)

Mark Roosevelt, on the other hand, was sure that the plan for Pittsburgh that he submitted was a winner. He was right. The Pittsburgh school system won $40 million.

The third winner was Memphis, which got $90 million. The last winner was College-Ready Promise, a coalition of five charter networks in Los Angeles, where the Gates people and every other reform group had all but given up on getting the teachers' union ever to agree to anything. College-Ready got $60 million.

The Pittsburgh school system was lauded in the Gates Foundation announcement for its "collaborative relationship with the teachers union," a local unit of Weingarten's AFT. The collaboration had produced a Teacher Effectiveness Reform Plan that included tying student test performance to teacher evaluations, along with as many as eight in-class observations, which would produce a Research-Based Inclusive System of Evaluation (dubbed RISE) that would "exit" ineffective teachers and link tenure decisions and compensation to student achievement. The Gates grant would also be used to recruit noncertified but highly qualified "Teach for Pittsburgh" teachers in science and math and for special needs students.

The Hillsborough and Memphis plans were similar to Pittsburgh's, though with some local variations.

Bill and Melinda Gates, who had reviewed each winning proposal page by page before signing off on the choices, had scattered their money smartly. The winners were a traditional strong union industrial city in the North, Pittsburgh; a less-union-friendly Southern district, Hillsborough County, that is a good mix of urban (Tampa) and suburban and is the country's eighth largest school district, with 192,000 students and 12,500 teachers in 248 schools in a state that, thanks to Jeb Bush, had already begun initiatives such as tracking student performance to schools and teachers; a smaller Southern city, Memphis, where the union was an NEA affiliate; and a charter network in the middle of what was perhaps the city with the local union that had most successfully rejected reform—Los Angeles.

In Hillsborough, Pittsburgh, and Memphis the Gates people picked districts that were amenable to what they wanted to accomplish. They didn't take any chances. They made sure the school board was functioning well, without the kinds of divisions that could stall innovation. For the same reason, they made sure the school board and the superintendent got along. More important, they required that the union leader got along with both the board and the superintendent and would not only sign on in advance to the plan but also sit on each project's five-person steering committee with the superintendent. They were paying for change that was going to be hard enough with everyone pulling in the same direction. They wanted to make sure nothing or nobody was going to stand in the way.

At the national level, the NEA's Dennis Van Roekel had been barely involved in the Memphis plan; his locals are traditionally more independent. Because Tennessee is not a strong union state, its teachers' unions usually have less leverage to resist reforms like this, anyway, especially when so much money is being offered in return. Weingarten, on the other hand, told me that she was heavily involved in the negotiations with Roosevelt in Pittsburgh and with Hillsborough officials. Roosevelt and union leader Tarka in Pittsburgh and superintendent Elia and union leader Clements in Hillsborough told me that Weingarten had encouraged them to participate but had taken no part in the negotiations.

It seemed as if what Bill Gates had called his foundation's "riskiest" venture was panning out. Whatever Weingarten's direct involvement, the school systems and the unions had, indeed, been collaborating in the good-faith spirit that Weingarten had rightly pointed out rarely got the press attention that a fight attracted.

However, the two sides had in many respects so far simply agreed to agree. For example, precise details of the evaluation plans—exactly how test score results would be weighted versus those classroom observations, or how teaching subjects like music or art would be evaluated—had still not been hammered out. What was not spelled out in the press release was that while the unions and the school systems had presented detailed paths for establishing all of these accountability and effectiveness reforms and really did seem to be working collaboratively, they had not yet filled in the important blanks.

In addition to announcing these grants totaling $290 million, the Gates Foundation announced that another $45 million would be spent in those locations and in other selected school systems to launch the second stage in Bill Gates's quest for data: Kane and a team of researchers would fan out and begin to home in on what actually constituted effective teaching. They were going to recruit 3,700 teachers to volunteer to be videotaped and evaluated by expert teachers, to have their students interviewed by a crew of researchers run by Kane to get feedback how well they thought they were taught, and to have their student performance data studied. It would all be an unprecedented effort to see how the performance data squared with the video evaluations and the student surveys and then to come up with common attributes of those who did well on all three. Bill and Melinda Gates were determined to discover the secret sauce of good teaching.

The largest foundation in the world had now thrown a lot of chips at teacher effectiveness and accountability. An even deeper pocket was about to raise the bet nearly fifteenfold.

"They'll Do Backflips"

December 17, 2008

On December 16, 2008, the president-elect announced that Arne Duncan would be his education secretary. By now the choice surprised no one. Indeed, in retrospect it seemed to be one of those presidential appointments that never should have been in doubt.

Duncan, who had just turned forty-four, has a passion for education that he didn't acquire professionally as an adult. When he was a child, his mother ran an after-school program for disadvantaged children in Chicago. (His father was a psychology professor at the University of Chicago.) "I spent my life in a church basement watching my mother trying to educate kids everyone else was giving up on," he says. "I'm so fortunate that I was able to see that this is possible since I was a baby." Midway through Harvard (where he graduated magna cum laude), Duncan took a year off to help his mother while he worked on a thesis on the urban underclass.

The most striking thing about Duncan beyond his six-foot-five height is a steadiness mixed with a kind of laconic cheerfulness. Rhetorically, he is not Klein or Rhee. He doesn't throw the reformers the raw meat likely to get Tilson hitting his blog jubilantly at midnight. He is the big guy who doesn't think he needs to flaunt it.

Yet Duncan is not an instinctive compromiser either. In one of our interviews, when I asked him if it was true that he seemed to be trying to romance or bear-hug Randi Weingarten over to his side rather than pull her or run over her, he said without hesitating, "I try to bear-hug everyone. But at the end of the day this is about the children, not about the adults. If the adults want to cooperate, fine. If not, that's too bad. We have to do this."

Duncan had co-captained Harvard's basketball team, and although not good enough to be a pro, he played for almost four years in pro leagues outside the United States, mostly in Australia.

A year after he returned to Chicago, childhood friend John Rogers Jr., who is also a good friend of Obama's, asked Duncan to run an after-school program for disadvantaged children that Rogers's successful venture capital firm was launching at one of Chicago's worst schools. When the school itself was shut down in 1996, Rodgers and Duncan reopened it as a turnaround school.

Three years later, Duncan went to work for the then-head of the Chicago schools, Paul Vallas—who would ultimately join TFA's Sarah Usdin and Louisiana education superintendent Paul Pastorek in the post-Katrina drive to create a new school system in New Orleans. When Vallas left and Duncan was picked by Mayor Richard M. Daley to run the Chicago schools in 2001, he pushed hard to close failing schools and replace them with new, smaller turnaround schools or charters. It was during this time that Duncan, via Rogers, became friends and basketball buddies with State Senator Barack Obama.

In his second book, *The Audacity of Hope*, Barack Obama recounts a visit to the Dodge Elementary School, a persistently failing Chicago school that had been successfully designated for turnaround, which, he wrote, opened his eyes to the need and potential for substantive education reform. Dodge is where the president-elect held the December 17, 2008, press conference nominating his friend to the cabinet. Most press accounts of the announcement featured prominent quotes from Joe Williams praising Duncan's support for charters and merit pay. Williams and the three DFER founders—Curry, Petry, and Tilson—were ecstatic.

The morning after the Duncan announcement, Higginbottom (who was about to become White House deputy domestic policy chief), Melody Barnes (who would be her boss as policy chief), and Duncan got on a conference call with Schnur, who was still in Washington, and with Robert Gordon, who had also just been officially appointed to the Office of Management and Budget. The incoming administration was targeting an overall stimulus plan of nearly $800 billion, of which, as suggested in mid-November by the stimulus transition staff, $100 billion might be allocated to education aid. If they went relatively easy on the requirements for most of it—85 percent was again mentioned—and doled it out to the states based on traditional population formulas, they could then get tough on how the other $15 billion was allocated.

Schnur had already thought about this, a lot, and had talked about it with Gordon and Michael Johnston, among others.

Let's have a contest, Schnur suggested. We'll give money to the states that present the best education reform plans. But it has to be a real contest, requiring real plans to win.

Look at what Gates had just done, Gordon, added, describing what Pittsburgh, Memphis, and Hillsborough had agreed to in the Gates Foundation competition.

Duncan remembered that when the Bush administration had distributed a few competitive grants, he had achieved many years' worth of reform in a few months because his team had been so eager to win, even though the grants involved piddling amounts that were rounding errors in his Chicago schools budget. "These contests can really work," he said

This time, someone added, the competition would be billions of dollars and high visibility—involving governors desperate not only to win a merit badge but also to fill huge budget gaps. "They'll do backflips," someone said.

Schnur began writing what would become the three-page memo and thirty pages of backup that would go to Obama.

As 2009 began and the inauguration approached, Schnur's friends at Democrats for Education Reform had no inkling from him, although he talked with them almost every day, about the stimulus contest plan that was in the works. They knew that education was going to get a big chunk of the stimulus money, but that was all they knew. Although an amazing percentage of the people the DFER transition memo had touted for high- and mid-level education positions had begun to be chosen to fill those spots, the DFER people and other reformers outside the growing administration circle had no sense of the rocket boost they were about to get for their agenda from what Schnur and Duncan were planning.

The other side was similarly clueless. On the morning of January 13, 2009, Sharon Robinson, the president of the American Association of Colleges for Teacher Education—a Washington group that pushes tighter teacher certification standards and other policies championed by Hammond and the unions—sent an e-mail alert to Washington lobbyists for the AFT and NEA. She urged them to push to have Darling-Hammond appointed as the top Duncan deputy—the "team of rivals approach" the DFER memo had warned of.

Robinson also noted rumors that Schnur, Wendy Kopp, and Andrew Rotherham—a reformer dating back to the Clinton years who was now an influential education consultant and blogger and who had helped edit the DFER transition memo—were being mentioned for top jobs. "The proposed team, if appointed, would be a grave disappointment for those of us who are hoping to change the education system in the interests of students," the education schools' lobbyist warned, adding, "This is not just the time to offer support for Linda Darling-Hammond. This is a moment when we need to let the transition team know that the circulated names of Kopp, Schnur, and Rotherham are not acceptable."

As the union lobbyists and their allies read Robinson's e-mail, Schnur was grinding through a draft of his plan for the contest, which he had dubbed "Race to the Top."

Meanwhile, Darling-Hammond had resumed teaching at Stanford. (She says she had no interest in a job in the administration, because she had to remain in California for family reasons.) That didn't mean that the race was a done deal. There were still the Democrats on Capitol Hill to contend with.

"Why Are We Doing This? Didn't We Win?"

January 29, 2009, Capitol Hill

The January 29 meeting in which Obama signed off on the Race to the Top ended at about 2:00. Schnur and Duncan then headed up to Capitol Hill to brief their most likely Democratic ally—George Miller, the California congressman and Education Committee chair whose failed TEACH Act had been a mini-version of what the new administration was about to propose. This had to happen quickly. The stimulus bill was on the fastest of fast tracks.

Schnur had worked with Miller for years on education projects, and Miller says he regards Schnur with almost fatherly affection as "one of the great public policy talents." Even before the Oval Office meeting, Schnur had quietly briefed Miller and Alice Cain, Miller's top staff person, on the possible plan to use stimulus money for a reform "contest." He knew they supported it.

The problem was that committees like Miller's write laws that set policy. They don't dole out money. That's the province of the appropriations committee and subcommittees, and the chair of the appropriations committee was David Obey of Wisconsin. Obey is about as traditional a Democrat as there is, and he had always worked closely with the NEA and AFT, whose political action committees have contributed heavily to his campaigns. (In 2006 and 2008, when he won reelection easily, the two unions gave him $40,000.) Equally important, as a longtime senior appropriator, Obey believed, as Miller puts it, that "appropriators, not presidents, decide how and where money is spent."

This was the pothole discussed at the Oval Office meeting. Schnur and Duncan were proposing that Duncan's department, not Congress, decide which states would get the Race's jackpot. And it had to be clear to Obey that his home state of Wisconsin—where Milwaukee had one of the country's worst-performing, union-controlled, reform-averse school systems, and which had a highly restrictive state law governing charter schools—had little chance of sharing in the money.

Obey was not happy, and, as usual, he made no effort to disguise it. Why were they proposing a George Bush–like plan that scapegoated schools and teachers, when what was needed was money to keep all teachers on the payroll and even add more? According to one congressional staffer, "Basically, Obey's reaction was, 'Wait a minute. Why are we doing this? Didn't we win?'"

Schnur, always low-key and respectful in situations like this, stressed that their proposal was "only" 15 percent of the $100 billion that would be sent to schools. That's $15 billion, Obey shot back. An Obey staffer said they might consider some kind of project, but it would have to be a "lot less" than that.

Within days—and after Rahm Emanuel had what he says were several heated discussions with Obey—Obey agreed to a $5 billion contest, a third less than their original request yet still a giant sweepstakes.

"He could have slammed it down," Miller says. "It's remarkable that he agreed. His whole life he's been an appropriator who controlled everything, but I guess in deference to the new president and the fact that this was only $5 billion in an $800 billion bill providing $100 billion to education, he let it go."

Another reason Obey relented was Miller, who played good cop to Emanuel's bad cop. "George told Mr. Obey that this is really serious and we really need this," says Cain, Miller's top aide. "And people really respect him. That really counts." It also didn't hurt that Miller is probably the member of Congress closest to then–House Speaker Nancy Pelosi.

Emanuel had remarked at one point in the deliberations over the Race that in a Democratic-controlled Congress, a bill that the California and New York delegations didn't want usually had slim chances. Yet this one—a direct challenge to those congressional delegations' strongest support group, the teachers' unions—was about to slide by, buried in a larger bill that all Democrats supported, and with the teachers' unions not seeing it coming.

"Such Criteria as the Secretary Deems Appropriate"

February 13, 2009, Capitol Hill

As soon as they got the go-ahead, a team led by Cain from Miller's office and Schnur representing Duncan, plus aides and lawyers from Miller's and Obey's shops, began drafting the section of the economic stimulus package that would become the Race to the Top. The drafting became an all-nighter, primarily because money cannot be appropriated by Congress unless it is to be spent for a purpose that has already been authorized by some statute. Threading that needle was a major challenge.

The hunt began to find some law or other that would allow money to be spent to reward states for initiating merit pay plans for teachers (as Miller's rejected TEACH Act had explicitly attempted to do), or for building data systems to track student performance and link it to individual teachers. Through the night, they came up with various laws that they shoehorned to provide them the ostensible authority to spend this money. For example, the old Bush No Child

Left Behind law had required states to report on how they were addressing inequities in the distribution of "well-qualified" teachers
in disadvantaged communities. By linking test data to teachers, this
money would help figure out who these "well-qualified" teachers
were, they rationalized. The America Competes Act of 2007, which
created a President's Council on Innovation and Competitiveness,
was rolled out to justify encouraging the improvement of state curricula standards.

This didn't require a lot of verbiage. In fact, the shorter the better, given how they were stretching the meaning and intent of those
old laws.

On February 13, the stimulus package was approved by Congress. It was 1,079 pages. The $100 billion education section was
nine pages. The $5 billion* Race to the Top section tucked into
those nine education pages was two and a half pages. Most of it was
taken up by an incomprehensible citing of the statutes associated
with those prior laws that supposedly gave Congress the right to
dispense the money to encourage the reforms that Miller and the
administration had in mind. The section carried the innocuous title
"Innovation Grants," which were to be dispensed, the provision said
matter-of-factly, according to such "criteria as the Secretary deems
appropriate."

What was by far the largest competitive grant program in American history was also the vaguest. Schnur and Duncan had a huge,
blank canvas.

Until that afternoon, when Duncan and Schnur held a briefing
about it for education reporters, few in the education community
outside the tight Duncan-Schnur circle—including the teachers'
unions' Washington lobbyists—had any idea the reform contest was
coming. Even the fact that Schnur surfaced on the call as a "consultant" to Duncan came as a surprise.

Duncan told the reporters that his fund was "a once-in-a-lifetime opportunity to do something dramatically better." He also unveiled the catchy name—"Race to the Top." In a city where interest
groups like the education community gossip and fight over a $5 mil-

---

* Actually it was $4.35 billion, plus another $600 million for a related Schools Innovation
Fund.

lion or $10 million grant award, the race was now on to figure out what this multibillion-dollar Race to the Top was actually going to look like.

A month later, on March 10, Obama provided vague clues in a speech to a Washington meeting of the Hispanic Chamber of Commerce. Invoking Lincoln's building of the transcontinental railroad during the Civil War, he made the case that America could and should, despite the economic crisis, get to work on "doing a far better job educating our sons and daughters" because we had "let our grades slip, our schools crumble, our teacher quality fall short, and other nations outpace us."

Therefore, Obama declared, "We will end what has become a race to the bottom in our schools and instead spur a race to the top by encouraging better standards and assessments. . . . But let me be clear," the president continued. "If a teacher is given a chance or two chances or three chances but still does not improve, there's no excuse for that person to continue teaching. I reject a system that rewards failure and protects a person from its consequences."

On their way back from the speech, Obama and Duncan made an impromptu stop at a national conference of state school superintendents. Duncan came to the podium and was introduced as "the Secretary of Education accompanied by the President of the United States," whereupon Obama emerged from behind a curtain, spoke informally to the group for about five minutes, and urged them to compete in the Race.

With that speech and the highly unusual surprise presidential drop-in at the school chiefs' meeting, it was now becoming clearer in the Beltway's education circles that the president himself was serious about education reform. What was not clear was how far the administration would push that agenda with this grant money. The president had been short on details, and Duncan, then and through the remainder of the spring, would be similarly vague.

Yet for Duncan, Schnur, and Michael Johnston, who was working with Schnur on framing the Race, there wasn't any doubt about how far and how hard they intended to push. With the cause of their lives having just been codified into a law signed by a president who shared that cause, they intended to make the grant money the ultimate in leveraged investment capital. The $5 billion they

had been allocated constituted less than 1 percent of what state and
local governments spend on education in a year. However, if they
wrote tough enough rules for getting it—rules that required the
winning states, desperate to plug their budget deficits, to deliver on
real reforms—they really could seize what Duncan had called this
"once-in-a-lifetime opportunity."

Back at the Department of Education, the grind of making that
happen would now begin. While Washington and much of the rest
of the country focused on legislative battles over health care and the
economy, not much would be heard about the Race, as Schnur and
squadrons of the department's staff struggled with the details of
translating presidential rhetoric and the bullet points of the reform
agenda into an effective government grant program. They were
joined by Robert Gordon, newly ensconced at the Office of Management and Budget, and monitored by Higginbottom, now at the
White House. Because this was the largest grant program ever that
required applicants to compete for the money based on the merits of
their proposals, rather than be entitled to it based on some population formula, getting it right was not going to be easy. How would
the merits of the plans be defined and measured? And who would
measure them?

"Things I Can't Change
from This Building"

April 2009, Denver

Michael Johnston had turned down an education job in the Obama administration, where by now he would have been working on those rules for the Race. He wanted to stay in Colorado. However, he had been getting increasingly involved in education politics, including an education summit he had helped organize with Sarah Usdin in New Orleans in 2006, the incoming Colorado governor's education transition committee that same year, and, of course, his work on the Obama campaign, capped by Obama's appearance at his school in May 2008 and his efforts with Schnur on the transition in creating the Race.

In the spring of 2009, Johnston got immersed in a political issue that hit closer to home and produced a more frustrating result. Because of what he was seeing and hearing at his high school, he was among those pushing for a bill in the Colorado legislature that would allow children who were in the country illegally but had successfully graduated from high school to qualify for the same free admission to state colleges offered to Colorado citizens. "I was watching it being debated all spring," he recalls. "I had all these undocumented kids who would say to me, 'Why should I sign the Commitment Board if I can't go to college even if I get in?'"

In April the bill was defeated in the state senate by one vote. "One of my smartest kids came up to me in tears," Johnston says. "'What do I do now?' he asked. I didn't have an answer."

It was then that Johnston concluded that "there are lots of things I can't do from this building. There are things I want to take to scale."

Johnston was not thinking in a vacuum. Colorado state senate president Peter Groff, who had also been a speaker at the DFER

Denver pre-convention rally (and had been named in the DFER transition memo as a good candidate for an administration education job), had just been appointed one of Duncan's assistant secretaries. His vacant state senate seat would now be filled by a selection committee. Although the seat in the racially mixed district had long been filled by an African American, Johnston decided to go for it.

An added lure was the coming Race to the Top. Johnston knew, he says, that "all the action was going to shift to the state level when states filed their applications."

Johnston, the only white in the four-person race, mounted a vigorous campaign in what is usually a sedate selection process. He met with nearly all 146 members of the selection committee and ran a grassroots letter-writing and e-mail campaign. It culminated in a rousing Obama-like speech on May 12, 2009, about racial unity and equality, to the panel in a room filled with supporters. He won easily.

Now he was determined to make fixing public education his mission at the state capital. He was about to get guidance, and ammunition, from fellow reformers at the New Teacher Project, the organization Rhee had started before going to Washington.

Widgets

June 2009, New York City

In June 2009, the New Teacher Project published an explosive report that was the result of a painstaking examination, financed in large part by the Gates Foundation, of the personnel files of twelve school systems of varying sizes across the country, including Denver's. Titled *The Widget Effect: Our National Failure to Acknowledge and Act on Differences in Teacher Effectiveness,* the report began by quoting a *New York Times* editorial from 1936: "Whether these incompetents [in the school system] were unfit to teach at any time, or have been rendered unfit by the passing years, is a matter of opinion. The question is, why are they allowed to remain?"

"In the 73 years since," the foreword to *The Widget Effect* continued, "we have made little progress toward answering the question of why poor instruction in our schools goes unaddressed."

The report's lead author was Daniel Weisberg, who had recently left his job as Klein's deputy in charge of labor relations to become general counsel of the New Teacher Project.

"Our schools are indifferent to instructional effectiveness," the study declared. In plain English, it said what Bill Gates had concluded after his meeting with Tom Kane and Robert Gordon: A huge sector of our economy—in this case the sector having to do with preparing our children to function as adults—didn't care about who was productive and who wasn't. (In fact, 3.2 million K–12 teachers constituted not only the country's largest profession, but the largest single occupation other than retail sales people or cashiers.)

In a section labeled "All Teachers Are Rated Good or Great," Weisberg described what his researchers had found in examining the results of teacher-rating processes across the twelve sample school districts, which included relatively small districts, such as Toledo, and large ones, such as Chicago, in addition to Denver. It was exactly what he had known to be the case in New York: In districts that had a binary, satisfactory-unsatisfactory system, 99 percent of teachers received a satisfactory rating. Even in the few districts that attempted a broader range of rating options, 94 percent get one of the top two ratings and less than 1 percent were rated unsatisfactory. This was because, the study found, most ratings are the result of cursory, once-a-year classroom observations of a teacher by a principal or an assistant principal.

"These data," the report added, "often stand in sharp relief against current levels of student achievement. For example, in Denver schools that did not make adequate yearly progress (AYP), more than 98 percent of tenured teachers received the highest rating—satisfactory. On average, over the last three years, only 10 percent of failing schools issued at least one unsatisfactory rating to a tenured teacher."

It was an echo of what Michelle Rhee had told me about teacher ratings in Washington when she took over: "When I came here, all the adults were fine; they all had satisfactory ratings. But only 8 percent of eighth graders were on grade level for math. How's that for an accountable system that puts the children first?"

The New Teacher Project report then laid out a road map for "a comprehensive performance evaluation system." It included the recommendation that for dismissals, "an expedited one-day hearing should be sufficient for the arbitrator to determine if the evaluation and development process was followed and judgments made in good faith."

I happened to read *The Widget Effect,* with that prescription for a one-day process, in July 2009, just before I spent a morning at an arbitration hearing involving a teacher whom Klein and Weisberg had sent to a Brooklyn Rubber Room almost a year before. Her arbitration had begun six months earlier, with hearing days scheduled only once or twice a month (in accordance with limits on the pace of hearings imposed in the union contract). The morning's proceedings focused first on a medical excuse that the teacher had produced for not showing up at the previous day's hearing. An earnest young lawyer from the Weisberg-created Teacher Performance Unit pointed out that the doctor's letter was eleven days old and therefore could have had nothing to do with her supposedly being sick the day before. The defense counsel, paid for by the union, replied that the letter referred to a chronic condition. The arbitrator said that he would reserve judgment.

Next came discussion among the lawyers and the arbitrator about Defense Exhibit 33Q, a picture of the teacher's classroom. The photograph showed a neatly organized room, with a lesson plan chalked on the blackboard. However, under questioning by her own lawyer, the teacher conceded that the picture had been taken in consultation with her union representative one morning before class, after the principal had begun complaining about her. A report from an independent expert, who had been hired, as required by the union contract, to observe the teacher in class before charges could be brought against her, was then offered into evidence. The report said that as of a month before the teacher was removed—and three months after the independent expert started observing and counseling her, and long after this picture was taken—the teacher had still not "organized her classroom to support instruction and enhance learning." This was an expert approved by the teachers' union.

That night, in reviewing the 5,044 pages of transcript covering the previous twenty-nine days of hearings, I found that nearly a day had been taken up on the question of whether the teacher had had "custody" of her teaching manual. Proving custody of the manual was presumably required to establish that it was her fault that she had allegedly failed, despite repeated warnings, to fill out report cards, correct student work, do lesson plans, follow the curriculum, or manage her class.

It was also alleged that she had appointed one of the biggest kids in the class to administer corporal punishment to other children who misbehaved; one of her defenses was that she did this to teach the children self-governance.

By now this teacher's arbitration process had dragged on longer than the O. J. Simpson murder trial. The pendulum—which had been at one extreme in Albert Shanker's day, when teachers were at the mercy of their employers—had swung fully to the other side.

It was no surprise, then, that the New Teacher Project's recommendation of a one-day process (along with recommendations for rigorous, frequent classroom observations and evaluations of teachers), juxtaposed against all of the report's unprecedented research into the actual evaluation practices of so many disparate school districts, became the talk of the education community. The "widget effect" became a favorite catchphrase.

Three weeks after the New Teacher Project report was published,

Duncan was booed at a National Education Association convention when he mentioned student test data and went on to say that "inflexible seniority and rigid tenure rules . . . put adults ahead of children. These policies were created over the past century to protect the rights of teachers, but they have produced an industrial factory model of education that treats all teachers like interchangeable widgets."

In that talk and in one a few days earlier at the Aspen Institute, Duncan signaled that this Democratic administration was serious about reform. Yet he still offered few details.

At the same convention, NEA longtime general counsel Robert Chanin gave a valedictory speech on the eve of his retirement. He sounded a defiant, if candid note. His union was effective he said, "not because we care about children, and it is not because we have a vision of a great public school for every child. NEA and its affiliates are effective advocates because we have power. And we have power because there are more than 3.2 million people who are willing to pay us hundreds of millions of dollars in dues each year because they believe that we are the unions that can most effectively represent them . . . protect their rights and advance their interests. . . . When all is said and done," he continued, "NEA and its affiliates must never lose sight of the fact that they are unions, and what unions do first and foremost is represent their members." The crowd stood and cheered.

The Toledo Example

One of the cities covered in the New Teacher Project report was Toledo, the Ohio city that Shanker had singled out for praise in 1985 for instituting a peer review program under which senior teachers evaluated their colleagues and targeted some for retraining or even dismissal. In 2011, Weingarten would remind me of the Toledo program, citing it as an example of the kinds of reforms that she and other enlightened union leaders supported. Toledo, she told me, "still weeds out bad teachers more aggressively than anything Joel Klein has ever suggested."

Actually, it seems to be more an example of how simple, checkable facts are sometimes scarce in the education reform debate.

Weingarten's Toledo claim was partially backed up by a report on the website of the Project on the Next Generation of Teachers run by the Harvard Graduate School of Education (although it had nothing to do with Harvard education professor Tom Kane). For years, the Harvard-branded website had extolled the virtues of the program and reported that it produced higher rates of dismissals than systems where school management evaluated teachers. That in turn led to the Toledo program's being cited by think tanks and others in the education community as a model of reform.

However, in *The Widget Effect* Toledo was reported to have had just one tenured teacher dismissed during the two years studied, while the Toledo school system and the Harvard website had routinely reported numbers for that category that were significantly higher and were the basis for the claim that the union's peer review system was rigorously effective. In fact, Weingarten had told me that Harvard had done independent studies of the program confirming how rigorous it was.

When *The Widget Effect* was published with its Toledo numbers, Weingarten and the AFT, as well as the Toledo local unit of the AFT, immediately complained, citing the Harvard numbers. When Weisberg and New Teacher Project president Tim Daly responded to the complaints by trying to reconcile their numbers with Harvard's, they discovered that the Harvard numbers were based *not* on the Harvard researchers' having examined the actual personnel records, as the New Teacher Project had, but on the union's and the school system's self-reporting of the numbers to Harvard. The self-reporting had included, among other inaccuracies, the counting of substitute teachers who had quit or had no longer been offered assignments as "dismissals of tenured teachers."

Asked why she had not disclosed initially that the numbers were based on self-reporting rather than an examination of the actual records, Harvard professor Susan Johnson, who runs the research project, told me she thought that "would have been obvious, but I do remember asking one of my assistants to add that disclosure, which I guess never happened." Asked to name the assistant, she hung up.

Agreement in Pittsburgh

Toledo might have been a reform mirage. Pittsburgh wasn't. On July 1, 2009, a new contract went into effect between the Pittsburgh school system and the Pittsburgh Federation of Teachers. It included provisions for everything outlined in the Gates Foundation plan.

To be sure, a few of the details still had to be filled in for the performance-based compensation pieces, including, for example, exactly how teachers in subjects such as music or the arts, for which there were no standardized tests, would be evaluated. All of that had to be completed by July 1, 2011, when the compensation provisions of the contract would take effect. But the overall structure, including how different levels of compensation would be paid and how various levels of the new career ladder would work, had now all been ratified in detail.

As for the remaining issues, Jerri Lynn Lippert, the school system's chief academic officer, who oversees the negotiation and implementation of the Gates plan, told me that, if anything, the process has brought both sides closer. "Everyone is working in a totally friendly, collaborative way," she said. "Our folks come back from the [teacher/ school system] committees that are meeting on these issues and consistently report progress. . . . There is a lot of brain sweat here, but there is a real sense of common cause. We all really want Pittsburgh to be a leader."

Hillsborough County, Florida, seemed to be making the same progress. After the Gates grant was awarded, new issues came up that the two sides succeeded in resolving, sometimes after locking themselves in a room for hours. For example, as they focused on the details of the compensation tiers and career ladders they had agreed on in principle, superintendent MaryEllen Elia's people wanted a provision that any teacher judged unsatisfactory two years in a row would get moved down a peg in the tiers they had created, just as any teacher who did extraordinarily well two years in a row would move up. Union leader Jean Clements pressed successfully for it to take three bad years for a teacher to be moved down, but only two to be moved up. One of the school system's arguments for performance as opposed to seniority-based compensation was, as one Hillsborough official put it, "You don't pay Derek Jeter or Michael Jordan [in their early years] less than some veteran because they don't have as many years on the job." True, but you also don't typically knock a top athlete down after just two off seasons, Clements countered.

That these types of remaining details were being resolved, while the last ones—how to give merit pay to music teachers—seemed on their way to being hashed out, demonstrated how far the reform agenda had come. It seemed that private foundation investments were actually going to bring change. Could investments by a government bureaucracy also produce results?

The Opposite of Venture Capital

July 24, 2009, Washington, D.C.

Measured against other Washington bureaucracies, the Department of Education, with only one large building housing five thousand employees, is relatively small. In fact, it's the smallest cabinet-level federal agency.

That didn't stop the department from issuing 147 dense pages of regulations on July 24, 2009, to implement the two-and-half-page Race to the Top provision of the stimulus bill.

Following the passage of the bill, Schnur had helped Arne Duncan recruit Joanne Weiss, another member of his reform network, to run the program. Weiss's résumé was perfect. She had been the chief operating officer of the NewSchools Venture Fund, a San Francisco–based nonprofit venture capital group that pools money from wealthy for-profit venture capitalists (such as John Doerr, the founder of Silicon Valley's Kleiner Perkins Caufield & Byers) who want to support school reform. Over the years, the fund had raised hundreds of millions of dollars and poured it into some of the best charter school networks, including KIPP, Green Dot, Aspire, and Harlem Success. Additional millions had gone to ventures such as Sarah Usdin's New Schools for New Orleans.

Weiss's job had been to vet those investments and oversee a staff that provided advice, support, and even recruiting help to the organizations that got the money.

The logic of Schnur's choosing Weiss was impeccable: The person who had vetted education investments for the world's toughest moneymen and then made sure those investments actually performed was now going to pick the state reform plans that seemed most likely to pay off.

The problem is that investing venture capital and giving government grants might as well be on two different planets. On the government grant-giving planet, Weiss wasn't going to get to vet anything herself.

Venture capitalists can make funding decisions based on a variety of factors: how they perceive a business's competitive environment, the size of its potential market, whether the technology will work, what the operating and capital costs are likely to be, and the record of the entrepreneurs who are going to run it, as well as whether these entrepreneurs display the right mix of discipline and passion when they make their pitch for the money. Much of that calculus ultimately comes down to gut decisions, or at least decisions not based wholly on spreadsheets and other paperwork. Maybe the guy making the presentation lights up the room with his passion. Perhaps a good friend at another firm says he is investing, too. Or maybe the group members sitting around the table sense, based on something they've read or heard from a friend who they think has a great gut, that demand for this product may be approaching the proverbial tipping point.

Similarly, Schnur, Duncan, and Weiss might have been able to sit in a room before any state filed an application and easily list the ones to whom they thought dispensing their $5 billion education reform kitty would produce the best return. But when it comes to competition for the public treasure, those kinds of intuitive decisions by political appointees, or even civil servants, aren't allowed, because they could also mean money dispensed to political cronies or to recipients who paid bribes or promised jobs to family members. The process has to be transparent and conducted on a rigidly regulated playing field, with the decisions made by disinterested "experts" who have no conflicts or potential conflicts of interest.

That Washington versus Silicon Valley dynamic is what produced the 147 pages of rigid rules for the contest, supplemented by thousands more pages of Department of Education restrictions governing how all department grants are decided.

To manage all that, Weiss had hired a handful of young aides who would work with her and larger teams of career staffers in the department's legal, grants, and elementary and secondary schools offices.

They basically had two jobs. First, they had to figure out the criteria for scoring the applications, such as what attributes would be looked for in a state's proposed reform plan and how much weight would be given to each. Second, they had to decide how to find experts to apply the criteria by giving each application a score.

The career people were there to enforce the rules governing how people like Weiss and her aides went about those two jobs.

Rules such as FACA.

FACA stands for the Federal Advisory Committee Act, a 1972 law that the federal General Services Administration website says is meant to "to ensure that advice by the various advisory committees formed over the years is objective and accessible to the public." That sounds right. After all, if the president appoints a committee of outsiders to advise on energy policy, wouldn't we want to know who its members are and require that its meetings be public?

When Duncan, Schnur, and Weiss began thinking about who would choose the winning entries, they quickly settled on using outside experts rather than the department's staff. This was not unprecedented for federal grant programs and certainly understandable for one involving this much money to be handed out based on the stimulus statute's vague standards.

Weiss envisioned that these outside vetters would engage in a collaborative process. A five-person team would review three or four states' proposals and come up with a preliminary rating but would then have a chance to discuss its relative merits with the teams looking at other states. Ultimately, they would end up with the whole group ranking all of the proposals from best to worst. That way, the scores they awarded would have context, rather than be determined by each team in isolation. This might prevent one team of easygoing vetters from awarding a higher score to a state than a team of tougher vetters would have awarded.

Given Weiss's venture capital experience, this was an obvious requirement. Venture firms typically meet once a week to discuss the various pitches that each partner has heard lately, and they compare them in order to decide how to dispense the firm's money.

That's where FACA butted in. The department's grant application lawyers ruled that those kinds of group conversations would transform the process. Instead of simply providing an "objective" score for each state against a rubric of requirements in the application, the vetters would now be making "subjective" judgments about the merits of one state plan versus another. That would turn the vetters into an "advisory committee," thereby opening the entire process to the public, requiring minutes to be taken, public notice to be given of each session, and otherwise turning the process into the equivalent of a town hall. There was a prolonged legal debate about it. Weiss lost.

The collaboration idea was scrapped. The teams would have to work in isolation, meaning states that drew a tough team were more likely to lose out to states that got lucky with a more generous team.

Then there was the question of who the vetters would be. Weiss and her staff decided early on that there would be five assigned to read each application, with each state's score being the average of the five vetters' scores.

Because Weiss and her staff expected thirty to forty states to apply and wanted each team to read three or four state applications (in order to provide at least some comparative context), they ended up seeking about sixty vetters. They got fifty-eight, each of whom was paid $5,000.

The regulations governing who the vetters could be were encyclopedic. To protect against conflicts of interest, Department of Education rules required that the fifty-eight could not only have *no* interest in the outcome of their decisions but also not even an *appearance* of a conflict, both in terms of financial interest and in terms of potential bias based on positions they might have taken on education issues. Screening for that became a ten-step process, organized around fourteen pages of rules and checklists. It involved thirty-five department employees in four separate checks for conflicts, carried out by personnel from three divisions of the department.

As it turned out, not even that was enough to satisfy the propriety police. A Government Accountability Office report would later criticize the department for its lax approach to choosing the vetters. The GAO complained that "the Department [of Education] did not perform a check of selected RTT [Race to the Top] peer reviewers against the General Services Administration's (GSA) Excluded Parties List System (EPLS) or adequately document formal approval of its peer reviewer roster prior to the beginning of the application review process."

Although it did not meet the GAO standards, the gauntlet that the vetters had to run pretty much eliminated people involved in operating school systems, those who were in any way active in Schnur's reform network, or those who had consulted for any state or local school systems. That left:

- Education foundation staff members, but not at places (like the Gates Foundation) that finance reform projects
- Think tank staffers, but not ones who had ever taken positions on the issues involved or were associated with think tanks that had taken such positions
- Education professors, but not professors (like Kane of Harvard) who had studied the reform initiatives being evaluated in the states' proposals
- Long-retired educators

The vetters were officially called "peer reviewers." Yet in terms of experience and knowledge, they were unlikely to be the peers of the school systems' leaders, like Paul Pastorek and Sarah Usdin in Louisiana, who would be framing their states' proposals.

Another rule required that the vetters could read only within the four corners of any proposal. Like jurors who must rely only on the evidence actually presented in court, they could not draw on any knowledge they had gained apart from reading the proposals they were judging. For example, if a vetter knew or had heard that a state was proposing to compensate teachers in a way that a state law did not allow (many states required lockstep, seniority-based compensation), he or she could not take that into account, nor could he or she assess whether existing union contracts would allow the states to do what they promised to do.

Worse, the department lawyers told Weiss that the people on her staff who would advise the vetters and monitor their deliberations could not read the proposals submitted by each of the states. There was another regulation that forbade them from doing this, Weiss was told, because that might make them biased in advising the vetters on how they should be doing their jobs.

Then there was the larger, more complicated issue of what would be required in the state applications.

Duncan, Schnur, and Weiss quickly made one threshold decision. Rather than offer vague suggestions about the reforms they
were looking for, they were going to be prescriptive. Extremely
prescriptive.

"We basically turned the application into a primer on education
reform," Weiss explains. "We plugged into a list of things that reform people out there wanted to do."

Working through the spring, sometimes pulling all-nighters,
Weiss and her staff produced draft after draft of different sections.
The drafts were then reviewed by Gordon at the Office of Management and Budget and by Schnur, and then by Duncan. They then
debated how much each factor would count in the overall score.

The result was a scoring system, totaling a maximum of five hundred points, that tracked the reform network's agenda with exqui-
site specificity, establishing six broad areas of reform, which were
then divided into nineteen subcategories, with each given a maximum point allocation depending on how important it was believed
to be in achieving real reform.

Although it was in nearly impenetrable language that reflected
all the cooks—including the lawyers—in the drafting kitchen, it
was a state-of-the-art blueprint for achieving the reformers' agenda.
It was unrelentingly prescriptive, requiring narratives, milestone
charts, timetables, and budgets specifying what the state had done
and was going to do to meet each of the reform goals. Also required,
importantly, in an appendix, were memoranda of understanding,
or MOUs, that the state had to get its school districts to sign proving their commitment to implement the state's plan if the state won.
There were boxes to check for which school districts and which
unions in which school districts had committed to the MOU.

At an average of two hundred to three hundred pages for the proposal and three hundred to five hundred pages for an appendix con-
taining information like the MOUs, each state's plan was typically
twice as long as this book.

The reformers loved how densely prescriptive the application was
(as did the army of education industry consultants who would be
retained to help the states make sense of it all). The winning plans
would need to have all the elements that groups like Democrats
for Education Reform had been pushing, and the elements of the
research and pilot projects that foundations, like Broad's and the

Gateses', had been financing. In fact, the race mirrored the four-venue contest Gates had just conducted, the one that Hillsborough County and Pittsburgh had won. Only it was the Gates contest on steroids.

The key categories for which the five hundred points would be allocated were:

- The states' plans for taking over failing schools and turning them around (including providing incentives so that the most effective teachers would want to work at those schools)
- The states' plans for improving curriculum standards
- The extent to which a state fostered a climate for innovation, which specifically included allowing charter schools to flourish
- Most important, the states' plan for creating data systems to track students' progress and then using the data so that teachers (and principals) could be compensated and promoted based in part on the data and be retrained and, when necessary, dismissed if they were found to be ineffective

"It's all about the talent," Duncan told me as the rules were being written. Thus, the highest number of points—138—would be awarded for a state's plans with regard to building data systems and using the data, plus rigorous classroom observations and other tools, to evaluate teachers and compensate, promote, or dismiss them accordingly.

When these point-by-point rules were issued on July 24, everyone suddenly knew how serious Duncan was.

To telegraph the point, several weeks before the rules were issued, Duncan had announced that no state would even be allowed to apply if it had a law on the books forbidding the linking of student test scores to individual teachers. "Someone told me about those firewall laws, and I said, 'You gotta be kidding me. Are you serious?'" Duncan recalled. "That was just a nonstarter."

This meant that if Wisconsin, California, and New York, where state legislators, at the behest of the teachers' unions, had passed laws putting up those firewalls between student data and teachers, did not repeal the laws by the January 19, 2010, deadline for applications, they need not apply.

Even before the July 24 release of the full rules package, the Wisconsin legislature had repealed its law because of the firewall disqualification. Now Duncan was staring down California and New York.

When Duncan held his July 24, 2009, press conference launching the Race and unveiling the rules, two things happened almost immediately.

First, everyone in education—state superintendents and school district leaders, union leaders like Weingarten of the AFT and Van Roekel of the NEA, reformers, Democratic and Republican politicians—was shocked at the specificity of the requirements, not to mention the demand for repeal of the firewall laws in the Democratic Party's two major strongholds, California and New York, as the uncompromising price of admission.

Second, the media soon became entranced by the contest aspects of the "race" in a way that not even Schnur had imagined. This phenomenon was buttressed by the release by Duncan's office of estimates, based on their relative student populations, of the total amount that each state might receive if it won the race. Suddenly, competing and winning became a way to plug each state's budget gaps. In fact, the potential winnings looked like a lot more than they really were.

For example, the press reported that New York stood to win $700 million. Indeed, Governor David Paterson quickly put receipt of that $700 million into his budget for the new year, where it went a long way toward plugging a $2 billion deficit. Aside from the fact that New York was by no means a sure winner, the rules of the Race were that the $700 million was to be doled out in equal parts over four years, and that half of it was to be given to local school districts. Half of $700 million is only $350 million, which is what the state would get to keep after distributions to school districts. A fourth of that, accounting for the fact that the grant was to be doled out over four years, is $87.5 million for that first year, barely 1 percent of New York State's budget.

Moreover, under the rules, that $87.5 million was actually supposed to be spent on new projects directed at implementing the state's Race to the Top proposal (such as building better data systems), not to fill a gap for expenses already budgeted. Nonetheless, most media reports on the lure of the Race would focus on how Paterson might get a $700 million windfall to plug that year's budget hole.

That kind of media attention was hardly restricted to New York. Across the country, local news stories in states that had little chance of winning an education reform contest—from South Dakota to Montana to Mississippi—carried reports, often with sports metaphors, of states "suiting up" for the race, a story line enhanced by the involvement of governors, who, after all, were the ones whose names would be attached to the contest applications. And, as in New York, both the politicians and the headline writers dramatically overstated the impact of the money at stake.

Indeed, through the summer and fall of 2009, Duncan's unveiling of the rules ignited such unprecedented hoopla around education reform that the issue suddenly became so hot that it was no longer the exclusive province of the reform network. In multiple forums and at multiple levels of government—town, city, state, federal—Americans became engaged in a rare substantive debate over a major political and policy issue. Even the American Enterprise Institute (AEI), a leading conservative think tank, was impressed by what the Obama team had done to elevate what was usually a Republican issue. AEI published a white paper that complimented the administration for raising the profile of these issues and reported that a search of the newspaper archives included in the Nexus database had found 222 references to "teacher tenure reform" in 2009 compared with 559 in all of the prior thirty-seven years.

Health care might have been topic A on Beltway talk shows, but everywhere else the education reform Race was on, with what would become forty states and the District of Columbia trying to outreform each other in time to submit a killer proposal by the January 19, 2010, deadline. The reform network across the country was now ready to seize the moment and take center stage helping to craft these plans. Bill and Melinda Gates similarly stepped up, doling out $250,000 to each of twenty-four states that their foundation decided were poised to submit the best plans. The money would enable these contestants to hire suddenly prosperous consultants to help craft their plans.

The pundits and editorial writers were on board, too. They were impressed by Duncan's rules for the contest—though some were skeptical that he would actually stick to his guns. They had seen this reform movie before. A month after the rules were announced, a *New York Times* editorial, sent by Tilson to his e-mail list, weighed in this way:

> The most important provision—the one that should be non-negotiable—requires states to show how student achievement will be taken into account when judging teacher performance. . . .
>
> Of course, those systems need to be sensible and fair. But the country will never get where it needs to be if we take the approach—as union leaders have sometimes done—that student test scores should be out of bounds when it comes to judging teacher effectiveness. That is an indefensible position. The unions can either help to create this system, or get left behind.
>
> In the past, the federal government talked a good game about requiring reform in exchange for federal dollars, then it caved when it came time to enforce the bargain. This time, Mr. Duncan has proposed using a closely calibrated evaluation process under which states get points for reforms they have made and points for changes they promise to make—as well as conditional financing that can be pulled back if the states fail to perform. Mr. Duncan should hold fast to that plan.

The unions were on the defensive to an extent unheard of since Al Shanker had won his first contract nearly fifty years earlier. Most Democratic governors, not to mention almost all Republicans, were suiting up for the race promoted by their Democratic president, looking for ways to fill their budget gaps and come out winners in what was now a media-intense contest. The unavoidable subtext was that they had to demonstrate their commitment to rolling back the protections their teachers' union supporters had come to take for granted.

That didn't mean the unions were going to roll over. As union officials pored over the fine print of the Race regulations, they came to realize just how "prescriptive" Duncan, Schnur, and Weiss had made their contest, then mounted a campaign to discredit it. On September 29, 2009, Weingarten would tell the *Washington Post*'s

Nick Anderson that now that she had examined the Race to the Top plan, "It looks like the only strategies they have are charter schools and measurement. That's Bush Three." The NEA called it a "disturbing federal intrusion. . . . We cannot support yet another layer of federal mandates that have little or no research base of success and that usurp state and local government's responsibilities for public education." It was at the state and local levels that the unions would now go to work, making sure that each state's proposed plans did not undermine all that they had won over the years. Among the key battlegrounds would be Michael Johnston's Colorado.

"Outcomes, Not Achievement"

December 9, 2009, Denver

From the moment he had taken his seat in the Colorado state senate in May, Michael Johnston was determined that there would be one issue on which this most junior of junior legislators could make his mark: Race to the Top. Johnston hadn't simply come to the senate as an ardent, seen-it-in-the-trenches education reformer. He also knew the Race goals cold, because he had worked on them, and he knew that they were intended to make legislatures like the one he had just joined step up.

Johnston immediately sketched out a plan for legislation that would require teachers to be measured for effectiveness, half by test scores and half by other rigorous processes, such as intense classroom observation. They would get four or maybe five rankings, ranging from noneffective to effective to outstanding. No teacher would get tenure until judged effective for at least three or maybe four years in a row, and a tenured teacher judged ineffective for two years in a row could be dismissed. Top-rated teachers would receive extra pay and move up to the rank of senior teacher or mentor. Also, teachers' effectiveness would be linked to the graduate schools they had attended so that the effectiveness of those schools, too, could be ranked.

Johnston thought he should at least start the process of drumming up support for the bill by trying some collaboration. On December 9, 2009, he met with officials of the Denver Classroom Teachers Association, an affiliate of the National Education Association. Although Weingarten's American Federation of Teachers was seen as being more moderate, or less completely hard-line, on reform issues, the NEA dominated teaching in Colorado, with some 38,000 members compared with 2,000 for Weingarten's Colorado affiliate. Besides, in 2009 the Denver unit of the state NEA had

agreed to a modified performance pay plan of its own and the NEA
had not interfered. So Johnston thought the local NEA was a good
place to start the conversation.

He and a member of his staff met with Henry Roman, the Denver union leader. Ever deferential and soft-spoken, the thirty-five-
year-old new senator asked Roman to outline his vision of a plan
for winning the Race to the Top. According to notes of the meeting
taken by a Johnston staffer, Roman insisted that any plan include
these core principles:

- "Teachers leading together in collaborative ways."
- "Teachers in charge of their own destiny and accountable to
  each other."

That did not seem like a Race-friendly approach. Worse, Roman
insisted that any change in the plan negotiated in Denver in 2009—
which included nothing about tenure reform and was at best a too-
soft version of pay based on performance—would happen, if ever,
only after that contract expired in 2012, long after the January 2010
deadline for submitting Race applications.

Johnston now knew he was going to get opposition from the NEA.
He had mentioned to Roman that he might send him a draft of what
he was working on when he had nailed down more details and gathered some co-sponsors. Now he wondered whether that might simply be tipping off an adversary.

However, Johnston did get something out of the meeting. Roman
had suggested that the bill should talk about "outcomes" rather than
"achievement," because performance seemed to imply that only testing was being considered in gauging a teacher's performance. Johnston liked that language tweak; it helped defuse the testing issue.

For the next several weeks leading up to the Race application
deadline, Johnston circulated his bill among legislators and the governor, Bill Ritter, a Democrat for whose campaign he had worked
in 2006 as an education adviser. He even met with and got the head
of the Colorado unit of Weingarten's AFT tentatively and quietly to
agree to sign on if the bill was introduced and some issues could be
worked out. That was significant symbolically, but without the far
larger NEA unit's support, Ritter and his staff refused to push the
bill.

However, Ritter did agree to appoint a commission to consider how to hammer out all the elements of Johnston's reform proposals so that they could propose legislation at some later time. And Ritter's staff did push through the part of Johnston's proposal that would link student performance through teachers and back to the education schools where the teachers had gotten their degrees, so that education schools would now be publicly accountable for the teachers they produced, even if the teachers weren't yet accountable. That piece of reform, the governor told Johnston, along with the establishment of his commission, plus the teacher performance pay contract negotiated in Denver, would be enough to carry the day. Johnston, who knew the criteria cold and the people in charge of implementing them, doubted it, but he was game to try.

Colorado was not the only state that would try to finesse the rules of the Race.

"Obfuscating the Issue . . . Fooling the Reviewers"

January 5, 2010, Washington, D.C.

On January 5, 2010, a staff person at the Council of the Great City Schools, a Washington lobbying group of urban school districts, sent an e-mail to people at school systems whom he knew to be believers in education reform, alerting them to something he was seeing in various drafts of the states' Race to the Top proposals. As required, the states were promising all kinds of reforms related to teacher compensation and accountability in their plans, which was great. However, there was a problem buried in the memoranda of understanding, or "MOUs," that were required to be attached as an appendix to the proposals. The MOU was supposed to outline the specifics of what each participating school district in the state would be responsible for doing. And, to ensure that the commitments were real, the head of the school district *and* the relevant local union leader were asked to sign it.

The staffer's e-mail alert said that he had heard that many states had inserted a clause in the MOUs that matter-of-factly stated that everything in the MOU was subject to, and would be superseded by, any existing collective-bargaining agreements. In other words, if the union contract required seniority-based compensation or did not allow evaluations based on student test scores, then everything promised in the proposal was one big never-mind.

The problem was that the people vetting these proposals would have no way of knowing this, because, under the rules, even if they were inclined to read through all the material in the appendixes and saw these escape clauses, they were not allowed to read the collective-bargaining agreements or anything else not submitted in the proposal.

"It appears that various states have structured their proposals . . .

to obfuscate the issue and possibly fool the grant reviewers," the e-mail warned. "I believe this entire area is a moving target with many state teacher unions attempting to get wiggle room ... in order to protect their CBA [collective-bargaining agreement] positions," the e-mail concluded.

The next day another memo circulating among the same group attached an Excel spreadsheet quoting the language being buried in the plans of more than a dozen states in order to demonstrate what was going on. The spreadsheet quoted the different varieties of weasel words proliferating across the country.

Two days later, a memo circulated among Joel Klein's staff, who had just read a draft of the New York State Department of Education Race to the Top proposal. It was titled "The Failed Promise of New York State's Race to the Top Application" and listed places where the application attempted exactly the kind of "wiggle room" the concerned Washington staff aide had spotlighted. For example, under the all-important "Great Teachers and Great Leaders" section of the application, which was all about teacher accountability, it cited this excerpt: "Promise: develop teacher ... evaluation and compensation systems, which will include annual evaluations using various measures including student achievement and/or growth data, *consistent with collective bargaining agreements*" (emphasis added).

Of course, the union's collective-bargaining agreements in New York City and throughout the state prohibited all of that.

Joel Klein read all of this and began to think the Race to the Top might become a farce.

The Race rules put a premium on a commitment by a state's school districts, especially the largest ones, to the work plan envisioned in the application. The memo sent to Klein and others on his staff argued that the plan was a charade and that Klein should not sign on to it. Klein agreed.

Klein's not participating would be mortally embarrassing, but it was the least of the state's problems as it hurried to prepare its Race application.

A Shriek on Park Avenue

*January 16, 2010, an apartment on
Park Avenue in New York City*

The person in charge of preparing New York State's Race to the Top proposal was John King, the senior deputy commissioner of the state Education Department. King is not the kind of person one would expect to find in a high position in New York's education department. It is a notoriously byzantine bureaucracy that made the place Joel Klein inherited at 110 Livingston Street look like a Silicon Valley start-up.

Schooled in Brooklyn (his father was the first African-American principal of a Brooklyn school) and a graduate of Harvard College and Yale Law School, King was a founder of the Roxbury Preparatory Charter School in Massachusetts. He then became managing director of the highly regarded Uncommon Schools charter network, and was holding that position when, amid lots of competition, he impressed the crowd as one of the most compelling speakers at the DFER forum at the 2008 Democratic convention in Denver.

King was now working for David Steiner, the state education commissioner. Steiner, a longtime academic and expert in curricula standards, has a résumé and a subdued personality that are the opposite of King's. Steiner's education department was largely under the control of the legislature, which was in turn controlled by the teachers' union stalwart protector, Assembly Speaker Sheldon Silver. Silver's legislature appoints the state Board of Regents, which oversees the department.

"Navigating all of the competing interests in New York is a lot different than any other job I have had," King told me, referring to his work putting together the Race to the Top application. With "all of the limits we had with the laws and collective-bargaining agreements in place and the political reality of the legislature," preparing New York's application "was difficult and frustrating."

One frustration centered on charter schools.

Although other reform criteria counted for much more, the contest measured a state's amenability to charters, allocating up to 38 of the 500 points to charter-friendly states. With New York State now twelve charters away from hitting its 2007 limit of two hundred (and likely to hit it with new charters to be issued in 2010), not lifting the cap threatened the state's application.

So King was pushing for the change, as was Merryl Tisch, the chancellor of the Board of Regents. Tisch is a knowledgeable and well-connected educator and part of the billionaire Tisch family that controls the Loews Corporation. She had been appointed by Speaker Silver but was sympathetic to the reformers and had been instrumental in bringing in King as the de facto chief operating officer of the state's education department.

At about midnight on Saturday, January 16, Tisch answered the phone in her apartment on Park Avenue and let out an ear-splitting shriek. She recalls that her husband, James, who is the chief executive of Loews, thought someone must have died. What Merryl Tisch was reacting to was a draft of a bill concerning charters that had just been e-mailed around by Silver's state assembly staff. The draft superseded a bill that the reformers, as well as Governor David Paterson (who had been an early ally of Democrats for Education Reform), thought was going to be a simple lift of the cap.

In fact, the first paragraphs seemed to do just that. However as with what the unions and Silver had tried during the 2007 cap-lift fight, a closer reading revealed so many conditions, or "poison pills," imposed on new charters that it would now become much harder to start charters than it was under the current law.

Among those conditions was a requirement that before any charters could co-locate in a public school building, the parents in the public school would have to approve by a majority vote the taking of their space. "This was a nonstarter. If you have an extra bedroom in your house because a child moved out, would you ever vote to allow someone else to move in?" asked John White, one of Joel Klein's deputies (and another TFA alum) who handled the co-locations. "The union, with ACORN and the Working Families Party, will always be able to get out that vote," he added.

Another provision stated that the authority to grant charters would now rest solely with state Education Department, whose

Board of Regents was controlled by Silver. That authority was now shared with the state university's well-established Charter Review Board and with Klein, who had a strong advisory role in approving New York City charters.

With three days left before New York's application was due, it was clear that Silver and the Democrats were choosing to side with the union over winning what the media had headlined was a $700 million windfall that the race offered Tisch's financially strapped state. Thus, her shriek.

Tisch struggled in the final hours to reach a compromise. She urged Klein to give up on co-location and agree to allow a cap on charters in what were called "certain communities" where charters were proliferating. This meant Harlem and a few other areas, such as parts of Brooklyn and Albany. These were places where the number of parents—and, therefore, voters—with children in charter schools was fast approaching critical mass. "If Joel would give up on co-location and look at doing something on saturation, it would sure ease all the tension," Tisch told me as the deadline neared. "The charters are supported by billionaires. Let them buy buildings."

Klein refused. "Co-location is why charters are able to exist," he explained when I asked about Tisch's compromise suggestion. "Buying and outfitting a new space for a school would cost the charters $20 million to $40 million each in New York, which the law does not allow the city to pay for, even if we could, which we can't. . . . That's billions of dollars for just two hundred more charters. . . . This is space that we demonstrate is not being used. But," he added, "if Merryl and Jimmy [Tisch] want to buy some buildings, that would be great."

Moreover, in Klein's view, a saturation cap meant not only taking parent choice away from parents in the communities that needed it the most but also holding down exactly the political movement he was trying to build: parents who understood that charter schools could deliver real education to their children.

"If it's something someone doesn't agree with, they call it a poison pill," Sheldon Silver told me, adding that he "supports charters, but to me the real need remains supporting public education with the resources to lower class size."

• • •

There would be no deal. When Republicans in the evenly divided state senate, backed by crucial support from two stalwart DFER Democrats, refused to pass the Silver version of the bill with all of its conditions, any prospect of lifting the cap was dead. The two sides stopped negotiating the day before New York's application was due.

The last-minute crisis over the charter cap—which, again, counted for only 38 of the 500 race points—grabbed headlines all over New York, with the union being blamed for sabotaging the state's effort to get a fast $700 million from Washington. Yet the state went ahead with its application—a 902-page submission that had problems far beyond the unremoved charter cap.

For starters, New York's application featured comic over-statements—New York has been recognized for its "ability to move poor performing teachers from the classroom," for example—that even the most clueless vetter was unlikely to believe. Also, the document was so much the product of a bureaucracy that not even King had gotten control of that, as the *New York Post* gleefully reported, the state's proposed budget for its $700 million grant listed $200,000 worth of new furniture, including fifteen "executive desks" costing $3,000 each and twenty-four "executive chairs" costing $550.

More important, the proposal contained significant omissions and misstatements, all of which were the product of King's game effort to finesse the grip the unions had on public education in his state. Much of it had to do with exactly what had been forecast in that earlier memo warning of the applicants' plans to bury a "subject to collective-bargaining agreements" condition in all of its promises.

The states had been instructed to check boxes on a grid to signal which of their local school systems had signed those memoranda of understanding, or MOUs, agreeing with the state to implement each of the many initiatives their plans promised if the state got the Race money. To make this expression of commitment unambiguous, the application included the exact MOU that was to be signed. That was part of the 147 pages of regulations.

The contest instructions also stated that if the wording of the MOU for any local school system was changed to make it "conditional," the box should *not* be checked.

New York checked all the boxes for all of its school districts for all of the initiatives on the grid it submitted. However, in the 559-page appendix to its 343-page application, New York included the MOU that actually had been signed by all of its school districts. It was worded almost exactly like the federal government's MOU—except that after reciting everything that would be done to link student tests to teacher evaluations, and to compensate teachers and move them up on a career ladder according to those evaluations, the New York MOU inserted this qualifier: "consistent with any applicable collective-bargaining requirements." Then for good measure, at the end of the entire MOU this sentence was added to cover everything: "Nothing in this MOU shall be construed to override any applicable state or local collective-bargaining requirements."

Of course the UFT's collective-bargaining agreements in New York City, as well as union contracts in much of the rest of the state, explicitly prohibited exactly the reforms promised in the application. Changing that was the point of Duncan's contest.

When I asked Merryl Tisch about this, the New York State Regents chancellor pointed to another added sentence, in which each school system and the union agree to negotiate any necessary contract changes in "good faith."

That's the "way we solved that," she told me.

"Right," Klein said when told of Tisch's explanation. "That's like telling a woman you'll marry her in the morning."

Moreover, it turns out that Michael Mulgrew, who succeeded Weingarten as head of the city's UFT after she went to Washington to run the AFT, refused to sign even that altered MOU.

On January 17 and 18 (the application deadline was January 19), there were a series of intense negotiations between Mulgrew's staff and Klein's staff and then Mulgrew and Klein, in which Mulgrew seemed to have yielded and agreed to an adequate teacher evaluation regimen. Then, just as the applications were due in Washington, Mulgrew submitted to Klein a completely redone version of the MOU that outlined a teacher evaluation program that would be totally voluntary and that contained a provision declaring that "student performance data shall not be a factor in decisions regarding individual teacher compensation."

"If this weren't so tragic it would be funny," Klein e-mailed his top aides after he saw the new Mulgrew draft. "In addition to gutting teacher eval, they want to get control of school closures, including an immediate moratorium," he added, referring to his key initiative of closing failing schools and reconstituting them as mini-schools under the management of groups like New Visions. Mulgrew, out of the blue, had apparently proposed to eliminate that as part of the deal. "Honestly, I don't know whether to laugh or cry," Klein wrote.

A few weeks later, I asked Mulgrew over breakfast, "If Arne Duncan was sitting here with a check ready to give to New York, and he said he'd give it to you if you promise to allow test scores to be tied to compensation, would you make the promise?"

"No. I'd tell him we have to negotiate with the guy up the street," Mulgrew replied, referring to Klein, "to come up with a fair system first. But I could not promise him that we could."

"Would you promise to support a repeal of the state law requiring layoffs to be done only on the basis of seniority?" I asked, referring to another controversial issue and potential factor in the Race scoring.

"No, that's the law," he said.

Nonetheless, the box on the state's application signifying the UFT's agreement to the standard MOU that pledged to support everything the state was promising was checked. Under the juror-like rules governing their review process, the vetters would have no way to test the veracity of those checked boxes.

Klein says he didn't want to sign the MOU, because the caveats made it meaningless, but he ultimately went along so as not to "seem like a spoilsport."

It was Steiner, as commissioner of the New York State Department of Education, who signed the application attesting to its accuracy.

The former dean of the Hunter College School of Education in New York, Steiner seemed at sea dealing with the maelstrom of New York education politics whenever I spoke with him. He offered no explanation for why the boxes were checked, other than that his staff had subsequently looked at other applications and found that Florida, Massachusetts, Pennsylvania, and Illinois also checked the boxes, "based," he said, "on a future commitment to collectively bargain." He's right. California did the same thing.

"We made the attorney general of each state sign an assurance that everything in the application was accurate," Joanne Weiss told me when I asked about all the boxes that were checked inaccurately to indicate school district and union commitments to implement the plans in the proposals. Actually, the regulations that Weiss and her team drafted required only that the attorneys general certify that any statements made in the application *about existing state law* were accurate, a point emphasized by a spokesman for then–New York State attorney general Andrew Cuomo when I asked about New York's inaccurately checked boxes.

Weiss also said that no one in her office checked the accuracy of the assurances, as conveyed by the checked boxes, before the awards were announced. One factor the vetters were allowed to consider, which counted for up to 45 of the 500 points, was the extent of "stakeholder" buy-in demonstrated by the states. In practice, this meant the degree to which the school districts as well as the unions across a state signed on to the MOUs. This meant, perversely, that a state that had gotten all of its unions to sign on to an MOU that really didn't obligate the teachers to do anything new—because in the small print the MOU promised not to override any current collective-bargaining agreement—could score higher than a state that had laws or regulations allowing it to do what it needed to do to meet the Race's requirements, regardless of whether the unions agreed and signed the MOUs.

By now many states other than New York had done a lot to clean up their acts in advance of their Race applications. In the first week in January, the California legislature had convened to repeal its "firewall" law not allowing test scores to be linked to teachers.* California also passed a unique "parent trigger" law, allowing a majority of the parents at any school defined by No Child Left Behind to be failing to vote to have the school turned into a charter school.

Michigan, the cradle of American unionism, passed laws lifting its cap on charter schools, tying test scores to teacher evaluations, and allowing the state to take over persistently failing schools. "This

---

* New York did not repeal its firewall law but argued that this was unnecessary because the law was due to expire in July 2011.

is a game changer forever," the Michigan education superintendent told the Associated Press.

In all, while most of American domestic political debate through 2009 was focused on the war over health-care legislation, thirty-four states would make important changes in their education laws or regulations in response to the Race; this was an unprecedented wave of reform as well as an unprecedented demonstration of federal leverage. The reform network—TFA alums, DFER members, Schnur's other contacts—was involved in drafting or pushing most of those changes across the country. Tilson's now almost daily e-mails could hardly keep up with all the action.

Nor could Randi Weingarten keep up with all the fires she was trying to put out.

The Feinberg Gambit

January 12, 2010, Washington, D.C.

On January 12, 2010, Randi Weingarten chose Washington's National Press Club to make what an American Federation of Teachers press release billed as an unveiling of "New Approaches to Teacher Evaluation and Labor-Management Relationships."

The centerpiece of the speech was dramatic. Weingarten announced that she had hired Kenneth Feinberg to devise a fair and streamlined process to handle cases in which school districts wanted to dismiss tenured teachers. In Washington, Feinberg had become known as the master mediator of excruciating dilemmas. He had successfully run the September 11 Victim Compensation Fund for the George W. Bush administration and then had been assigned by the Obama administration to overhaul compensation plans for executives at the bailed-out banks. He would soon be appointed to handle claims from victims of the Gulf oil spill. Weingarten's obvious message was that hiring Ken Feinberg meant that she meant business. Yet by equating the issue of removing the worst teachers from the classroom with dilemmas such as how much money to award different victims of the 9/11 attacks (should the family of a fallen stockbroker get more than the family of a janitor?), Weingarten was also elevating what the reformers thought was a simple issue.

Less than three weeks later, Weingarten deployed Feinberg in what became an unforgettable media appearance that epitomized her disarming willingness to engage when confronted with even the most hostile audience. Weingarten appeared on the MSNBC show *Morning Joe*, which, amid all the activity surrounding the Race, had taken up education reform as a pet cause. She was brought on following the replaying of a segment aired the week before with Deborah Kenny, the founder of the successful Harlem Village Academy charter network, and recording artist John Legend, who is a Harlem Village board member and passionate education reformer.

Host Joe Scarborough began the chat with Weingarten by recounting how impressed he was when he had visited one of Kenny's schools. He rattled off the school's test score statistics. Then he read from a column by *Time*'s Joe Klein blasting the teachers' union for sabotaging the New York Race to the Top application, and, particularly its sandbagging of the charter cap raise. Weingarten, as if entranced by a media coach who had told her to smile and accentuate the positive no matter what, sat there calmly, as if chatting about the weather. Asked about the poison pills in the charter bill the union had promoted, she said that the union had tried to lift the cap and that she herself ran a charter school.

The most memorable moment was when Carl Bernstein, of Woodward and Bernstein fame, prefaced his remarks by saying he was the son of a union man, then, making no effort to hide his contempt, asked her why teachers' unions were held in "such disregard. . . . The perception is that you all over the years have put job security in front of the welfare of kids." Was everybody wrong about how they were blocking more charter schools and other reforms, such as lifting tenure protections for bad teachers? he asked angrily.

Weingarten, still smiling and deploying her trademark hand gestures (the favorite being cradling her fingers into a pyramid), replied that the economy had made everyone unhappy and "everybody really wants to make sure we help all of our kids." Then she pulled her ace. Saying that she, too, favored reform of the tenure system, she declared that "no other than Ken Feinberg, who's known to really solve the problems of America" had been retained by her to work on the problem of creating a process for dealing with accused teachers. As the barrage continued, Weingarten referred again and again to the "overhaul" of the tenure process she now had Feinberg working on.

About six weeks later, I had dinner with Feinberg, about whom I had written extensively in covering his prior assignments. When I asked how he was going about attacking the problem of ineffective teachers, he seemed dumbfounded. His assignment, he explained, was only to come up with a suggested plan for dealing with teachers indicted for crimes or accused of other serious misconduct. Should they be kept on the payroll while their criminal charges were pending, and if so, how long? His job had nothing to do with a process for adjudicating a principal's charge of incompetence, which was obviously the larger, harder issue. A year later, Weingarten would announce the results of Feinberg's study. His eleven-page memo, for which he was paid $75,000, dealt only with outlining a new timetable for a process for removing teachers indicted for crimes or accused of sexual improprieties or striking a student.

Weingarten thought that the media backlash against her and her union—induced by all the activity surrounding the Race, such as the fight over the charter cap in the media capital of the world—had reached a peak with that *Morning Joe* inquisition. "I remember it as very depressing, a new low," she would later tell me. "I mean, Carl Bernstein was treating me like some kind of Nixon villain."

Weingarten's media troubles were just beginning. She was about to become a Hollywood villain.

School Reform:
The Movie

A week before Weingarten's *Morning Joe* appearance, a documentary called *Waiting for Superman* was previewed in advance of a fall release at the Sundance Film Festival, the annual showcase for independent movies in Park City, Utah, founded by Robert Redford. It was written and directed by Davis Guggenheim and produced by Lesley Chilcott. Guggenheim and Chilcott had made big names for themselves with *An Inconvenient Truth,* the global-warming manifesto featuring former vice president Al Gore. Guggenheim had also directed pilot episodes of the television series *The Unit* and *Melrose Place,* as well as the biographical movie about Barack Obama shown at the Democratic National Convention.

Guggenheim and Chilcott had been working on *Waiting for Superman* since the spring of 2008, when Jeffrey Skoll, the founder of Participant Media, had asked them to think about doing an education reform documentary. Skoll, whose mother was a schoolteacher, was the first employee and later president of eBay. In 2004, he dedicated a substantial portion of his haul from eBay stock options to start Participant as a vehicle to fund movies that he believes have an important social purpose and might also make money. Participant had provided seed money for *An Inconvenient Truth.*

Guggenheim had initially been wary of Skoll's idea because he had done a documentary in 2001 about schoolteachers that few people had watched, in part because it had premiered on public television five days after the September 11 terrorist attacks. However, Guggenheim started to warm to the project as he began to think about the public schools he drove by every day in Los Angeles on his way to dropping his kids off at their private school. Why was a liberal like him keeping his children out of the schools everyone else had to go to? Chilcott, who had worked as a teacher in Japan for a few years after college, persuaded her partner that they should at least investigate the possibility.

Luckily for them, one of the first people they met as they explored the idea was Geoffrey Canada. Canada is the magnetic founder of the Harlem Children's Zone, which combines charter schools with wraparound social services (such as advice for new mothers and preschool education programs) in a part of Harlem that Canada has designated as his target community. A Harvard Education School graduate, Canada is so articulate, so smart, so impassioned that he could make a movie about actuaries come alive. "He blew us away," Chilcott recalls.

So did Michelle Rhee, one of the next people Guggenheim and Chilcott consulted. Because she is almost always unconcerned with filtering what she says, Rhee is a sound bite machine.

As the lure of these characters began to get Chilcott and Guggenheim hooked, they happened to read a May 25, 2008, op-ed column by the *New York Times*'s Thomas Friedman, in which he described a scene from a lottery being held at the SEED charter school in Baltimore. Eighty boys and girls were to be chosen for places at the school from among three hundred applicants. It all depended on whether their numbers, written on Ping-Pong balls rolling around a bingo cage, were picked from the cage.

"It was impossible to watch all those balls tumbling around inside the cage and not see them as the people in that room tumbling around inside, waiting to see who would be the lucky one to slide out and be blessed," Friedman wrote. "There's something wrong when so much of an American child's future is riding on the bounce of a Ping-Pong ball."

Friedman had introduced his column this way: "Every once in a while as a journalist you see a scene that grips you and will not let go." Chilcott and Guggenheim had the same reaction. Now they had a story line. They would follow families entering a charter lottery and tell the stories of the winners and losers.

"I always look for a personal way to tell a story," Guggenheim says. "No matter how abstract or obtuse it got, I knew I could always cut back to those kids and their families."

As they moved ahead with their filming, they found that they actually had two story lines. First, was the lottery, which Guggenheim says he called "Other People's Children" to remind him of his challenge in getting adults like him to think about children, unlike his own, who had no choice but the failing public schools. Second, there were all the eye-opening facts about America's failing school systems and the causes of their failure. The more they read and the more they talked to people like Harvard's Tom Kane, or Canada and Rhee, the more they felt compelled to lay all this out somehow. Guggenheim called that second story "The Folly of the Adults" to underscore the theme, he says, that "the system worked for the adults but not the kids."

That second story line started to become its own, second documentary featuring animated characters and graphics to illustrate student performance comparisons between the United States and other countries, how class size did not affect student outcomes, or how principals passed off bad teachers to other principals because the tenure system prevented them from being fired.*

It was as they were gathering the material that they came up with the movie's title. Guggenheim and Chilcott had been stunned that their researchers had not been able to find a single book that spelled out exactly what it takes to be a good teacher. "It amazed me that no one seemed to know what the formula was, even though people like Kane knew that there definitely were good teachers and bad teachers," Chilcott recalls. One day they asked Canada about that, and he said that great teaching is not magic but hard work, attention to detail, experience, and maintaining high expectations for kids for whom the expectations have always been low. When he was a kid living in the Bronx, Canada continued, he always dreamed that Superman would come and carry him off to a better life. "Well, there's no waiting for Superman in the real world," he explained.

---

* The producers picked up a version of the phrase—"passing the lemons"—coined by Lombardi, the Queens middle school principal, while interviewing former Milwaukee schools superintendent and Marquette University education professor Howard Fuller. Fuller referred to it as the "Dance of the Lemons." So they showed animated lemons jumping from one schoolhouse to another.

In the fall of 2009, Guggenheim and Chilcott began combining the two story lines—the lottery families and the broader case for education reform—into one movie. As they were finishing their first cut, they received word that they had been invited to show the film at Sundance.

Another education reformer they had interviewed earlier in the fall had been Bill Gates, who had surprised them with his mastery of all the data and how swept up he was in the issues. So they decided to add some buzz to their presentation by inviting Gates to join them and Geoffrey Canada on the stage following the Sundance screening for a panel discussion with the audience.

Waiting for Superman became the talk of Sundance. In fact, after screening it in advance, Paramount Pictures announced the day Sundance opened that it had bought rights to distribute the movie. On the last day, it was announced that the movie had been voted the Audience Award for best documentary.

The movie's family interviews and lottery scenes, shot in Washington, Los Angeles, Baltimore, and New York (including Harlem Success), were every bit as moving as Thomas Friedman had found them. And Canada and Rhee were as riveting on film as they had been when Guggenheim and Chilcott had met them. On camera, Rhee sat back in a chair in her office and said, "Forty-six thousand kids are counting on you, and most them are getting a really crappy education."

Chilcott's and Guggenheim's use of the "animated facts" turned spinach into ice cream, providing as digestible an overlay of the dry scholarship and bureaucratic dynamics of education policy as any movie could hope for, while the scenes of union-sponsored ACORN troops protesting the expansion of charters at co-located sites in New York created an irresistible good guys/bad guys contrast.

And then there was Weingarten. Chilcott and Guggenheim were thrilled (and amazed) when the AFT gave them the right to use footage the union had taped of her giving a rousing speech to a union audience attacking those who said the union was blocking reform. It was an over-the-top stem-winder, during which the camera panned in on her almost spitting out her words. Weingarten came off in the film as "something of a foaming satanic beast," a reviewer for *Variety* wrote.

The much more hard-line Van Roekel of the NEA, who is a bore as a speaker, didn't make it into the movie.

The final touch was a great sound track that featured a song at the end, John Legend's "Shine": "Let them [these beautiful minds] shine. Let them shine on."

In all, it was a relentlessly compelling case for the reform argument, a masterful mix of fact and emotion.

The movie was set for a fall rollout through Paramount, and in the months preceding it, the studio would screen it for select "opinion leader" audiences across the country to build buzz. In April, after they had made some more edits, Guggenheim and Chilcott screened it for Randi Weingarten. "I was shocked by the way it demonizes teachers," she told me. That, along with the producers' failure to show places like Toledo and Pittsburgh where the union was promoting reform, would be her refrain as she framed a public relations campaign against the movie. Guggenheim and Chilcott, of course, maintained that they might have been critical of the union, but not of teachers.

As always, Weingarten tried to bear-hug her adversaries. She had lunch with the producers after she saw the film and asked them if the movie was now completed or if she could make some suggestions. She backed off immediately when they said it was indeed finished. Their lunch continued, with Weingarten chiding them for their lack of perspective, but expressing sorrow, never anger. She ended up appearing with them on panels to discuss the movie and would even write her own chapter for a companion book they published when the movie was released. In it, she praised the movie lightly, saying the "challenges it laid bare hit home so powerfully," while regretting that it didn't include the good work so many union teachers do or cover the reform efforts the union has been involved in. She mostly wrote about how collaboration is necessary for reform to work.

Bill Gates was so enthusiastic about *Waiting for Superman* that the Gates Foundation gave a $2 million grant to Participant Media, which, according to the grant document, was meant "to execute a social action campaign that will complement Paramount's marketing campaign." The money financed, among other projects, a website urging people to "take action" by writing elected officials and others to demand school reform. Gates made the funding decision long after the movie was completed, and he had no role in the movie's content, according to him and the producers. Eli Broad's foundation also chipped in to help promote the movie.

Meantime, another drama was playing out in Rhode Island.

Firing Everyone

In January 2010, reform-minded Rhode Island schools superintendent Deborah Gist, a veteran educator who had been in the job six months, decided that she had to do something about one of her state's worst high schools. Gist, a graduate of the Broad Foundation Superintendents Academy, declared Central Falls High School—which had graduation rates of below 50 percent, and where 7 percent of eleventh graders were doing math at grade level—a failing school. Under the No Child Left Behind requirements, this meant that the school district had to execute one of four types of turn-around plans: closing the school and dispersing the students, closing the school and turning it into a charter, choosing a "reform" model of removing the principal and firing all the teachers, or trying a "transformation" alternative that would force radical change at the school but preserve the teaching staff.

By early February, Central Falls district superintendent Frances Gallo had decided to try the most moderate step—the transformation alternative. So she asked the teachers' union to agree to a longer school day with more training and more tutoring, but with no extra pay. When the union refused, Gallo said she would have to go to Plan B, the reform model, which meant all one hundred teachers and administrators would be fired.

The union still refused. So on February 12, Gallo announced that all of the teachers were fired, effective at the beginning of the next school year in September. "We're very confident that we are following both the state and federal laws very carefully," Gist, the state chief, said. "In fact, it's the expectation both in state and federal law that we take these steps."

The Central Falls local union is an affiliate of Weingarten's AFT, and Weingarten, who says she learned about the confrontation only as it was about to blow up, immediately stepped in to express her outrage that the teachers were being scapegoated. Doing something this disruptive was unfair to them and bad for their students, she said.

As the standoff continued, things for Weingarten turned from bad to worse. Speaking at a Washington event meant to highlight the stimulus funding being offered to school districts that develop turnaround plans for persistently failing schools, President Obama declared, "If a school continues to fail its students year after year after year, if it doesn't show signs of improvement, then there's got to be a sense of accountability. And that's what happened in Rhode Island last week."

In a chatty Q&A later in 2010 with Politico, the Washington political newspaper and website, Weingarten would be asked what her strongest body part was. She singled out her legs, because, she said, she's "always walking a tightrope."

At first read, that tightrope seemed to be about satisfying her union members while still giving in enough to the reformers to ease the pressure. Obama's sharp comments about Central Falls suggested a second tightrope she had been walking: pushing back on the Obama education agenda without criticizing the Democratic administration so much that there would be a complete rupture of the union's relationship with the Democrats. This typically took the form of rebuking the president's advisers or attacking a policy, such as Race to the Top, while never attacking the president by name.

With Obama's statement about Central Falls, Weingarten jumped off that tightrope. Obama's comments "do not reflect the reality on the ground," she told the *Washington Post*. "We know it is tempting for people in Washington to score political points by scapegoating teachers, but it does nothing to give our students and teachers the tools they need to succeed," she added in a written statement. She would later tell me that the Obama intervention in the Central Falls dispute was, along with *Waiting for Superman*, one of the low points of her career.

About eight weeks later, Weingarten was instrumental in negotiating a settlement at Central Falls, in which the teachers agreed to do the extra work for no extra pay.

"My Baby Is Reading"

February 22, 2010, PS 30, Harlem

At 5:30 in the evening on February 22, a brushfire in the battle over education reform played out in a packed, raucous gym at PS 30 on 128th Street in Harlem, which hundreds of folding chairs had transformed into an auditorium. Unlike the one in Rhode Island, this battle wasn't about getting union teachers to agree to do more or be fired. It was about having them work in the same building with teachers who had already agreed to do more.

Harlem Success Academy II, where Jessica Reid had taught first grade during the 2008–2009 school year, was growing out of the space it shared with another public school and had to move. Actually, it had needed to move the year before and was slated to go to another school that Klein had wanted to close, but the teachers' union had successfully sued to hold up the closure because the city had not submitted sufficient documentation to justify it.

Klein's relocation office had now targeted PS 30 and had documented that it had more than enough vacant space to accommodate Moskowitz's school. However, a hearing was still required to be held by a local Community Education Council, so that school officials could hear the community's views before giving their final approval, after which another hearing (scheduled two nights later) would be held by a citywide panel to sign off on all pending co-location decisions across the city.

By the time of this hearing on a cold February night, Klein and his team, not to mention the mayor, had spent nearly eight years unambiguously espousing and implementing a policy of encouraging successful charters and allowing them to co-locate in unused public school space. Yet just the setup of this event—the ordering of the speakers, who got to sit where, and even who got to post signs on the walls—provided a telling snapshot of how tenaciously the school's bureaucracy and the union to which it had been accustomed to answering were hanging on.

The Community Education Council was typically made up of parents in the traditional public schools. Most of the logistics were handled by members of this council, plus officials of the school district and the principal—all civil servants, and all understandably bothered by the prospect of Moskowitz taking some of their space and some of their children. They had called the meeting for 5:30, yet they had allowed the teachers' union to send supporters in early to fill the sign-up sheet for people who wanted to speak.

When parents from Harlem Success (or parents who hoped to win a lottery to get their children into the new spots opening up at Harlem Success) were allowed in, they ended up so far down the list that the first of their speakers wouldn't be heard until about 8:00. The union troops had also been allowed to hang banners: "HSA GO AWAY, WE DON'T NEED YOU," "PRIVATE DONATIONS: A WAY TO CONQUER US," "P.S. 30 SHOULD STAY." (No one was proposing to take away PS 30—only to use the space created by the reality that its enrollment was about a third less than it had had ten years before.)

Somehow, all of the anti-Harlem Success people had ended up with seats at the front of the room.

Although Moskowitz and one of her aides had managed to grab two chairs about five rows from the front, all of the Harlem Success parents, plus a contingent of Harlem Success teachers, were sitting in the back. Yet they were not hard to find. Most were wearing Harlem Success's signature orange T-shirts and hats, and most had banners or signs, which they had to hold up because they had not been allowed to post them. Among them was Jessica Reid.

Reid had started the new school year in August 2009, having moved from Harlem Success II (whose space needs were the subject of this hearing) to Harlem Success I, so that she could return to teaching the fifth grade. It wasn't just that Moskowitz wanted to put Reid with the older students whom Reid preferred teaching. The decision was more strategic than that. At the end of the fifth grade the following June, the students would be taking standardized tests whose scores would have to be submitted with Moskowitz's first application to renew her charter. Moskowitz wanted to ace the scores, and she thought that Reid—whom Moskowitz and other Harlem

Success supervisors had quickly identified as a star—could help make that happen.

Moskowitz might have been sitting quietly off by herself, but she had not been outdone by the union in planning for this event. The signs she and her teachers had suggested the parents display pulled no punches. "BAN POLS PROTECTING BAD SCHOOLS," one said. "RESPECT US. WE COUNT," another declared. "I ♥ PARENT CHOICE," said dozens of others.

And then there was the sign held up by one mother who told me she had composed it on her own: "MY BABY IS READING."

Many of the parents balanced their young Harlem Success children on their laps. One six-year-old was holding his own sign, which repeated "RESPECT US" and added a parenthetical comment below it: "I CAN READ THIS."

The boy's father, who said he worked as a porter in an apartment building and is a union member, was mystified that any parent would want to stop the expansion of a school like Harlem Success in his community. "Once they sit down and see the environment and see how these kids are improving, there is no way they would oppose this," he said, rocking his first grader on his lap.

Moving to the back of the auditorium, I began to see what Moskowitz had pulled off: Though one would not know it from the speakers' roster, the orange rows seemed to outnumber the others by about four or five to one.

At the front table, a local school district official began by reading the report from Klein's office that unambiguously detailed the availability of the space and charted how it would be divided so that both schools could operate smoothly. Although this document was ostensibly the topic of the meeting, the boos from the front rows pretty much drowned out the reader.

The report had been prepared by John White, the Klein deputy (and a TFA and Broad Superintendents Academy alum) in charge of, among other things, efforts to accommodate charters. He was leaning against a wall at the side of the auditorium unnoticed and unknown to those gathered to argue over his work.*

---

* In May 2011, White would leave New York to become the superintendent of the New Orleans Recovery School District.

The first speakers were orderly. They were children who said they attended PS 30. All were wearing beanies with a UFT logo. "PS 30 is a good school, and I don't want to see it taken away," said one. "The teachers and students here are like my family," another said. Maybe, but PS 30 ranked near the bottom third of all New York City elementary schools in student performance, while Harlem Success was at the top. Just 33 percent of PS 30 third graders were up to state standards in reading in the 2009–2010 school year, while 40 percent were proficient in math. Besides, no one was trying to "take away" PS 30.

Another child, reading from a note card, declared "Charter schools don't belong here. We don't need you." The front rows drowned the hall in whistles and cheers, while the orange T-shirts and hats in the back sat quietly. When I tried to ask one of the children who told her that her school was going to be taken away, I was blocked by her mother, who told me that she was a teacher at the school.

One contingent was sitting up front cheering, whistling, or booing whenever the other opponents of Harlem Success did. But they didn't seem to have their hearts in it, or, for that matter, to have much of a stake in the argument. They were all wearing hard hats from three construction union locals based in Queens. "I really don't have any views on this," a man wearing a yellow hard hat, with a Laborers Local 79 decal and American flag fixed on it, told me. "We were just sent here to give support to the union."

As parents from PS 30 followed the child speakers, the rhetoric was turned up. One parent got the front rows cheering by talking about the "invasion" backed by people "not from our community." A second parent attacked the "signs of the intruders. . . . You come in with your bright colors and try to move in here against our will."

Another launched a full-throated attack on Moskowitz because she is "not from this community." (Actually, she lives in Harlem.) This was followed by someone who said, "Trying to take our space is like asking for an extra pound of flesh." Cheers and whistles erupted from the front rows. Moskowitz didn't flinch, though the HSA teachers in the back, including Reid, looked at each other.

"The whole thing was so depressing," Reid would later recall. "And I think the Harlem Success parents were really embarrassed. This is their community."

Next up was a fiery speaker who seemed to want to use the event to launch some kind of campaign for local political office. In an argument that was hard to follow, he compared the decision that was going to be made tonight to *Brown v. Board of Education,* the Supreme Court decision outlawing school segregation, asserting— actually, screaming—that allowing Harlem Success to move in would reverse *Brown* because Harlem Success takes only "certain" students. (The hard-to-follow part was the idea that being chosen in a lottery is like being chosen on the basis of race, which is what *Brown* was all about.) "Gentrification is coming to our schools," he screamed. "Don't let them do this."

The other problem with his speech is that it dragged on for so long that even the pro-union timekeeper at the front table intervened. This caused the front rows to erupt in chants of "Let him speak," followed by efforts to grab the microphone from him and then for him. For a while the event became something of a Jerry Springer show.

It took about fifteen minutes for things to calm down and for the speeches to resume, and it took more than two hours after that for most of the Harlem Success speakers to get to speak, during which time they were routinely jeered.

The most articulate speaker on the union side was Brian Jones, thirty-two, who teaches drama and calls himself "a union activist." Jones represents some of what Weingarten had to contend with internally in walking her tightrope. He was handing out literature from a group called GEM, which stands for Grassroots Education Movement. The GEM flyer attacked charter schools and the education reform movement as being the handiwork of "billionaires like Bill Gates" who were trying to privatize public education.

GEM was formed, Jones explained in a subsequent interview, by teachers who fear that Weingarten will compromise with the reformers. For example, any kind of performance pay, he said "would pit me against other educators. I'm not a stockbroker." Besides, he added, it is impossible to measure a teacher's impact on children, especially against other factors such as "the quality of the parents" and even whether the parents "are getting the proper mental health care." What about teachers who are obviously incompetent or even misbehaving in class? "If the teachers in the school had more power, they could deal with that holistically," Jones said, "without driving [a teacher] onto the streets into poverty."

After the speakers were finished at about 10:00, the Community Education Council declined to vote on the co-location. It was only an advisory decision, anyway. When Mayor Bloomberg took over the schools, groups like this had been largely stripped of all actual power.

I left the hearing early so that my wife and I could meet friends for dinner at an Upper East Side restaurant that is frequented by journalists and other media people. It was about an eight-minute cab ride. When we started to explain to our dinner companions where we had been and the fight we had seen, they had no idea what we were talking about. Few of those sitting at the other tables probably would have had any idea either. As Klein liked to say, many who lived on the east, west, or south sides of Central Park already had school choice, because they could afford to send their children to private schools. So it was easy to see why they would have no clue that a grassroots revolution over public education was in progress eight minutes away, involving those who lived in places like the north side of the park. Most Harlem parents had long been dissatisfied with their public schools. Now that they were seeing that there was a far better alternative, dissatisfaction was turning into disgust. And the realization that some of their public officials might be trying to snuff out that option was making them tea party–like angry.

"Someone Like Senator Perkins Has to Know That"

February 24, 2010, New York City

The same battle over co-location was fought on a much larger stage two nights later. On February 24, 2010, in an auditorium in Manhattan's Chelsea neighborhood, Klein and a citywide education policy panel sat on a podium for a hearing about all the upcoming co-location decisions in New York's five boroughs, including the Harlem Success move. The decisions were a foregone conclusion; the mayor and Klein controlled this panel.

Nonetheless, the UFT had brought shop stewards and local Democratic officeholders, as well as teachers and parents from the public side of some soon-to-be-shared buildings.

Again, these anti-charter people were far outnumbered by parents and teachers from a half dozen different charter school networks. Harlem Success's orange T-shirts were now joined by equally bright colors worn by KIPP, Democracy Prep, Achievement First, and other charter schools, whose parents and students filled the seats and aisles of the 1,600-capacity auditorium. They were in for a long night; many of the schools had hauled in pizzas for the parents and children and crates of soft drinks. All of that, plus the whistling and jeering—and the two union-affiliated women dressed as clowns off to the side, apparently to protest the clowns (Klein and the mayor's education policy panel) sitting at a table up on the stage—gave the hearing all the solemnity of a carnival.

Because Klein's people controlled the podium this time, the order of the speakers was evenly divided. And the pro-charter signs were more varied, because they'd been prepared by lots of teachers and parents from lots of charters.

"Charter schools are public schools, too, and they should not be treated any differently," said Kayla, a second grader, as she clutched the microphone. "Children like me should be allowed to go there so they can go to college and become the first female"—she paused for several seconds—"you know, the first female whatever." Even some of the union people thought that was cute.

"My son never misses a day at school," a KIPP mother said. "Even when he's sick, he says, 'Mom, just pack the Motrin.' It's very sad," she continued, "to be pitted against my neighbors."

Midway through the night a little girl came to the microphone, which her mother lowered for her. "My name is Tiana Wynn, and at my Harlem Success school they teach us to share and care about each other. Why can't you?" The charter part of crowd erupted in cheers for the five-year-old.

"I've got one child in a charter [Harlem Success I] and have had two in public schools," Tiana's mother, Bernice, told me a few weeks after her daughter's public-speaking debut. She was sitting behind a desk in the optician's shop on Lenox Avenue in Harlem that she runs with her husband. "There is no comparison. Tiana is in kindergarten and already reading books and writing stories."

"Someone like Perkins has to know that we know that," added her husband, DeJuan.

DeJuan Wynn was referring to his state senator, Bill Perkins, who is the legislature's leading opponent of charter schools and had been instrumental in killing the lift of the charter cap in Albany just before the Race to the Top filing deadline.

A year before that Albany battle, in 2009, Perkins had led a fight to strip Bloomberg of the mayoral control over the schools given to him in 2002, which the Albany legislators had conveniently set up to "sunset" unless they voted to renew it. The protests by Perkins and others that Bloomberg's "dictatorial" control had hurt the schools hadn't prevailed. Student scores and graduation rates had been going up, and there was a strong enough consensus that putting the schools back under the old Board of Education made no sense. In the end, even Weingarten publicly supported keeping control with Bloomberg, despite having encouraged the initial opposition by Perkins and other politicians who were the beneficiaries of the union's support.

One would think that, if nothing else, the arithmetic of education politics in Harlem would have pushed Perkins the other way, toward the Wynns' view. Like Tiana Wynn, about 20 percent of all age-eligible Harlem children were enrolled in charters by 2010, and there was such demand among the parents who were Perkins's constituents that 14,000 more (probably another 20 or 25 percent) would submit applications in the 2010 spring lottery for only 2,700 open seats. This means that more than 11,000 kids just in Harlem, who presumably had parents who were Perkins's constituents, would be turned away because charters had not been allowed to continue to expand.

It's no surprise, then, that earlier in February, Perkins had been faced with a march on Albany organized by Democrats for Education Reform, Moskowitz, and other charter school leaders to protest his and his colleagues' opposition to lifting the charter school cap. Perkins—who has repeatedly been endorsed by the city and state teachers' unions in Democratic primaries, where their money and the troops they can deploy to get out the low-turnout vote is crucial—had not budged.

When I asked him about charter schools and other aspects of education reform following my visit with Tiana and her parents, Perkins seemed so flummoxed that it was hard to escape the conclusion that he has calculated that the union can still produce more for him on Election Day than people like the Wynns can.

Sitting next to a poster of Barack Obama with the headline BROTHERS FOR BARACK in his office on 125th Street, Harlem's main thoroughfare, Perkins said it was "stupid and unfair to blame unions when the reason the schools in this community are failing is that they lack resources. . . . The president is wrong on all of this, and this Race to the Top that Duncan and those folks talked him into is just so misguided."

What about union rules that allow ineffective teachers to be paid the same as others and be protected by tenure, or rules that allow senior teachers to transfer out of schools in high-needs communities like his? Would he favor changing any of those rules?

"I don't see those as issues," he answered. "These are just ways that the right wing is trying to bust unions."

Ignoring the charter lotteries, which at this time of the year were the talk of his community, Perkins said charters were "skimming the cream of the community." That explained their higher test scores, which he said were "highly suspect" anyway.

"People have to start to think about what a racket charters are," he said, "and how a lot of rich people are making money off of them. If they are so good," he added, "why aren't they putting charters in the rich neighborhoods south of Ninety-sixth Street?"

Charters "divert money from public schools," Perkins added. "We have to focus on improving the public schools for everyone. Choice creates a diversion. It divides the community."

Perkins himself benefited from parent choice. He graduated from Collegiate, a prestigious private Manhattan boys' school. However, he said, "That is irrelevant. There is nothing wrong with a mother wanting her children to get the best education."

"Parent Choice = Parent Power"

February 27, 2010, Harlem

To the left of the Harlem Globetrotters scoreboard in a sprawling armory on 143rd Street in East Harlem, a banner had been hung on the morning of February 27, 2010, declaring PARENT CHOICE = PARENT POWER. Another poster featured President Obama and declared that he had been a product of "parent choice." (The president had attended a private school in Hawaii.)

Thousands of parents had trudged through the drifts from a blizzard that had hit the day before to come to the Third Annual Harlem Parents United Education Fair and try to pick a school for their children. Twenty-five charter schools had set up exhibit tables full of brochures and other materials, as had several parochial schools and even a few of the traditional public schools. Harlem Success's orange-and-blue glossy one-pager featured waist-up shots of a smiling boy and girl in the HSA uniform, urged parents to come in for a visit, and included the following sales points:

- We are PUBLIC CHARTER schools.
- It is FREE to attend.
- It's EASY AND FAST to apply online.
- 100% of 3rd graders passed the NY Math Exam.
- 95% of 3rd graders passed the NY State ELA [English and reading] exam.

Below that was a headline announcing, "We have FOUR schools in Harlem and are opening THREE NEW SCHOOLS for the 2010–2011 SCHOOL YEAR.*" The * led the reader to smaller print at the bottom, which said, "Subject to government approval." The lead speaker of the morning was about to talk about that.

As the parents, some with children in tow, read through brochures and asked teachers and headmasters like Moskowitz how their schools worked, Joel Klein, in a blue blazer and open-collared shirt, walked into the hall. He hugged Moskowitz, embraced the man who runs the Catholic archdiocese schools, then greeted friends from Harlem Village Academy and Democracy Prep. Soon he was surrounded by parents and children who recognized him. It was as much of a rock star welcome as any balding, sixty-four-year-old antitrust lawyer is likely to get in Harlem (or anywhere). The parents quietly and simply thanked him. He seemed almost to tear up when one kid, who said he wanted to be mayor, thanked him, too. One parent gathered a group of six small children to stand around Klein for a picture.

Klein moved onto a stage set in the middle of the armory and took the microphone from Moskowitz, who had introduced him. "I'm thrilled to be here today to see so many of you," he began. The room turned silent, eerily so for such a cavernous hall with so many people milling about, accompanied by so many children.

"Think how much has changed," Klein continued. "Think of a decade ago and how few choices parents had. . . . The reason you have these great choices is that so many people have come to Harlem to create so many great schools that Harlem is now literally the school choice capital of the United States. . . . The quality of your child's school no longer depends on his zip code. . . . But we still have more to do," Klein added.

"We have people who are trying to stop us as we try to keep adding these great schools. So it's only going to continue to change if every one of you stands up and tells your elected officials and the bureaucrats and all the others who aren't making the decisions that they need to make, to let school choice continue so that we don't have to have lotteries. It'll only continue if you stand up to your elected officials. Then, there will come a day when everyone here really has a full, fair choice. It's starting here in Harlem, but you have to fight to continue it."

Another speaker was less subtle. Daniel Clark was introduced as the field director of a grassroots political group called Parent Power. "We are the silent majority," he declared. "It's time for us to wake up and organize. We shouldn't have to go begging for equal space and equal funding. We have to wake up so the Bill Perkinses of the world will know not to mess with charter schools."

After he left the stage, Clark, who said he runs "a small entertainment business that is getting smaller by the minute," explained that his son had had a "really rough time" in the fifth grade, including an incident that "terrified me," when a group of boys had smashed his son's head against a bathroom sink. He had complained to school officials, to no avail, he said. Then he got a flyer in the mail—the charter schools use some of their private donations to blanket the neighborhood with flyers—about Democracy Prep, a highly regarded Harlem-based charter network founded in 2006, whose motto is "Work Hard. Go to College. Change the World."

"I knew nothing about any of this until I got that flyer," Clark says. Since his son won the lottery and enrolled there more than a year ago, "he has really blossomed. He was such a shy kid, but now he's a different person. . . . The atmosphere is so different. It's quiet. Everyone is nice. . . . He used to be afraid to go to school. Now he looks forward to the Saturday sessions.

"Perkins is a pretty interesting guy," Clark continued. "He wonders why all these schools are north of Ninety-sixth Street. Well, they need to be. Last year there were 542 applications for 81 seats at Democracy Prep. That's a civil rights issue—allowing parents like me who are not rich a choice for their children. . . . Perkins supports a public school that my son has to walk past every day that is so bad that they throw stuff at him from out of the windows. Why does Perkins support that school and not us? UFT. UFT. UFT. He knows better, but he thinks he needs the UFT to protect him. Well, I don't think he understands that passion of parents like me. But he will. That's our organization's purpose—to go after people like Bill Perkins."

Clark's group had already received a $20,000 contribution from Democrats for Education Reform, with the prospect of more money on the way to fuel a Democratic primary campaign against Perkins in September.

Clark's chances of getting a candidate to make a successful run against Perkins looked good. As the *Wall Street Journal* analyzed the math in an article a few months later, in 2006, 23,000 people voted in the Democratic gubernatorial primary in Perkins's senate district. There were now at least 10,000 children in Harlem charter schools, and another 10,000 to 14,000 were likely to lose out in the lottery coming up this spring—an estimate that does not account for those who lost out in prior lotteries. If each of those children has just one parent living in the district who was eligible to vote and could be mobilized over an issue that certainly seemed to galvanize the thousands of parents in the armory that morning, the numbers seemed stacked against Perkins—especially if Democrats for Education Reform's donors joined the cause.

DFER's presence was already visible in the armory. In addition to the charter brochures, volunteers were handing out postcards, financed by DFER, for those attending to fill out and send to the

Democratic state senate president John Samson, demanding that "Albany STOP treating us as 2nd-class citizens."

The reform movement's political power seemed unstoppable that morning in the Harlem armory. But the unions were about to play their own Nixon-to-China card.

Going Over to the Other Side

February 26, 2010, Washington, D.C.

On February 26, 2010, the *Washington Post* reported that "for those who believe that performance pay and charter schools pose a threat to public education and that a cult of testing and account-ability has hijacked school reform, an unlikely national spokes-woman has emerged. Diane Ravitch, an education historian, now renounces many of the market-oriented policies she promoted as a former federal education official with close ties to Democrats and Republicans."

An anti–education reform blog appearing on the *Post*'s website, called *The Answer Sheet,* supplemented the article with a triumphant report that Ravitch had "credibility with conservatives [which] is exactly why it would be particularly instructive for everyone—whether you have kids in school or not—to read *The Death and Life of the Great American School System.* Ravitch, who has spent some forty years in education, explains how she went from supporting No Child Left Behind and its testing and accountability regimes to be-coming a vocal critic who thinks the very things she once backed are destroying public schools."

Reading the book and talking to Ravitch were disappointing for a writer hoping to find articulate arguments from the other side of the reform movement. It was easy to tell what Ravitch was against: She made fun of the "billionaire boys' club"—Gates, Broad, the Waltons (the Wal-Mart family), the hedge funders—who, she said, funded charter schools and other reforms as a favorite fad. She cited evidence from a national study showing that charter schools as a whole were an even mix of successes and failures, though she ig-nored the studies that showed that where the chartering process was carefully overseen, as in New York, the schools generally performed better—in fact, much better—than public schools. She also ignored the central evidentiary value of charters like KIPP or Harlem Success: They proved that intense, effective teaching could overcome poverty and other obstacles and that, as Klein liked to say, demography does not have to be destiny.

Ravitch said that the charter schools that did well cherry-picked the most motivated students, and explained away the randomness of the lottery by arguing that the act of entering a lottery demonstrated unusual motivation by the students and their parents. This might have made sense but for research done by Tom Kane and published more than a year before her book was published, in which he compared data in Boston for students who had entered the lottery and won with data for those who had entered and lost. In other words, he controlled for this "motivation" factor. The result: The students who won and went to charters scored higher in subsequent years than those who lost. Same demographics, same motivation, different result.

And like Linda Darling-Hammond, Ravitch saw TFA as a bunch of ill-prepared dilettantes and snobs who flitted into and out of schools for a couple of years, abusing their students and disrupting normal school staffing processes. In fact, by now there was abundant independent research showing that, although teachers with at least three years of experience were generally more effective than all rookies, the TFA corps generally did better than non-TFA teachers in their initial two-year stints.

Ravitch was also against kids' being overtested and teachers' teaching to tests in order to win their performance pay. Those were, indeed, valid concerns. However, as Jessica Reid pointed out when we were discussing Ravitch's book and testing, "The kids in my class are going to have to take tests to get into college, and then take tests if they want to be doctors or lawyers. Tests suck. But they are a fact of life, and these kids start here with all of the disadvantages imaginable stacked against them. What's wrong with helping them learn and preparing them, and then having tests that prove that they have learned, when the assumption, without the tests, will always be that they aren't equipped for college or anything else? Do test make kids nervous? Of course, but these kids have to be prepared for all kinds of things along the way, including tests, that are going to make them nervous. And if tests are also used to help tell someone whether I am a good teacher, why is that bad? Just because tests aren't perfect doesn't mean you should not use them at all."

Those were all the things Ravitch was *against*. Other than a constant refrain for better curriculum standards and more research to see what might really work, it was impossible to tell from her book or our discussions what Ravitch was actually *for*.

Nonetheless, her book instantly became the unions' answer to the surge in reform hoopla caused by Race to the Top and the buzz emanating out of Sundance about *Waiting for Superman*, which was scheduled for a full release in the fall as the school year started. Whenever someone from the reform side was booked on a talk show or quoted in a news article, Ravitch was often sitting there or quoted there, too. The anti-reformers had their own Nixon-to-China story.

Randi Weingarten told me that she spoke with Ravitch often while she was preparing her book and urged her to take her message far and wide as soon as it was published, "because she had an important story to tell that no one else could tell." Weingarten and her union did in fact help to get the story out.

From February 2010 through March 2011, Ravitch would make fifteen speeches across the country, according to a schedule found on her own website, to local, state, or national units of the teachers' unions, plus nine to other groups—such as associations of local school boards or principals and a think tank funded by the NEA— that were also squarely in the anti-reform camp.

Asked if she charged the unions whose cause was given such a lift in her book, Ravitch said, "Don't you charge for your speeches?" (Answer: Not if it's a group whose issues I am covering, or might cover, in any way as a writer.)

A spokesman for the Florida Education Association told me that Ravitch was paid $10,000 for her speech to that group. Other unions declined to discuss her fees.

Ravitch told me that the Florida speech was the most she was paid to speak to any one group and that her total speaking fees from union groups during this thirteen-month period were $50,000–$60,000. She told me in April 2011 that she had "an even fuller" schedule of speeches slated for the remainder of the year, although she declined to say how many would be paid for by union groups. "I was married to a wealthy man," she said, referring to Richard

Ravitch, a successful construction company executive, real-estate developer, and banker, who served as New York's lieutenant governor from 2009 to the end of 2010, and from whom she is divorced. "I live very comfortably. This is not about the money. I'm seventy-two and don't need money. If I want to speak to a group I'll do it for free or for a few thousand dollars if that's all they can pay."*

In her media appearances as the counterpoint to the reformers, Ravitch was identified only as an education historian and professor at New York University, not as someone who had accepted multiple speaking fees from the unions whose interest she was defending.

As education reform became a hot topic in the lead-up to the announcement of the winners of Round One of the Race to the Top, Ravitch became the unions' best counterpunch.**

* In an e-mail following this conversation, Ravitch told me that she was donating her speaking fees to a pediatric oncology program, dedicated in May 2011, in memory of her son, who had died of leukemia at age two.

** Following the initial publication of *Class Warfare* I became aware that Ravitch believed that my account was intended to suggest that she changed her position on education issues in order to garner speaking fees—and that some readers might also have gotten the same impression. This was neither what I had written nor what I believe. Rather, the issue I am addressing is the disclosure of Ravitch's receipt of fees following the publication of her book during a period when she was appearing in the media and discussing educational reform issues. My view is that fees received from interested groups on one side of a hotly debated topic should be disclosed when an expert such as Ravitch appears in the media to discuss that topic and to take the same side as those groups.

A "Baffling" Round One

Louisiana State Schools Superintendent Paul Pastorek, fifty-six, is one of the most highly regarded school leaders in the country. A Republican lawyer who had quietly volunteered in the New Orleans schools while he litigated for corporate clients at a New Orleans firm, Pastorek had been appointed to the job by Democratic governor Kathleen Blanco. Although Pastorek, who had been general counsel of NASA in the George W. Bush administration, can dial down and be low-key when he wants to, he can also be a tough guy to stand in the way of.

Louisiana had seized the New Orleans school system in the aftermath of Hurricane Katrina. About eighteen months later, Pastorek had been appointed superintendent following the death in office of his predecessor. He had since redefined the New Orleans schools around the twin pillars of Sarah Usdin's charter portfolio model and the state-run Recovery School District schools, which he had recruited highly regarded urban school reformer Paul Vallas (Duncan's predecessor in Chicago) to run. Thus, the consensus among the education reformers was that if any state was a shoo-in to win the Race to the Top Sweepstakes, it was Louisiana.

Pastorek, Vallas, and a state education department staff that included TFA alums, with help from Jon Schnur and Usdin, threw themselves into framing a detailed, impressive Race proposal that was able to cite great data systems, changes in state laws that facilitated measuring teacher effectiveness, and a plan for (and a record of) turning around failing schools. On top of that there was New Orleans's record of creating a great environment for effective charter schools, as well as achieving terrific improvements at the schools put under the control of the Recovery School District.

The graphs presented in a massive appendix to Louisiana's Race application showing the progress at each school in the post-Katrina recovery district were stunning. Pastorek and his team used some Gates money to get the McKinsey consulting firm to sprinkle the proposal with buzzwords like *nimble, crisp,* and *delivery chain,* and spiff up the graphic presentation, but they mostly did the drafting themselves. They finished it off in one grueling January session in an empty conference room at a New Orleans school they commandeered to review each page of the 260-page proposal (and 418-page appendix) with no interruption.

So it was no surprise that on March 4, 2010, Louisiana was on the list when Duncan announced the sixteen finalists out of forty-one applicants that had survived the first cuts in the Race to the Top contest and would soon come to Washington and make oral presentations for the final leg of the competition. Nor was Florida, home of Jeb Bush's years-long reform push, a surprise. Nor was Tennessee, where Democratic governor Phil Bredesen had pushed a comprehensive teacher evaluation bill through the legislature.

But New York?

New York, along with other laggards, such as Kentucky and Pennsylvania, had made it into the finalists' group, a group that Duncan said, in announcing the finalists, were all examples "for the country of what is possible when adults come together and do the right thing for children."

New York, which had not lifted the charter cap?

New York, which had peppered its promises with those "subject to collective-bargaining agreements" escape clauses that meant it was promising nothing?

New York, which had not even eliminated its firewall separating student performance data from the students' teachers? (The state's application argued that because the law setting up the firewall expired in July 2011, it was not relevant.)

When the news of Duncan's sixteen selections broke, Joe Williams of Democrats for Education Reform wrote an e-mail to his supporters, titled "Dear Education Warrior," saying he was "baffled."

Joel Klein sent friends and close staff members an e-mail saying, "You can't make this stuff up."

"When I heard that New York was a finalist, it convinced me that this Race to the Top is a charade," Anthony Lombardi, the Queens middle school principal who had informally tutored Klein, told me.

Frederick Hess, a highly regarded American Enterprise Institute education expert, wrote in *National Review Online* that "our earnest secretary of education . . . repeatedly bragged last year how tough he would be. He promised, 'It's going to be a very, very high bar. People won't believe it until we do it.' . . . Well, Duncan had his first test last Thursday. . . . And Duncan failed in grand fashion."

By now Jon Schnur had ended his stint as a Duncan adviser and gone back to running New Leaders for New Schools. He was no longer in touch, he told me, with Duncan and others at the department because he was advising states on their applications and wanted to avoid any appearance of a conflict. Nonetheless, he told his friends not to worry. He pointed to a statement Duncan had made in announcing the sixteen finalists in which he said he was "setting a high bar" for the ultimate winners and that "we anticipate very few winners in phase one."

"Arne will lower the boom," Schnur promised, "when he decides how many actually get past the finals and win. It'll be two or three. Watch."

As with his assurances when Linda Darling-Hammond had been named head of the Obama education transition team, Schnur thought he was telling the truth, based on everything he knew about Duncan. But he wasn't sure.

The press certainly took the announcement of the first-round winners seriously. Across the country, headlines in the fifteen states and the District of Columbia announced their hometown winners triumphantly and promoted the coming final phase—the contenders heading off in mid-March to make their oral presentation to the vetters in Washington—as a showdown akin to college basketball's March Madness.

"Big News: We Are Finalists for Race to the Top Millions," crowed the *Atlanta Journal-Constitution Online,* reporting that Georgia had made the list. The *New York Times* was more circumspect, saying that New York's "placement among the finalists had been anything but certain" and quoting Regents chair Merryl Tisch as saying that New York now had to pass a law lifting the charter cap in order to win an award.

In fact, the vetters would not be allowed to consider any laws passed or any other changes that happened following the filing of the applications in January. However, Duncan had said that the contest would be conducted in two rounds. This was only Round One. Round Two would accept applications at the beginning of June for awards to be given out in late August; this meant that states like New York, if they did not win in Round One, would still have a chance to clean up their acts. This is part of what had led Schnur to believe Duncan would "lower the boom" in Round One and give few awards; he would use that tough approach to get places like New York to get more serious about Round Two. That might have been true, but for now it looked as though New York and other states with poor proposals had gotten a free pass by being named finalists. After all, hadn't Duncan just said they had all done great work?

The Murder Boards

Weekend of March 12–14, 2010, Washington, D.C.

On Capitol Hill, the prep sessions that the staffs conduct for government officials called to testify before congressional committees are often called "murder boards."

Backed by money quietly kicked in by several reform-friendly foundations (such as the Broad, Walton, and Gates Foundations, as well as the Great Lakes–based Joyce Foundation), Schnur and his network had decided to help prepare representatives from their favorite states that were finalists in the Race. The goal was to polish their PowerPoints and arm them with sharp answers for even the roughest questions by the vetters. With the press talking about how key public officials were "suiting up" for the showdown—in some cases, even governors were accompanying their school superintendents to Washington—and with Duncan's rules having heralded the Q&A as a pivotal aspect of these all-important presentations, this kind of final tune-up made sense.

Among those making up these murder boards were education policy staff people from the Aspen Institute. Aspen's CEO, Walter Isaacson, is an ardent reformer and New Orleans native who had been instrumental in organizing the post-Katrina overhaul of his city's schools. Among the states that participated were Louisiana, Tennessee, Colorado, Illinois, Rhode Island, and Florida, and the District of Columbia (although Rhee was highly skeptical of her chances because her union contract was still in limbo). Even New York joined the group, because of deputy state commissioner John King's connections to the reform network. King thought his state had little chance of winning, given its pre-application failures with the legislature and the teachers' union, although his boss, David Steiner, thought that all the work they had done in data systems and curriculum strengthening might carry the day.

Pastorek of Louisiana told me the day after his state was declared a finalist on March 4 that he welcomed the chance to prepare for the vetters this way, but that the only "wild card in this, as far as I am concerned, is who these vetters are. None of them seem to have real experience." The murder boards might know their stuff, he thought. Would the vetters?

The Australian

March 17, 2010, 8:30 a.m., Holiday Inn, Washington, D.C.

At 8:30 a.m., Mayor Adrian Fenty, Michelle Rhee, and three other officials from the District of Columbia filed into a conference room at the Holiday Inn, across the street from the Department of Education in Washington. Pastorek, Vallas, and their team from Louisiana waited in another conference room down the hall.

Steiner and King from New York took their seats in a third room, accompanied by Regents chair Tisch and one other state education official. Joel Klein had refused to participate, so Tisch had also recruited Robert Hughes of New Visions, the organization Klein had used to establish his themed mini-schools, as a substitute. Of course, the very existence of Hughes's successful yet limited organization, with its strategy of working around the larger school system, epitomized the need for the systemic reforms that the Race was trying to encourage and that New York, as evidenced by Klein's absence, was not able to deliver on.

The District of Columbia did not deserve to win, because of its standoff with its union, which had refused to participate in the application. Yet Rhee's plans for taking over and turning around the district's worst schools were solid and based on what she has already done with failing schools, as were her plans to build data systems. Moreover, her credibility and her and her mayor's determination to force contract improvements on the union should have counted for something.

Rhee's most persistent questioner was Sharon Harsh, who pressed her, Fenty, and the other D.C. panelists on a number of organizational issues that seemed to have little to do with education reform, and seemed oblivious to what Rhee had already accomplished or to the success of the flourishing charter network in Washington. Harsh works on the staff of the Appalachia Regional Comprehensive Center, where, her bio states, "she manages state liaisons and content specialists who provide technical assistance to the state education agencies in Kentucky, North Carolina, Tennessee, Virginia, and West Virginia."

At the Louisiana session, Pastorek's most skeptical vetter was Alan Ruby, a senior fellow for international education at the University of Pennsylvania Graduate School of Education. The key items on his résumé prior to his arrival at Penn are his years working at the World Bank and as Australia's deputy secretary of employment, education, training, and youth affairs. Professor Ruby would later acknowledge in an interview that he vetted Louisiana, but he rejected the notion "that my questions were hostile or skeptical." He apparently* ended up giving Louisiana a score of 349 out of 500, 38 points lower than the score California, which did not make it into

---

* Note that I refer to how Ruby had "apparently" scored Louisiana. I can't be sure. Duncan released a list of the Round One vetters with their biographies, but he refused to disclose which ones judged which states or awarded which scores and wrote which comments. Thus, I had to make suppositions about Ruby, which are based on Pastorek's identifying him at the oral presentations, where there was a nameplate in front of him. Duncan also required the vetters to sign broad nondisclosure agreements prohibiting them from talking to the press; most either adhered to the letter of those agreements or refused in interviews to allow me to use their names or the names of the states they vetted. Asked how he could explain shielding publicly paid officials from publicly explaining their individual decisions to spend taxpayer money, Duncan cited the "transparency" of having made all the applications, scores, and comments public and said, "It's a set of folks together making the decisions." Race to the Top chief Weiss interrupted to add that "it's also to prevent these guys from having all kinds of undue pressure brought to bear on them."

the finals, got from one of its vetters, despite the fact that California's widely panned application committed to do nothing to link teacher pay to performance until 2012 and even then promised to do it for only 10 percent of the state's teachers—and only if the unions agreed.

In the New York hearing room, John King's muted, nervous presentation was nothing like the booming talk he had given at the Democrats for Education Reform event in Denver, when the Democrats had met to nominate the man whose new administration had proposed the Race. His boss, David Steiner, lamely explained the absence of Klein by saying he preferred having "folks on the ground" doing reform, like Hughes of New Visions.

As the ninety-minute presentation dragged on, King's performance, which I later saw on a Department of Education videotape, looked increasingly like a hostage video. "We were all struggling," King recalls. "We thought we had a great proposal in terms of what we could control—like curricula standards and data systems—but the areas we could not control because of the contracts and laws were difficult."

Sessions like these, which depended on the vetters' being able to read between the lines of the PowerPoints, illuminated the implementation risks inherent in this kind of a grant program. However, the Obama administration already saw the Race, with all the reform debate and activity it had stirred, as a clear winner. Thus, the administration was hatching a plan to embed it permanently in federal education policy.

"Varnish on a Sinking Ship"

March 17, 2010, Capitol Hill

Because the Race to the Top money was part of the emergency economic stimulus package, it was only a temporary program, albeit one that would extend for four years because the funds were to be paid in four yearly increments as states implemented their programs. Even before the Round One winners were announced, the administration launched a campaign to make reform contests permanent.

The Elementary and Secondary Education Act (ESEA) is the Lyndon Johnson Great Society bill that had begun providing significant aid to state and local school systems. Each year as the money is "authorized" by Congress, lawmakers can tweak it to change how the funds are to be spent. That's what Congressman Miller and Senator Kennedy had tried to do with their TEACH Act to encourage teacher-merit-related reforms. And it's what George W. Bush had done with No Child Left Behind; it was a resetting of ESEA.

On March 17, 2010, Duncan, riding the wave of enthusiasm about the Race, submitted a plan to Congress to change ESEA again to provide permanently that a portion of the money would be directed at competitive grant programs similar to Race to the Top.

David Obey, the turf-sensitive chair of the Appropriations Committee, who had allowed the Race to be slipped into the $800 billion stimulus package, was noticeably distressed. (His reaction could not have been helped by the fact that his home state of Wisconsin had not even made the finals of the Race). Referring to how school systems across the country faced staggering deficits and how what they needed most were the resources to avert layoffs in order to maintain all-important class size, Obey declared that the "request includes over $3.5 billion for new and untested initiatives, for which you will control how the funding is allocated to states, school districts, and other providers. In times like this, we need to worry about our core foundational programs, which go out by formula and are widely shared across the nation. A school district's ability to attract funds should not depend up on its capacity to write a grant application.

"When the sailboat is sinking," Obey added, "my top priority would not be to put a new coat of varnish on the deck."

For now, the Obama/Duncan initiative was dead.

Meantime, everyone in the reform community was waiting to see which states were going to get some of that varnish.

Two Winners

March 29, 2010, Washington, D.C.

Jon Schnur delivered again. On March 29, 2010, Duncan announced that only two states had won Round One. As Schnur had promised, the education secretary had lowered the boom, cutting off the winners at the number two score of 444 out of 500. He said he had picked only two because he wanted to set a high bar in this Round One, so that states applying for grants in Round Two later in the spring would push even harder.

Of the two states that won—Delaware and Tennessee—only Tennessee had been picked by the reformers to be a likely winner. Delaware had been a bit of an unknown. It didn't have a lot of TFA alums working in the system, and Schnur had only passing contacts there. Besides, what had happened to Louisiana, which finished in eleventh place? And Florida, which finished fourth? Or Rhode Island, which came in eighth? They and all the other states would have to go back and redo their applications for Round Two. Or, as a few ultimately would, they could give up and drop out.

Although he had not had a good feeling after the questioning from Professor Ruby, his toughest vetter, during the oral presentation, Pastorek was still shocked that Louisiana had been left out. For a few days, he was in such a funk that Schnur had to talk him down as he considered dropping out. One of Schnur's arguments was that Duncan had already signaled that ten to twelve more states were going to get awards in Round Two. Even if Pastorek stayed at eleventh, which seemed improbable, that would still make him ninth, with the two top-scoring states now removed from Round Two. Pastorek decided to stay in.

Now everyone began to pick through the tea leaves from Round One to prepare for Round Two.

It turned out that the oral presentations, with all that preparation before the murder boards, hadn't mattered, even in Pastorek's case. When the winners were announced, the Education Department released a tally of all the scores, as well as the vetters' scores before the oral presentations and then how they had changed after the oral sessions. Except for Delaware, which gained 16 points on the 500-point scale, no state moved more than 7 points, or 1.4 percent. And although the top two switched places (Delaware moved ahead of Tennessee into first), Duncan's decision to choose only two winners would have yielded the same two had the much-prepared-for in-person presentations never taken place. Michelle Rhee would still have finished dead last among the sixteen finalists. Pastorek, who actually moved up 7 points after the presentations, apparently because he impressed the vetters other than Ruby, would still have finished eleventh.

Even first-round winner Delaware broke the rules, and its vetters didn't seem to notice. Like New York, Delaware checked all the boxes for indicating union support in its thirty-eight school districts, even though its appended MOU, like New York's, made its commitments conditional on union collective-bargaining agreements being negotiated "in good faith." However, in Delaware, while the core of its commitments—such as how teachers would be evaluated—were to be defined with input from the union, the proposal had pointed out that under state regulations revised for the Race, these terms could ultimately be imposed by the state without union sign-off. The collective-bargaining caveat in the MOU, Delaware teachers' union president Diane Donohue told me, "has to do with other, smaller aspects of the plan, like extending school days at turnaround schools, which I am sure we will agree on." Besides, Donohue went to Washington with Delaware officials to assure the vetters of her union's commitment to the entire proposal—which could have been why Delaware's scored jumped a bit after its presentation.

"We worked on the application all summer, built on a ten-year legacy of reform," Delaware governor Jack Markell, a Democrat, told me after he received the news of his state's $119 million win. In its application, Delaware was able to point to regulations that had been beefed up for the Race: The plan promised that beginning in the 2011–2012 school year, no teacher would be rated "effective" who did not meet targets connected to student test score improvement (as well as other subjective measures, like evaluations of lesson plans and classroom management) over the school year, and teachers could be removed if they were rated "ineffective" or "needs improvement" two years in a row.

"We know testing has to be part of the evaluation process," teachers' union head Donohue told me. "This is a culture change that has been happening over the years and came to a head with Race to the Top."

Delaware immediately was able to draw down one-eighth of its $119 million, representing half of the first of the four yearly payments. The state then had ninety days, until June 28, 2010, to submit a formal overall statement of work, called an SOW, with a detailed schedule. That document then had to be approved by the Department of Education's Race to the Top monitoring office in order for Delaware to start drawing down the rest of the money over the next four years.

From the sidelines there was talk among the reform network and the consultants—who, like the reformers, had mostly never been in Delaware's orbit—that such a small state education department with such small school districts would have trouble coming up with these complicated data-driven plans at all, let alone by the end of June.

There was less skepticism about Tennessee, which had been favored by the reformers to win and was awarded $500 million. Following the announcement of the Race rules, Tennessee governor Phil Bredesen, also a Democrat, had pushed the legislature to pass laws allowing more charter schools and making student test scores 50 percent of annual teacher evaluations. Bredesen closely consulted with Schnur throughout the entire process.

Tennessee's statewide teachers' union ended up supporting both bills. Bredesen later explained the new politics of education in his state to me in a familiar way: "For me there's a little bit of a Nixon-goes-to-China feel about it, because I had done a lot of things that teachers were quite happy with over the years. My argument to them was that this is coming from a Democratic administration.

"This is not a Republican idea anymore. I told them that I know this goes at the core of what you and your colleagues have been protecting over the years," Bredesen continued. "But now, we're all going to have to evolve. It's coming, and you can either help to structure it, or you can fight it, and it won't be as good."

Bredesen then pointed to an earlier development in his state that, he said, had "broken the ice": the 2009 Gates Foundation $90 million grant to the Memphis school system—the state's largest—as part of the foundation's four-venue contest. The money had been given to Memphis after the school system and its union agreed that 35 percent of the teachers' performance ratings would be based on student test scores.

As the education community picked through the score sheets, many began to see that although the oral presentations might not have counted, the differences among the vetters certainly had. Their written comments, which were included in the publicly released score sheets, were often wildly inconsistent, as were their scores. For example, there was Ruby, the Australian former deputy labor and education minister, who apparently gave Louisiana a score 38 points lower than the highest score given to California's hapless proposal, at the same time that another Louisiana vetter gave Louisiana a higher score (457) than Delaware's winning average score of 455. One vetter gave New York a breathtaking 454, which was 10 points ahead of second-place finisher Tennessee's average score of 444 and even with winner Delaware. That vetter praised the breadth of commitments by local school systems and their unions that New York's application listed.

A few days after the scores were released, the New Teacher Project recommended that monitoring of the vetters' work in the upcoming second round should be made "more robust" and that the highest and lowest scores out of the five should be eliminated, so that outliers could not unduly influence the results. That change would have put Louisiana in sixth place in Round One (Delaware and Tennessee would still have scored first and second).

Duncan didn't budge. "My biggest fear," Duncan told me when asked about the New Teacher Project recommendations, "is that you throw out the outliers. You need people who are willing to say the emperor has no clothes, or this is a brilliant idea." The vetters, Duncan maintained, with his best game face, had done a "phenomenal job."

The reformers were also concerned about Duncan's statements after the results were announced praising the unions for having cooperated in both winning states. They worried that by emphasizing how the unions had bought into the plans of Delaware and Tennessee, Duncan was suggesting that union buy-in could make or break a proposal. After all, they reasoned, why should it have mattered that in Tennessee, as the governor explained, the unions went along after seeing that the legislation was going to pass anyway? And should it matter that in Louisiana the union did not support the legislative changes if the laws had been passed anyway, which meant that Pastorek could deliver on his promises?

This buzz over whether Duncan was putting an undue premium on union buy-in that would lead to watered-down, union-supported proposals in Round Two moved Schnur to write an op-ed in the *Washington Post* trying to knock down the collaboration idea. He noted that the states that had scored third and fourth in Round One were Georgia and Florida, which had not had union buy-in. Duncan, too, tried to tamp down the collaboration fear, citing the Georgia and Florida finishes and telling reporters whenever asked that, as he put it to me, "What we want are the plans that touch the most children. Ideally we want the adults working together, but at the end of the day this is about reform."

Yet some of that collaboration perspective did seep into how the vetters had scored the states in Round One, at least according to one reviewer. The 500-point score sheet had a discrete place where stakeholder buy-in was to be taken into account for up to 45 points, with most states getting 25 to 45 points. That means that only about 20 points for buy-in were typically in play—or *should* have been in play—related to union support. Yet one vetter who was willing to be interviewed about this issue—Michael Johanek, who, like Ruby, teaches at the University of Pennsylvania Graduate School of Education—readily told me he thought "there were plenty of places throughout the application, probably hundreds of points' worth, where if you believe you can't do successful reform without teacher enthusiasm you could take that into account." Professor Johanek would not reveal which states he vetted, but his perception of the scoring rules—not to mention his equating of a union leader's signature with "teacher enthusiasm"—might have been telling.

Adding to the worry that Duncan, or at least the vetters, counted union buy-in too heavily had been Duncan's statements after he announced the Round One winners that in Round Two he expected to give grants to ten to twelve states. There was still $3.4 billion left in the Race fund, he said, to emphasize the point. With that money scheduled to be awarded in the fall, at the height of the congressional election season when dispensing pork might be tempting, would Duncan reach so far down the scoring charts that he would award states that were not serious about reform?

Duncan did agree to one change from the first to the second round: After the Round One results were released and reports spread that the boxes indicating commitments to the MOU specified by the education department had been falsely checked, an Education Department announcement, noting "inconsistencies in some instances between the tables and narratives," said that the Race rules were being amended to require that any state in which a school district's commitment to implement any part of the state's plan was conditional on future collective-bargaining agreements should mark C in the relevant box on the grid, rather than Y or N.

In Colorado, Michael Johnston agreed with that change in the rules. He was determined that his state was not going to have any C's on its application—because he was going to push through a state law that would make participation in teacher evaluations and other Race requirements anything but conditional.

Back on the Horse in Colorado

March 30, 2010, Denver

Michael Johnston hadn't been surprised by Colorado's loss (the state had finished fourteenth among the sixteen finalists). Governor Bill Ritter, for whom Johnston had worked as an education adviser in his 2006 campaign, had punted in February on supporting Johnston's far-reaching reform proposal. He had praised Johnston's ideas and his efforts, but then appointed a Council on Educator Effectiveness that was supposed to consider and refine it quickly. Ritter had set a deadline of March 1 for the council's first meeting. On March 1, the council's members hadn't been appointed.

Nonetheless, Johnston was sure he could bring his state over the finish line in Round Two. If anything, he thought, the loss in Round One by a state whose major school system, Denver, had been a leader in negotiating a teacher performance pay plan, albeit a modest one, would be an impetus for Colorado now to do what was necessary to win. That meant somehow getting the legislation Johnston had drafted passed in time for the June 1 Round Two application deadline. Pass the law, and the state would have a killer application. The governor's cop-out earlier that had limited the application to citing the impending deliberations of his council obviously wasn't enough, even though both state teachers' unions had endorsed that plan. Finishing fourteenth in the Race had proved that.

So the day after the disappointing Round One result was announced, Johnston started over again in pushing his comprehensive bill. He met with a teachers' union leader—but not with Henry Roman, the head of the state's largest NEA-affiliated teachers' group, with whom he had met fruitlessly before. Instead, he sat down with Brenda Smith, who runs the tiny AFT affiliate, which represents two thousand teachers in the state's Douglaston school district.

Johnston had reached out to Smith before through a local Democrats for Education Reform lobbyist whom executive director Joe Williams had hired. Smith had said that with some changes, she thought she could end up supporting the bill. It was not much of a reach. Smith, a veteran teacher, had made no secret of the fact that she believes in reforms such as pay for performance. In fact, she had already negotiated such a plan in Douglaston.

Johnston and Smith met after lunch in a senate committee hearing room in the Denver capitol on March 30, 2010, the day after Colorado lost Round One. Smith outlined for Johnston how she thought she could support the bill if he helped her out on a few issues.

For the next six weeks, Johnston and Smith and their staffs met repeatedly to work on Smith's concerns.

Finally, Smith said she was ready to sign on, but that she wanted to run it by Weingarten's staff in Washington. Within days, she got Weingarten's encouragement to support Senate Bill 191.

Smith represented about 2,000 teachers in all of Colorado. The Colorado NEA unit, which had brushed Johnston off, represented 38,000, or 95 percent of the teachers. But Johnston was thinking about optic equivalency. Get one of the two teachers' unions, and the press would report that teachers were split on his Senate Bill 191. Get one of the two unions, and some Democrats would have political cover. They hadn't voted against the teachers. They had voted for something one union supported and one didn't.

Cynics could argue—and Michelle Rhee did, in talking to me about Weingarten's support for Johnston's bill in Colorado—that the compromise by Weingarten's AFT unit in Colorado was a mirage. Letting 2,000 of Weingarten's 1.5 million AFT members sign on to a reform package that was likely to become a high-profile national story made her look reasonable compared with the NEA. Yet it would not affect a meaningful segment of her members. However, Brenda Smith says that Weingarten was not heavily involved in her negotiation with Johnston, and Johnston says that even though he briefed Weingarten's staff in Washington by phone and sent them copies of his first and later drafts of his bill, "Brenda really seemed to be calling the shots."

Whoever at the AFT was doing what for whatever reason, within twenty-four hours of Colorado's Round One loss in the Race, the state's most junior senator thought he was on the way to giving Colorado a post position for Round Two. However, winning the symbolic support of *a* teachers' union was a long way away from overcoming the intense opposition of *the* teachers' union. The NEA was preparing a fight in the legislature of a kind that had rarely been seen in Denver.

Democrats for Education Reform had a fledgling Colorado unit that would raise and spend a fraction of the NEA's money to fight off the union's attacks. But in New York, DFER was about to win an arms race for the first time.

Billionaires Trapped in an Elevator

April 6, 2010, New York City

When New York submitted its weak Race to the Top application, Democrats for Education Reform executive director Joe Williams sent around an e-mail and posted this blog, titled "New York Belches in RTTT Competition":

> *Friends:*
>
> *When I was a freshman in college, one of my buddies woke up one morning after a rowdy night on the town and decided, while doing a "walk of shame" back to our dorm, that he was going to join a 10-k run that was starting in the middle of our campus. He was hungover (probably still drunk from the night before, but so was I so details are fuzzy), out of shape, and he looked terribly out of place at the starting line. While everyone else was suited up for a marathon, my pal was wearing cut-off jeans and a ripped shirt. On his feet, rather than running shoes, he was still wearing the docksiders he had worn the night before—and no socks.*
>
> *He ran for about a half mile and then vomited on the sidewalk.*
>
> *It simply wasn't meant to be.*
>
> *I thought of my friend a lot in the last couple of days, as I watched the New York State Legislature do the governing equivalent of puking up a bunch of Jagermeister on the sidewalks of Albany in the way that it handled itself in dealing with the federal "Race to the Top" contest.*

A few days later, Joel Klein decided to help Democrats for Education Reform by going to a meeting of the board of the Robin Hood Foundation in New York.

Robin Hood is a uniquely New York charity. Founded in 1988 by, among others, billionaire venture capitalist and hedge-fund trader

Paul Tudor Jones II, and governed by a board that is a who's who of megarich Wall Streeters and media people, Robin Hood raises more than $100 million annually, much of it at a lavish black-tie ball held at the Javits Convention Center. The ball features an auction, where billionaires and mere millionaires bid against each other for all kinds of platinum novelties, such as golf dates or lunches with A-list celebrities, or a private party for twenty-five with the Jonas Brothers. In the last dozen years, much of Robin Hood's funds have gone to support charter schools. Klein's message to the Robin Hood board (and then to other billionaires around town whom he knew to be sympathetic to school reform) was simple: You are wasting your money giving it to charter schools if you don't also invest in Albany, because Albany is going to kill off the charter movement if you don't do something to counterbalance the power of the teachers' unions.

"Democrats for Education Reform was doing okay with guys who could give five or ten thousand bucks," Klein recalls. "But the Robin Hood people and others like them are a big notch up. They could give a hundred thousand or a half a million. We needed those people."

On April 6, 2010, a group of exactly those people, plus DFER's Joe Williams and Bradley Tusk, a New York Democratic political consultant DFER had retained, convened over drinks at the Fifth Avenue apartment of Kenneth Langone. Langone, the burly venture capitalist who had co-founded Home Depot, chaired Geoffrey Canada's Harlem Children's Zone charter network. Canada was also there.

About fifteen potential donors were in the room, including Paul Tudor Jones and Stanley Druckenmiller, who had run George Soros's hedge funds. Williams and Tusk laid out a pitch for a media blitz (they even played a sample commercial) and door-to-door canvassing campaign to take place over the next six weeks, aimed at getting the legislature to override Sheldon Silver and the teachers' union.

Canada, who says the meeting "was more billionaires than I had ever seen in one room," told them that it was "absolutely necessary" to do this, that it was time to stop being naïve about the politics of what they were involved in. "You guys are the ones who can stand up to Shelly Silver and the union," he said. "And if you don't, then everything we're doing is in danger."

The cost of doing it right, said Tusk, was $8 million to $10 million. For starters, they needed at least a half million from everyone in the room.

Langone, Druckenmiller, and Jones immediately said yes. The others would chip in the same or lesser amounts, as did a few Klein/DFER targets who had not come to the meeting, including media mogul Rupert Murdoch, whose *New York Post* had long been beating the education reform drum.

Everyone had taken pains to arrive inconspicuously, in large part because the Democrats for Education Reform plan for this money was right out of the playbook of former George W. Bush political guru Karl Rove and other conservative political activists: They were going to put the millions into the type of political action fund (called a 501[c][4]) that did not have to reveal its donors. That way, the unions couldn't attack their campaign as a plot by Wall Street billionaires to take over the public schools.

Everything seemed to be going as planned until they stuffed themselves into the elevator as they left Langone's elegant co-op building. The elevator got stuck between floors. No amount of tinkering by the doorman after they rang the alarm worked. They waited. The building superintendent couldn't get the elevator to budge either. Fire trucks had to come, sirens and lights blaring as they hurtled down this quiet section of Fifth Avenue at Seventy-fifth Street. "It was the damnedest thing," Langone recalls. "Really hilarious. How many billions of dollars do you think were stuck in that elevator?"

Despite their less than subtle exit, the billionaires' donations never became public. Yet the impact of their money was swift. It ricocheted through New York political circles. By the end of April, waves of commercials were blaring over radio and television stations in New York City, Buffalo, and Albany, calling for parent choice and "accountability in the classroom," and demanding that Albany politicians stop kowtowing to the teachers' unions so New York could win its $700 million in Race money. "Albany should do what's right," the ads proclaimed. "There are 700 million reasons why."

Tusk, the consultant (who was paid $75,000 for his three months of work), recruited people to go door to door in state senate and assembly districts held by Democrats who were thought to be persuadable, or whom the DFER wanted at least to shake up. The canvassers would explain the charter cap lift issue and ask people to contact their Albany legislators.

The goal wasn't so much to have the assemblymen and senators actually pestered by their constituents in order to change their votes as to let them know that there was a new force on the ground. It was a potent message. State legislators, especially in New York, aren't used to having people knocking on voters' doors talking about them. Some manpower was even devoted to Speaker Silver's district—just so he would hear about it.

One evening a DFER canvasser knocked on a man's door in Brooklyn to urge him to call State Senator Kevin Parker. "That's me," Parker said. "It's about time you guys started doing this." Another woman answered the door and used her cell phone to patch that canvasser through to her son, Assemblyman Karim Camara, also of Brooklyn. Camara is a key Democrats for Education Reform supporter who, in fact, had introduced a bill to lift the charter cap.

It took about two weeks for the billionaires' money to begin to pay off. In the midst of it all, Perkins held a state senate committee hearing in Manhattan—he claimed it was because his constituents were complaining about charter schools—to "investigate" what he said he had heard was profiteering and test score irregularities at the charters. It was so heavy-handed that it backfired, comically. Hundreds of charter school parents and supporters were stranded on lower Broadway, not allowed into the office building where Perkins had convened the hearing. They included John Petry, the hedge-fund investor, Harlem Success co-founder, and key force behind DFER. He was stuck, in shirtsleeves, on the sidewalk because Perkins's staff and the UFT had given the building's guards only the names of union supporters who were to be allowed upstairs. Even officials from Klein's department of education were barred.

The press mostly stayed on the sidewalk, too, not covering the testimony upstairs from members of a supposed parents' community group whose website went dark soon after the hearing. Instead they interviewed the charter school parents and people, who, like Petry, had been forced into convening a spontaneous street rally.

By now, Petry and Democrats for Education Reform were gearing up to find a candidate to run against Perkins in the fall Democratic primary; this was also reported in some of the stories about Perkins's "hearings."

By mid-May, negotiations started again in Albany about lifting the cap.

"When the ads went up and Silver started hearing about people ringing doorbells, the people in his office called our people and said we have to try to settle this," recalls a key teachers' union lobbyist.

"By early May, we knew that Shelly had told [UFT president Michael] Mulgrew to make this go away," Williams of DFER told me. This was, he said, becoming "a fun fight for the heart and soul of the Democratic Party in New York."

Randi Weingarten wanted none of that fight. She had mostly stayed out of the debate over the charter cap lift earlier in the year in her hometown, when the state was racing to deal with it in time for the Round One Race application. She had talked about it only when asked, as she had been on *Morning Joe*, and then had lamely said that she favored lifting the cap and that the union's poison pills in its January proposal—to require all parents to approve co-locations and to limit charter-granting authority to the Regents (whom Silver largely controlled)—were simply meant to make charters more accountable. Privately she told friends and associates that she was embarrassed by the charter fight, that Mulgrew (her UFT successor) was taking the union down in a battle he shouldn't be waging. With all the money pouring in from the other side, she was now certain she had been right. She urged Mulgrew to relent.

Once again, Merryl Tisch, the Regents board chair, was in the middle. And once again, the union/Silver side began its compromise discussion with its list of poison pills. It would raise the charter cap but only with so many conditions attached that current charters would be endangered and new ones would be impossible to start. This time, Klein and the Bloomberg administration's lobbying team in Albany knew that the equilibrium had shifted. With the DFER ads filling the airways, and with the press, led by the *New York Post*, headlining the union's effort once again to torpedo the Race application, they were not going to negotiate.

On May 29, again in the dead of night, Silver relented. Faced with a rare revolt among his own nervous Democratic assembly members, he allowed a clean lift of the charter cap to go through the assembly, and after that it sailed through the state senate. The reformers had outspent and outgunned the teachers' unions.

"This is a bend in history's arc, caused by the Race," Klein told me the next day.

However, as with the Round One application, lifting the limit on charter schools was a secondary issue, although it received all the headlines. The larger issue had to do with the state laws and union contracts that didn't allow performance pay, evaluations based on test scores, or pretty much anything else that the Race application demanded. Through the spring, as the June 1 application deadline for Round Two approached, all those involved knew they had to do better than submitting anything like that same MOU again—the one with all the conditional paragraphs making everything subject to laws and contract provisions that negated it all.

As the two sides circled each other to see if they could make some kind of deal, they did at least bury the hatchet on what had remained the most indelible artifact of the union's straitjacket contract: On April 15, 2010, Mayor Bloomberg, Klein, and Mulgrew held a press conference to announce what their press release billed as a "Breakthrough to Eliminate 'Rubber Rooms.' " The two sides had agreed to add more arbitrators, limit procedural and other technical disputes during the hearings (such as the one I had witnessed about whether a teacher had had custody of her teachers' manual), and otherwise streamline the process by which teachers were either cleared and returned to the classroom or dismissed. Moreover, while those hoped-for shortened hearings were pending, teachers would be assigned to clerical or other duties, not go to those Rubber Rooms to do nothing.

It sounded good. Yet the teachers would still be on the payroll while their hearings played out. And it was not at all clear from a close reading of the new rules that the hearing process would, in fact, be streamlined in practice. Nor was it clear that those administrative duties would amount to anything more than having the accused teachers sit by themselves somewhere doing nothing rather than sit doing nothing in a group where a reporter could find them.

However, while the verdict was pending on whether this deal on Rubber Rooms was a real advance in teacher accountability, a deal Michelle Rhee was completing in Washington with another local affiliate of Weingarten's AFT was an unambiguous win for the reformers.

Rhee's Breakthrough

April 7, 2010, Washington, D.C.

The school district where Randi Weingarten was most involved in dousing the reform fires of 2010 was Washington, D.C. In part, this was because the local AFT affiliate there was so divided by rivalries within its own leadership that she had almost had to take it over. It was also because this was the nation's capital and Weingarten's hometown now that she had moved from the UFT in New York to run the AFT. And then there was the fact that on the other side was Michelle Rhee, the *Time* magazine cover girl with the broom. Weingarten disliked Rhee intensely yet, as always, felt compelled to engage.

Weingarten had refused for nearly two years even to allow her members to vote on Rhee's proposal that they could make a choice: Opt into a new performance-based pay system and get huge salary increases and the chance for a bonus on top of that, but give up tenure protections; or opt out and receive no big salary increases and no bonuses, yet keep tenure protection.

Weingarten's biggest problem was the way the plan would split her teachers between those who chose the new plan and those who didn't. Unions are about unity, and Rhee's proposal threatened to divide her people, plus set a national precedent in the nation's capital. Weingarten was willing to accept some performance pay and even a lessening of tenure protection if she could avoid that split into two camps.

For several months she and Rhee were locked in intense negotiations with a mediator, former Baltimore mayor Kurt Schmoke, trying to figure a way out.

On April 7, 2010, Rhee and Weingarten announced a settlement that, when read closely, actually achieved more than Rhee had sought in her original offer. Despite efforts by both sides to save face for the union by preserving the *language* of tenure (language that was intensely negotiated), the new contract unambiguously, if subtly, stripped tenure of its core job security protections for *all* Washington teachers, not just those who opted into the performance pay plan.

In one respect the settlement looked like a win for Weingarten, because there was now no explicit language splitting the teachers into "red" or "green" groups, depending on whether they opted for the higher pay for performance.

However, two clauses inserted into the new contract now made it possible for Rhee to fire *any* teacher with tenure, no matter which track he or she chose (lockstep compensation or performance-based pay). Either way, if the teacher was evaluated as "ineffective" for one year or "minimally effective" for two years, he or she could be fired. The criteria used to define "ineffective" or "minimally effective" would be, according to another clause in the new deal, "a non-negotiable item," determined solely by Rhee and her staff. In other words, Weingarten avoided splitting her members explicitly into two camps by giving up tenure protection for *all* of them.

The new contract is a "home run for Michelle," Klein told me the night he heard about it. "I'd kill for that contract."

When an article I wrote about the 2010 education reform battles, called "The Teachers' Unions' Last Stand," appeared in the *New York Times Magazine* about a month later, Weingarten had two principal complaints. The first, which she expressed that night in e-mails to Rhee and to me, was that I had misreported the outcome of this Washington deal by writing that Rhee had achieved more than she had originally sought. She wanted Rhee to correct me, because, she said she feared my report would endanger the union's ratification of the deal. (The teachers ultimately voted 80 percent to 20 percent in favor of it.)

In a robust round of e-mails that night and the next day, Weingarten not only neglected to mention the new pay-for-performance provisions in her demand for a correction, she also cited a provision in the prior D.C. contract to assert that Rhee had gotten nothing more than she already had in terms of her authority to remove bad teachers. This was plainly wrong; the small print of the old provision was far different and created exactly the red-tape obstacles that the new contract unambiguously removed—both for teachers who opted into the performance bonus plan and for those who didn't.

Weingarten had recently hired Michael Powell, who had described himself to me the first time we spoke as a "crisis communications" specialist. Powell's biography on the AFT website says he has "developed strategies for Fortune 500 companies—including for Nextel, when its communication devices failed to work during 9/11," and that he "helped the state of California with its message and media campaign to address an energy crisis that had resulted in rolling brownouts." The morning after the *Times Magazine* article came out with that assessment of Rhee's victory over Weingarten, Powell began a phone conversation with a comment that summarized the crisis he and Weingarten were trying to manage: With the union's positions being attacked from all sides, she somehow had to steer her members to more moderate stances without having them rebel against her. Otherwise, the union risked being destroyed altogether. Thus, Powell declared, "Randi is trying not to be the next president of the UAW [United Auto Workers], and you sure aren't helping her."

Weingarten's second complaint—and it was equally vehement—was that I had quoted her as criticizing President Obama when, in fact, she said, she had criticized "the Obama administration." This was incorrect, too, though the hairsplitting was telling. In both instances her complaints were understandable, as was her urgency. She was still trying to walk the twin tightropes of allowing reform while not losing her constituency and criticizing Obama's policies without taking the further step of criticizing Obama, which in her calculus would fracture her union's relationship with a Democratic president.

Despite Weingarten's complaints, the outcome of her negotiation was clear. Rhee had won a breakthrough that was certain to help her in Round Two of the Race.

In Colorado, Michael Johnston was on the same path with a state law that matched what Rhee had just achieved with her new contract.

"He Met with Everyone"

April 12, 2010, Denver

By the time Michael Johnston introduced his sweeping education bill in the Colorado state senate on April 12, 2010, he had, says Colorado AFT president Brenda Smith, "met with everyone—and listened to everyone." He had lined up the Democratic speaker of the assembly and persuaded the president of the senate, who opposed the bill, to agree to allow it to be put up for a vote. This forced the still-wavering Governor Bill Ritter into a tough spot. "I know I will persuade the governor," Johnston told me that week. Even if he did, he still had to get enough Democrats to go along with the near-unanimous support he expected from the state's senate and assembly Republicans because the Republicans were a minority in both houses.

Johnston got Democrats for Education Reform to pay for a poll that showed that jaw-dropping majorities of Colorado voters supported evaluating and paying teachers based on performance, opposed tenure laws that prevented firing ineffective teachers, and otherwise overwhelmingly agreed with every provision of his proposed law. Eighty-one percent "strongly agreed" or "agreed," for example, with the statement that "because of tenure there are bad teachers we just can't get rid of." Seventy-eight percent "strongly agreed" or "agreed" that "tenure should be based primarily on student achievement."

Johnston put those poll results into a loose-leaf briefing book whose other sections included a step-by-step, plain-English explanation of the bill; comments from the Round One vetters criticizing Colorado's lack of a law that backed its stated intention in its first-round proposal to evaluate teachers based on merit; news clips, editorials, and magazine articles making the reform arguments; and the New Teacher Project's analysis of Round One stating that Colorado needed to pass Johnston's bill to win Round Two. He carried it all around the state capitol, meeting with legislators one by one.

Colorado AFT president Smith was by now firmly behind the bill. According to Smith, Johnston had "stuck to his basic ideas, but he has a way of doing it that makes people like him. And in areas where there were issues that I cared about, he listened."

For example, the Johnston bill required that teachers who were judged "ineffective two years in a row" be dismissed, even if they had tenure. Smith wanted to strengthen the training (called "professional development" in education bureaucracy lingo) that teachers would get after the first year, so that they could have a better chance to improve. Who could be against that? Johnston agreed.

Smith, after consulting Weingarten and her staff in Washington, also accepted the idea that teachers who were laid off from one school could not be forced on a principal at another school. This was the problem Johnston had confronted as a principal at his first school. Smith also agreed that if these teachers did not find new jobs in new schools within eighteen months, they would be removed from the payroll. That addressed the problem of "reserve teachers" lingering on the payroll forever—something that Klein had not been able to get Weingarten to relent on in New York.

Similarly, Smith was willing to sign on to getting rid of last in/ first out—the union clause prevalent around the country that required that in the event of layoffs teachers had to be let go in reverse order of their seniority, regardless of their performance ratings. (This LIFO issue would become a flashpoint in the reformers' fight with the unions in 2011, as layoffs loomed across the country.) As with the issue of laid-off teachers' staying on the payroll forever, Smith's acceptance of an end to LIFO was worlds away from the hard-line positions Weingarten and the UFT's Mulgrew were taking in New York.

Smith explains it this way, referring to the snowballing support on both sides of the aisle that the mild-mannered rookie senator was building in Colorado: "You never want to be run over by a train. . . . Too often, we in the union just say no instead of leading the charge."

Weingarten explains it differently, and predictably, praising the parties with whom she works out these compromises and in the process blaming her bigger adversaries, with whom she takes the hard line: "Where you have an environment of trust, you can agree to these types of reforms. We always do. But where you have a Joel Klein, you can't engage this way." Her union represents 100,000 teachers in New York and 2,000 in Colorado.

Weingarten's counterpart in the larger National Education Association was having none of this compromise talk. The NEA, with 38,000 of Colorado's 40,000 teachers, adamantly opposed Johnston's bill. NEA head Dennis Van Roekel—whose state unit had given more than $500,000 to Democratic Colorado legislators in 2008—even flew in to Denver to testify against it. And, in a twist that would put to the test Secretary Duncan's promise that collaboration would never be the determining factor in judging Race to the Top applications, Von Roekel vowed that the NEA unit in Colorado—again, representing 95 percent of the state's teachers—would not support or sign any MOUs for Colorado's Round Two application if Michael Johnston's bill passed.

In New York, Regents chair Merryl Tisch was determined to get a law *and* get the union's sign-off. The latter, of course, was necessary, because, unlike in Colorado, in New York the Democratic-controlled legislature was not going to pass anything without the union's agreement.

A New York Breakthrough— or Mirage?

May 11, 2010, Albany

While the press and most politicians in Albany were focused on the fight to lift the charter schools cap in time for the Round Two Race application, due June 1, 2010, Tisch and John King, her handpicked deputy superintendent of the state education department, were working not only on the charter cap but also on a far more difficult obstacle. How were they going to get the New York City's UFT and the New York State United Teachers (NYSUT) to agree to allow teachers to be evaluated, compensated, and even dismissed based on their performance, as measured in large part by student test scores? Mulgrew of the UFT had repeatedly said this was a nonstarter, as evidenced by his gamesmanship with the Race application's MOU in January. The state teachers' union, which was largely controlled by Mulgrew and the UFT in any event, had taken just as hard a line.

Tisch and King were an unlikely yet effective team. She seems to know, and be willing to negotiate with, everyone in New York politics, including Assembly Speaker Silver (who had appointed her). Tisch simply refused to concede that it couldn't be done. King, the Brooklyn-born former charter school leader, knew the issues cold and is the kind of soft-spoken always-serious person who, when sitting next to Tisch, made it especially hard to brush Tisch off, even for Mulgrew.

Tisch tried to convince Mulgrew that this was his chance to be a statesman and leave a legacy. It was an unlikely tack to take with the gruff former Brooklyn vocational education teacher, who seemed to be nothing like Weingarten when it came to scoping out the bigger picture.

Beyond that, Tisch and King reminded Mulgrew and his staff

of the new Race-stimulated political climate. The press was attacking the union almost every day for endangering the state's Race application. The legislature had caved with regard to the charter cap, following the DFER ad attack. Washington's teachers had caved. Colorado's legislature seemed on the brink of passing unprecedented reform. In fact, almost three dozen states had now taken a whack at the teachers' unions with new reform laws or rewritten regulations in response to the Race. Did Mulgrew really want to be on the wrong side of history? Did he want reform to be done to him, instead of working with Tisch and King on negotiating it?

Mulgrew and his team agreed to try to negotiate something. From mid-April through the night of May 10, intense talks were held, with King—constantly consulting Klein and his staff, while not giving them any kind of veto—pushing Mulgrew's staff to agree to changes to the New York laws regarding teacher evaluation, compensation, and tenure.

On May 11, 2010, reform seemed to have come to New York. King's office issued a surprise press release announcing "New York State Education Department Proposes Race to the Top Legislative Reforms with Support of New York State United Teachers and the United Federation of Teachers."

Under the agreement, a new teacher evaluation system would be enacted into law with the support of the union. It would include the following provisions:

- Forty percent of the evaluation would be based on student test data.
- The remaining 60 percent would be based on "locally negotiated processes," such as classroom observations.
- Using the new evaluation system, teachers and principals would receive one of four ratings: "highly effective," "effective," "developing," or "ineffective." The evaluations would "play a significant role in a wide array of employment decisions, including professional development, tenure determinations, selection for leadership opportunities, supplemental compensation based on a career ladder, and termination."
- Those rated "developing" and "ineffective" would receive additional support through a customized improvement plan.
- Teachers and principals with a pattern of ineffective teach-

ing or performance—defined as two consecutive "ineffective" ratings—could be charged with incompetence and considered for termination through an expedited hearing, during which "a pattern of ineffective teaching would constitute very significant evidence of incompetence and could provide the basis for removal."

• The hearing would have to be completed within sixty days.

"New York's chances of winning Round Two of the federal Race to the Top competition will rise dramatically if the legislature acts rapidly on this proposal," Tisch exulted.

The legislature quickly passed the law, now that it had the unions' go-ahead.

It seemed an extraordinary capitulation for Mulgrew, who praised the plan for its use of objective criteria. Just two months earlier, he had told me over breakfast that he could never agree to any kind of data-linked evaluation plan, even if Arne Duncan were sitting there with us ready to hand him a check.

Whitney Tilson immediately trumpeted the news to his e-mail followers: "Some GREAT news from NY today—this is HUGE! Kudos to Steiner, King, and Tisch—and, yes, to the unions! (You see, I CAN give credit where credit is due—I just wish it was more often . . .)."

For Joel Klein, who got the details of the agreement as it was announced, it seemed too good to be true.

If, like Klein, you read the small print of teachers' union agreements with skepticism, it *was* too good to be true.

The actual draft of the proposed change in the state education law had a catch: Nothing in the law could override existing union contracts. The UFT's contract with New York City had expired in 2009, but under another state law, it remained in effect until Mulgrew agreed to a new deal. That meant that if he didn't agree to a new contract, none of these changes would happen.

King and Tisch had a ready answer for that, when I asked about it: Sooner or later, they told me, Mulgrew would have to agree to a new contract, because until he did his teachers would not get a raise. And any new contract had to be consistent with the new law. Klein and his staff knew that this was true, but they also knew that sooner was likely to come later. Mayor Bloomberg had said he needed to freeze teacher and other salaries in light of the city's budget crunch. Thus, the leverage offered by the lure of a lucrative new contract was not likely to be available anytime soon. Besides, under the lockstep seniority-based compensation formula, which was the bedrock of the existing union contract, teacher salaries went up automatically the more years they worked. So they would get raises anyway, without a new contract being negotiated.

There was an even bigger catch. The new law explicitly stated that until the 60 percent component of a teacher evaluation governing the non-testing components of the evaluation was agreed to in negotiations by the union and the local school system, *no part* of the evaluation system could be put into effect. So Mulgrew simply had to stall, for example, on how classroom observations would be conducted, which was an inherently complicated issue. (Would the teachers get advance notice? What types of paperwork would accompany the observations? Who would do them? Could the observers' conclusions be appealed through the long grievance process?) He could negotiate these issues for a few years until the reform fervor died down and then get the legislature to change the law again.

Within a day, Klein and his staff were e-mailing each other and their reform friends, such as Rhee, grousing that the Tisch-King-Mulgrew deal—which didn't even try to break the seniority lockstep compensation system by tying the evaluations to compensation, let alone do anything about LIFO—was almost meaningless, or would at least be meaningless for the next few years, when all the changes promised in the Race application had to happen.

However, it all looked good and got great press. Even Klein, worried that he would look as if he were trying to sabotage the state's winning of the Race's $700 million prize (a quarter to a third of which would go to the city), praised the agreement, though he did mention its conditional nature to some reporters. When the *New York Post* and *Daily News* followed up with editorials questioning how great the deal was, Tilson sent a follow-up to his e-mail list quoting the editorials and calling the agreement "dubious."

Mulgrew clearly agreed: Soon after Tisch and King announced the landmark Albany deal, the following explanation of the agreement appeared in the Q&A section of the UFT members' website:

Throughout the process, the role of collective bargaining is maintained, and, in many ways, strengthened. All of the elements comprising the composite score must be developed through state and local negotiations. The agreement states that the new teacher evaluation and improvement system would also be a "significant factor" in employment decisions such as a career ladder to positions such as lead teacher, mentor or coach that could lead to supplemental compensation, promotion into administrative positions, and tenure determination. . . . But how the evaluations will figure into those decisions must be determined locally through collective bargaining. If no agreement can be reached, the old system will remain in place.

Even Van Roekel of the NEA probably would have bought into a law in Colorado with loopholes like that.

Rocky Mountain High

May 12, 2010

Whitney Tilson was having trouble keeping up with all the good news. Reform seemed to be breaking out everywhere. On May 12, 2010, Colorado fell. Johnston's bill passed 27–8 in the state senate, after the assembly had voted for it a few days before. The governor immediately said he would sign it.

"Teacher-Evaluation Bill Approved in Colorado; Mike Johnston, Superstar" was the subject heading of Tilson's e-mail to his reform list. "I know I'm totally over-using STOP THE PRESSES!" he wrote, "but there really are AMAZING, UNPRECEDENTED things happening all over the country almost every day. The latest is the new teacher evaluation and tenure bill passed by the Colorado legislature. . . . It is a model for the entire country."

Johnston's strategy—get all Republicans and then, aided by a DFER lobbyist and using his loose-leaf binder full of polls, data, press clips, and plain English arguments, pick off just enough Democrats—had worked the way Democrats for Education Reform had always thought it could.

The lopsided final vote masked what was among the hardest-fought battles in Colorado history. The Colorado unit of the NEA had poured hundreds of thousands of dollars into radio ads attacking the bill and Johnston. Teachers swarmed into the capitol, staging demonstrations and lobbying their legislators. Diane Ravitch flew in to give two speeches saying the bill "demonized" teachers.

The debate on both floors was often emotional and sometimes over the top. One senator who supported the union declared that linking teachers to the test scores of children who were the products of poor and often dysfunctional families was "like blaming a baker who gets flour filled with maggots."

"He really didn't just say that, did he?" Johnston gasped to people who were standing next to him on the senate floor.

When the bill passed, the NEA made good on its threat to withdraw its support for the second Race application. One of Johnston's senate allies quickly labeled it a "tantrum" that might cost the state $175 million.

The union representing 95 percent of Colorado's teachers would no longer be signing its MOU. Then again, with the new law passed, its cooperation was no longer required. Teachers would be vigorously rated, with 50 percent of the rating linked to test data, and they could be advanced or fired based on these ratings. Duncan had said he cared more about effective plans for reform than about whether all the adults were getting along. Colorado had now passed that test just in time for the June 1 application deadline.

In that sense it seemed that Colorado had now vaulted even past Florida, which had finished fourth in the first round. A month earlier, when the Florida house and senate passed a bill roughly equivalent to Colorado's, Florida governor Charlie Crist had vetoed it. His veto was a testament to the union's continued power and Crist's changing political calculus. Crist was in a hotly contested Senate race and was about to drop out of the Republican primary to run as an independent. He would now need teachers' union support. He had originally favored the bill, which was championed by former governor Jeb Bush. Now Crist explained that he had decided to kill it because "the people spoke, and they spoke loudly." Those on the other side pointed to a ferocious lobbying campaign by the state teachers' union that generated more than 100,000 e-mail messages and phone calls to Crist's office.

Bush was, he says, "disgusted" by Crist's capitulation. Because of Bush's work, Florida still had one of the nation's best data systems in place, and many of its larger school systems—such as Hillsborough County (which includes Tampa) with its Gates-funded commitment—were already embarked on Race-friendly reforms. Crist vowed to get the unions to sign on to a modified plan. Yet his veto of the tougher plan had to hurt the state's Race chances. Florida's rejection of what Colorado had embraced cheered team Colorado.

• • •

For both national unions—Van Roekel's NEA and Weingarten's
AFT—these battles in Colorado, Florida, New York, and other
states over reforms designed to win the Race money would become the focus, and rallying cry, of the coming summer gatherings
of their delegates from across the country. As with Duncan at the
NEA in 2009, Democratic presidents or their secretaries of education had traditionally been honored speakers at these conventions.
Not this year.

"Honored, Humbled, Hopeful—and Horrified"

NEA president Dennis Van Roekel, a former math teacher from Arizona, is usually affable and soft-spoken. He was none of that in his speech to nearly seven thousand delegates in New Orleans on July 3, 2010. Van Roekel began by recalling for the delegates that when they met a year ago, before the release of the Race to the Top rules, "I was still inspired by the election and all the change it promised. . . . Oh, we were ready for change," he shouted. "We were ready to leave No Child Left Behind behind us forever! . . . Oh, we were ready for change, and we had hope. Well, a few things got in the way of that hope and the change.

"In states," he continued, "like Louisiana, Colorado, and Florida, some policymakers propose laws that disrespect educators and trample employee rights and call it education reform."

Turning to the federal government, Van Roekel laced into the Obama administration: "While we applaud the administration for its commitment to fund education, our members are frustrated by the disconnect between what they need each day to support their students and the federal policies that hold up struggling students as 'products to be tested.' Why deliver Race to the Top . . . in ways that incite chaos in the states, give insufficient time to plan, challenge our contracts . . . and cause the teachers in Central Falls, Rhode Island . . . to be fired?"

Echoing the defiant speech of his general counsel the year before (who had said that what the NEA does "first and foremost is represent its members"), the NEA leader reminded them of their strength in numbers, as he urged his delegates to vote yes the next day on a motion to repudiate Education Secretary Duncan (which they did) and, more important, to gear up for an all-out fight in Washington.

"Do the math," he said. "There are 3.2 million of us and 535 of them"—100 in the Senate and 435 in the House of Representatives—"That's 6,000 NEA members for each member of Congress. I say we can and we will influence the outcome of this debate. . . . Imagine you and thirty of your best friends arriving at your Senator's district office. . . . Imagine every Representative getting hundreds of e-mails every single day. . . . Speak up. . . . We simply cannot sit it out. . . . Let's demand the right to be the ones in charge. . . . Seize the moment!"

Saying she remained "deeply honored" to lead her union, "humbled by the contributions you make on a daily basis," and "hopeful that we can overcome the formidable obstacles before us," Weingarten told her AFT delegates in Seattle five days later that she was "shaken to the core—in fact, I am horrified—by the immense threats to public services, particularly public education, that exist in the corridors of power in this country."

Referring to a remark Rhee had made in *Waiting for Superman,* Weingarten continued, "I never thought I'd see the superintendent of a major city's school system call public education, and I'm quoting here: 'crappy.'

"I never thought I'd see a Democratic president, who we helped elect," Weingarten continued, "and his education secretary, applaud the mass firing of 89 teachers and staff in Central Falls, Rhode Island, when not a single one of the teachers ever received an unsatisfactory evaluation." (To the reformers, of course, that was the point: A school could completely fail to educate its children while all the teachers would get thumbs-up ratings.)

"And I never thought I'd see a documentary film about helping disadvantaged children in which the villain wasn't crumbling schools, or grinding poverty, or the lack of a curriculum, or overcrowded classrooms, or the total failure of No Child Left Behind. No, the villain was *us.*

"Taking abuse shouldn't be the job description of more than 3 million public school teachers who work hard every day to do right by their students," Weingarten continued. "I don't know if I should call the people attacking us, quote, 'reformers,' as they'd like to be known—or performers, which might be more accurate.

Because many of them seem more interested in engaging in political theater than constructive conversation. So I'll just call them the 'blame-the-teacher' crowd."

Weingarten went on to list all the reforms that teachers stood for, emphasizing that teachers want only what is good for children. She took a swipe at charter schools as the "lovely" education equivalent of "boutiques" that are "selective in their enrollment." Then she demanded that accountability be applied to school system administrators and principals, not just to teachers.

Two days later, she was back at the same venue in front of the same crowd, but to present a different message. As her convention was winding up, Weingarten climbed back onto the tightrope. She pivoted from the red meat she had thrown the delegates in her opening speech and introduced as her invited speaker the patron saint of the reformers, Bill Gates.

There were boos, even some rump demonstrations in the hall, protesting Gates. Weingarten stared them down, insisting that everyone be respectful.

Gates had never met Weingarten and, he says, never been to a union convention.

"Bill was confident going in," recalls a Gates Foundation staffer who helped Gates prepare his talk. "But let's just say that when he saw the demonstrations he was a little shaken. He looked at me as if to say, 'What have I gotten into?' "

The hall quieted down. Gates delivered a careful, eloquent speech that emphasized the positive yet did not duck the core issues separating him from his audience.

He started by praising the AFT for its cooperation in Hillsborough County and Pittsburgh. "You have surprised a lot of people lately," he began, "by launching reforms with a long list of unexpected partners. Melinda and I are proud to have our names on that list."

Then he rolled out his data, with their evidence that the union's solution—more teachers and smaller class size—was not the key to better schools. "Since 1973, we have doubled per-pupil spending," he said. "We've moved from one adult for every fourteen students to one adult for every *eight* students. Despite these efforts, our high school scores in math and reading are flat. Our graduation rates have plunged from 2nd in the world to 16th. And our fifteen-year-olds now rank behind 22 countries in science and behind 31 countries in math.

"Yet," Gates said, "I believe the conditions are ripe for dramatic improvements in our schools." The examples he cited were the charter schools that Weingarten had dismissed as "lovely boutiques" two days before: "There are a growing number of public schools—including charter schools—that," he declared, "smash old prejudices about what low-income and minority students can achieve. They give us models to study, understand, and spread." The audience was silent.

Then Gates offered the compliment that represents a trapdoor for an audience of teachers active in their union—that they count, even if they don't want the accountability that should attach to people who count. "Most important," he said, "I believe that the field of school reform is finally focused on the right strategic lever. There is an expanding body of evidence that says *the single most decisive factor in student achievement is excellent teaching.*"

Gates poured on some humility: "I have to admit, that is not where we started. Our work in schools began with a focus on making high schools smaller, in the hope of improving relationships to drive down dropout rates and increase student achievement. Many of the schools we worked with made strong gains, but," he added, "others were disappointing. The schools that made the biggest gains in achievement did more than make structural changes; they also improved teaching." He did not add that those improvements had come, as in Klein's initiative with New Visions in New York, by replacing the incumbent teachers in the large high schools with a more mission-friendly staff for the mini-schools.

Gates then described a forty-thousand-teacher poll his foundation had done that found that the rank and file themselves wanted more feedback and better evaluations. (He did not mention that the same poll also found that most teachers did not think tenure decisions correlated with teacher effectiveness.) The message here was that the delegates, who are union activists, were trailing their members when it came to wanting change. "The heart of the challenge," he declared, was "how do you set up a system that helps every teacher get better?"

The country's richest man offered more flattery: "A lot of people who've never been in front of a classroom think they could just walk in one day and teach a course. That's nonsense. I've had one brief, informal experience in teaching that was rather humbling. I tried to teach science to two kids at the same time. I couldn't do it. So I taught them one at a time. I guess that's the ultimate in class size reduction." The audience laughed. "I could make that change because they were my own children, and I was trying to supplement their regular courses. I enjoyed it. My students did their homework. They didn't disrupt class. Parent-teacher contact was high. In other words, conditions were pretty optimal"—more audience chuckles— "and *still* it was hard. If you told me I had to teach thirty students, I don't know how I'd do it. I have watched great teachers keep thirty students riveted for an hour. That takes dazzling skill."

Gates then described what his foundation, with the cooperation of the AFT locals, was doing to understand and replicate that dazzling skill in Pittsburgh and in Hillsborough County, calling out the two AFT local leaders there by name for praise.

He urged the delegates to help all teachers become great teachers, then closed with the more difficult part of his message: "But there is another way you can make a difference. Many teachers say they know someone who—even after getting the support needed to improve—simply doesn't deserve to get tenure. You owe it to your profession and your students to make sure that tenure reflects more than the number of years spent in the classroom. It should reflect the quality of work you *do* in the classroom—and that means student achievement should be a factor in decisions about tenure.

"No one can choose a world without change," Gates concluded. "We choose only whether we drive change or react to it. . . . Not every teacher is eager for change. Not every local wants reform. If you want teachers' unions to lead a revolution in American education, please remember: sometimes the most difficult act of leadership is not fighting the enemy. It's telling your friends it's time to change."

The audience applauded politely. Weingarten later told me she was relieved Gates had been received as graciously as he had. She was still trying to walk the tightrope.

"She's de Klerk in South Africa. We Have to Help Her."

July 17, 2010, Columbia University Graduate School of Education, New York City

On July 17, 2010, the Hechinger Institute at Columbia University's Teachers College, which aims to help journalists understand education issues, convened a daylong training session for newspaper reporters who cover education. One of the panels, on current school reform issues, featured Weingarten and Arne Duncan's assistant secretary for communications, Peter Cunningham, as well as Lillian Lowery, the secretary of education of Delaware, which had been one of two Race to the Top Round One winners. (The finalists for Round Two had not yet been announced.)

Given Weingarten's denunciation of the Obama administration and Race to the Top nine days earlier, this promised to be a lively session. It wasn't.

Cunningham, who was Duncan's public relations aide in Chicago and is a tough political operative who grew up in New York as the son of a powerful Bronx Democratic political leader, opened by saying that the reporters needed to look beyond the "conventional wisdom." The controversy between the administration and the unions was "overrated," he said. "Reform is all about the unions cooperating. . . . What we really need to do in American education," he intoned, "is all work together, and we are."

Weingarten—whose rhetorical pauses and hand gestures (including patting the arm of the person sitting next to her) were on full display—agreed. "The pivotal operating theory in education," she said, pausing to close her eyes for a moment, "is working together. Which is totally boring to your editors." She then came out for good curricula, "shared responsibility," and "conditions to alleviate barriers to success." In passing, she took a swipe at Race to the Top as being "all about charters and closing schools." Cunningham ignored her.

Secretary Lowery from Delaware, a veteran teacher and school administrator, praised the Race, saying, "The money is not the big driver. The big driver is the focus it gave us to change. . . . If we're going to continue to do what we've always done, we're going to get the same results we've always gotten. . . . For years, the only people accountable for growth were the children. That's unfair." She also rebutted a drive-by swipe Weingarten had taken at Teach for America, saying she'd be glad to get as many of its recruits as she could.

Except for Weingarten's saying that Ken Feinberg would soon be solving the accountability problem, Cunningham and Weingarten ignored Lowery. Their message was collaboration.

Cunningham, in fact, helped Weingarten near the end of the session by seconding her point that many charter schools were terrible.

"We view Randi as something like a de Klerk figure in South Africa," a key reformer told me when I asked him about the Weingarten/Cunningham kumbaya session. He was referring to F. W. de Klerk, the white South African president who had helped end apartheid. "We need to support her and give her room."

A few weeks later I would see the same de Klerk treatment up close, when I sat on a panel in Washington on education reform. Weingarten was one of the speakers, as was James Shelton, an Education Department assistant deputy secretary. Shelton had worked for Klein in New York (and had been on the Democrats for Education Reform transition memo list for department job slots). He is an ardent and much respected member of Schnur's reform network.

When the moderator asked me to respond to something Weingarten had said about wanting what was best for kids, I casually asked her why, if she believed in ensuring quality teaching, she still supported the laying off of teachers during a budget crunch based only on seniority—in other words, the "quality-blind" last in/first out regimen. Before Weingarten could answer, Shelton laced into me for focusing on "divisive issues of yesterday rather than the real issues of how we move forward." At the time, LIFO was actually an issue for tomorrow, with so many state and local budget crises looming. Shelton seemed really angry. We were sitting two feet apart on bar-stool-like chairs, and the veins were popping out of his neck. I almost thought he was going to slug me. He then praised Weingarten as someone who was looking forward, whereupon she praised him back.

As soon as the program ended, Shelton unclipped his microphone, took me aside, shook my hand, and said, "Thank you so much. What you were saying is just so important. Randi tries to finesse these issues. But you cut through all of that by calling her on the details. It's really important to cut through her bullshit."

It seemed that by now Shelton was so in sync with the education department's de Klerk tap dance with Weingarten, and so sure that people like me understood it, that he didn't appreciate the irony of his off-mike change of tune, let alone see any need to explain it. He assumed we both knew that we had just participated in a show, each of us playing his part.

The maestro in the choreography remained Shelton's boss, Duncan, who continued to pull no punches yet seemed intent on negotiating de Klerk's peaceful, if gradual, surrender.

The Quiet Revolution

On July 27, 2010, Arne Duncan went to Washington's National Press Club for a speech that would accompany his announcement of the nineteen finalists (out of thirty-six entries) for Round Two of Race to the Top. Mingling in shirtsleeves among the assembled Washington education industry insiders (plus several school district chiefs and sympathetic union officials from across the country whom his staff had invited), Duncan seemed completely relaxed, as he usually does.

His speech was titled "The Quiet Revolution." It was a theme suggested by White House Chief of Staff Rahm Emanuel, who did not think the administration was getting enough credit for its education initiatives and all the change it had instigated across the country. Emanuel had been inspired by a column in the *New York Times* by David Brooks a month earlier praising the "catalytic" effect of Race to the Top.

Brooks and Emanuel had a point. The fact that so many states—thirty-four by now—had enacted what a year or two ago would have seemed like radical education reform laws in defiance of the teachers' unions did make this a revolution. It had not exactly proceeded quietly in terms of lobbying in the various state capitals, but its significance had largely eluded the national press and others based in Washington.

Duncan stressed a key Obama theme: Education reform was all about making America competitive in the new century. What was most notable was that when he took questions afterward, he casually answered one about what he thought of the new contract Rhee had negotiated that had eliminated core tenure protections in Washington and initiated performance pay for teachers based on rigorous evaluations. He called it "a breakthrough." Again, no hot rhetoric, but no flinching.

The list of the nineteen Round Two finalists released by Duncan's department with the text of his speech included all of the anticipated contenders, such as lead prospects Colorado and Louisiana, as well as the finalists from Round One, including New York. The only surprise was not which states were eliminated but that a few consensus non-contenders, such as Hawaii and Maryland, had made the cut.

Whatever the loopholes in New York's new teacher evaluation law that gave the union almost total control over when or if it could be implemented, the state had at least lifted its cap on charters—something that Eva Moskowitz was already taking advantage of with plans to expand her Harlem Success network.

"Teach Like Your Hair's on Fire"

August 5, 2010, the Bronx

On August 5, 2010, Eva Moskowitz began the writing workshop on the fourth day of a three-week training and orientation session for 250 new and returning Harlem Success Academy teachers who would be teaching in seven Harlem Success schools that fall. She asked who had not studied the previous night's reading material and had not completed the associated written work. (Everyone had been given a loose-leaf course book, with day-by-day lessons; today's included boxes to fill in from yesterday's simulated mini-lesson, such as "What are the pre-mortems and fixes of this lesson; what could go wrong and how could I prepare?") One new teacher in the auditorium raised her hand. "Thank you," Moskowitz said. "Integrity is really important."

Moskowitz then began a riff on the importance of "teaching the writer, not the writing. . . . Fix the piece of writing for a scholar, and the kid's not going to go to college," she warned. "You have to do everything you can to convey that writing is the most magical thing you can learn. We write to show ideas. We believe in the power of ideas and we have to pass that on."

One way to do that, she stressed, was "to talk to the children in the same language that you talk to adults. Do not infantilize. That doesn't mean you don't ham it up for second or third graders. . . . You should do all of that, and use analogies, to make your teaching point. But," she added, "remember the objective. Kids remember what they were thinking about in class. If you use a costume with a hat to illustrate a point, will they remember that hat, or remember the point?"

In a classroom management workshop for new teachers,* Da-

---

* These new teachers included some Teach For America recruits, but at Harlem Success they would be assistant teachers who would not run a classroom. Harlem Success allows only teachers with teaching experience, which could include one year as an assistant teacher at HSA, to be lead teachers in a classroom.

nique Loving, who was in Wendy Kopp's first class of TFA recruits
and who is the principal of Harlem Success Academy IV, lectured
the four young men and twelve young women (four were African
American, three Hispanic, and two Asian) about how Harlem Success uses the "joy factor" to keep the children connected. This includes tactics such as competitions, songs, dances, rhymes, raps,
jokes, and "suspense and surprise" wherein the children have to
solve a mystery. It all had one serious purpose—to teach whatever
the day's lesson was. As with Moskowitz's warning about the costume, which Loving repeated, they had to make sure they were
never diverted from that purpose. "The joy factor is not just singing
and dancing. You have to check constantly for understanding, which
can be a disheartening thing to do at the beginning, but you have to
do it."

After showing a video of an HSA lesson, Loving went around the
room, asking the teachers to pick out the moments where the teacher
had deployed especially good or weak tactics. Then she talked about
HSA's "Get Positive" tools—"scholar of the day" awards, compliment cards posted on a board in front of the class, calls home to
parents, classroom cheers, or dance parties—all meant to reinforce
daily acts of student achievement. The last one was the one most
routinely used: The teacher would tell a student to "kiss your brain,"
meaning kiss your finger and touch it to your head, when the child
made a particularly good comment in class.

The overall goal, Loving said, is to be so active, so creative, so
intense that "there is no chance for the children to lose interest. You
have to "teach like your hair's on fire," which, she explained was a
phrase coined by Rafe Esquith, the Los Angeles–area teacher who
inspired KIPP founders Dave Levin and Mike Feinberg when they
heard him speak in Houston in 1993.

In another workshop, the new teachers broke into small groups
to practice lessons. A group leader would pick a subject and ask one
or two of the group of five or six to do a two-minute lesson about it.
The leader would then pick apart the teachers' performance.

One of those leaders was Jessica Reid, who was slated to begin
her new job as an assistant principal at Harlem Success Academy I a
few weeks later.

Reid had done so well in the 2009–2010 school year, when she was put back into a fifth-grade class, that Moskowitz had decided to make her a leadership resident (or assistant principal) at Harlem Success I, supervising grades three through five.

Reid's debut teaching teachers was all business. She gently critiqued two mini-lessons, then redid them her own way for the group. Although, at twenty-eight, she was barely older than her mentees (and looked the same age as or younger than all of them), they were riveted by her performance. Groups at other tables in the large hall off the auditorium peered over to catch her act, too.

When I saw Reid perform that day, I was carrying around a book that one of the instructors I had met at a Bronx TFA training institute had suggested I read. It was *Teach Like a Champion* by Doug Lemov, the managing director of the Uncommon Schools charter network.

Teach Like a Champion had been celebrated in the *New York Times Magazine* for its insights into effective teaching. It lists forty-nine basics of running a classroom, such as writing the key takeaway of the day's lesson on the blackboard, involving all the students by calling on them rather than waiting for them to raise their hands, and focusing the lesson plan on what the teacher wants the *students* to do rather than on what the *teacher* plans to do.

I read the book in August as I was about to begin my tenth year teaching a journalism seminar at Yale College. As I jotted down what I thought to be Lemov's ten most basic pointers—which seemed obvious once he articulated them—I realized that for nine years I had batted zero for ten. I also realized that teaching a seminar of Yalies—in fact, a seminar where I got to choose fifteen highly motivated students from among the eighty to one hundred who applied—was shooting fish in a barrel compared with what American public school teachers, especially those in communities where many children don't live in homes with lots of books and educated parents, have to do every day.

I also realized that despite my new interest in teacher accountability and what I was learning about the need for rigorous observations of teachers in the classroom, I had never been observed by any supervisor at Yale.

I was not alone. In the midst of a discussion a few weeks later with Tom Kane of the Harvard Education School about his work for the Gates Foundation organizing teams of researchers to observe teachers in classrooms in Pittsburgh, Hillsborough County, Memphis, and elsewhere, I asked how long he had been teaching classes at Harvard. Nearly twenty years, he replied. Had anyone ever observed him in class? Never.

Five days after Jessica Reid performed for that group of HSA recruits, New York educators from a much higher pay grade would put on an equally bravura performance in Washington.

Klein's and Mulgrew's "Wonderful Negotiation"

August 10, 2010, Washington, D.C.

At 8:30 on the morning of August 10, 2010, the New York State Race to the Top team was back for its Round Two oral presentation to the vetters. But this time state education commissioner David Steiner, his deputy John King, and Regents chair Merryl Tisch had shed Robert Hughes of New Visions and another education department official so that they could add none other than Michael Mulgrew, the UFT head, and Joel Klein.

Tisch and King were thrilled that all of their work lifting the charter cap and, more important, forging the teacher evaluation agreement had gotten Mulgrew and Klein into this room.

The vetters* seemed thrilled, too. This session had all the rigor of a celebration compared even with the easy time New York had had in Round One, when the state's weak proposal had somehow made it into the finals.

Tisch celebrated all the new cooperation that had gone into the new proposal. Klein—now having agreed to be a team player because the farce of the Round One MOU had been eradicated, even if by what he believed to be an agreement still full of loopholes—dismissed his battles with the union as if they were history and all was forgiven. He even praised Mulgrew for working with him to close and replace low-performing schools, despite the fact that the UFT had regularly opposed Klein or even sued him when he had tried to replace failing schools or break them into smaller units. In fact, as they sat there that morning, the UFT had just defeated

---

* This was not the same team that had vetted the first New York proposal. Overall, there were sixty-seven vetters for Round Two, compared with fifty-eight in Round One, of whom thirty-six vetted both rounds. No vetters were allowed to vet the same state twice.

Klein in his appeal of a suit that had blocked the closing of nineteen such schools after the union cited a failure by the city to document the need for the closings sufficiently, thereby delaying the closings by a year.

Mulgrew praised the value of testing and objective data, declaring that Klein and the union "just did a wonderful negotiation" to come up with a new teacher evaluation system.

Actually, they had done no negotiating at all. Klein later told me that he and Mulgrew had not met or spoken once during the process by which the State Education Department had forged the agreement.

It was an amazing performance. King, who had looked like someone making a hostage video in the Round One presentation, was ebullient, topped only by Tisch.

No vetter asked about the escape clauses that said that nothing would supersede the current union contract and that none of the reforms would go forward until the two sides agreed on all of the non-data aspects of the evaluation process. No one noticed that the state had not checked C, for conditional, as was now required when it came to specifying the unions' commitment. No one asked about the statement on the UFT website that plainly said that the way in which teacher evaluations will figure into compensation, career ladder, tenure, and dismissal decisions "must be determined locally through collective bargaining," and that "if no agreement can be reached, the old system will remain in place." Under the rules of the Race set by Duncan and Weiss, the vetters weren't allowed to know or consider this, because that website statement, of course, had not been included in the application.

Although the setting, with the New York presenters sitting in front of a backdrop of red and gold curtains in a Holiday Inn conference room, was reminiscent of Russian television, this had the feel of a Hollywood scam movie like *Catch Me If You Can*.

The vetters weren't equipped to catch anyone. One was so clueless that, apparently not knowing who Klein was, he asked why the president of the local school board in New York City—which was abolished in 2002 in favor of the mayor-controlled department of education, run by Klein—had not signed off on the plan. The New York delegation had trouble hiding their smirks.

• • •

Louisiana made its presentation on the same August morning, and Colorado took the floor that afternoon. Both had solid laws in place that did not need further agreement from the unions. It had all been resolved in black-and-white statutes. Yet each state had a much rougher time than New York.

The first two questions from the Louisiana vetters to Pastorek, the state superintendent, were about how the state could pull off what it was proposing if local school districts had not signed on. Pastorek patiently explained that, in essence, the new state law made that irrelevant. The districts, and the union, had no choice. That was the purpose of the law. And because they had no choice, they were already quietly sitting down to work with him on the evaluation plan.

The other vetters kept at it, wondering how the state could achieve its reform goals unless everyone was on board. Pastorek, his frustration mounting, also pointed out that the schools in the largest district, New Orleans, were mostly controlled by the state through its own Recovery Schools District or by reform-minded charters.

When Colorado arrived for its presentation in the afternoon, the skepticism became a barrage. The first five questions were about the lack of union sign-on. How could Colorado achieve what it promised if the union representing 95 percent of the state's teachers had not signed an MOU and had refused to endorse the plan? Because we have a law, replied Colorado education commissioner Dwight Jones, who tried multiple ways to say the same thing in responding to basically the same question. Jones also stressed, as Pastorek had, that because the law was in place, the unions had now agreed informally to sit with him and provide input. The difference was that their input was now no longer a veto, because of the law.

As soon as Johnston, back in Denver, heard about the grilling, he told the Colorado team not to worry. The law he had drafted was the *law*. It was good that the vetters had aired their skepticism so that the Colorado team could address it head-on.

Pastorek wanted to believe the same thing. The law has to count for something, he told Schnur in several postmortem conversations. Of course it will, Schnur assured him.

Although the vetters' sessions with these officials were videotaped and made publicly available, these television shows were not exactly ready for prime time. Even the most dedicated education bureaucrat would have had trouble staying awake through these arcane discussions. However, in Los Angeles a team of reporters was working on a project that would thrust education reform and the issue of teacher effectiveness and accountability into the headlines in a way that directly touched hundreds of thousands of parents.

From Inside Baseball to
Public Accountability

August 14, 2010, Los Angeles

In 2000, the Times Mirror newspaper chain, including the flagship *Los Angeles Times*, was sold by the Chandler family of Southern California to the Chicago-based Tribune Company. Tribune went deep into debt to pay far too much for newspapers that were about to go into an Internet-induced tailspin, and in 2007 the combined company was sold to a debt-laden real estate developer, who plunged it into bankruptcy soon thereafter. These financial catastrophes had drastically reduced the capacity of the once-great *Los Angeles Times* to do trailblazing journalism. But not completely.

On August 14, 2010, the *Times* published what would rank in any era as one of its most important pieces of enterprise reporting. The article, the first of a series, propelled the issues of education reform and teacher accountability beyond the wonk debates within the education and political fraternities straight to the mass of parents who are the consumers of public education. It was classic journalism, meant to inform consumers of the quality of the products they were buying.

Jason Song, the thirty-two-year-old education reporter for the *Times*, had written an article in 2009 (before my article in the *New Yorker*) about Los Angeles's version of Rubber Rooms. He had found that in contrast to New York, where teachers accused of misconduct or incompetence had to report to several central "reassignment centers" every day, in Los Angeles most were sent to individual offices to do make-work and some were allowed to stay home while they remained on the payroll. That had gotten him interested in the whole issue of teacher accountability, and soon he had teamed up with *Times* investigations specialist Jason Felch and another reporter,

Doug Smith, to take a broader look. The bankrupt *Los Angeles Times* would end up giving them, and others whom they later brought into the project, a year to work on it.

As they began to do background reading, the two Jasons had the kind of epiphany Bill Gates had had in reviewing the scholarship on the same subject: Teachers could be measured for effectiveness. In fact, in some places, as reported in those early studies from Kati Haycock's Education Trust and the Hamilton Project (both of which the reporters examined), teacher effectiveness had already been measured. Then they discovered that the Los Angeles school system had exactly that kind of data, though it had never been studied or used: There were student test scores linked to a teacher identification number that could link student performance—and progress—to individual teachers, giving each teacher what the academics called a "value-added" score. In other words, officials of the Los Angeles school system could have told the city's parents how effective each of their children's teachers was, by name. But they hadn't.

If Song and Felch could get the data, the *Los Angeles Times* would.

The reporters met with Ramon Cortines, the schools superintendent. They were surprised when Cortines said it sounded like a good idea to him. He called his data office and told the staff to cooperate with the reporters. However, the reporters soon realized, as one of their editors on the project put it, that "when you talk to leadership in the school system, you're not talking to the people who count." The bureaucrats counted, and they balked at releasing anything.

A series of negotiations began between the reporters and the school system's lawyers. The reporters found out that the school officials were consulting with the union about the data request, which was not allowed under the state's liberal public records law. Either the records were public or they weren't; those who might be embarrassed by their disclosure were not allowed to weigh in. The *Times* pushed back. The school system offered a compromise: the data, but no teacher names, because naming names would violate the teachers' privacy.

The two Jasons insisted on the names. That was the point of their project. They argued that teachers' names were routinely listed on websites and in other public documents and, in any event, that teachers were public officials. The case for getting the data seemed open and shut. Taxpayer dollars had been spent collecting these statistics, and they had to do with the performance of public servants.

Finally, the school system relented as the *Times* was about to sue.

Now Song and Felch had to figure out how to use the data. Value-added scores are not a matter of simple math. Several factors—such as the demographics of the students in a teacher's classroom—have to be calibrated and controlled for to arrive at fair comparisons. They canvassed several universities and think tanks, asking whether such a value-added analysis was possible. Most said it was but warned against it.

"The academics were all nervous," Felch recalls. "They told us it was technically possible to publish a list with teachers' scores, but they were afraid. They were worried about the political impact. . . . They wanted to keep what they were doing within the academic community, to do this quietly. Maybe they would do a study so the school system could tell the teachers how they were doing, but the parents? That was too much. For years the academics had been doing this, but no one in the public knew anything about it. It was all a game of inside baseball."

Finally, they found an expert named Richard Buddin, who had published widely on the subject in peer-reviewed journals and was carefully vetted by the paper. Buddin built them their statistical model and analyzed the data. They paid him $50 an hour, in part with a grant from the Hechinger Institute at Columbia Teachers College. Between Buddin and other costs, the paper would end up spending about $50,000 on the project on top of the near-full-time salary for a year that the two Jasons worked on it, plus the time chipped in by other reporters, interns, and editors.

The August 14 launch of the series was the opposite of a journalistic drive-by shooting. The first story, "Who's Teaching L.A.'s Kids?" bylined by the two Jasons and Doug Smith, included examples of high- and low-scoring teaches, all of whom were given the opportunity to comment. The story began dramatically:

> The fifth-graders at Broadous Elementary School come from the same world—the poorest corner of the San Fernando Valley, a Pacoima neighborhood framed by two freeways where some have lost friends to the stray bullets of rival gangs.

Many are the sons and daughters of Latino immigrants who never finished high school, hard-working parents who keep a respectful distance and trust educators to do what's best.

The students study the same lessons. They are often on the same chapter of the same book.

Yet year after year, one fifth-grade class learns far more than the other down the hall. The difference has almost nothing to do with the size of the class, the students or their parents.

It's their teachers.

With Miguel Aguilar, students consistently have made striking gains on state standardized tests, many of them vaulting from the bottom third of students in Los Angeles schools to well above average, according to a *Times* analysis. John Smith's pupils next door have started out slightly ahead of Aguilar's but by the end of the year have been far behind.

In Los Angeles and across the country, education officials have long known of the often huge disparities among teachers. They've seen the indelible effects, for good and ill, on children. But rather than analyze and address these disparities, they have opted mostly to ignore them.

Most districts act as though one teacher is about as good as another. As a result, the most effective teachers often go unrecognized, the keys to their success rarely studied. Ineffective teachers often face no consequences and get no extra help. . . .

Highly effective teachers routinely propel students from below grade level to advanced in a single year. There is a substantial gap at year's end between students whose teachers were in the top 10% in effectiveness and the bottom 10%. The fortunate students ranked 17 percentile points higher in English and 25 points higher in math.

The article proceeded to put the data in a larger context, again letting a large chunk of America's parents in on the secret the academics had been discussing mostly among themselves for more than a decade:

- Contrary to popular belief, the best teachers were not concentrated in schools in the most affluent neighborhoods, nor were the weakest instructors bunched in poor areas. Rather, these teachers were scattered throughout the district. The quality of instruction typically varied far more within a school than between schools.

• Although many parents fixate on picking the right school for their child, it matters far more which teacher the child gets. Teachers had three times as much influence on students' academic development as the school they attend. Yet parents have no access to objective information about individual instructors, and they often have little say in which teacher their child gets.

• Many of the factors commonly assumed to be important to teachers' effectiveness were not. Although teachers are paid more for experience, education, and training, none of this had much bearing on whether they improved their students' performance.

Then the authors asked the teachers to comment, including the laggard, John Smith (his real name). "Obviously, what I need to do is look at what I am doing and take some steps to make sure something changes," he said.

In the same story, the *Times* announced that "later in the month" they were going to publish seven years of math and English test scores covering all teachers in the grades tested. The paper invited teachers to go to a special closed section of the website where they could view their scores in advance, privately, and then comment privately to the reporters or choose to have their comments run publicly alongside their names and scores when the data went public. The paper's tech team built a back end for that part of the website, manned by the interns, who would verify the personally identifiable information provided by the teachers who wanted to get in to see their scores.

"Some of the comments were really useful," Song recalls. "For example, we had not thought about team teaching and how if someone was team teaching it might not be completely fair to link those student scores to an individual teacher." They added a note on scores that were the result of team teaching.

In other cases, teachers e-mailed or got on the phone with them to say their scores couldn't possibly be right. The reporters walked them through the data and the scoring. "Sometimes, they said, 'Oh, I see,' or, 'Maybe, but those scores don't tell everything about me.' Other times, they just hung up," says Song.

What was most striking about the teacher reactions, both reporters say, is that most of the teachers they spoke with seemed never to have had any kind of meaningful feedback about how they were doing in the classroom.

The head of United Teachers Los Angeles, which is affiliated with both the NEA and AFT, had been asked to comment for the August 14 story as the reporters were preparing it. He had declined their request. "We were surprised that the union didn't see the potential impact of this," says Felch. "They kind of blew us off."

However, with the paper's announcement on August 14 that it was going to publish the entire database, the union publicly attacked the *Times* for an invasion of the teachers' privacy that would produce unfair assessments. The tests behind the scores were inaccurate, the union argued, and it was unfair to link tests to individual teachers in any event.

Weingarten weighed in, calling on the paper not to publish the data. She said she favored value-added assessments and even making them public, but only if the assessments were fair—and these assessments were not going to be fair.

As the controversy built following the first story and the announcement of the coming data dump, Duncan was asked by the *Los Angeles Times* what he thought. As with his and Obama's statements about the firing of the teachers in Central Falls, Rhode Island, Duncan didn't duck. He said it was only fair to parents that the data should be made public and that if the school system wouldn't do it, then it made sense for a newspaper to. "What's there to hide?" he asked.

On August 29, "No Gold Stars for Excellent L.A. Teaching," the article with the link to the database, appeared. An invitation to review the performance scores of thousands of public servants in what most agreed was one of the most important of all public service jobs was now splashed across the front page of the leading newspaper in America's second-largest city.

The publication of the full database was accompanied by an article that spotlighted high-scoring teachers, including Zenaida Tan, who was described teaching her students using a game she called Monster Math. After noting that Tan said her favorite movie was *Stand and Deliver,* about the legendary Los Angeles teacher Jaime Escalante, the story, bylined by Jason Felch, went on to say that Los Angeles has "hundreds of Jaime Escalantes—teachers who preside over remarkable successes, year after year, often against incredible odds. . . . But nobody is making a film about them."

The article focused on the methods and personalities of those the *Times* had identified as the city's 100 most effective teachers, and the accompanying database received 230,000 views on the Sunday (usually a low-traffic day for the website) that it was published. Yet the backlash from the teachers continued. The union even organized a protest in front of the *Times* building, demanding the database be taken down.

On September 27, the opposition became a firestorm when local news stations reported that a teacher who had had a moderately negative rating in the database had jumped off a bridge. Although there was no evidence linking the suicide to the publication of the data, the union organized a second protest in which the demonstrators angrily charged that the publication of the teacher's score had caused his suicide and again demanded the database be taken down. The paper held firm.

By the fall, New York's three daily newspapers began to get the same idea and asked the city for its records linking teachers to student performance. Klein was about to agree, when the UFT intervened and sued to stop publication. (The case has dragged on and was not resolved as of May 2011, although the newspapers seem to have the law on their side.)* It now seemed obvious that the *Los An-*

---

* In February 2012, following the courts' rejection of appeals by the United Federation of Teachers in New York City, the ratings were released for the 18,000 city teachers who teach in grades where tests that make up the value-added scores are given. The union's reaction was so furious that many of its Democratic allies pushed for legislation to keep future scores from being made public. As of May 2012 a compromise of sorts was being discussed by Governor Andrew Cuomo and legislative leaders in Albany, who were under intense pressure from the teachers' unions. Under the compromise, the scores would be released to parents but not to the public. However, how such a plan would work was unclear: Would parents considering which school to send their children to be allowed to see the scores? Would parents be penalized for revealing the scores publicly? Could they be penalized *(cont.)*

geles Times reporters had added a potentially explosive "consumer news" ingredient to the school reform movement. Across the country newspapers were likely to demand the same information about their communities' teachers.

The controversy presented another example of what reformers use as their basic argument: A school system's highest priority should be the children (and their parents), not the adults who work in the schools. Making performance scores public might embarrass some teachers or even unfairly stigmatize them because some of the ratings may be inaccurate. But those negatives are outweighed by the benefit to the children and their parents of getting a read on how their teachers are performing and holding teachers accountable.

Yet sometimes even reformers worry about the adults—if they are the adults in question. By 2010, Teach For America had poured so much effort into recovering from its early lapses in training and supporting its corps members that it had perhaps the best data system anywhere measuring its teachers' performance.* So I asked Wendy Kopp if she would make the data available to the parents of the children the corps members were teaching, or if she would make it available to schools that were preparing to hire her teachers once they left their two-year stints at TFA. In fact, why not just publish the scores on her website?

Kopp replied, uncharacteristically, through a spokesman. The spokesman said that TFA does not release its performance data because he said, "it would cause all kinds of morale issues. These are for our internal use only."

---

in any way that did not violate their First Amendment rights to comment on the work of publicly paid officials?

Following the controversy generated by the release of the New York scores, and with the 2012 election approaching, Education Secretary Duncan backpedaled on his prior support for releasing the data, telling *Education Week*, "There's not much of an upside there, and there's a tremendous downside for teachers. We're at a time where morale is at a record low. . . . We need to be strengthening teachers, and elevating them, and supporting them."

* The person now in charge of all TFA's training and quality control was Steven Farr, the TFA recruit who had been teaching on the Rio Grande in Texas and been so jarred by Linda Darling-Hammond's article attacking TFA. Farr had gone on to Yale Law School and then taken a series of increasingly senior jobs at TFA.

"Arne, Here's the Column
You've Been Missing"

August 23, 2010, Washington, D.C.

Beginning the week of August 16, the Race to the Top state-by-state scores for Round Two—the average scores of the five-person team vetting each state—had been trickling into Joanne Weiss's office at the Department of Education. Under the rules established by the lawyers, the vetters didn't know how their assessments of the states they judged compared with the scores awarded to other states. Only Weiss and her staff had a feel for who was coming out on top.

As more of the vetters began to rank the scores and forward them to Weiss, near-panic set in at her office. By August 20, a Friday, Weiss decided she needed to get Duncan up to speed. Earlier in the week, Duncan had been given a peek at the scores, but the column indicating which state had which scores had been blocked. All he had seen was that the scores for Round Two were coming in higher; the top score was 471, compared with 454 for winner Delaware in Round One. Three states, in fact, had higher scores than Delaware. And whereas sixteen of forty-one entries in Round One had scored over 400 on the 500-point scale, it now appeared that nineteen of thirty-six Round Two entries had. That seemed like good news: The states had taken the requirements seriously and gotten their acts together, in part with all that new reform legislation enacted across the country. So they had submitted plans that the vetters could score higher. What could be bad about that?

In order to shield Duncan from any accusations of tipping the scales, he was not involved in the scoring. He had the authority under the regulations to override the vetters' scores and make grants as he saw fit, but he had vowed not to do that.

Weiss told Duncan that he needed to see the column he had not seen yet—the one listing the states alongside the vetters' rankings. There are problems, she told him. Big problems.

On August 23, Duncan and other senior department officials convened with Weiss at the conference table in his office. Weiss unveiled her chart for the first time with the states' column filled in.

Number one, with 471, was Massachusetts. Although the state had scored only thirteenth the first time, with 411, its place on this list was not surprising. Massachusetts has long been known to have the tightest curriculum standards in the country and one of the best student achievement records.

The first shocker was number two: New York.

The vetters who had given Mulgrew, Klein, Tisch, King, and Steiner such an easy time in their oral presentation had given New York 465, up from its fifteenth-place 409 in Round One. It wasn't so much that New York should not have been a Round Two winner; whatever loopholes and obstacles remained in the state's plan, it had been improved dramatically since Round One. But 465 points? A second-place finish?

Obviously, lifting the charter cap had helped by giving the state an extra 9 points in that category. The bigger difference was the new law about teacher evaluations and tenure: New York got 54 out of 65 possible points in the category related to how heavily local school districts and their unions were committed to the state's plan, including 28 points out of a possible 28 for "using evaluations to inform key decisions."

The vetters' written comments praised New York's proposal for having gotten so many school districts and unions to sign on to the new MOU, even though that MOU was framed solely by the requirements of the new state law—which contained the loophole, as clearly explained on the UFT's own website, for existing contracts to stay in place until a new one was negotiated, as well as the loophole that nothing would change until *all* of the local aspects of each evaluation regimen were negotiated with the union.

On top of that, Mulgrew's affable participation in Round Two—his citing of that "wonderful negotiation" with Klein—seemed to have boosted the state's scores across the board, apparently because at least some of the vetters thought, contrary to Duncan's instructions, that union buy-in, or claimed buy-in, made all aspects of a state's plan stronger.

The number three finisher was an even bigger surprise: Hawaii. Two senior members of Duncan's staff told me that the score given to Hawaii was "bizarre."

Hawaii had finished twenty-second in Round One, with a dismal 364. Based on its record and the plan it submitted, that had made sense. As far as anyone could tell, the state had done little in the way of new laws, regulations, union agreements, or anything else to improve its plan. Now the vetters had ranked it number three, with 462, which was higher than the score of either of the Round One winners. Weeks later, people like Jon Schnur would still be mystified about Hawaii, though the vetters' comments provide one clue: They were so impressed that Hawaii has a single, unified state-run, statewide school district—which by definition guarantees 100 percent "school district" participation in whatever plan the state implements—that they did not seem to spend much time examining details of the plan.

One of those details was a letter "of support" from the Hawaii State Teachers Association, the local affiliate of the Race-hostile NEA, that said, "We have signed Agreement of Concepts in which we agree to further discuss facilitating reforms needed in the targeted schools on a smaller scale. These reforms," the letter continued, "would guide and inform statewide implementation efforts." In short, they were committing to nothing. With no laws in place, like those in Colorado or Louisiana forcing reforms in areas such as teacher evaluation and performance pay, that should have eliminated Hawaii.

In the key area of "improving teacher and principal effectiveness based on performance," Hawaii got 58 out of 58 from the generous vetters, who apparently again paid no attention to that escape clause in the union's letter.

Three vetters I spoke with, one of whom vetted Hawaii, said that on their teams a pattern developed: One vetter would have a particularly strong view and push one or more others toward his or her side. In the case of Hawaii, one vetter had insisted that Hawaii's

statewide school district had made its ability to deliver on whatever it promised "a slam dunk, by definition." In the other cases,
reported by the two other vetters, who say they vetted eight states
between them, the vetters with the insistent views were veteran academics who expressed skepticism that any reform could happen, or
in one case should happen, without the wholehearted cooperation of
the teachers' unions.

The states ranking fourth through tenth were mostly not sur-
prises, although Ohio at number ten and Maryland, ranked six, did
raise eyebrows around Duncan's table. Florida's fourth-place finish, following the governor's veto of a strong law, was seen as ironic,
though understandable, given the state's rich reform history and
data systems as well as Governor's Crist's immediate formation of
a committee to fix the law a bit to get the teachers on board to pursue a strong reform agenda in a state where much had already been
achieved, thanks to Jeb Bush.

Weiss explained to Duncan that, based on the budgets that the ten
states at the top of the scoring chart had submitted, giving grants to
them was as far as they could go down the charts before the money
ran out. There could only be ten winners.

And that was the problem. The two states everyone in the room
assumed would win easily—Louisiana and Colorado—weren't in the
ten. Louisiana was number thirteen and Colorado was an incredible number seventeen, scoring even below California's laughable
plan.

The vetters' insistent questions during the Colorado and Louisiana oral presentations about union buy-in were reflected in their
general attitude about the two states' plans and were especially
costly in scoring categories involving the core reforms aimed at
making teachers more accountable for their performance.

Colorado got a 37 out of 45 for securing stakeholder commitment to those reforms, even though one would think that an ex-
pansive, tough state law obligating that commitment regardless of
the unions' wishes should have yielded a perfect score. Louisiana,
which had passed an equally tough, detailed law, got a 35.

When it came to "improving teacher and principal effectiveness
based on performance," Colorado got a 43 out of 58. Louisiana got a

48, well below Hawaii's perfect 58 and the 54 awarded to New York, despite the loopholes in New York's new law.*

"There is no chance that Mulgrew will negotiate these reforms anytime soon," one of Bloomberg's senior staff people told me in explaining the New York strategy. "What everyone wanted was to avoid the headline that they were responsible for not getting the money. After that, who cares?"

Duncan was surprised and upset about Colorado and Louisiana. He thought they were among the states most committed to real reform, and that they were the two states that had done the heaviest lifting to pass laws in response to the Race. Dinging them would send a terrible message. "Is there anything we can do?" he asked the group. "Anyone have any ideas?"

Weiss—who by now was highly frustrated by how difficult the process had been, compared with the decisions she had been able to make at the school reform venture capital fund where she had previously worked—walked Duncan and the group through three choices they had to fix the problem.

First, Duncan could simply overrule the scores, but everyone quickly dismissed this option. Given the department's commitment to make all of the vetters' scores public, it would discredit the elaborate process they had gone through and draw howls and accusations from the states (and their congressional representatives) that would now lose if he overruled the scores.

The second choice was to cut each state's budgeted grant allocation by some fraction so that Duncan could have enough money to reach lower down the list and scoop up Louisiana and Colorado. No scores would be changed, but these lower-scoring states would now be winners, too. The problem was that this would require a cut of about 20 percent for each state to get to Louisiana and more than 40 percent to get to Colorado. That would mean breaking a prom-

---

* Had Colorado and Louisiana been given the perfect scores that they deserved in just those two categories, Colorado would have finished in the top ten, and Louisiana would have finished fifth. And if New York had gotten penalized by only 20 points for the conditions that attached to its ability to deliver on the new law, it would have finished below Louisiana and about even with Colorado. Add back just a few more points to correct the undue skepticism about the Colorado and Louisiana laws and the optimism about New York's proposal that permeated other scoring categories, and New York would have been a loser, while Colorado and Louisiana would have ended up near the top.

ise to the states that had worked so hard to come up with plans—a promise about how much they would get if they won. Also, it would sweep in some states, such as number sixteen, California, that definitely did not deserve to win. It was bad enough that some seemingly unworthy states had already won. With this plan many more of them would get the money. Duncan would be breaking his vow to set a "high bar."

Third, they could reach lower down the list by deciding that the grants should be for three years, not four. However, that would still not yield enough money to sweep in Colorado. And, again, it would be changing the winnings promised to the contestants.

None of the alternatives was palatable. That the group spent time seriously considering the last two demonstrated how frustrated they were about what had happened to Colorado and Louisiana.

Duncan ended the meeting, giving the go-ahead to announce the winners the next day, August 24. He would now call every governor who had made the finals, as well as key members of Congress from states affected by the decisions—the winners and losers—and tell them the good or bad news. He'd also call the Democratic senator from Louisiana, Mary Landrieu, and the Democrat from Colorado, Michael Bennet, to break it to them.

The call to Bennet was especially difficult. Bennet had been the superintendent of the Denver schools before being appointed to fill the Senate vacancy created when incumbent Ken Salazar was appointed secretary of the interior. Education reform was Bennet's big cause in Denver and in the Senate. Michael Johnston, who had followed him by ten years at Yale Law School (where Bennet was editor in chief of the *Law Journal*), was a protégé of Bennet's.

The Obama administration considered Bennet—a soft-spoken, whip-smart venture capitalist before he took over the Denver schools—to be a rising star, but one who needed help because he was running in a hotly contested Democratic primary and then in a swing state if he survived the primary. His Democratic opponent was supported by the Colorado Education Association, whose withdrawal of support from the Race application had apparently doomed it. Now Duncan had to deliver the news that his primary opponent was going to be able to argue that Bennet had failed to deliver for his state on his signature issue.

"I appreciated Arne's call, and there still is no bigger supporter of him or Race to the Top," Bennet says. "But I told him there was no way on the planet that Colorado shouldn't have won. Yes, I wished he had overturned the results, but I didn't ask him to."

"Arne made the right call in not messing with the results," said Johnston, weeks after he learned that Colorado had lost despite his new legislation. "It was a terrible decision by the people who judged us, but if Arne had screwed with the results it would have undermined the credibility of the whole program."

Meantime, Colorado, Louisiana, and other states, such as Washington, announced that they were moving ahead with their Race to the Top reform program even without the Race money.

Looking across the Round Two score sheets, it is easy to conclude that if, as Churchill said, "Democracy is the worst form of government except for all the others that have been tried," competitive government grant programs, in which the money is dispensed by objective and disinterested (and therefore not fully knowledgeable) judges, may be the worst way to dole out taxpayer money except for all the others.

Still, it was possible that the lure of the money might get unlikely states, such as Hawaii or Maryland, and continuing battlegrounds like New York to deliver. And there was no denying that there and in the other winning states the process of engaging in the contest changed laws and regulations, produced plans to overhaul school systems, and strengthened the political movement and will to do so. This is also true in places that lost—obviously Louisiana and Colorado, but also Illinois, Washington State, and, to a limited extent, even California.

Nonetheless, the obvious misfires in the judging of the contest raised the question of what the winners would now actually do with the money they won. Would and could they implement their plans?

Weiss and Duncan had attached a tight set of deadlines to the grant awards for final implementation plans, called Statements of Work, to be submitted and approved, and then for when each step in the plans had to be completed. States that missed these deadlines risked not getting the next installment of their grants, or even being asked to give back money they had received. To be sure, that is always the case with federal grants, yet actual performance, let alone performance on schedule, is typically the exception rather than the rule.

Duncan had told me just after the Round Two awards were announced that he was "perfectly willing to ding states that did not deliver. We'll hold the money back in a heartbeat if we have to." First-round winners Tennessee and Delaware were supposed to have had their plans in and approved by June 28, 2010. As of the end of August, when the Round Two results were announced, neither of the Round One winners' plans had been approved but both states had gotten their first installment of the grant.

In a white paper praising the broad impact of Race to the Top in pushing the reform agenda across the country, the conservative American Enterprise Institute had warned that "the history of federal education policy is replete with well-intentioned and initially promising attempts to effect positive change on schools, but it remains extraordinarily difficult to drive change from the national level all the way down to the classroom level."

The paper went on to note, "The Department of Education has long lacked the staff, resources, and technical expertise to provide sustained supervision and guidance [of] state compliance with federal education programs. While its programs and grant expenditures have grown dramatically in the past thirty years, [the Department of Education] staff of 4,199 was 44 percent below the 7,528 employees who administered Federal education programs . . . in 1980, when the Department was created. Ironically then, even as [Race to the Top] seeks to expand states' administrative capacity to implement education reform, it may be undone by the lack of adequate administrative capacity at the national level."

Soaring Dreams, Street-Level Politics

September 8, 2010, New York City

On September 8, 2010, Democrats for Education Reform's Joe Williams sent his e-mail list an exuberant fund-raising message titled "DFER: Bursting the Dam." His message would have been unimaginable the night in 2005 that Barack Obama showed up to speak at the DFER cocktail party, and it provided an amazing contrast to the day in 1994 when Congressman George Miller was voted down 434–1 when he suggested that teachers be certified as qualified to teach their subjects and be eligible for a modest performance pay plan.

"In the last three years," William began, "Democrats for Education Reform alone has pumped more than $17 million into political advocacy at the federal, state and local levels." This included $10 million DFER had raised for the media and canvassing campaign and other activities in New York, $500,000 to help Michael Bennet in his Colorado Senate primary (which he won in a close race in August, before winning an even closer general election fight), and money to support local races and DFER field units in California, Michigan, Indiana, Rhode Island, Ohio, Wisconsin, and Washington State.

"Alumni of programs like Teach For America are beginning to run for office," Williams continued. "Reformers have assumed positions of influence at the federal and state levels of government. We're closer than we've ever been to bursting the dam that has prevented progress in K–12 education. To be sure, since the 1983 release of the federal report *A Nation At Risk*, there have been small but valuable political fissures in the dam. But the dam itself has remained strong enough to stop widespread reform. The 2008 election of President Barack Obama created unprecedented political conditions, which now make fundamental reform of public education a possibility. The first-ever Democratic president elected without significant support of teachers' unions (the American Federation of Teachers, which backed Hillary Clinton early on, spent millions trying to knock Obama off the ballot), Obama has governed with unusual credibility and freedom."

Williams then explained how Race to the Top had "produced more simultaneous fissures in the dam than we've ever seen. Cash-strapped state legislatures, hoping to win a chunk of nearly $5 billion in federal prizes, passed more education reform legislation in eight months than they had in the previous eight years. . . .

"In the aftermath of some of these 2010 reform battles, elections will determine whether this wave of reform is politically sustainable," Williams concluded. "Leaders who supported reform must be protected, or the old (and highly effective) story line will emerge once again: Promote education reform at your own political peril. On the other hand, infusing the ranks of state and national government with more reform-friendly leaders will propel education reform even further away from the era when political martyrdom was commonplace. . . . Continued success in the political arena in 2010 and 2011—at a time when difficult local and state budgets will continue to force some tough discussions on education policy—have the potential to burst the dam once and for all."

On the morning that Williams sent that e-mail, I traveled to one of the front lines of that political battle. For several months, Basil Smikle—a smart, well-connected African-American Ivy League son of a Queens teacher and UFT member—had been talked about as the answer to pro-union, anti-charter Harlem state senator Bill Perkins. Smikle, a thirty-eight-year-old political consultant, had worked as a political operative for Senator Hillary Clinton and Mayor Bloomberg. All summer, he had gotten good stories in the local press, following a May send-off in a Whitney Tilson e-mail urging reformers to dig into their pockets for "this outstanding person."

"Taking Perkins out," Tilson had written, "would be huge, both morally and politically. . . . Bill Perkins, you are going down for the high crime of taking children in your care and throwing them under the bus!"

Since then, Smikle had out-fund-raised Perkins, drawing more than $200,000 in contributions to Perkins's $175,000. This had prompted the *Wall Street Journal*, in reporting that reformers had raised a total of $600,000 for New York state candidates, to name the Smikle-Perkins race as one to watch.

That made sense to me, based on a long breakfast I had had with Smikle near his Harlem headquarters in August. The insurgent candidate had crisply rattled off the district's election demographics (he lived there and had coordinated the Bloomberg campaign there), talked about endorsements he was about to get, and opined on what he called Perkins's aloof relationship with the community and his thin support.

At 7:00 a.m. on September 8, 2010, I stood about ten feet away from Smikle as he awaited those entering or emerging from the busy subway station at 110th Street and Lenox Avenue. There were six days left before voters would be choosing him or Perkins in the primary. He stood there casually, holding a cup of Starbucks coffee. A volunteer mumbled, "Come meet Basil, running for state senate," then tried to hand each passerby a brochure, which about one third bothered to take.

Curiously, the brochure said nothing about charter schools, let alone about Perkins's fight against them; the only reference was a vague mention of "school choice and educational opportunities" among six bullet-point clichés ("protect senior services," "fight for social justice").

As the people hurried by, Smikle said, in a voice just north of a murmur, "Hi, I'm Basil. Need your vote next week." Some press reports had described Smikle as a local version of Barack Obama, which in terms of his résumé and good looks he might have been. He seemed that morning to have taken the comparison to mean he had already been elected.

A woman hurried up the subway station stairs, clutching two little girls. Each wore the distinctive Harlem Success Academy uniform. They were obviously headed to Eva Moskowitz's and Jessica Reid's school, eight blocks up Lenox Avenue. Smikle nodded at the mother. "Hi, I'm Basil, running for state senate." With her girls tugging her down the block, she barely acknowledged him.

I trailed after her and asked if she knew anything about the state senate race. She didn't. I asked if she knew that her state senator,

Bill Perkins, had been leading the fight to limit the expansion of charter schools like Harlem Success. She said she hadn't heard that either. Now she seemed interested, but she had to get the kids to school.

"Those were Harlem Success uniforms," I told Smikle when I came back.

"Sure, I know that," he said. "It's one of the schools I am in this race to fight for."

Why hadn't he told that woman that? He looked at me blankly, then said something about how that was not how he liked to campaign.

Geoffrey Canada of the Harlem Children's Zone and Eva Moskowitz believed that Smikle should have spent his campaign face time standing in front of the charter schools every morning and afternoon as parents dropped off and picked up their children. Neither thought it appropriate to give him their mailing lists of parents, but Moskowitz sent out mailers to parents reminding them of the primary and the two candidates who were running and what their positions were on charter schools. Yet Smikle told me he mostly "stayed away from being right in front of the schools" and had limited his street campaigning mostly to subway stops or similar encounters like the one I had just watched.

"We need tough fighters in these campaigns," Moskowitz told me that week. "We can't win with candidates like this. This guy just didn't campaign, and the hedge-fund guys don't know what they're doing when it comes to street politics like this. It's all about shoe leather."

Six days later, on September 14, Perkins beat Smikle in the primary 76 percent to 24 percent. He got 17,000 votes to Smikle's 5,000. The total vote was lower than the number of children—24,000—in Harlem charter schools or on waiting lists because they had been turned away from the charters in lotteries. Translating charter children into votes by their parents had proved to be undoable, not only because of Smikle's less-than-compelling performance but also because many parents in Harlem are not registered voters or, in fact, may not even be citizens eligible to vote. Perkins, on the other hand, benefited from an avid get-out-the-vote phone bank campaign supported by the teachers' union.

"Next time," said Moskowitz, who formed her own political action committee after Smikle's loss, "we have to do everything to organize the parents, register them, and get out the vote."

One of her colleagues, Seth Andrew, who runs the Democracy Prep charter network, immediately set out to organize that effort. Andrew, who had allowed one of his staff members to take a leave and help Democrats for Education Reform's get-out-the-vote efforts for Smikle, organized "Democracy Builders," a charter parents' advocacy group, which, in addition to Democracy Prep, quickly signed up fifty-four charter schools in Harlem, Brooklyn, and the Bronx. Within a few months, approximately 5,000 parents had joined the program, which is intended to train them to participate in and testify at public hearings, write to elected officials, and organize voter registration drives around the issue of charter schools and parent choice.

Rhee Rejected

September 14, 2010

Bill Perkins's rout of Basil Smikle wasn't the only defeat for the reformers. September 14 was also primary day in Washington, D.C., and Michelle Rhee's boss, Adrian Fenty, was in a hotly contested Democratic primary (which in Washington is tantamount to the election) with City Council leader Vincent Gray.

Fenty had a lot going for him. He had shaken up a city bureaucracy—not just the school system, but also police, sanitation, and other basic services—that needed shaking up. Yet along the way he had acquired a reputation of being heavy-handed and aloof. In other words, like his schools chancellor, he was not big on collaboration.

Gray had picked away at that vulnerability and in doing so decided to focus on one issue: what he called Fenty's and Rhee's divisive tactics in running the schools. Gray said that he supported fixing the schools, but that he would go about it more collaboratively.

This seemed a curious point of attack. The schools were clearly doing better. Test scores and graduation rates were up, and Rhee had built a national following as someone who might be taking no prisoners but was getting the job done.

However, Washington, D.C.—where, according to a Gallup poll taken a month before the primary, 38 percent of the adults worked for the federal or local government, which probably meant most households had a government worker—is not the best place to run for reelection on a record of challenging the prerogatives and job security of civil servants.

Those voters, many of whom constitute a vibrant African-American middle class, had gotten a harsh reminder of the Fenty/Rhee approach in July, when, with no warning, Rhee used her new power derived from the contract she had negotiated with Weingarten to fire 226 teachers—

about 5 percent of the teachers in the district—for poor performance. "That was a seminal day in this whole movement," Klein told me the next morning. "That's the day the music stopped for these people."

Rhee also deployed her new teacher evaluation regimen to warn 737 others that they had been judged "minimally effective." She gave them a year to improve or face dismissal. It was as if she was trying to prove to Fenty what she had told him the first time they met—that hiring her would be a "political disaster."

By August, a local poll had showed Fenty trailing Gray. Rhee soon got firsthand information that the poll was on target. Her fiancé, Kevin Johnson, who is a well-known African-American former basketball star and was now the mayor of Sacramento, came to Washington one weekend to knock on doors for Fenty in African-American neighborhoods. Johnson reported back to Rhee that although Fenty, like Gray, is black, he had detected strong resentment with a racial overtone having to do with the Korean-American schools chancellor.

Although Weingarten's AFT poured more than a million dollars into the Gray campaign to unseat Fenty and Rhee, Democrats for Education Reform and its allies didn't put money into Washington until the last minute, because it had seemed unimaginable that their superstar's boss could be in trouble. Yet the Fenty campaign was well financed, and in the end it wasn't money that made the difference so much as Fenty's and Rhee's tin ears when it came to the politics of education reform.

"We were so sure that what we were doing was right, and we could see the numbers that proved it," says Rhee, referring to student achievement gains, not voter polls, "that we didn't pay any attention to the political aspect of getting that message across. We thought the results would take care of all that."

On September 14, Fenty lost to Gray by ten points.

Although Rhee publicly said she was not sure if she was going to leave, and Gray said he had not made a decision about asking her to stay, within days she had decided to move on. She was going to take on the job of spreading her political message nationally. With Klein's help, she met with sympathetic financiers to solicit backing for a national political action committee that would be a DFER-like group on steroids. She and fiancé Johnson decided grandiosely that she would raise $1 billion to push her cause and never again get caught short when it came to getting the message out.

In fact, within a few weeks, and well before she officially announced her intention not to work for Gray, some of those backers were already quietly funneling seed money into Democrats for Education Reform's 501(c)(4) (meaning the donors would be anonymous), with the understanding that once Rhee officially announced her own new group, the money would be transferred to it.

The reformers were, of course, concerned that Rhee's departure would set back what in their view was the great progress they had achieved in Washington. There was even speculation that foundations such as Broad's or the Walton family's, which had pledged the funds to support Rhee's groundbreaking opt-in teacher bonus program, would pull out.

Mayor Gray's appointment of Kaya Henderson—Rhee's top deputy and another TFA alum—as interim chancellor eased those worries, at least temporarily.

"I'll E-mail Your Dad and Tell Him"

September 14, 2010, New York City

While the air was coming out of Basil Smikle's and Adrian Fenty's campaign balloons on September 14, Jessica Reid began the morning at 7:30 by hugging about two dozen of her 235 third, fourth, and fifth graders as they trooped in for breakfast in the cafeteria that Harlem Success Academy I shares with PS 149.

She was more tired than usual, because she had been up the night before buying nail polish remover and then squeezing it into little packets she could give to more than a dozen girls who had been violating the school's rule against brightly painted nails.

"I saw you got a really good grade on your vocab test," she said to a quiet little boy with thick glasses. "I'll e-mail your dad and tell him." The boy broke into a huge smile.

"He's in the fourth grade," Reid whispered to me, "and was in the fourth grade last year, too. We could have pushed him through, but we held him back, because our goal is to get him into college, not push him through. It turned out to be the best thing for him. He's totally blooming this year."

As the children ate their muffins or cereal and drank their milk, Reid pored through an eighteen-item to-do list, which consisted of compliments or criticisms she hadn't had a chance to discuss with her teachers the day before.

A "+" in the margin meant a compliment—for example, one teacher had improved the efficiency of the "transition" process by which her students move from their chairs, push the chairs under their desks, and get down on the rug to begin paired discussions of the reading. A "Δ" meant something needed improvement, such as one teacher's not having explained clearly enough how to round numbers up or down.

At about 7:55 Reid stood up, looked around the room to see who was reading while eating, then clapped three times. Silence. She stood in front of the group and announced that Boston College (all classes are named for the college their teacher attended) "has earned a compliment card because they have the most scholars reading this morning." Then she walked over to one boy deep in the *New York Times* and gave him a personal compliment for being so engrossed in the paper.

As we walked off to a class, Reid explained that the school tries to lavish praise incessantly on even the small things, "so that everyone will keep doing them." As she passed a parent in the hall, she grabbed her hand to congratulate her because her daughter "is doing so fantastically."

"We also get on them for little things, like even minor uniform infractions," she explained. At Harlem Success, the students start the day with green cards posted under their names in front of the room. If a student does something wrong, such as talking out of turn or not completing part of a homework assignment, the green comes down and a yellow card replaces it. Something really bad— like missing homework altogether, or earning three yellows—gets a red card and a call to a parent. (If for some reason a parent isn't sufficiently involved, Moskowitz will hunt for another relative or even a volunteer to become the student's go-to person for the school.) A student who stays on green all week earns a "green machine" award and gets a "green machine" cheer from the class at the end of the week.

At the University of North Carolina classroom, Reid watched for a few minutes, whispered a compliment to one student for her "awesome eye contact," then quietly walked up to the projector the teacher was using and removed the page. "It had the main idea for today's discussion, and I didn't want them to see it until they formed their own ideas," she whispered to me when she returned. As the children "transitioned" to the floor for their one-on-one discussions of the reading (after which they are supposed to tell the class what they think the main idea was), Reid interrupted, "Scholars, I noticed yesterday that in many of your pairs it's always one of you who speaks to the other first. I want you to reverse that today, please. Okay, now turn and whisper."

The children had obviously learned a protocol for these conversations. As one listened, the other was supposed to tap his or her head when he or she had an idea and was ready to speak. And always, the response began with either "I agree" or "I disagree."

Soon it was time for the duos to present their ideas to the class. When others wanted to respond to the idea presented, they also patted their heads, so the teacher knew they wanted to chime in.

The book was about a boy named Todd who lived in a foster home. Todd had a mean foster father. When one little boy referred to the foster father as "white and rich," another patted his head rapidly and got called on. Reid is always telling the students to present "proof" for their ideas, and this student wanted to know, "What's your proof that Todd's family is white?"

"Because," the first boy replied, "it talks about him wearing a robe and slippers. That makes him seem rich, so he must be white."

Now a little girl patted her head. "There are black people who have robes and slippers, too," she said.

When the class ended about thirty minutes later, Reid and the University of North Carolina teacher huddled together, smiling and talking excitedly about how well the class went. The only equivalent I could think of was how pumped up television news producers get after they pull off a show that they think really connected with the audience. These teachers and Reid seemed to think of every class period as a major production.

Six weeks earlier, Harlem Success had announced that although New York State had drastically raised the "cut scores" needed to be judged proficient in math or reading (which had dramatically set back the proficiency rates for Klein's schools), Harlem Success students had continued to ace the exams. Eighty-six percent were proficient or better in English, and 94 percent were proficient or better in math in the 2009–2010 school year that had ended last June.

On the other side of the building at PS 149, the numbers were 29 percent and 34 percent.*

Kayrol Burgess-Harper, the principal of PS 149, who had taken over last January, was determined to make things better. Beginning in

---

* When the scores for 2011 were reported in August 2011, Harlem Success actually improved on that performance across a variety of measures.

September she began sending weekly e-mails to her teachers, hoping to rally them to the cause, which she summarized this way at the end of each e-mail: "We will continue to do our best until every member on staff wants his/her son, daughter, niece, nephew, cousins, and neighbors to attend our school."

Burgess-Harper's e-mails singled out teachers who had "good classroom environments" that the others should visit and learn from, celebrated the initiation of swimming classes for second and third graders, and congratulated two teachers for getting a small grant from J.Crew to help buy extra supplies for the third graders. Other e-mails announced a program to send curriculum information to all parents (an idea she got from Harlem Success), thanked a teacher for starting a "perfect attendance" bulletin board on the first floor for all students to see, reminded the teachers to submit their "star student of the month" with "a synopsis, so these students may be highlighted," and offered a pizza party to the class that achieved 100 percent parent attendance at the upcoming parent-teacher conferences.

She also tried to confront challenges. One e-mail complained that "some teachers who do not receive the ratings they thought they should discussed this with a parent and sent the parent to advocate on their behalf. Please note that parents do not have the training to decipher what constitutes a quality lesson. This behavior is highly inappropriate."

On multiple occasions she had to remind teachers to do lesson plans, and once she had to write a long plea that teachers "who have difficulty conferring" with their students in order to give them feedback should seek her assistance. "Please note," she added, "that conferring with students is non-negotiable. . . . Let us continue to treat other people's children the way we want our children to be treated."

In that same e-mail she had to deal with a complaint lodged by the school's union representative and some of the teachers. They didn't like it that tutors from the Harlem Children's Zone (HCZ)—Geoffrey Canada's organization that, in addition to running its own charter schools, supplied tutors to Harlem public schools—were eating in the teachers' lounge. By contract, the lounge was reserved for teachers only. "Let us not forget," Burgess-Harper told the teachers, "that it is through HCZ that most of our students are tutored. . . .

Without this partnership, we would lose valuable resources, which our parents depend on, and a drop in enrollment means a cut in teaching staff. . . . [I]t is creating bad blood that makes this partnership seem like a catastrophe. . . . Let us . . . not allow our joy to be taken away by a few outliers."

It was petty rear guard actions like this, or what Klein described as the "thuggery" of "putting hits out on principals" with calls to the school system's anonymous corruption hotline, that had convinced Klein, as well as Rhee, that the unions would bend only to superior power, not through persuasion or compromise, because they could not be trusted to live up to any compromises.* With the national rollout of *Waiting for Superman* approaching, the differences between the most combative reformers and those more inclined to compromise would become clearer because the debate would now play out on a more media-intense, public stage.

* By 2012, Burgess-Harper was no longer the principal of P.S. 149.

The "Mujahideen" and the Moderates

Fall 2010–winter 2011

Waiting for Superman opened on September 24 in theaters across the country, following a September 20 send-off on the *Oprah Winfrey Show*, where Bill Gates, Michelle Rhee, and producer Davis Guggenheim appeared. It was the beginning of a publicity triumph for the movie, including magazine cover stories, television specials, community viewing parties sponsored by charter schools and reform groups (often organized through a splashy website partially funded by the Gates, Broad, and Walton foundations), and generally positive critical reviews.

In anticipation, Weingarten and Michael Powell, her "crisis communications" specialist, circulated a long memo to the media two weeks before, providing their take on the film. Another, arguably more compelling if less lavishly produced, documentary on the same subject—*The Lottery*, which focused on Moskowitz's Harlem Success applicants, and was financed by reform-sympathetic donors and produced and directed by Madeleine Sackler—also opened at about this time. Powell had a lot of crisis to contend with.

His media memo, signed by Weingarten, elicited a point-by-point rebuttal by Whitney Tilson in an e-mail to his followers and to the press. The dueling memos nicely framed the arguments of the two sides, as these sample exchanges illustrate:

POWELL/WEINGARTEN memo. It is shameful to suggest, as the film does, that the deplorable behavior of one or two teachers (including an example more than two decades old) is representative of all public school teachers.
TILSON REBUTTAL. I've seen the film three times and it doesn't suggest this. This is just what the unions always do whenever

anyone says a word about bad teachers: distorts it into an attack on ALL teachers.

POWELL/WEINGARTEN. Guggenheim makes only glancing reference to the poor achievement of most charter schools, despite the abundance of independent research showing that most charter schools perform worse than or only about as well as comparable regular public schools. Nevertheless, he illogically holds them up as the ticket to a good education for disadvantaged students.

TILSON. We could have a spirited debate about whether charter schools, as a whole, are better than comparable public schools—the short answer is that in states with strong charter laws like NY, they are; in states with lousy charter laws, they're not—but that's not the issue. *Waiting for Superman* is focused on schools that PROVE, beyond any doubt, that demography is NOT destiny and that schools CAN change the life trajectories of kids, even the most disadvantaged ones. This is really, really hard and . . . there are probably only a few hundred schools in the country that are achieving such outcomes—and guess what, the vast majority of these schools are charter schools, so it's hardly surprising that the movie focuses on these schools.

POWELL/WEINGARTEN. The most effective solutions didn't make it into the film. In other words, Guggenheim ignored what works: developing and supporting great teachers; implementing valid and comprehensive evaluation systems that inform teaching and learning; creating great curriculum and the conditions that promote learning for all kids; and insisting on shared responsibility and mutual accountability that hold everyone, not just teachers, responsible for ensuring that all our children receive a great education.

TILSON. I would actually largely agree with Randi here (though she's missing the critical elements of setting high expectations and building culture/character), except she has the first sentence exactly backward. It should read: "The most effective solutions *made it into* the film." In other words, the successful schools the film highlights are doing EXACTLY what Randi calls for: they're developing and supporting great teachers (and getting rid of ineffective ones); they've developed rigorous and fair evaluation systems so that every teacher AND every student knows exactly how they're doing and what they need to do to improve; and they hold EVERYONE accountable, from teachers, to principals/administrators, and yes, to parents and students as well.

Like Rhee, Tilson enjoys confrontation. Jon Schnur is the opposite. Later in the fall, Schnur accepted an invitation to meet with the National Education Association's state delegates and national officers at a retreat in Miami. The invitation itself from the hardline union was a sign of how much had changed.

"He must have begun every other sentence by thanking them for inviting him or praising them for engaging in the conversation," said one person who was at the Schnur session. Schnur ignored what he later told a friend were "some of the crazies in the room, like the people from Louisiana who yelled that the New Orleans schools had deteriorated since all the post-Katrina changes."

Schnur's pitch was direct, if soft: "Even if you don't buy all of our arguments, you should engage with us and work with us. It will only make what we do better for the kids and better for teachers. You can choose between getting behind Barack Obama, who deeply cares about education and teachers, or a Governor Christie,"* he added, referring to New Jersey Republican Chris Christie, who was rapidly building a national following by targeting the teachers' unions in his state.

Actually, Schnur admired Christie, and one of Schnur's longtime cohorts in the reform movement—Christopher Cerf, who had been Klein's deputy—was about to become Christie's education superintendent. However, Schnur was trying to see if he could turn some of the NEA's leadership into de Klerk–like figures who would, as the South African president had done with the end of apartheid, yield to and get behind the inevitable without more fighting.

Joel Klein took the opposite approach. In November, George Parker—the Washington, D.C., union leader who, with Weingarten,

---

* This is a paraphrase, based on the accounts of two people at the meeting.

had negotiated that concessionary deal with Michelle Rhee—was voted out of office. The man who beat him had vowed to roll back the contract Parker and Weingarten had agreed to. "I think any union president that is pushing and getting in front of reform takes a risk, and I took a risk," Parker said after the election.

Klein's reaction, he told a friend, was that "part of me thinks it's a good thing if the mujahideen come in and polarize the debate still more so we can win this once and for all." Of course, he was referring to the Islamic radical warriors kiddingly, but Klein's willingness to engage in the fight when others might have compromised was no joke—and had yielded great results as he confronted the unions or maneuvered around them (by encouraging charters or reconstituting failing high schools) when they tried to block him. In his view, as he wrote in a June 2011 account of his tenure in the *Atlantic Monthly*, "collaboration is the elixir of the status-quo crowd."

Rhee, of course, was dismayed by Parker's defeat, though she knew that the man who beat him was making empty threats about overturning the contract. Yet as a general matter, she shared Klein's approach, and then some. To her, the last months of 2010, with all of its reform advances, and the coming of 2011 weren't about negotiating a peaceful compromise. It was all about storming the remaining barricades. On December 6, she announced her hoped-for billion-dollar political action group, called StudentsFirst, with a cover article that she wrote in *Newsweek* titled "The Real Battle for School Reform Begins Now."

"Despite a handful of successful reforms, the state of American education is pitiful, and getting worse," she wrote. "The children in our schools today will be the first generation of Americans who will be less educated than the previous generation."

Comparing the teachers' unions to the National Rifle Association and the pharmaceutical and tobacco industries, Rhee declared, "Though we'll be nonpartisan, we can't pretend that education reform isn't political.... During the civil-rights movement they didn't work everything out by sitting down collaboratively and compromising.... This is the time to stand up and say what you believe, not sweep the issues under the rug so that we can feel good about getting along."

Rhee quickly gained traction, with support not only from Democrats for Education Reform and its usual backers but also from a group of Republican governors—including Rick Scott of Florida, Mitch Daniels of Indiana, and Christie of New Jersey—who announced that she was consulting with them on their education initiatives. Rhee also supported Governor Scott Walker's winter 2011 effort in Wisconsin to curtail public employee collective bargaining. Meantime, Karl Rove's conservative political action group, Crossroads Grassroots Policy Strategies, jumped on the bandwagon with a television ad campaign on the cable news channels supporting the Republican governors' attacks on the unions and featuring the 2009 speech by the NEA general counsel in which he had proclaimed that the NEA's priority was its members' interests, not "a vision of a great public school system for every child."

When I first met Jean Clements, the union leader in Hillsborough County, Florida, who had fashioned the compromise that had won her school district the Gates Foundation grant, we sat at a table in her office on the ground floor of a housing project the union runs for low-income retirees. The cover of *Newsweek* featuring Rhee and her call to arms was sitting on the table staring up at us. When Clements saw me looking at it, she said, "Yeah, we're not exactly two people who take the same approach to things." Yet, as when Pittsburgh superintendent Mark Roosevelt had invoked the specter of someone like Rhee forcing change on the teachers, both Clements and Hillsborough superintendent MaryEllen Elia said that the ferment and threat that Rhee had stirred up had helped them get the teachers behind their reform program. Put simply, the spear carriers and the moderates seemed to be playing tandem roles.

Rhee appeared on *Oprah* the day *Newsweek* came out and got so many donations—100,000 within forty-eight hours, totaling more than $1 million—that they blew out the computers serving the "donate" section of the StudentsFirst website, which actually was a section of the DFER website, because DFER was still serving as the fund-raising conduit for Rhee's start-up organization. Meantime, she had gathered more than $100 million in donations or pledges from heavy hitters such as Eli Broad, Rupert Murdoch, Julian Robertson, Ken Langone, and the Fisher family that had founded the Gap (and was a major KIPP benefactor).

Rhee's spectacular launch, and the fact that in March 2011 the new Washington mayor, Vincent Gray, formally announced that he was appointing Rhee's former deputy as the chancellor, suggested that Mayor Fenty's loss and Rhee's departure as chancellor might turn out to be a net plus for the reform movement.

However, through the fall of 2010, for every one or two steps forward for the reformers, there seemed to be at least one step back.

One was a particularly important: the departure of Joel Klein.

On November 9, Klein announced that he was resigning as New York City's schools chancellor, effective December 31, and going to work as a senior executive at Rupert Murdoch's News Corporation, where he intended to get the media conglomerate into the business of creating and selling software and related technology products for educators. Klein says he had told Mayor Bloomberg over the summer that he hoped to leave sometime near the end of 2010 or the beginning of 2011, and he had told close friends the same thing. The announcement, therefore, was not a shock. Bloomberg's choice of a successor, Cathleen Black, was.

Black, who was the president of the magazine division of the Hearst Corporation, and her husband, lawyer Tom Harvey, are old friends of Bloomberg's. That was about the only connection she had that had anything to do with New York City government, let alone its schools. Black had been educated in parochial schools in Illinois, and her children had attended private schools in New York.

Klein's education résumé had been thin, too—a year as a Queens teacher and twelve years in Queens public schools. However, he had also been involved in public policy and politics as a private Washington lawyer, White House counsel, the head of the Justice Department's antitrust division, and a member of the D.C. mayor's kitchen cabinet.

Black's main experience at Hearst—an intensely private and privately held company—and at other publishers before that had been selling advertising and, later, supervising teams of ad salespeople.

More important than their respective résumés, Klein had been hired at a time—2002—when Bloomberg and everyone else trying to overhaul public education was essentially writing on a clean slate. There were no "experienced" education reformers and few cutting-edge education system managers. By 2010 there were.

Merryl Tisch, a longtime friend of Bloomberg's, had one such experienced person in mind: John King, her deputy state education commissioner. King attended Brooklyn public schools, then Harvard College and Yale Law School. After that he had started his own charter school and then had been managing director of the Uncommon Schools charter network. He is also African-American and, as deputy superintendent, had gained experience working with all the players on the New York education scene.

Tisch was furious that Bloomberg had picked Cathy Black out of the blue. She was not alone. Across the country, teachers, school administrators, and especially reformers felt insulted that Bloomberg thought so little of their work that he assumed anyone could step in and do it. King was so upset that he refused to participate in the process whereby the state education department had to issue a waiver for Black to be certified for appointment because she did not have the requisite education credentials. That job was left to his boss, Commissioner David Steiner, who embarrassed himself in a long interview with the *New York Times* in which he publicly agonized over the decision—which was a foregone conclusion: Tisch told him he had to issue the waiver because the law requiring the waiver was inconsistent with the idea of mayoral control of the schools.

Steiner's public vacillation did not bode well for his prospects for getting the UFT's Mulgrew not to exploit the loopholes in the state's new reform law. Nor did Bloomberg's having not picked a chancellor like Klein bode well for how far the city would continue to push the education reform agenda during Bloomberg's remaining three years. Although he reported to the mayor, Klein had had his own views and constituency that enabled him to serve as at least a partial counterweight to what had been City Hall's more conciliatory stance.

Black's initial months on the job did not quiet those concerns. She did little more than tour schools and attend public hearings, where on several occasions she made gaffes that the press latched onto and that caused the staff Klein had left behind to begin polishing their résumés. Just three months into her tenure, after a significant core of Klein's staff had already resigned, Bloomberg fired Black and replaced her with Dennis Walcott, a deputy mayor who had been a City Hall liaison to Klein.

Walcott's role had been that of a behind-the-scenes Bloomberg deputy who arbitrated disputes among Klein's and Bloomberg's people over how strong a stand to take against the union. Bloomberg's choice of Walcott—who has been a New York City public schools student, teacher, parent, and grandparent—to replace Black left open the question of whether he would now assume Klein's tough, independent posture, or whether, as Bloomberg's appointment of his friend Black had seemed to signal, he was put there so that City Hall could dial back the push against the union that Klein had led.

In a less ambiguous, positive development for the reformers, the same day that Black was fired, State Commissioner Steiner resigned, clearing the way for his tougher, more competent deputy, King, to succeed him. King was officially appointed to the top spot in May 2011.

Klein's impending departure in December 2010 triggered multiple retrospectives on his tenure, almost all positive. Even Weingarten e-mailed him the night of the announcement, saying he "should take a bow."

Klein seemed moved by her gesture. "I fought with her, and there are a lot of things I don't like about her," he told me the next day. "But this is a real person, not some caricature or figurehead. She's up late at night and dashes off that e-mail to me."

The state's decision in 2010 to score its standardized tests much more stringently (a decision Klein supported) had reversed some of the city's test score gains recorded since he had taken office in 2002. Yet the gains were still substantial. And they were going in the right direction at a time when so many school districts in New York and around the country were standing still or going the other way.

Across New York, principals trained in Klein's Leadership Academy were in place and injecting new energy and expectations into a system that needed both, strengthening the prospects for further progress. High school graduation rates had increased, and Klein's move to break up large, failing schools and put them under the management of organizations like New Visions, which could choose new teaching staffs, had undeniably improved education for tens of thousands of students.

And then there was what Klein, with Bloomberg's complete backing, had done to promote charters. The antitrust lawyer had seized on the idea that even poor parents deserved choice instead of the public school monopoly. He had pushed quality charters—with co-locations and the fights to lift the cap—in a way that, as investor and Democrats for Education Reform co-founder Boykin Curry had marveled, "was the rare instance of a public official trying to give up turf."

Whitney Tilson, Curry's DFER co-founder, blogged a paean to Klein on the eve of his departure that covered his accomplishments in New York and also toured the country identifying people who had worked for Klein who now ran their own school systems: in New Jersey, Baltimore, New Haven, Rochester, and, of course, until recently Washington, D.C. This was Klein's "lasting legacy," Tilson concluded.

Yet Klein himself was ambivalent about that, again reflecting his storm-the-barricades view. He pointed to two of those places where, he told me, his people had not been tough-minded enough and had compromised too much with the unions. "I like to say that there are big minds and strong minds," he explained. "All of them had big minds, but not all had strong minds."

A few weeks after he had left office, I asked Klein why he had seemed so unrelenting, so wary of compromise. "I always made it a point to get out into the schools and spend time with children, and it always moved me," he said. "It still does. And when you see those kids and then think of the people who are trying to block them from getting the education and opportunity that you and I had, it has to make you angry. . . . It pisses me off because these kids don't have time for these compromises."

Just before Klein's last day, he walked over to an office to find out about his retirement funds. Although as chancellor he was obviously not covered by the union contract, one aspect of his benefit package was, he was told, aligned with something in the contract: He could withdraw the funds he had contributed into a 401(k) plan if he wanted to, but if he left them in the education department's fund, he would be guaranteed a return of 8.25 percent. Forever.

"How can you guarantee 8.25 percent?" Klein asked.

"Because the union contract says that teachers who contribute into this fund [in addition to the other, larger pension fund set up for them that the city contributes to] are guaranteed 8.25 percent," the fund clerk told him. "If the investments fall short, the city has to make up the rest."

Klein had just learned about a benefit written into the union contract that was another underfunded time bomb.

"Who else but Bernie Madoff guarantees 8.25 percent a year permanently?" Klein chuckled.

After the announcement of Black's appointment, the UFT's Michael Mulgrew told a November 2010 meeting of a community group sympathetic to his union that "mayoral control [of the schools] is due to sunset in three years, and there is no way it is coming back." As for Black, Mulgrew said that he had told "City Hall" that "the same morons you are depending on to guide her educationally are the morons who guided Klein." However, Mulgrew assured his audience, "City Hall" had told him that Black had been appointed because the mayor "wants the noise around education to die down."

The same day, one of Klein's deputies told me that "Mulgrew is now really pumped up. There is no chance he is going to negotiate the reforms [called for in the new state law]. Everyone knows that."

Others were more optimistic. John King, the newly promoted state commissioner, said that "sooner or later he is going to have to have a new contract and then he will have to negotiate those evaluations." Indeed, it is hard to imagine that three or five years from now, Kayrol Burgess-Harper, the principal on the PS 149 side of the building housing Harlem Success I, isn't going to be able to pick her teachers and motivate them more effectively, and that even more charter schools will not have proliferated around her, allowing parents still more choice while reminding them and everyone else that free schools don't have to mean failing schools.

Then again, pendulums do swing; three years from now, New York will have a new mayor, who will probably have been chosen in a Democratic Party primary, a venue in which Mulgrew's union has always had great influence.

In New York and across the country, the last two years had seen sweeping change in the laws, the rules, and the political dynamics of public education, as well as a dramatic shift in public consciousness. But the fight was not over. Two steps forward, and one or maybe two steps back for the reformers is likely to be the way this battle continues to play out. That was certainly how things looked as 2010 ended. There was lots of activity, and lots of reasons for both sides to cheer, or to be alarmed.

Punch, Counterpunch

Winter–spring 2011

Across the Hudson River from New York, the news as 2011 began was that Facebook founder Mark Zuckerberg had pledged $100 million to the Newark school system so that Democrats for Education Reform stalwart (and friend of DFER co-founder Boykin Curry) Mayor Cory Booker could work with Republican governor Chris Christie in order, says Curry, "to explode the number of charters in Newark." It certainly was futile ground. Newark's bureaucracy and union contracts are such that it spends even more per student in its public schools than New York does, with worse results.

Launching all those charters may not be easy. In March 2011, after Booker announced his intention to steal a page from Klein's playbook and co-locate the charters in public schools, the head of Weingarten's AFT unit in Newark vowed to the *Wall Street Journal* that "there isn't going to be any way that there will be co-existence with charter schools while I'm breathing."

In Rhode Island, newly elected governor Lincoln Chafee, a Republican turned independent, seemed poised to go in the opposite direction from his predecessor, Donald Carcieri, a Republican who had pushed reform and presided over his state's winning Race to the Top application. Chafee had supported Obama, and the president returned the favor by not endorsing his Democratic opponent, who is a DFER member. Soon after he assumed office, Chafee announced that he wanted to take "a pause" on expanding charter schools. He was wary of charters "undermining and cherry picking and skimming off the top of our public school system," he explained. Chafee, who had been endorsed by the state units of the NEA and AFT, said that he was inviting Diane Ravitch up to advise him. He also quickly removed the pro-reform chairman of the state Board of Regents; and the job of education commissioner Deborah

Gist, who had supported the firing of the Central Falls High School teachers, was thought to be in jeopardy. However, as of May, the specter of losing Race to the Top money that the state had already won seemed to have caused Chafee to hesitate on scuttling Rhode Island's reform plans, and Gist was still in her job.

Meantime, neighboring Massachusetts, which had also won Race to the Top money, proceeded with its ambitious implementation, but Connecticut, which did not win the Race, scrapped its plans, citing a lack of funds.

And in New York, not only had the UFT's Mulgrew not budged by the spring of 2011 on negotiating a new contract that would allow the state teacher evaluation law to be implemented in New York, but the Rubber Room reform that he, Klein, and Bloomberg had announced a year earlier seemed to have morphed into a lot less than had been touted.

True, only 83 of 744 teachers in the Rubber Rooms a year earlier were still on the list of those who had been put on "Temporary Reassignment," which was the official designation for Rubber Roomers. That was the headline—only 83 of 744 Rubber Roomers still left— that the Department of Education conveyed when I first inquired.

However, of the 661 teachers no longer on this "reassignment" status, only 33 had been terminated following an arbitrator's decision. Another 154 had been allowed to resign or retire (typically in return for receiving some kind of severance payment and being able to keep their pensions), or had been dismissed because they had not had tenure.

This means that 474—or 63 percent of the original group of Rubber Roomers—had been, in the education department's terminology, "returned to service." Some were put back into classrooms. But in a deft bureaucratic shell game, most of them—272 of these 474 cases—were simply added to the Absent Teacher Reserve list, where they were still paid to do nothing.* In other words, they had been moved from one list of idle teachers to another list of idle teachers, but the new list has no bothersome arbitration hearings or even a

---

* The Absent Teacher Reserve had previously consisted only of the group of teachers who were "excessed" out of one school but were not hired by any principal at another school. These were the teachers Klein had tried unsuccessfully to get Weingarten to allow him to remove from the payroll after a deadline of a year.

theoretical possibility of termination: Teachers can stay on the Absent Teacher Reserve payroll forever.

Put simply, the hearings for these accused Rubber Room teachers were indeed moving faster, but the results were that most of the teachers were being returned to teaching or kept on the payroll while not teaching. "That's what happens when these arbitrators have to be approved every year by the union," Klein says. The union could argue that the fact that so few teachers have been dismissed proves they had been unfairly accused. However, the time I had spent with people in the Rubber Rooms and reading their case files leaves me believing that the safeguards built into the process to protect teachers and thwart principals have survived.

Moreover, the city appeared to have let up on Klein's aggressive posture that had sent 250 to 300 teachers a year to the Rubber Room in the first place; just 155 had been removed from class in the year following the big announcement of the April 2010 agreement.

Asked about these statistics in May 2011, Mayor Bloomberg said he knew that most had been kept on the payroll but assumed they had been sent back to class. Told that so many had simply been shifted to the Absent Teacher Reserve, he readily conceded that the Rubber Room deal he announced with the union the prior April had worked only in the sense that the arbitration process had been speeded up and "the press doesn't have a Rubber Room to write about." But, he added, "Whether or not [the former Rubber Roomers still on the payroll] are doing any work, I have no idea."

In California, Governor Jerry Brown, the just elected Democrat who had received strong support from the teachers' unions, removed seven of the eleven members of the state education board, all reformers. One of the replacements was a teachers' union lobbyist. And a new state education superintendent, also backed by the unions, took office, having beaten reformer Gloria Romero. (Romero was subsequently hired by DFER to run a California DFER unit.)

However, on December 7, a surprising counterforce emerged in California. Speaking to an education conference in Sacramento, Los Angeles mayor Antonio Villaraigosa laced into the teachers' unions—and cited an unprecedented credential giving him special credibility:

> Why, for so long, have we allowed denial and indifference to
> defeat action? I do not raise this question lightly, and I do not
> come to my conclusion from a lack of experience. I was a leg-
> islative advocate for the California Teachers Association, and
> I was a union organizer for United Teachers of Los Angeles.
> From the time I entered the California State Assembly and be-
> came Speaker, to my tenure as Mayor of Los Angeles, I have
> fought to fund and reform California's public schools. Over the
> past five years, . . . there has been one, unwavering roadblock
> to reform: UTLA [United Teachers Los Angeles]. . . . Union
> leaders need to take notice that it is their friends, the very peo-
> ple who have supported them and the people whom they have
> supported, who are carrying the torch of education reform and
> crying out for the unions to join them.

Villaraigosa told me that he had started to change his views about
the union in 2005, when Eli Broad had sponsored a local political
action fund and voters started asking the then–mayoral candidate
whether unions were an impediment to fixing the schools. He had
begun thinking generally about education reform even earlier, he
said, in the late 1990s, "when I saw that George Miller [the Bay
Area congressman] and Ted Kennedy were getting into it. If these
guys were for it, maybe it wasn't so bad."

Villaraigosa was "radicalized," he said, when he became mayor
and began to dig deeper into the schools, which he knew was peril-
ous because the schools were mostly the turf of the teachers' unions,
for which he had worked as a lobbyist and which contributed approximately $1 million to his mayoral campaign.

"I started talking about this to the union right after I got
elected," he said, "and always it was the same old song. 'We need
more money. You don't understand. These kids are poor. These kids
are English-language learners.' Well, I did understand, because I
was one of those kids.

"I'm a lot different than the governor of Wisconsin," Villaraigosa
added, referring to Scott Walker, who had ignited protests in Wisconsin in early 2011 not only by going after the pay, benefits, and working condition protections of public employees, especially teachers, but
also by trying to take away their rights to bargain collectively at all.

"I'm not Scott Walker," the mayor repeated. "I was the child of these people, their offspring. Now they have been weakened by their offspring and it has hit them in the mouth."

Through the winter and spring of 2011, Villaraigosa was immersed in efforts to turn Los Angeles into what he calls "the new epicenter" of reform. He had eased out the incumbent superintendent and brought in John Deasy, a highly regarded reformer who had been deputy director of the Gates Foundation's education projects and before that superintendent of three different school districts.

The mayor was also heavily involved, along with Democrats for Education Reform, in raising money for reform-minded candidates running for five contested seats on the seven-member Los Angeles Unified School district board. When the votes were counted on March 8, two of the reform incumbents had won, one of the two union-supported candidates had beaten the most avid reformer, and the other union-backed candidate was forced into a runoff with the candidate supported by the mayor. Thus, the mayor had at a minimum kept a 4–3 majority on the board, which could become a 5–2 advantage, depending on the runoff. And his new zeal for the reform cause, along with Deasy's arrival as superintendent, was likely to propel a major reform drive in Los Angeles for the remainder of his term, which ends in 2013.

Moreover, a bill passed by the California legislature in response to the pressure for reforms generated by the Race to the Top was now bearing fruit. The so-called "Trigger Law" allowed parents in a school judged under federal standards to be persistently failing to petition to have the school turned into a charter. The legislation had barely survived a Sacramento lobbying campaign by the supporters of teachers' unions, who dubbed it a "lynch mob" law.

In February 2011, parents at a Compton, California, middle school pulled their trigger, igniting a legal battle with school officials and the union, who questioned the validity of their petitions. The parents were supported by a growing California organization called Parent Revolution, run by Ben Austin, a former Clinton aide and charter school veteran (who was one of the state education board members removed by Governor Brown). Austin's group and the Trigger Law seemed to be creating a grassroots movement around school reform that had rarely been seen anywhere else—and that was buttressed by the controversy and new public awareness stirred by the *Los Angeles Times*'s August publication of those teacher effectiveness scores.

That all of this was happening in California—which for so long had been a teachers' union stronghold and a bastion of failing public schools but was now being pushed in the opposite direction by the state's leading mayor—was especially significant.

At the same time, Villaraigosa had been meeting with Arne Duncan and his staff to persuade them to let Los Angeles apply as a district—rather than require the state to apply—if Duncan was able to get Congress to authorize a 2012 round of Race to the Top. Even the unions—under pressure from the mayor and from the publication of the *Times* teacher data—had expressed a new willingness to compromise on teacher evaluations.

"With Deasy here now, we'll win it," the mayor said, referring to the possible new Race to the Top competition. Potential movement in California, or even just Los Angeles, would affect so many children and so change the political landscape that it would dwarf the impact of whatever problems states like Hawaii or Delaware had in meeting their Race to the Top commitments.

Another front for the reformers, with major political implications, was opening up on the other coast, on Manhattan's Upper West Side.

In the fall of 2010, Eva Moskowitz announced that she was launching Upper West Side Success Academy, a charter school to be housed in the middle of a community that, while it included many poor families, also included much of what was left of Manhattan's middle class, as well as many wealthy, liberal Democrats. After the typically chaotic process, in which the city bounced it from one prospective co-located school to another, ample space was found at a high school on West Eighty-eighth Street, smack in the center of a middle- and upper-class neighborhood, where families with children approaching school age scraped together the money necessary to pay for private schools, moved to the suburbs to find good schooling, or tolerated the area's mix of well-performing and poorly performing schools.

Because the district included (to the north) many impoverished families in Harlem, and because everyone from the district was eligible to be admitted by lottery, Upper West Side Success promised to open up another front in the battle for public school choice. This would be a charter school that provided not only a dream alternative for the poor but also an almost unheard-of alternative for the middle class: classrooms that would have standards and test results equivalent to those of the best private schools in Manhattan but that would cost nothing—because these classrooms were in a public school open to everyone, which is what charter schools are. Plus, it offered rare diversity because it would attract lottery applicants from across the district.

Moskowitz knew she was filling a need. The poor and middle class in New York both lacked alternatives to the traditional public schools or the expensive private schools. This was confirmed by the hundreds of applications that soon poured in.

Klein, among others, immediately also appreciated the political brilliance of what she was doing. Moskowitz was taking the battle south of Harlem to a community that had far more political clout than the usual venues for charter schools and where politically aware parents would be an important new ally. For these probable liberal Democrats, for whom support of unions was instinctive, the debate they might have read about occasionally in the past few years over charter schools in Harlem would now become a debate about *their* children. The appeal of the charter option for middle-class New Yorkers obviously would spread beyond the Upper West Side to similar neighborhoods in Manhattan and the other boroughs, where parents were increasingly finding their children relegated to waiting lists at those public schools that were still regarded as providing good teaching.

UFT leaders and community elected officials who had benefited from the union's support in Democratic primaries, such as the local councilwoman, rose up to protest the co-location. They even got one local parents' group to join them. Together, they made the usual arguments: that there was not enough space (which was not true), and that the co-location would cause tension (which would be true if they caused it). They added a third argument, which was unusual for this Manhattan bastion of liberalism—that the charter school would attract "outsiders" into the community. As more parents sent in applications, their protest petered out to the point that one highly publicized street demonstration organized in December, which called on thousands of West Siders to protest Moskowitz's school, attracted about two dozen people.

Meantime, other local politicians began to recognize the squeeze Moskowitz had put on them: Should they side with the union that had played a key role in getting them into office, or respond to the yearning for a better school by parents who were arguably more sophisticated (and had higher voter turnout records) than many in Harlem? Thus, City Council speaker and likely 2013 mayoral candidate Christine Quinn told attendees at a private Democrats for Education Reform luncheon in December that she favored the school but had not yet "figured out how to formally announce my position." She never did. And one of her probable mayoral election opponents—the always press-hungry Manhattan borough president Scott Stringer, who had won his job running against Eva Moskowitz with the union's all-out support—would not come to the phone when I called to ask his position. He had a spokesman issue a statement in which he "deplored the controversy" generated by the new school.

One day in December, I watched the potentially transformative political impact of Upper West Side Success play out. To drum up applications, Moskowitz had invited prospective parents to tour another of her schools farther up the West Side, in Harlem, to get a taste of how Harlem Success operated. Sixteen parents—three African American, two Asian, the rest white—gathered in a science room to hear Moskowitz talk about her schools. One man in a black cashmere overcoat, who was glancing at his BlackBerry, looked as if he might have stopped by on the way to his law firm or investment bank. Most of the others were carrying briefcases or backpacks and also looked as if they were on the way to work. One told me he was an editor at a magazine, another a software marketer, a third a graphic designer. Their eyes seemed to widen as Moskowitz offered details about the "unique design of the school."

- "In regular Department of Education schools it is incredibly challenging for principals and assistant principals to get out of their offices and into the classroom, but here we have business managers who take care of all of that, so that we can observe four or five classrooms a day."

- "In the regular schools, the teachers get one day to prepare for the school year, but here we take thirty days."
- "We teach science in every grade—you are sitting in a first-grade science class—and we teach everyone chess, because my son has serious language-learning deficiencies but great strategic abilities, and we could never have learned or developed that without chess."
- "In a traditional school, if it's forty degrees or colder no one goes outside into the schoolyard, because it's too cold for the adults. Not us."

In January 2011, the co-location of Upper West Side Success was officially approved by the citywide panel, chaired by Cathleen Black.*

Still another positive development for the reformers came as a result of the financial bind facing state and local governments at the beginning of 2011. School districts across the country were going to have to implement teacher layoffs. In most major cities, union contracts required that layoffs be done on the last in/first out, or "LIFO," basis, meaning the most junior teachers would be the ones to go. In fact, the teachers' unions over the years had successfully lobbied in eleven states, including California and New York, to cement that protection into state law.

As issues go, there was broad consensus that this restriction was the least defensible of all the teachers' unions' job protections. The UFT's Mulgrew had told me that it was necessary to prevent principals or school systems from targeting senior teachers because they get

---

* The union soon sued to block the school, arguing, as usual, that the paperwork documenting the availability of the co-located space was insufficient. The suit, which could only delay the school but not ultimately block it, was finally thrown out by a judge on August 12, 2011. The first students arrived on August 24, 2011. The school proved to be so successful and popular that in April 2012, Upper West Side Success received 2,199 lottery applications for 89 seats.

Despite a renewed flurry of lawsuits and fierce union opposition, in 2012 Moskowitz received approval to open new Success Academies in two more mixed-income neighborhoods, both in Brooklyn, beginning in August 2012. Some of the UFT-backed suits against the schools were pending as of May 2012.

In April 2012, all of the Harlem Success schools combined received applications for 1,200 seats from 12,300 children.

paid the most and, therefore, would yield the most savings if fired. Weingarten also defended LIFO with the argument that it protected against age discrimination. That may have been true in the first half of the last century, when these restrictions were put in place, but it plainly isn't true since the passage of the federal age discrimination act in 1967. Not only is that kind of discrimination now illegal, it is also the easiest discrimination claim to sue an employer for. If an employer lays off one hundred people and they are disproportionally old, it's almost an open-and-shut case, with the simple age data as Exhibit A. It's not anything like the difficulty of proving discrimination in one-by-one hiring decisions, where the evidence is more difficult to gather and intent is harder to prove.

Moreover, this argument called attention to the overriding aspect of the union contracts' compensation system that had by now fallen into such disfavor—that these senior teachers got paid more just because they were more senior.

Finally, it was easy to show, and the unions' opponents did this repeatedly, that firing the most junior teachers would disproportionately reduce the staffs at the schools in the most challenged communities, because senior teachers didn't want to teach there (and could choose not to because their seniority gave them site preference, too). In other words, LIFO not only forced "quality-blind" layoff decisions, as the opponents liked to put it, but also was perversely geared to hurt the schools that needed the most help and the least disruption.

Across the country, newspapers and newscasts ran stories of young "teachers of the year" or idealistic, effective TFA teachers facing layoffs.* Rhee quickly targeted LIFO as her best point of attack for her new organization. In New York, former chancellor Klein had agreed to become chairman of DFER's Education Reform Now, its 501(c)(4) fund. With help from Mayor Bloomberg, Education Reform Now quickly rounded up millions from donors, including Eli Broad and Rupert Murdoch, and began a series of media blasts urg-

---

* TFA was probably going to suffer badly from LIFO, and many reformers were surprised and even angry that Wendy Kopp did not come out swinging against it. "Do I really need to?" she asked me. "It should be obvious how I feel, but we have to work with these school systems and teachers every day."

ing Albany to end LIFO. Meantime, Bloomberg mounted the bully pulpit at City Hall.

Why is this listed as a positive development for the reformers? Because LIFO really was like apartheid. In the post–Race to the Top world of 2011, it was indefensible and forced the unions into a fight that they not only were going to lose, sooner or later, but that also would make them look less credible the longer they kept fighting.

Through the fall of 2010 and winter of 2011, Duncan and his staff were thrilled by what they had done in their first two years and by how the president was lately becoming even more of a cheerleader for these initiatives. "We got dozens of states to change their laws and regulations; we got members of Congress from fifty states to pay for reform in eleven states and the District of Columbia, which never happens around here; and we've created a brand and a cause that the president is out there promoting every day," said one of Duncan's top aides. "Not bad."

Perhaps. Yet, as of April 2011, Duncan's office had had to approve what the official Department of Education document called seven "adjustments" to the time line that Delaware had promised in its Race to the Top proposal. In all cases the "adjustments" postponed the deadlines.

Hawaii asked for and was granted ten such "adjustments." The state had yet to draft its promised plan for teacher evaluations, let alone get the unions to agree to it.

As of the beginning of April, three of ten Round Two winners— Georgia, New York, and Rhode Island*—had not yet had their post-award plans approved for how they would implement everything they had promised, even though these had been due at the end of November and should really have just been restatements of their proposals. More important than the paperwork, New York City was not a day closer to putting in place the evaluations its new law supposedly guaranteed, because the UFT's Mulgrew was still holding out. "All of the agreements related to how they [New York State] won the Race to the Top money are just not going to happen," Bloomberg told me in May 2011.

* Rhode Island's Statement of Work was approved on April 8, 2011.

Meantime, some school districts in winning states threatened to drop out, and some did drop out, despite the MOUs they had signed. Their reason was that they were finally focusing on what they would have known had they stopped and done the math when the Race began: that they were in line for small amounts of money and actually had to spend it to cover the costs of the efforts they had promised.

"This is not the windfall we were expecting," the superintendent of the Longwood school district in New York told local reporters when he found out he would receive $239,000 spread over four years. Another New York school board president called his $53,000 a year "crumbs from the feast." Still, both districts ultimately stayed signed up. That was not the case in Jones County, Georgia, which decided that $143,000 a year doled out over four years was not worth the effort of negotiating evaluation formulas and merit pay for teachers, let alone the cost of building the associated data systems— all of which, of course, had been spelled out in the application.

Still, despite many complaints about the "crumbs," the falloff from the original declarations of participation was modest; of the thousands of districts that originally promised to participate with their states in the Race, those with about 1 percent of the students in the winning states dropped out.

A bigger issue than districts officially dropping out was what those that stayed in were actually doing. Some states, like Florida, seemed well on their way; districts across the state were already heavily engaged in new teacher-training programs and technology purchases aimed at providing better monitoring of student progress. The legislature had passed a law making good on the state's promise that test scores would count 50 percent toward annual evaluations of teachers, which would be used for compensation and tenure decisions. And, of course, there was the ongoing Gates-funded work on teacher evaluations and merit pay being done by union leader Jean Clements and superintendent MaryEllen Elia in Hillsborough County. It was moving at a pace that was roughly a year ahead of the state's schedule.

However, getting many of the other states to crack the whip on their supposedly participating districts was proving to be a problem, not only in tiny Delaware, Hawaii, and Rhode Island, but also in many districts in Ohio, Georgia, North Carolina, Maryland, and, of course, New York. The problems were such that Duncan's department had to award two "technical assistance" contracts worth $42.9 million to a consulting firm that was engaged to help the states figure out how to comply with their own Race plans.

On the other hand, there were other steps forward for the Race's agenda.

- Klein announced just before his departure that New York City was immediately going to start using test scores to evaluate new teachers when they were considered for tenure. The Race-inspired decision by the legislature to allow the "firewall" law (prohibiting the linking of test scores to teacher tenure decisions) to expire gave Klein the power to do this, even if the city still had to negotiate with Mulgrew on using scores for the evaluation, compensation, and potential dismissal of already tenured teachers.

- In an effort organized by the National Governors Association, standards for a "common core" curriculum were tentatively adopted by forty-three states plus the District of Columbia in 2010. This was the result of the Race to the Top's having awarded points to states that participated in standards-setting efforts like this. The common standards momentum continued through the beginning of 2011, as the Obama administration financed the development of tests to match the core curriculum, and as advocates pushed a follow-up plan, organized in part by the Albert Shanker Institute (a think tank run by the AFT), to expand the grades and subjects covered. This kind of push for unity of standards among the states would have been unthinkable in the days when Ronald Reagan believed public education should be the province of individual state and local school districts, or when Arkansas governor Bill Clinton struggled at that Charlottesville White House/National Governors Association Education Summit just to get the states to agree on broad common goals. Many conservative Republicans—including John Kline, who took over as chairman of the House Education Committee in 2011 after the Republicans won control of the House—still shared Reagan's preference for localism. Yet the common curriculum movement, which was supported by many other Republicans, such as Jeb Bush, and spurred by the Race and President Obama's repeated warnings that America was now competing in a global talent market, seemed unstoppable.*

- As with Hillsborough County, in Memphis, Pittsburgh, and the group of charter networks in Los Angeles that won the Gates Foundation teacher effectiveness grants, the promised reforms seemed to be proceeding on schedule. The difference might have been that these districts were chosen more intuitively than the bureaucratically driven selection of Race to the Top winners. The decisions had been made by a knowledgeable foundation staff overseen by the pragmatic Bill and Melinda Gates. And they were districts, not states, which eliminated a layer of bureaucracy and allowed the foundation staff to monitor each program closely before checks for additional installments on the grants were written.

- In December, Tom Kane, who runs the Gates Foundation's education research, announced the first results of the foundation's $45 million effort to have thousands of teachers videotaped in class so that expert teachers could examine the tapes and evaluate the teachers. The students were also given extensive feedback surveys. The initial results were that the grades given the teachers from the videos and the feedback from the surveys were consistent with each other and also consistent with the value-added scores Kane had calculated by tracking the test score progress of the same teachers' students from the beginning to the end of the school year. In other words, the test data—often attacked by the unions as unfairly serendipitous—seemed to match ex-

---

* However, through the spring of 2012 the national Republican Party seemed to retreat almost completely from the idea that public education was a federal issue. The candidates running in the primaries for president tried to out-do each other to be the most in favor of the federal government staying out of K-12 education. Former Pennsylvania senator Rick Santorum even argued that the states should not be involved in K-12 issues, which should be left entirely to local school districts or home-schooling parents. Although eventual nominee Mitt Romney, alone among his competitors, voiced muted support for George W. Bush's No Child Left Behind, he, too, expressed opposition to a continued strong federal role in K-12 education.

pert teachers' classroom evaluations (based on the videos)
and even the students' evaluations (based on the surveys).
Combining all three seemed to offer a promising and unas-
sailable formula. Moreover, the video aspect of the effort allowed the observations to be done remotely, enabling real
experts to do them efficiently, which was better than rely-
ing on local teachers to have the necessary expertise and
objectivity.

- Rahm Emanuel, who pushed the Race as President Obama's
chief of staff, was elected Chicago's mayor in February 2011.
Emanuel had made education reform a key campaign promise. In April, Emanuel's ability to push his agenda beyond
even how Villaraigosa hopes to push his in Los Angeles was
dramatically enhanced when the Illinois legislature passed a
sweeping reform bill the mayor-elect had advocated. The law
eliminated last in/first out layoffs. It also allowed school districts across the state to award tenure based on performance,
to dismiss tenured teachers for poor performance in a streamlined process, and to extend the school day—which in Chicago
had been shortened by the union to the point where Chicago
children were spending 270 hours (or about forty school days)
a year less in class than New York City's undertaught students. The surprising turnaround in education politics in the
Democratic bastion of Illinois came after the teachers' unions
overplayed their hand and alienated Democratic legislative
leaders by withdrawing all financial support to them in retali-
ation for the Democrats' support of a relatively modest pension reform proposal in the cash-strapped state. Emanuel says
he plans to implement these reforms quickly and also begin
using Schnur's New Leaders for New Schools and other outside groups to do all the recruiting of school principals. "What
happened in Illinois was staggering," says Duncan, who had
run Chicago's schools before becoming education secretary.
"I could never have imagined it. These guys didn't win the
[Race] money, but they just kept on moving."

- In addition to Emanuel, a driving force behind the Illinois
bill was Stand for Children, an increasingly influential education reform group whose emergence was, itself, another

positive development for the reform movement. Run by Jonah Edelman, the son of Children's Defense Fund founder Marian Wright Edelman, Stand for Children was so effective in lobbying (and in raising more than $3 million in political action committee funds in the state) that the unions were forced to capitulate and negotiate with the reformers. Stand for Children had also played a major role in pushing reform laws in Arizona and Tennessee, as well as Michael Johnston's bill in Colorado. "We bring all the political tools to the office," says Edelman. "Strategic selection and recruitment of candidates, grassroots organization of parents and educators, digital and traditional media, and money for candidates and lobbyists. In Illinois, we had eleven paid lobbyists."

- Democrats for Education Reform was continuing its own surge as a heavyweight counter to the teachers' unions. In May 2011, when the New York State agency that monitors lobbying issued its annual report, DFER was found to have outspent the United Federation of Teachers and New York State United Teachers combined, spending $6.6 million for its 2010 media blitz and an army of Albany lobbyists, compared with $6.2 million dispensed by the unions. Of course, as Michael Bloomberg told me, the reformers "have to learn to use that money to fight as ruthlessly as the unions do, not with facts and position papers." But with Michele Rhee's just-formed StudentsFirst now gearing up in her quest to raise a billion dollars, the unions' historic status as the overwhelmingly dominant force in public education politics seemed to be over (assuming the donors funding the reform movement keep at it rather than treat their cause as a passing fad).*

- Ironically, the reforms enacted into law in Louisiana and

* Through the end of 2011 and the first half of 2012, Rhee continued to raise money and forge alliances with political leaders, including strident anti-union Republican governors across the country. Meanwhile, on the heels of a front-page *New York Times* article on March 20, 2012, about how all the candidates slated to compete in New York City's 2013 Democratic mayoral primary were already courting UFT leader Michael Mulgrew, Rhee announced the formation of a New York unit of StudentsFirst. Its unabashed purpose was to raise funds to counter the UFT's political influence. The board of Rhee's new group included Joel Klein, Eva Moskowitz, and Geoffrey Canada. Mayor Bloomberg's former chief Albany lobbyist was chosen to run it.

Colorado, the two states jilted in the Race, were also proceeding on schedule. According to Michael Johnston, because "we budgeted money in the law as if we would lose," all plans were moving ahead and, in fact, the provision not allowing the forced placement of teachers into schools where principals don't want them was already in effect. In Louisiana, Jon Schnur was working closely with state officials to implement every aspect of the state's Race plan.

- Moreover, in Louisiana, Duncan's department had awarded a major "innovation grant" to Sarah Usdin's New Schools for New Orleans umbrella organization, which partly made up for the state's loss in the Race.

Although many of the states that won the Race were already behind in their timetables, even the slowest were taking significant steps toward reform. And many—I'll guess eight or nine of the twelve winners—will get most or all of their plans implemented by 2012 to 2014, which is basically on time, given the need to build databases and collect two years of test scores and other evaluation measures (such as classroom observations) before beginning to compensate and promote (or fire) teachers based on those scores. Supporters of the Race would argue that while keeping to schedules and the letter of the plans is important, what was more important was all the change in laws and regulations that the Race had spurred across the country—in thirty-four states. Moreover, they pointed to the change in public consciousness and sentiment about these issues, particularly the core reform of paying, advancing, promoting, or firing teachers based on rigorous evaluations.

They were right. With $600 billion spent on public education in the United States each year, sprinkling $5 billion out there payable over four years amounted to about two-tenths of 1 percent of annual spending. This meant that the Race produced not only actual reform, in which some or all of the plans would be carried out, but also, and more important, the ultimate "leverage" of a powerful marketing campaign that galvanized politicians, parents, and the press around an issue that had been festering for years.

"We didn't create all of this movement," says Duncan. "We simply unleashed it. There was all this pent-up demand. People in their hearts knew that what was going on in our schools was bad. Wrong. Immoral. We ended up with almost as much change in states that didn't win the money—sometimes even more—than states that did win the money. It wasn't about the money. It was about creating a climate that gave states and districts and politicians permission to do what was right."

As Duncan struggled through the winter and spring of 2011 to get the tightfisted new Republican Congress to approve his reduced plan for a second Race in which districts, not states, would compete, there was talk in the reform network and even among some on his staff and in the White House (which regarded the Race as its major domestic success) about whether he should boost his chances of winning over congressional Republicans by making an example of one of the lagging Race states, such as New York. Maybe he should withhold payment on a next installment of the grant or even demand that funds already paid be sent back to Washington. Although this is almost never done with federal grants except in cases of fraud, it seemed a perfect way for a president who had vowed to change the way Washington worked to look as tough as any Republican with the federal purse, while again putting what was thought to be the administration's trophy initiative in the spotlight.

"This is hard work," Duncan told me in April. "There's a reason this took five decades. So I am less worried about getting it done on time than getting it right." Asked specifically about New York and the probability that New York City would not have an agreed-on teacher evaluation plan anytime soon, much less have implemented it, Duncan refused to comment on any particular state but said, "If we see folks are not making progress we have a moral and financial obligation to stop funding them. And we will."

As of May 2011, Duncan had not yet clamped down on any state, but he had publicly endorsed the threat by the Delaware department of education to withhold funding from the state's largest school district, which was wavering on its commitment to adopt a teacher evaluation plan.*

* As of May 2012, the Department of Education had, according to *Education Week*, placed Hawaii on "high risk" status for "significant performance issues." *Education Week* reported that the department had "found that the state had failed to hit key milestones in every part of its application, but particularly in its promises to secure a collective bargaining *(cont.)*

• • •

In a coup negotiated as part of the last-minute budget deal worked out between the President and the Republican Congress in April 2011, the Obama administration was able to win another $1.25 billion in the 2011 budget year for education reform incentives.* Duncan planned to use the money to offer states relief from some of the burdens of the old No Child Left Behind law in return for enacting specified reforms that these funds would help finance, and for a contest for states related to early childhood learning innovations. Duncan did not get the authority to run a Race to the Top–like reform contest among school districts rather than states—but he and his team hoped to try that next year.

Meanwhile, the secretary continued to be the un-Klein and un-Rhee, bear-hugging his potential opposition. He scheduled regular breakfasts with Van Roekel of the NEA and Weingarten of the AFT, and he traveled the country for press events congratulating local school chiefs—and, when possible, local union leaders, including Clements in Hillsborough County—for their reform efforts.

Boykin Curry, the hedge-fund investor who had helped start Democrats for Education Reform, was of two minds about all of this. He liked all of the Race to the Top activity, but over breakfast one morning he reflected the view of an increasing number of school reformers, such as Usdin in New Orleans and Moskowitz in Harlem, in expounding what he called his "Hong Kong theory." Hong Kong, he explained, had demonstrated that free markets and

---

agreement with its teachers' union so it can pilot and implement statewide a new teacher-evaluation system based, in part, on student performance."

New York, after fits and starts in negotiations in Albany aimed at forcing the unions to agree to the promised evaluation plans, was still almost completely stalled.

And across the country, all twelve winners had applied to the Department of Education for a minimum of three amendments each (and a total of 64 for the twelve). The amendments typically cut back on their promised plans and extended their timetables, most of them significantly. Duncan had yet to demand the taxpayers' money back, but he had slowed the spigot so much in light of the slow progress that only 14 percent of the $4.35 billion allocated to Race to the Top had been dispensed, with "the bulk of the early money," according to *Education Week*, having gone to consultants who were working on honing and rejiggering the winners' plans.

* The Obama administration's point person in this negotiation with the Republican-led House was Robert Gordon, the co-author of the Hamilton Project paper on teacher effectiveness who had recently been promoted to executive associate director of the Office of Management and Budget.

capitalism worked so well that neighboring mainland China had seen the comparison and been motivated to throw out communism, not reform it. "It's like Aeroflot," he said, referring to the hapless Russian airline. "They can't fix it. They have to scrap it, just the way we scrapped the old airline regulatory system in the U.S. in the 1970s and created a competitive market that now allows people who work in Costco to afford to get on a JetBlue or a Southwest Airlines plane and go see their relatives."

The supposed wonderfulness of American commercial aviation aside, what Curry meant was that the old notion that charter schools could be small laboratories for reform should be discarded and replaced with a bigger idea. He believed that charters had to gain critical mass, as they had in New Orleans, Washington, D.C., and Harlem, and as he wanted to have happen in Newark with Mark Zuckerberg's Facebook money. Only that would create the kind of truly visible demonstrations of schools that work and the accompanying critical mass of parents that would force the old system to be thrown out.

"We are fast reaching that moment," Curry assured me, "when things will flip, and all schools will be charters, or be forced to act like charters. We've got all of this momentum now, with the Race, with Obama, with DFER, and now with Michelle's new group. It's amazing how fast this is now happening."

The turnarounds in New Orleans, Washington, and Harlem were, indeed, extraordinary. The question, though, was how all that momentum could be sustained and spread beyond a few "Hong Kongs." That wasn't simply a matter of politics. Curry's exuberance aside, there were enormous practical issues associated with "scaling" a turnaround of public education.

A Marathon, Not a Sprint

Dave Levin, the co-founder of KIPP, was giving me a tour one afternoon of KIPP Infinity in upper Manhattan, which is considered to be one of the best of KIPP's ninety-nine schools across the country. After he bemoaned the school's co-location tensions, he echoed Curry in marveling at all that had happened in the eighteen years since his friends and family "couldn't understand why a Yalie would go teach in some ghetto school in Houston. . . . We've got a Democratic president and Race to the Top. We've got all these wonderful schools in places like Harlem. We've got two movies"—*Waiting for Superman* and *The Lottery*—"taking up the cause. We've got Oprah, you name it."

"So you must feel pretty good," I said.

"Well, that's it, I don't," he replied. "I'm still failing 60 percent of the time."

Levin explained that although the 40 percent college graduation rate of KIPP students who had gone through the charter network's eighth grade (and were now old enough to have completed college) was multiples higher than the equivalent rates for students who lived in these communities, it still meant he was failing 60 percent of the time, by his standards.

"It's really sad and outrageous what's happening to the children on the other floors of this building," he added, referring to the co-located public school. "But we're failing a lot, every day, on *this* floor, too. I know it's happening even as we speak. And these kids aren't helped by movies or Oprah. They depend on what we do here."

To make his point, he grabbed a piece of paper to take notes and walked me into the back of one of his classrooms. It seemed to me like most KIPP classrooms—full of focused, connected children with a magnetic teacher in front of the room. To Levin, though, there was a lot wrong with this picture.

Twenty minutes later, after we had left the room, Levin rattled off four things he had seen misfiring: an imperfect bulletin board, three students whose eyes were wandering, the teacher turning her back to face the blackboard, an incomplete reading log.

"Making all those things work is the job," he continued. "It's exhausting and it's not exciting, but it's what you have to do."

Levin acknowledged that he was at least free to try because he was not straitjacketed by a union contract. He could hire and fire as he pleased, set the work hours he needed, move the staff around—everything he needed to do to make KIPP work. "That's totally true," he said. Then he stopped, looked up, and delivered a dose of reality: "If you tore up every union contract in the country," he began "that would just give you the freedom to try. It's a prerequisite, but that's all. Then you would have to train and motivate not 70,000 or 80,000 teachers"—the number teaching in the most effective charter schools—"but 3 million teachers," the approximate number teaching in American public elementary and secondary schools.

Levin compared the situation to the Iranian oil crisis of 1978. "Remember the gas lines? That was when we should have done something about energy," he said, "because it takes that long. But we didn't. This is the same thing. You had *A Nation At Risk* in 1983, and we basically did nothing. With the energy crisis we had everyone waiting on line for gas and we still did nothing. Here we had kids hidden away in classrooms, where most people expect them to fail anyway, and we did nothing. . . . Now we finally seem motivated, but it's going to take a long time."

Another way to look at that time line was a calculation sketched by Mark Roosevelt, who ran the Pittsburgh schools. If, through evaluations and other means, he could improve his teaching talent each year by retraining or removing 60 to 80 ineffective teachers out of his group of 2,200 and replacing them with better recruits, it would still take ten years to re-fortify a third of his workforce. That would make a significant difference, and it would be worth the effort. However, that's a hard gulp for politicians who typically risk only big fights, such as union confrontations, for tangible short-term payoffs. That was why the Gates money, which is not available to systems countrywide, had been so important to Roosevelt. It's why Race to the Top, which offered less money per winning school district but lots of glory for winning politicians in winning states, worked. But even if the Gates- or Race-inspired reforms were implemented around the country—and worked—Roosevelt's calculation demonstrated that it was going to take a long time to revive American public education.

It wasn't as if Roosevelt could do it any faster in Pittsburgh. If he removed 5 to 10 percent of what he judged to be his worst-performing teachers each year, instead of 3 or 4 percent, where was he going to find and train that many qualified replacements?

In the summer of 2010, when I heard Arne Duncan remark that "you can't fire your way to the top," I thought it a clever turn of phrase intended to mollify the unions. Duncan was actually making an important point. For, as Levin explained, the bigger hurdle is that "you can't expect 3 million people, or even a half million, to be as talented as our [KIPP] teachers are, or as willing to work these kinds of hours and do this as intensely as they do. You have to devise support systems, with great management and great technology, to make moderately talented people better. You can't do this by depending only on the kinds of exceptional people we have around here who pour themselves into this every hour of every day."

"Everywhere I travel to give speeches," says Diane Ravitch, "I meet thousands and thousands of teachers who typically grew up in the cities and towns where they teach, and went to education schools near there. They're the ones we are going to have to depend on next year and ten years from now, not some Ivy Leaguers who are doing it for a year or two. If you took every single Ivy Leaguer, you couldn't fill a fraction of our classrooms." She's right about that.

"I feel overwhelmed, underappreciated, and underpaid," one Harlem Success teacher told me. "I work from 7:30 to 5:30 in the building and then go home and work some more. I get disrespectful pushback from parents all the time, when I try to give their kids consequences. I get feedback from my leaders [supervisors] who demand that I change five or six things by the next day. I think we are doing a great job, so I keep at it. But there is no way I can do this beyond another year or two. . . . Eva [Moskowitz] says Harlem Success is going to grow to forty schools. I don't see how they can possibly do that. This model just cannot scale."

Moskowitz says that although not everyone is cut out for this work, "to say that we can't scale this is like saying we can't build the Brooklyn Bridge because it's hard. We're a tougher country than that. . . . Sure, we have turnover, but our teachers make good money; we pay for them to take dial cars home if they work late; and we buy them perks, like massages every other month or so. And they can advance quickly. . . . I have leadership residents [assistant principals] who are twenty-eight years old and making $100,000 or $120,000, who get six weeks' vacation. How bad a career path is that?"

On January 19, 2011, I met one of those leadership residents, Jessica Reid, for a drink to talk about burnout, among other issues. She quickly volunteered, "I know I can't do this forever. And I know if I had a child I couldn't do it. As it is, it is screwing up my marriage."

Already thin, Reid said she was losing weight and never seemed to be able to get away from her work. She recounted how the night before she had had to get off the treadmill during one of her now rare weekday trips to the gym—and, therefore, had been late for dinner—in order to spend a half hour "arguing with a parent who thought I was being too hard on her daughter for not completing her writing assignment.

"I had marked it incomplete and asked her to bring it home to her mother and have her initial it because she had not written all the way down to the bottom lines and included the conclusion," she explained.

In urging Reid to ease up, the child's mother reminded Reid that her daughter had trouble writing.

"*Exactly*," Reid had replied. "That's why she needs to do these assignments, or she's not going to college."

That had happened Tuesday night. Reid and I talked about it Wednesday night.

On Sunday, I learned that Reid had resigned from Harlem Success over the weekend, citing issues related to her health and her personal life. A month later, she used the word *sustainable* a dozen times in explaining her sudden decision to me—as in, "This wasn't a sustainable life, in terms of my health and my marriage."

The woman who had said, "You can never sit down," had had to sit down.

That Reid had tried to sprint through Levin's marathon was understandable. Geoffrey Canada often says that we have to treat the children's lives being stunted by failing schools as an emergency. We have to act now, urgently. Who wouldn't feel compelled to sprint?

Canada is an extraordinary person. So is Dave Levin. And Wendy Kopp. And Jessica Reid. So are thousands of spectacular, equally driven teachers in traditional public schools across the country. We can be led and inspired by extraordinary men and women in these charter or public schools. But they will lead us to the right place only if we can figure out a realistic way to motivate and enable the less than extraordinary in the rank and file to respond to this emergency. We can't do that by requiring them either to sprint or stand aside.

The lesson, then, of Reid's dropping out of the race at Harlem Success is that unions run by people like Jean Clements in Hillsborough County and by Randi Weingarten have to be enlisted in that fight because unions are the organizational link to enable school improvement to expand beyond the ability of the extraordinary people to work extraordinary hours.

In fact, if Michael Bloomberg really wanted to go for a touchdown in education reform in his remaining years in office he could try the ultimate Nixon-to-China play: He would put Dennis Walcott, his replacement for the failed Cathleen Black, back in his deputy mayor's job and make Randi Weingarten the schools chancellor. She's smart and almost certainly knows that the way to fix public education is to make the rank and file perform better. She knows exactly where and how to fix the union contract so that it rewards performance and enhances professionalism. She knows that the shelf life is rapidly expiring on her standard dodge that she, too, wants to change lockstep compensation, LIFO, and overprotective tenure rules, but that this can be done only if all sides collaborate to develop truly fair evaluation systems. She has well-deserved credibility with teachers. She obviously cares about her place in history. "I hope my career is on an arc like Al's," she told me in one of our last interviews, referring to Albert Shanker.

As chancellor, Weingarten would have to shed her habit of making offhand overstatements that can easily be disproved by reporters who would now see her as a bigger target, but she's proved to be a savvy political player who can hold her own in any arena or in front of any camera. I can see her now standing with Bloomberg, as she accepts the job, declaring that times have changed; that we face a true crisis in educating America's next generation; that we have to move ahead with tough teacher evaluation systems even if tests and other aspects of the evaluation process can't be perfect and even if management has to impose it the way management does in every other professional workplace; and that she's going to lead a new era of professionalism and accountability in teaching that is, as her favorite phrase goes, "good for children and good for teachers." Only now her constituency would be the children (and Bloomberg).

A traditional Democrat's appointing Weingarten would be seen, correctly, as a big step back from reform. Bloomberg's appointing her—and loudly pushing her to complete the job of reform that he stepped back from when he undermined Klein and yielded to her in the 2005 and 2007 contract negotiations—would be seen as exactly the opposite. And, if, as is likely, a Democrat succeeds Bloomberg, he or she would have a hard time forcing this fiercely loyal Democrat, with her now proclaimed reform agenda, from office.

Asked if she would take the job, Weingarten said, "Being chancellor in New York has to be one of the most important jobs and best jobs anyone could have in life. Anyone who really cares about educating public school children would take that job." But could she really go over to the management side? "I manage a lot of people right now. . . . A good union leader has to be able to walk in management's shoes."

Weingarten then added that Bloomberg had asked her to take the job "many years ago," but that she had declined because at the time "it would not have been credible." (Bloomberg says he never spoke with Weingarten about being chancellor, adding, "It's a really stupid idea. Never in a million years.")

This Weingarten-as-chancellor fantasy aside, the fact is that unions and their leaders can and should be enlisted to help stand up those in the rank and file who are well-motivated and able but are not extraordinary. That doesn't mean yielding to the unions' narrow interests; it means continuing to enhance the political climate and, with it, the backbone of the political leaders who negotiate with the unions, so that the unions will yield to the interests of the children their members are supposed to serve.

Waiting for that to happen is not an excuse for inaction. Waiting for *the* scalable solution, as the hedge funders would call it, is no better than waiting for Superman. Geoffrey Canada, Michelle Rhee, Dave Levin, and the Jessica Reids of the world have helped thousands of children in the emergency room. More should be encouraged and enabled to do so.

But having great care in an emergency room is no substitute for fixing the health-care system.

Assuming that half the 4,900 charter schools now serving 1.7 million students are doing lifesaving work, that would add up to 850,000 lives being reclaimed. That is multiples more than the country's twenty best universities can claim. And it's probably more lives saved than the best-funded, most effective government medical research program can claim.* So the importance of charters shouldn't be discounted. It's well worth celebrating, in many movies.

However, there are about 50 million American public school students in 95,000 K–12 schools. If just half of them need the kind of intensive care offered by the good charters because they lack the supplemental support that more affluent families can provide, that would require overhauling schoolrooms serving more than twenty-five times as many children as those charters serve, in 47,500 or more schools. That cannot be done charter by charter; it takes the infrastructure of the public school systems. And whether those schools are charter schools or traditional public schools, that means finding, training, and motivating 1.5 million teachers and some 47,500 principals.

Mounting and training an army that large requires the kind of intense focus on minute-by-minute teaching practices that characterizes the best charters. However, it also means creating working lives and career paths for teachers that will motivate a good portion of them to stay for more than a few years. In a world where career changes are the norm and serve to reenergize every workplace, that may not mean they stay for twenty or thirty years, but it should mean they are there for at least five or ten.

This is crucial. If there is anything to be learned from spending

---

* Moreover, charters don't cost taxpayers any extra money; in fact, as Eva Moskowitz will eagerly remind you, in most states they are typically funded with fewer taxpayer dollars than are allocated per student to traditional public schools.

two years trying to figure out public education, it's not just that the teachers who are hanging on for twenty or thirty years caring only about their pensions and tenure protection are toxic. It's also that teachers get far better at what they do when they've been doing it for more than a year or two. Working long, hard hours helps. But it takes preparation, training, lots of feedback and introspection, and high expectations—in addition to some element of classroom charisma, whether low-key or flamboyant—to turn a hard worker into the kind of great teacher we all had in one classroom or another. A handful may have all that on their first day in class. Most don't. It's a building process that requires time.

Jessica Reid's plan was to move up from teacher to assistant principal to principal, and she quickly got two thirds of the way there. Given what we have seen Moskowitz go through since she started in 2006—grueling hours of fighting bureaucratic hassles and push back from everyone threatened by her schools' performance—it's hardly clear that the life of a principal at a school that is on this mission is currently sustainable over the long term, either.

When I first asked Moskowitz about potential burnout, we were meeting at 5:00 in her office the day before Thanksgiving, 2010. She showed me her reading assignment for later that night and through the Thanksgiving weekend. She had to vet a dense "Education Impact Statement" that the Department of Education had drafted outlining its plan for co-locating one of the new schools she planned for the following fall. "I have to read and re-read this, because the unions will sue to invalidate this if there's even a typo or some trivial fact wrong," she explained, "and the department always screws these up.

"This is the kind of crap I deal with every day," she said. "So I guess asking me about burnout is a good question. Some days I don't know."*

True, the Race to the Top and the political blossoming of the re-

---

* Apparently, Moskowitz isn't burning out just yet. As of May 2012, she had plans to expand her Success Academy network from eight schools in 2010 to twenty-one across New York City by August 2013. Among these are two more (opening in August 2012) in mixed income neighborhoods in Brooklyn that immediately upon receiving approval became lightning rods for multiple UFT-backed lawsuits.

form movement have shined the light on the obstacles people like
Moskowitz face, and this has partially eased her way. Rhee's new
group will add to that momentum. The balance of power has clearly
shifted. It needs to shift more. Then the question becomes how to
sustain that new balance.

It's clear that when Albert Shanker began to try to push the
pendulum of union-management relations back from one extreme in 1953, it ended up going too far in the other direction.
The emergence of the reform network and all the activity emanating from Race to the Top have now pushed it back the other
way.

However, beginning in the winter of 2011 in Wisconsin, it seemed
to some as if the pendulum in some places might be swinging toward the original, pre-Shanker extreme. In January, newly elected
Republican governor Scott Walker threatened the very existence of
teachers' (and other public employees') unions by seeking to eliminate almost all of their rights to bargain collectively. This was the
right that Shanker had won in 1961 in New York (and that Wisconsin public workers had won in 1959).

Diane Ravitch told me that Walker's push in Wisconsin and
similar moves by Republican governors in Ohio and Indiana
were "the natural extension of the so-called reform movement;
it's what they always wanted." However, Democrats for Education
Reform sided with the teachers' union in Wisconsin and against
the governor. This was not only good politics, but smart—and
consistent—education reform strategy. Governor Walker's fron-
tal attack on the union's right to represent its members may
please those who think no pendulum swung toward employers
can swing too far. However, it went beyond education reform
and, in fact, threatened to undermine reform by creating sympathy for union leaders who may not deserve it and by seeking to
eliminate organizations that could help make reform happen if
they keep being pushed in that direction.

There is a good argument to be made against public employee
unions, and the story of the teachers' unions in the last forty years
certainly helps make it: They end up having too much power in
negotiating for salaries, benefits, and work rules, because they are
negotiating with the public officials for whom they often play a piv-

otal role in hiring through the election process. Yet that ignores the role that teachers' unions—once they are reined in politically, as began to happen in the last two years—can play in fixing public education.

Tough legislation to trump the unions, such as that pushed by Johnston in Colorado, is necessary. But taking the next step and eliminating the unions is not likely to improve schools. In Colorado, having an organized group to talk to—the union—after the law was passed helped make the goals of the law a reality. An apt analogy would be the United States' mistake in disbanding the entire Iraqi army and government infrastructure after Saddam Hussein was overthrown. "The NEA has been more helpful to us in dealing with the challenges of implementing the new Colorado law than a lot of the bureaucrats in the school system," says Jonah Edelman, of Stand for Children, who fought the union over the Michael Johnston–sponsored legislation.

In Hillsborough County or Pittsburgh, having the union sitting at the table was not a capitulation by the reformers but a victory for reform. It was a victory that was won, it must be emphasized, not only by those who compromised with the union but also by the harder-edged fighters, like Rhee and Klein, who created the political climate in which the unions had to seek compromise.

If the country has to sign up the platoons that Dave Levin says are needed, then giving teachers some say, through their representatives, about their professional lives—not to reject performance pay, or make a principal accept a lesson plan written on toilet paper, but the ability to have a more balanced life than the one that sidelined Jessica Reid—is a long-term positive, not a negative.

Exhibit A may be Jessica Reid. Within a week of quitting Harlem Success, she had gotten a job as an "achievement coach" at a Harlem public school through a teacher she had befriended on a subway platform the year she started at Teach For America in the Bronx. That teacher is now a Leadership Academy–trained principal, and he hired Reid to observe his teachers in his elementary and middle school and coach those who need help. "In the morning I can now go jogging or have breakfast with my husband," she says. "It's still a lot of work, but it's sustainable at the same time that it's hugely satisfying."*

"We need great new school leaders, we need new systems, we need new structures, but at the end of the day all of that has to be geared toward developing and retaining great teachers and bringing new ones into the pool," explains Schnur, who has three children, the oldest of whom is in kindergarten in a New Jersey public school, and who says that school reform remains the "mission of my life." Schnur adds, "The unions need to be part of that solution. It's like the country's electronic grid. If you wanted to change it to deliver new, better products, you wouldn't just rip it out. You'd rewire it to make it capable of delivering those products."

Pendulums swing back violently when they have been pushed too far in one direction. That is what enabled Governor Walker in Wisconsin. But it has also hurt the teachers. The unions succeeded so well that they hurt their own members.

In the midst of the Wisconsin fight that stripped teachers and other public employees of most of their bargaining rights, there were multiple newspaper articles about teachers feeling under siege. On March 3, 2011, the *New York Times* profiled Erin Parker, a thirty-year-old second-year teacher in Madison, Wisconsin, who was making $36,000 a year. She said she planned to move home to Colorado, where she could afford to continue teaching because she could live with her parents.

"The jabs she had heard about her job had stunned her," the *Times* wrote. "You feel punched in the stomach," she told the paper.

In 2009, Madison, which was already feeling the budget pinch, had negotiated a new 178-page union contract with the teachers, giving them just a 1 percent raise. However, all other protections under the contract—including lockstep seniority-based pay, a four-stage grievance process, and three paid days to attend union conventions—were kept in place. In Milwaukee, the 2009 contract had frozen pay for the city's 5,600 teachers in the first year, before giving them 3 percent and 2.5 percent increases in subsequent years. The teachers were also required for the first time to contribute a

---

* As of May 2012, Reid was still working as a coach, though she was now coaching principals as well as teachers for a network of schools whose management the New York City Department of Education has outsourced to a nonprofit group called The Urban Assembly. "I've never been happier or healthier," Reid told me.

small amount—1 percent of base salary for individual coverage, 2 percent for family coverage—for health-care coverage. However, as in Madison, all of their work rules protections and fringe benefits, such as pensions, remained in place.

In Milwaukee, the cost of fringe benefits, especially pensions, is such that the average total annual compensation of a teacher is about $99,000. (The same data are not available for Madison, but based on a reading of its contract, the total would appear to be about the same.)

It is contracts like these that not only gave the governor his ammunition but also, on closer analysis, actually seem likely to drive people like Erin Parker from their classrooms, which is why turnover rates among junior teachers are so high.

After the *Times* article about her was published, Parker received what she says was "such an outpouring of support from students, parents, and even a member of the school board that I decided to try to stick it out for now." But a different kind of union contract might have made the job far more appealing to Parker than the one that she came so close to leaving, while also boosting the performance of Madison's public schools.

For starters, her contract could have been geared to pay her significantly more in salary if, as with most people in the workplace her age, her union had bargained for a standard 401(k) pension plan, to which she and her employer would contribute a certain amount each year. Instead the unions have continued to insist on pension plans that guarantee lavish benefits only to teachers who stick it out for the duration of their careers—perhaps because senior teachers are generally the most active in the union and typically have the highest turnout rates in union elections. (Parker did not vote in the last union election, which had a low turnout rate because it was uncontested.) Having to reserve less for pensions for the tenure-protected senior teachers would free up funds to give qualified junior teachers higher salaries. "I think they should restructure the contracts so that new teachers can be paid more and everyone could have a smaller 401(k) contribution that they could take with them," Parker says.

Second, Parker is a high school science teacher. Because science, along with math and engineering, has seen a shortage of qualified teachers, school reformers have repeatedly argued that teachers of these subjects should be paid more. The Race to the Top contest—citing the need for more science, math, and engineering talent as a matter of national security and global competitiveness—encouraged the same reform by offering points for states that demonstrated how, with higher pay and other measures, they were going to beef up the teaching of these subjects. However, the unions have consistently been against differential pay of any kind. As a result, Wisconsin's Race to the Top application included no differential pay for science teachers, nor does the Madison teachers' contract allow it.

Had her union been willing to negotiate a contract that was consistent with national policy and priorities, Parker would have been paid more than $36,000. Asked about that reform proposal, Parker said, "I don't agree with the union on this. It's only fair that those of us teaching high-need subjects should be paid more."

Third, the contract could have been changed to eliminate LIFO, which makes it possible that Parker will be fired soon, regardless of how good a teacher she is, because Madison may have to implement deficit-forced layoffs. In fact, LIFO forces more teacher layoffs than would otherwise be required if the layoffs were spread across all levels of seniority based on quality; because all the layoffs are now directed only at the most junior teachers with the lowest salaries, more have to be laid off to achieve the same savings. "Obviously, LIFO is a bad idea," Parker says. "It's so frustrating." For Parker, LIFO is the real punch in the stomach.

Fourth, there are the provisions in Parker's contract, and in contracts across the country, that require school systems to spend $5 billion a year, as much money as Race to the Top is spending over four years, automatically awarding salary increases to teachers who gain added academic credentials, such as graduate degrees. As Bill Gates pointed out in several speeches beginning at the end of 2010, this is despite the fact that all the data that people like Tom Kane have been gathering show absolutely no correlation between teacher effectiveness and these credentials. Five billion dollars spread among 3 million teachers would, itself, be a $1,700-a-year boost for Erin Parker, who has only a bachelor's degree in science. Spread it among the half that are performing the best, and it becomes an extra $3,400 for Parker, who, based on the support she received from parents after the *Times* article, seems like someone who would qualify for a performance bonus.

If the country sets a goal that teachers ought to be paid in some proportion to their importance, school systems could easily get to pay scales of $65,000 for a starting salary (the average now is about $35,000), going up to $165,000 for the most accomplished professionals. This could be achieved mostly by spending smarter, not spending more.* There are lots of pockets of multibillion-dollar expenditures like the payout for extra degrees embedded in the system that could be redirected. These include the costs of keeping teachers on payrolls while they await interminable arbitration proceedings before being dismissed, paying them for so many sick days (or in cash if they don't use the sick days), paying them to attend union conventions, and paying union representatives who do not teach classes.

If school systems stopped adhering to class size limits now that we know that class size counts less at the margins than the quality of the teacher in front of the class—Jessica Reid's classes were larger than those in the public school next door—and increased students per class by just 10 percent (while using technology to help manage the workload more efficiently),** they could produce savings that could add more than $10,000 to the average teacher's salary. This can be looked at another way, as Eva Moskowitz pointed out in a March 2011 op-ed in the *Washington Post*: New York City allocates $13,500 to her per pupil. Increasing class size by an average of just one student, therefore, would enable the city's schools to pay each teacher $13,500 more.

Distance learning allows students to take specialized courses on-

* An exhaustive study in 2010 by the McKinsey consulting firm found that if teacher salaries were raised to an average starting base of $65,000 and topped out at just $150,000, the portion of newly entering teachers in high-poverty schools who come from the top third of their college class would multiply nearly fivefold, from 14 percent to 68 percent.

** Joel Klein believes so much in technology's potential to improve teacher effectiveness that when he left his post as chancellor in New York, he joined Rupert Murdoch's media conglomerate, News Corporation, in order to start a division that would invest in the development of technology to allow teachers to monitor their students' homework and progress more efficiently and digitize their texts and other materials to make them less expensive, more interactive, more up-do-date, and better able to be shared with parents.

line or through video conferencing. The unions have resisted it by successfully lobbying for requirements that all teachers, no matter how specialized the subject, must teach their students in person. Changing this would save billions more that could be given back to Erin Parker and her colleagues. It would also improve student opportunities to take advanced courses.

And, yes, if the country invested new money, say 3 percent of the current public education budget, that would free up the equivalent of another $6,000 per teacher. But the appetite for investing that money will not materialize if it is seen as giving more to people with a civil service mentality.

That brings us to the fifth and most important step to keep people like Parker teaching: Madison's union contract could have substituted performance pay for lockstep seniority pay, as the winning Race to the Top states have said they will do. (Wisconsin finished twenty-seventh out of thirty-six in Round Two and offered no tangible plan for rigorous evaluations and performance-based compensation in its application.)

With a contract like that—which is what she would now get, thanks to Michael Johnston, if she does move to a teaching job in Colorado—Parker, who says she is confident of her teaching ability, would have been further encouraged to stay. And she would be less likely to feel "punched in the stomach" if the public perception of her work shifted to that of someone in a profession that values talent rather than longevity. "You'd be hard-pressed to find any good teacher here who believes in seniority compensation and wouldn't like to be paid for performance, assuming the testing and evaluations were fair," Parker says.

By the spring of 2011, an unlikely convergence of forces had made stunning headway in pushing the agenda that would keep the Erin Parkers of the world happily at work—and that *A Nation At Risk* warned nearly thirty years before was so urgent. They include TFA alums and other reformers in Schnur's network; academics like Kane; money people like Broad, Gates, the hedge funders, and the billionaires in the elevator; charter operators; parents from Harlem to Los Angeles who saw that there was an alternative to assumed failure for their children and demanded that they be allowed to pursue it; and Democrats who were willing to join Republicans like Jeb Bush in confronting the unions, including the Democratic president who set off the imperfect but pivotal Race to the Top.

Looked at from the perspective of how far they have come from Wendy Kopp's college thesis, from Jon Schnur's fruitless drafting of speeches for Al Gore and John Kerry, from Congressman George Miller's losing a 434–1 vote on teacher certification and performance pay, from Bill and Melinda Gates's or Eli Broad's early missteps in education philanthropy, from Joel Klein's inability to order his own human resources department to produce data on teacher effectiveness, or even from the Obama administration's creation of what at first blush looked to be just another government grant program, they should all be taking bows.

But this is only the first mile of the marathon.

How can they keep going? How can they succeed in putting the American dream back into America's classrooms?

First, they have to keep at the work of instilling in teachers the high expectations for all children that the successful charter schools have proved possible. Their relentless message and policy thrust—in legislation, contracts, pay scales, even simple teacher recognition programs—must be that teachers can no longer be babysitters or incremental helpers for children destined to fail. They must be the talented enablers of children who can succeed.

This means that while the reformers shouldn't disband the unions, they can't let up against unions either. They have to continue to push back against union leaders who want to de-professionalize teachers by requiring that they be treated as interchangeable widgets unaccountable for their students' fates. They have to make sure that a political climate that always puts children first becomes so ingrained that a politician who negotiates a contract allowing teachers to be protected from poor performance, or to refuse to allow their lesson plans to conform to a standard, will be treated like a politician who allows firemen to pick which fire alarms they answer.

At the same time, the sprinters like Geoffrey Canada, Dave Levin, or Eva Moskowitz, whose work is saving thousands of children, must continue to be encouraged and given running room. They must be allowed to keep pushing and to keep experimenting— whether it's with new classroom games and gimmicks, curricula improvements, better tests that measure broader dimensions of a child's progress, or new technology to enable them to do it all more effectively.

But the reformers must also understand that they can't rely on the sprinters alone. Whitney Tilson's exclamation-point-filled e-mails about this or that hero are great reading and give those extraordinary people the cheers they deserve. But they alone won't tell the ultimate story of how public education will be turned around. As Dave Levin would attest, that story will be slower moving, be filled with infinite small steps, maybe even be boring.

Hundreds of thousands, even millions, of teachers will have to be enlisted to run the marathon and be helped to the finish line. That requires not eliminating the unions that represent them but keeping the pressure on the unions and the politicians to create an environment where everyone can agree that our public school teachers can sit down once in a while—as long as they are committed to running the race and to being accountable for where they and the children entrusted to them finish.

Acknowledgments

As the source list that follows indicates, 152 people were interviewed for this book and allowed their names to be used. An additional 56 sources were not comfortable being cited by name. In all cases, people on all sides of the difficult issues I have attempted to explain in *Class Warfare* were generous with their time even though they typically had little of it to spare, and often despite my pestering them after hours or on weekends. The prime example of that cooperation may be American Federation of Teachers president Randi Weingarten. I may have spent more time with her than with any other source, over meals, on the phone and in animated e-mail conversations. I doubt that Ms. Weingarten and the others whose time I took will think I got everything right from their perspective, but I know that I could not have gotten any of it right without their cooperation. I owe them great thanks.

My interest in school reform began with an article about New York's Rubber Rooms that I wrote for *The New Yorker* in 2009. *New Yorker* editor David Remnick encouraged my return to magazine writing and provided terrific guidance in making the piece work, as did Katherine Stirling, a brilliant features editor at the magazine. Also, Tim Farrington, *a New Yorker* fact checker, was responsible for an important nugget of reporting in the article, something that the *New Yorker*'s rules did not allow me to credit him for in the piece (so I am doing it here). He, not I, tracked down the woman who had been sent to the Rubber Room for being drunk in class, and whom the United Federation of Teachers featured on its website as having been targeted only because she was a senior teacher with a high salary. This enabled me to speak with her and add her powerful quotes to the article and to this book.

Nearly a year after the Rubber Room article, my interest in Race to the Top and how it marked a coming-out party of sorts for the growing education reform network became an article in the *New York Times Magazine*. That could not have happened without the encouragement and fine editing of *New York Times* managing editor Jill Abramson and magazine features editor Vera Titunik.

This book also benefited from the work of many remarkable journalists at newspapers, magazines, and websites that cover education, particularly *The New York Times*, *The Washington Post*, *The Los Angeles Times*, *Time*, *Newsweek*, *The Atlantic Monthly*, *Education Week*, *The Hechinger Ed Blog*, *Eduwonk* (a blog by Andrew Rotherham), *Gotham Schools*, and Alexander Russo's *This Week in Education* online report. The more I learned about the issues they were covering, the more I grew to respect how well they did their work under the deadline pressure that someone writing a book doesn't face.

At Simon & Schuster several people on this perennially first-class publishing team made this book happen, starting with Alice Mayhew, who continues to be a reporter's ideal editor. Alice somehow supplies the perfect mix of big-picture enthusiasm and attention to the small stuff, page by page. (I still use a page of her edits of an old manuscript of mine for a journalism class I teach.)

Also at Simon & Schuster, Jonathan Karp provided early and important counsel on how to structure this narrative, then made sure that *Class Warfare* was published with S&S's trademark flair and professionalism. My thanks also to Roger Labrie for his sharp editing; to Rachel Bergmann for help in coordinating the publishing and editing process; to the extremely capable and diligent copy editing and production team of copyeditor Cynthia Merman, Mara Lurie, and Larry Pekarek; the design and art team of Akasha Archer and Jackie Seow; and the marketing and publicity team of Rachelle Andujar, Tracey Guest, and Kelly Walsh.

In addition, my friend and agent, Lynn Nesbit, provided great enthusiasm, direction, and counsel. In my own office, Janet Thomson provided key assistance in organizing my life around my day job and this project, in keeping my files straight, and in helping with research, as did Paul Needham, a former student who found materials online whenever I couldn't. Another longtime friend, Chicago journalist James Warren, dutifully read the draft and provided his own characteristically incisive edits and suggestions.

Finally, my wife, Cynthia, never stopped tolerating me and my constant demands that she read and fix multiple drafts. I cannot imagine how I could have done this book (or much of anything else over the last three-plus decades) without her sharp eye, wisdom, encouragement, and love.

DISCLOSURES

Here is some information about me and my relation to the subject matter and people in *Class Warfare* that might be interesting or useful to readers. I don't think it affected how I reported this book, but readers might want to know it in order to make their own decisions:

- I attended New York City public schools through junior high school, then went to Deerfield Academy, a private school in Massachusetts, as a scholarship student.
- My three children attended private schools in New York City.
- During a five-year period when I was not working as a journalist, my wife and I contributed to the 2006 Senate campaign of Hillary Clinton and the 2008 presidential campaign of Barack Obama. (We contributed to other candidates during that time, but none who have been involved in education issues.)
- My son teaches at a New York charter school, although I have never met or spoken with anyone associated with the school, do not write about the school in this book, and had nothing to do with his getting the job.
- Joel Klein and I have several close friends in common and have seen each other at many social events hosted by those friends. In addition, the company where Klein took a senior executive position after resigning as New York City's schools chancellor—News Corporation, whose chairman Rupert Murdoch is an ardent proponent of education reform—was an investor in Journalism Online, the company I co-founded and run. However, News Corporation had sold its investment, at a profit, by the time this book was written.

Sources

All sources were interviewed by the author. Their titles or affiliations are given for the time during which they were interviewed and/or the periods about which they were interviewed.

Abrevaya, Sandra—Office of Public Affairs, U.S. Department of Education

Adams, Patricia (pseudonym)—teacher sent to Rubber Room after alcohol abuse incident at Stuyvesant High School

Ali, Russlynn—assistant secretary for civil rights, U.S. Department of Education

Alter, Jonathan—columnist and senior editor, *Newsweek* magazine

Anagnostopoulos, Photo—chief of operations, New York City Department of Education

Anderson, Monique—parent of student at Harlem Success

Andrew, Seth—founder and superintendent, Democracy Prep Public Schools

Barone, Charles—director of federal policy, Democrats for Education Reform; former staff adviser to Congressman George Miller of California

Bennet, Michael—United States senator from Colorado

Bennett, William—former secretary of education

Berkeley, Carlton—speaker at New York City co-location hearing, February 22, 2010

Bersin, Alan—former superintendent of public education, San Diego; currently commissioner of customs and border protection, U.S. Department of Homeland Security

Best, Michael—general counsel, New York City Department of Education

Bloomberg, Michael—mayor of New York City

Bredesen, Phil—governor of Tennessee

Broad, Eli—philanthropist, Eli and Edythe Broad Foundation

Brodsky, David—general counsel, Office of Labor Relations, New York City Department of Education

Burgess-Harper, Kayrol—acting principal, PS 149, Manhattan

Bush, Jeb—former governor of Florida

Cain, Alice—former staff adviser to Congressman George Miller of California

Camara, Karim—member, New York State Assembly

Canada, Geoffrey—founder and CEO, Harlem Children's Zone

Cantrell, LaToya—president, Broadmoor Improvement Association, New Orleans

Carlson, Margaret—friend of Michael Bloomberg and Joel Klein; columnist for Bloomberg News

Carroll, Tom—president, National Commission on Teaching and America's Future

Casserly, Michael—executive director, Council of the Great City Schools

Cerf, Christopher—deputy chancellor, New York City Department of Education; commissioner, New Jersey Department of Education (since 2011)

Chilcott, Lesley—producer, *Waiting for Superman*

Clements, Jean—president, Hillsborough Classroom Teachers Association, Hillsborough County, Florida

Colvin, Richard Lee—director, Hechinger Institute, Columbia University Teachers College

Considine, J. C.—director of board and media relations, Massachusetts Department of Education

Costrell, Robert—professor, Department of Education Reform, University of Arkansas (public employee pension expert)

Cunningham, Peter—assistant secretary, U.S. Department of Education

Curry, Ravenel Boykin, IV—co-founder, Democrats for Education Reform

Daly, Timothy—president, New Teacher Project

Darling-Hammond, Linda—Charles E. Ducommun Professor of Education, Stanford University

De Costa, Dennis—lawyer, New York City Department of Education, Teacher Performance Unit

Donohue, Diane—president, Delaware State Teachers Association

Duncan, Arne—U.S. secretary of education

Edelman, Jonah—founder, Stand for Children

Einhorn, David—founder and president, Greenlight Capital; major donor to Democrats for Education Reform

Elia, MaryEllen—superintendent, Hillsborough County (Florida) Public Schools

Emanuel, Rahm—chief of staff to the president of the United States; mayor-elect of Chicago

Farace, Meredith—staff analyst, Race to the Top, U.S. Department of Education

Farr, Steven—former TFA teacher in Texas; chief knowledge officer (in charge of training), Teach For America

Feinberg, Kenneth—special master, BP Deepwater Horizon Disaster Victim Compensation Fund; consultant to Randi Weingarten

Felch, Jason—reporter, *Los Angeles Times*

Felder, Susan—principal, PS 40, Manhattan

Finney, Mara Lynn—Harlem Success Academy parent

Forte, Anne—Press Office, New York City Department of Education

Garcia, Daysi—principal, PS 65, Brooklyn, New York

Gates, Bill—co-chair, Bill & Melinda Gates Foundation

Gates, Melinda—co-chair, Bill & Melinda Gates Foundation

Goldner, Courtney—former TFA teacher in Arizona; TFA staff member and program director (New York district training liaison)

Gordon, Robert—executive associate director, White House Office of Management and Budget; former senior fellow, Center for American Progress; former senior adviser to Chancellor Joel Klein, New York City Department of Education

Greenblatt, Joel—founder, Gotham Capital; co-founder and board chair, Harlem Success Academy network

Gribbon, Francis—deputy commissioner for public information, New York City Fire Department

Guggenheim, Davis—writer and director, *Waiting for Superman*

Hamilton, Sarah—press secretary to Los Angeles mayor Antonio Villaraigosa

Haycock, Kati—president, Education Trust

Hegarty, Steven—communications officer, Hillsborough County (Florida) Public Schools

Higginbottom, Heather—deputy director, White House Office of Management and Budget; former deputy director, White House Domestic Policy Office; former deputy issues director, Obama '08

Huffman, Kevin—executive vice president, Teach For America

Hughes, Robert—president, New Visions for Public Schools

Isaacson, Walter—CEO, the Aspen Institute; board chair, Teach For America

Jaime, Mattias—researcher, Center for Responsive Politics

Johanek, Michael—professor, University of Pennsylvania Graduate School of Education; vetter in Race to the Top

Johnson, Susan—professor, Harvard University Graduate School of Education

Johnston, Michael—former TFA teacher in Greenville, Mississippi; co-founder, New Leaders for New Schools; member, Colorado State Senate

Jones, Brian—teacher at PS 30 in East Harlem and union activist

Jones, Marie—assistant principal, PS 149, Manhattan

Jupp, Brad—special adviser, Department of Education secretary Arne Duncan; former senior adviser to then–Denver schools superintendent Michael Bennet

Kahan, Richard—founder and CEO, Urban Assembly

Kahlenberg, Richard—senior fellow, Century Foundation; author of *Tough Liberal*

Kamras, Jason—chief of human capital, District of Columbia Public Schools

Kane, Thomas—professor, Harvard University Graduate School of Education; deputy director of education, Bill & Melinda Gates Foundation

Kenny, Deborah—chief executive, Harlem Village Academies

King, John, Jr.—senior deputy commissioner, New York State Department of Education

Klein, Joel—chancellor, New York City Department of Education

Kopp, Wendy—founder and CEO, Teach For America

Kudlow, Mark—spokesman, Florida Education Association

Langone, Kenneth—co-founder, Home Depot, major contributor to Democrats for Education Reform; board member, Harlem Children's Zone

Lasher, Micah—lobbyist for the New York City Department of Education, then for the City of New York

Lenker, Lydia—press secretary for the Governor Phil Bredesen of Tennessee

Levin, Dave—co-founder, Knowledge Is Power Program (KIPP); superintendent, KIPP New York

Lippert, Jerri Lynn—chief academic officer, Pittsburgh Board of Education

Lombardi, Anthony—principal, PS/IS 49, Middle Village, Queens

Markell, Jack—governor of Delaware

Marquis, Julie—deputy metro editor, *Los Angeles Times*

Martin, Carmel—assistant secretary for planning, evaluation, and policy development, U.S. Department of Education; former general counsel and chief education adviser to Senator Edward Kennedy

Miller, George—member of Congress from California

Miller, Matt—*Washington Post* columnist; consultant to McKinsey & Company

Montero, Vincent—construction union member present at New York City co-location hearing on February 22, 2010

Morgan, Barbara—Press Office, New York City Department of Education

Moskowitz, Eva—founder, Harlem Success Academy charter network (now called Success Charter Network); former member, New York City Council

Mulgrew, Michael—president, United Federation of Teachers

Orange-Jones, Kira—TFA coordinator, New Orleans

Ostrin, Steve—inhabitant of Brooklyn Rubber Room

Parker, Erin—science teacher, Madison, Wisconsin

Parker, Kevin—New York state senator from Brooklyn

Pastorek, Paul—superintendent of education, Louisiana

Petry, John—co-founder, Democrats for Education Reform; board member, Harlem Success Charter Network

Phillips, Vicki—director of education, College Ready in the United States program, Bill & Melinda Gates Foundation

Powell, Michael—assistant to the president for communications, American Federation of Teachers

Ravitch, Diane—author of twenty-four books on the history of education; former assistant secretary, U.S. Department of Education

Reid, Jessica—former TFA teacher in the Bronx; leadership resident (assistant principal), Harlem Success Academy I

Rhee, Michelle—founder and CEO, StudentsFirst; former chancellor of Washington, D.C., school system; former TFA teacher in Baltimore

Riley, William—director of communications, United Federation of Teachers

Robinson, Thomasina—inhabitant of Manhattan Rubber Room

Romero, Gloria—Democrats for Education Reform, California

Roosevelt, Mark—former Pittsburgh Public Schools superintendent

Rosen, Amy—president and CEO, Network for Teaching Entrepreneurship; education adviser to Newark mayor Cory Booker; former education consultant to the Bloomberg administration; former chief operating officer, New Visions for New Schools

Rotherham, Andrew—education consultant, Bellwether Education Partners; blogger, Eduwonk; member of President Clinton's education policy staff

Ruby, Alan—professor, University of Pennsylvania Graduate School of Education; vetter in Race to the Top

Saltzman, David—executive director, Robin Hood Foundation

Sardoff, Karen—New York City Department of Education, Office of Labor Relations

Scheiner, Brandi—inhabitant of Manhattan Rubber Room

Schnur, Jon—chairman and co-founder, New Leaders for New Schools; former adviser to Education Secretary Arne Duncan

Schumer, Charles—U.S. senator from New York

Sedlis, Jenny—director of public affairs, Harlem Success Academy Network

Shannon, Mary—sixth-grade social studies teacher, PS/IS 49, Middle Village, Queens

Shaw, Greg—senior adviser for strategic partnerships, Bill & Melinda Gates Foundation

Shelton, James—assistant deputy secretary, U.S. Department of Education

Siegel, Jay—arbitrator in New York City teacher dismissal case

Silver, Sheldon—speaker of the New York State Assembly

Smikle, Basil—candidate for New York State Senate in 2010 Democratic Primary; policy analyst

Smith, Brenda—president, American Federation of Teachers, Colorado affiliate

Smith, Craig—member, New York State Senate (through 2010)

Song, Jason—reporter, *Los Angeles Times*

Steele, David—chief information and technology officer and director for empowering effective teachers (the Gates grant project), Hillsborough County (Florida) Public Schools

Stein, Gideon—board member, Harlem Success Charter Network; board member, Future Is Now Schools (formerly Green Dot Public Schools)

Steiner, David—commissioner, New York State Department of Education

Tarka, John—president, Pittsburgh Federation of Teachers

Tilson, Whitney—co-founder, Democrats for Education Reform; blogger on education reform issues

Tisch, Merryl—chancellor, New York State Board of Regents

Usdin, Sarah—former TFA teacher in Baton Rouge, Louisiana; former TFA coordinator for Louisiana; head of New Schools for New Orleans

Valtchev, Ivan—inhabitant of Manhattan Rubber Room

Van Roekel, Dennis—president, National Education Association

Villaraigosa, Antonio—mayor of Los Angeles

Walsh, Patrick—United Federation of Teachers representative, PS 149, Manhattan

Weingarten, Randi—president, American Federation of Teachers

Weisberg, Daniel—general counsel, New Teacher Project; former head of labor relations, New York City Department of Education

Weiss, Joanne—chief of staff and former head of Race to the Top, U.S. Department of Education

White, John—deputy chancellor, New York City Department of Education

Wilkins, Amy—former executive director, Democrats for Education Reform

Williams, Chris—public affairs staff member, Bill & Melinda Gates Foundation

Williams, Joe—executive director, Democrats for Education Reform

Wolter, Celeste—fund-raiser, Smikle for State Senate (New York)

Wynn, Bernice—mother of Tiana Wynn and two children at a public school

Wynn, DeJuan—father of Tiana Wynn and two children at a public school

Wynn, Tiana—student at Harlem Success Academy I

Young, Lucius—network leader (including PS 149), New York City Department of Education

DESCRIPTION OF SOURCES WHO
REQUESTED NOT TO BE NAMED:

Eighteen present or former teachers at the Harlem Success Charter Network
Eleven inhabitants of the Rubber Room
Three friends of Joel Klein
Three vetters in Race to the Top
Three National Education Association officers or delegates
Three staff members in the Department of Education
Three staff members of local New York City elected officials
Two staff members working for Democratic members of Congress
Two friends of Jon Schnur
Two members of the White House staff
Two staff members working for Republican members of Congress
Two veteran New York City Department of Education officials
One staff member of New York State Teachers United
One officer of the United Federation of Teachers

Notes

Because efforts were made to make sources apparent throughout the text, this section is more limited than it would otherwise be. Source references are listed below only for material for which it is not obvious from the text what or whom the source is, or where it is not made clear in the text that the author relied on the reporting of others. Each name listed means that one or more interviews were conducted with that person.

References are not listed for unambiguous statements of fact, such as a date or an election result, nor are they listed if the material is obviously taken from a public event or public records, such as a budget, a union contract, or the transcript of congressional testimony. Similarly, if the text quotes from a television program or a newspaper article the reference is not cited here if the text makes the source of the article and the date clear.

When multiple sources are cited, they are listed in order of their importance. When the information is significant but in dispute, I have signaled those disputes in the text.

THE RACE

Oval Office meeting: Arne Duncan, Jon Schnur, Heather Higginbottom.

Schnur background: Jon Schnur.

Gore speech: Jon Schnur; Katherine Q. Seelye, "Gore Dangles Teacher Raises, but Attaches Conditions, Too," *New York Times*, May 6, 2000.

Schnur experience with Kerry: Jon Schnur, Heather Higginbottom.

Obama legislation: Senate Bill 2441, introduced March 16, 2006.

Yepsen article: "No Music to the Ears," *Des Moines Register*, February 12, 2007.

Schnur and Higginbottom present education reform plan to Obama: Jon Schnur, Heather Higginbottom.

Materials Obama reviewed: The author read them.

Miller position and Miller-Schnur conversation: George Miller, Jon Schnur, Alice Cain.

Weingarten background: Randi Weingarten.

Weingarten "would start confiding to friends": Randi Weingarten and two of her friends who asked not to be named.

JUICY WORDS

Jessica Reid's day and background: Author was present; Jessica Reid.

Shortcomings of teacher Reid decided to replace: Jessica Reid, Jenny Sedlis. (The teacher declined to comment.)

Setup and logistics of building that houses Harlem Success Academy I and PS 149: author's visits; Harlem Success Academy I charter application and renewal application.

Costs at Harlem Success and PS 149: Data supplied by the New York City Department of Education and by Harlem Success, including audited accounts provided by Harlem Success.

Teacher attendance records at the two schools: Supplied by the New York City Department of Education.

Test scores: Available at New York City Department of Education website.

Background of Kayrol Burgess-Harper: Kayrol Burgess-Harper, Lucius Young.

Practices and procedures at PS 149: Burgess-Harper, Marie Jones, Lucius Young.

THE EPIPHANIES

Reid experience at TFA in the Bronx: Jessica Reid; review of e-mails and excerpts of a diary and blog she maintained during that time.

Rhee experience in Baltimore: Michelle Rhee; the author also relied on *The Bee Eater*, an excellent biography of Rhee by Richard Whitmire (Jossey-Bass, 2011).

Levin Houston experiences: Dave Levin, Wendy Kopp; the author also relied on Jay Mathews's excellent story of the founding of KIPP, *Work Hard, Be Nice* (Algonquin Books, 2009), for much of this account and would not have known many of the right questions to ask Levin about his early teaching years had he not read Mathews's book first.

Sarah Usdin background and early experiences teaching: Sarah Usdin, Wendy Kopp, Walter Isaacson.

Michael Johnston background: Michael Johnston. Johnston wrote a memoir of his years teaching in Mississippi, *In the Deep Heart's Core* (Grove Press, 2002).

Data on education spending: U.S. Department of Education, National Center for Education Statistics.

Rubber Room: Much of this information is taken from my article in the *New Yorker*, August 31, 2009. My thanks to editors David Remnick and Katherine Stirling and fact checker Tim Farrington for their enormous help.

"BE OBEDIENT. BE GOOD. KEEP YOUR MOUTH SHUT."

Background on Shanker: The author relied heavily on Richard Kahlenberg's seminal biography of Albert Shanker, *Tough Liberal* (Columbia University Press, 2007). Anecdotes from Shanker's early days, such as his having been forced to watch for student shoplifters, are taken from this book. The author also interviewed Kahlenberg, who provided additional background material.

Comparison of teachers' salaries and the wages of car washers: Kahlenberg, *Tough Liberal*, then checked by the author.

Laws regarding pregnant women or tenure and the general treatment of teachers before the establishment of strong unions: The author relied on *New York Times* archives, the history section of the websites of the United Federation of Teachers, the Washington Teachers' Union, and the National Education Association. I also used two books that recount the history of teachers' unions: *Why Teachers Organized* by Wayne J. Urban (Detroit, MI: Wayne State University Press, 1982); and *Blackboard Unions: The AFT and NEA, 1900–1980* by Marjorie Murphy (Ithaca, NY: Cornell University Press, 1992). Whenever a law or regulation is mentioned, the author checked the original statute.

First New York City teachers' union contract: Whenever a union contract is mentioned, the author read the contract.

Ocean Hill–Brownsville dispute: Much of this account relies on Kahlenberg's *Tough Liberal*, although it is supplemented by a review of articles reporting these events in the *New York Times* and *New York Post*.

Shanker calling for four-day workweek: Kahlenberg, *Tough Liberal*, then checked by author's review of the archives of Shanker's "Where We Stand" *New York Times* columns.

Teachers' unions' pensions: Andrew Rotherham, Joel Klein, Robert Costrell, (who provided charts and data from numerous articles he has written and pointed me to the Missouri pension law change that counted the cost of health insurance as salary for the purpose of computing a teacher's pension).

Teachers' unions' increasing political influence: *New York Times* and *Washington Post* articles published during this time; Kahlenberg, *Tough Liberal*; and *The NEA and AFT: Teacher Unions in Power and Politics* by Charlene Haar, Myron Lieberman, and Leo Troy (Pro Active Publishers, 1994).

"The only honest thing to do would be to designate Shanker as [Schools] Chancellor: A. H. Raskin, "Shanker's Great Leap," *New York Times Magazine*, September 9, 1973.

"IF AN UNFRIENDLY FOREIGN POWER HAD ATTEMPTED . . ."

President Reagan's reaction to *A Nation At Risk*: Accounts published at the time in the *New York Times* and *Washington Post*; William Bennett; Kahlenberg, *Tough Liberal*.

Author's New York City school experience: This was at PS 104 in Queens.

50/40,000/130,000 dilemma: I first came upon this reference in the white paper "Creating Cover and Constructing Capacity" by Patrick McGuinn (American Enterprise Institute, 2010).

Clinton debates Shanker: "Arkansas Governor Defends Tests in Debate with A.F.T.'s Shanker," *Education Week*, April 10, 1985.

Shanker speeches and columns about education reform: Although I checked each of these in a Shanker archive maintained by New York State United Teachers, I first became aware of this material in reading Kahlenberg.

Two-thirds more per student: This is extrapolated from a statistical table published by the U.S. Department of Education's National Center for Education Statistics.

A "HOPELESSLY NAÏVE" THESIS

Kopp background: Kopp interviews, as well as her memoir *One Day, All Children*... (Public Affairs, 2001), from which much of the narrative around her thesis and the startup of Teach For America is drawn. All accounts in Kopp's book were checked, wherever possible and relevant, with third parties, such as people involved in the startup of Teach For America. In addition, I read Kopp's Princeton thesis.

Statistics on Teach For America alumni: Provided by Teach For America, then spot-checked independently.

A GOVERNOR AND A PRESIDENT TAKE CENTER STAGE

White House/Governors Education Summit: All documents issued by the conference and the White House; multiple newspaper accounts at the time, particularly from the *Washington Post* and the *New York Times*; William Bennett.

Clinton "Hula Hoop" quote: Edward B. Fiske, "Meeting on Education Starts Today in Virginia," *New York Times*, September 27, 1989.

Clinton "accountability" quote: Bernard Weinraub, "Hope and Dissent Blend in Education Conference," *New York Times*, September 28, 1989.

Clinton quote that "this is the first time in the history of our country..." Edward B. Fiske, "Remedial Work," *New York Times*, October 1, 1989.

PAYROLL TO PAYROLL

Further accounts of Teach For America startup: Wendy Kopp, Whitney Tilson, Sarah Usdin, Michelle Rhee; Kopp, *One Day, All Children*...; Kopp's thesis.

LIGHTING UP THE CAPITOL SWITCHBOARD

Congressman Miller's 1994 legislative effort: George Miller, Alice Cain, Andrew Rotherham, Jon Schnur, Carmel Martin; *Congressional Record*.

THE BACKLASH

Farr background and account of Farr's reaction to Darling-Hammond article: Steven Farr, Wendy Kopp, Linda Darling-Hammond.

SCHOOLYARD CLASSROOM

Levin prepares for Bronx KIPP: Dave Levin; visit to the site; Mathews, *Work Hard, Be Nice*.

Hatching of KIPP idea in Houston: Dave Levin and Wendy Kopp; Mathews, *Work Hard, Be Nice*.

Board of Education *Circular*: A veteran education department human resources official; Anthony Lombardi; the document itself.

THE NETWORK

Tilson background: Whitney Tilson, Wendy Kopp, John Petry, Boykin Curry, Dave Levin, Amy Wilkins, Jon Schnur.

Schnur and Johnston meet: John Schnur, Michael Johnston.

Account of New Leaders for New Schools: Jon Schnur; Michael Johnston; Eli Broad; New Leaders for New Schools published materials.

"DON'T WORRY; IT'S JUST A PARENT"

Klein first days as chancellor: Joel Klein, two longtime Department of Education staffers who wished to remain anonymous, Christopher Cerf, Dan Weisberg, Margaret Carlson, Wendy Kopp, Eli Broad, three friends of Klein's who asked not to be named.

Bloomberg's choice of Klein: Michael Bloomberg, Joel Klein, Margaret Carlson.

Klein-Bersin conversations: Joel Klein and Alan Bersin.

Kopp encouraged by Klein's plans: Wendy Kopp.

Klein encounter with Rhee: Joel Klein, Michelle Rhee, Wendy Kopp, Daniel Weisberg.

Klein, Broad involvement: Eli Broad, Joel Klein; public documents; documents and reports of Broad Foundation.

"THE UNION WON'T ALLOW IT"

Klein encounter with his human resources department: Joel Klein, two longtime Department of Education officials who asked not to be named, Michelle Rhee, Thomas Kane.

Klein relationship with Lombardi and Weingarten: Joel Klein, Anthony Lombardi, Randi Weingarten, Eli Broad; review of all Lombardi e-mails to Klein.

Klein negotiation with Weingarten: Joel Klein, Randi Weingarten, Christopher Cerf, Daniel Weisberg, Michael Bloomberg, a UFT official who asked not to be named.

Gates Foundation decision to fund New York City small schools program and Bill Gates's relationship with Klein: Bill Gates, Melinda Gates, Vicki Phillips, Joel Klein.

Klein encounter with principal: Joel Klein, Christopher Cerf.

"HOW COULD THE DEMOCRATS BE AGAINST THIS?"

Klein relationship with Jeb Bush: Jeb Bush, Joel Klein.

SEEING GEORGE SOROS'S APARTMENT

Formation of Democrats for Education Reform and encounter with Barack Obama: Whitney Tilson, Boykin Curry, John Petry, Joel Greenblatt, Amy Wilkins, Joe Williams; inspection of various Tilson and DFER e-mails.

NEW YORK REALITIES

Jessica Reid's frustration over school supplies: Jessica Reid; review of her e-mails.

Weingarten and Bloomberg talks: Randi Weingarten, Christopher Cerf, Daniel Weisberg, Joel Klein, Michael Bloomberg.

UFT expenditures: The union's financial reports as filed with the U.S. Department of Labor.

New York City's negotiations with Weingarten: Randi Weingarten, Daniel Weisberg, Joel Klein, David Brodsky, Michael Bloomberg.

Weingarten bragged about her access to Bloomberg: Daniel Weisberg, Christopher Cerf, Joel Klein, Randi Weingarten.

"OUR PARTY HAS GOT TO WAKE UP ON THIS"

Democrats for Education Reform continued growth and party with Obama: Whitney Tilson, Joe Williams, Boykin Curry, John Petry; review of Tilson e-mails.

CREATING A NEW SCHOOL SYSTEM THE HARD WAY

New Orleans schools pre- and post-Katrina: Sarah Usdin, Paul Pastorek, Wendy Kopp, Walter Isaacson; Kopp, *One Day, All Children . . .* ; Stacey Childress and James Weber, "Public Education in New Orleans: Pursuing Systemic Change Through Entrepreneurship," *Harvard Business Review,* March 31, 2010 (many of the statistics cited come from this excellent study).

THE POL AND THE MONEYMEN

Moskowitz City Council hearings: Eva Moskowitz, Randi Weingarten; articles in the *New York Times,* the *Post,* and the *Daily News.*

Moskowitz meetings with Petry and Greenblatt: Eva Moskowitz, John Petry, Joel Greenblatt; author also reviewed economic models prepared by Petry.

MOUNTING EVIDENCE

"Volatility guys" and explanation of research: Thomas Kane, Robert Gordon.

Organization of Hamilton Project: Robert Gordon, Thomas Kane, Jon Schnur.

MORE MONEY, NO HASSLES

2006 negotiation with UFT: Joel Klein, Daniel Weisberg, Randi Weingarten.

BUILDING HARLEM SUCCESS

Account of opening of Harlem Success: Eva Moskowitz, John Petry, Joel Greenblatt, Jenny Sedlis; newsclips from the *New York Times*, the *Post*, and the *Daily News*; author's review of Moskowitz e-mails.

Fight in Albany over charter cap: Eva Moskowitz, Joel Klein, Sheldon Silver, a lobbyist for New York City who did not wish to be named.

"THIS IS NOT A SELF-ESTEEM MOVEMENT"

UFT loan to Green Dot: American Federation of Teachers filing with U.S. Department of Labor for period covering August 1, 2008, through July 31, 2009.

MONEY MEETS DATA

Gates Foundation deliberations and Gates's meeting at Pierre Hotel: Vicki Phillips, Bill Gates, Thomas Kane, Robert Gordon. Note: While all four were present at the meeting, none took contemporaneous notes; the material in quotes is based on their recollections and, therefore, is unlikely to be a verbatim account.

$45,000 WELL-SPENT

Progress of Democrats for Education Reform: Joe Williams, John Petry, Boykin Curry; review of internal e-mails.

"FACELESS BUREAUCRACY"

Rhee's first days on the job: Whitmore, *The Bee Eater*; Michelle Rhee, two colleagues of Rhee who asked not to be named, Joel Klein; *Washington Post* and *Washington Times* articles reporting these events contemporaneously.

RHEE'S CHOICE: YOUR UNION OR $130,000

Rhee contract offer: Michelle Rhee, Randi Weingarten. Note: Weingarten disputes the characterization that she did not "let the offer be put up for a vote" as unfair. She says that it is standard in labor-management negotiations that a union does not send a contract to its members for a vote unless the union's leaders endorse the proposal.

TURNING AROUND THE USS *GATES*

Gates Foundation deliberations: Bill and Melinda Gates, Vicki Phillips, Chris Williams.

THE NEW DEMOCRATS

Democrats for Education Reform meeting in Denver: Joe Williams, Joel Klein, Jon Schnur, Jonathan Alter; review of DFER internal e-mails; audiotape of the event.

Sharpton fee request and Sharpton controversy: Joe Williams; review of internal DFER e-mails; Joel Klein. Note: Sharpton declined repeated, explicit requests to comment.

TWO RETURNS TO THE CLASSROOM

"When I found Adams to ask her about all of this . . .": I found Adams through the excellent legwork of *New Yorker* fact checker Tim Farrington: see Acknowledgments.

Weingarten called Adams: Randi Weingarten, Patricia Adams.

"WAKE UP, OBAMA JUST TALKED ABOUT YOU"

Rhee watches the debate, falls asleep, then gets calls and e-mails: Michelle Rhee, Amy Rosen.

"INSIDE BASEBALL"

DFER leaders' reaction to Darling-Hammond as transition head and strategy to respond to it: Joe Williams, Charles Barone, Whitney Tilson, Jon Schnur.

"WHAT DO YOU GUYS THINK YOU COULD DO WITH A HUNDRED BILLION?"

First word that $100 billion of stimulus was to go for education, including $15 billion for reform plans: Jon Schnur, Heather Higginbottom, Robert Gordon.

THE CHOSEN FOUR

Clements background and Gates Foundation competition and awards: Jean Clements, David Steele, MaryEllen Elia, Vicki Phillips; Gates Foundation documents.

"THEY'LL DO BACKFLIPS"

Duncan's background: Arne Duncan, Peter Cunningham, Jon Schnur.

Conference call about stimulus money: Jon Schnur, Heather Higginbottom, Robert Gordon, Arne Duncan.

Meetings on Capitol Hill: George Miller, Alice Cain, Jon Schnur, Arne Duncan.

Emanuel had remarked at one point: Arne Duncan, Jon Schnur, Rahm Emanuel.

Drafting Race to the Top legislative provisions: George Miller, Alice Cain, Jon Schnur.

Meeting of school chiefs: Peter Cunningham.

AGREEMENT IN PITTSBURGH

Progress in Pittsburgh: Jerri Lynn Lippert, John Tarka.

Progress in Hillsborough County: Jean Clements, MaryEllen Elia, David Steele.

THE OPPOSITE OF VENTURE CAPITAL

Decisions on framing Race rules and contest: Joanne Weiss, Jon Schnur, Peter Cunningham, two lower-level Department of Education staffers who asked not to be named.

Elaborate process for screening vetters for conflicts: This is spelled out in the Government Accountability Office's Report on the selection of the "peer reviewers."

Gates Foundation gives grants to twenty-four states: Vicki Phillips.

"OUTCOMES, NOT ACHIEVEMENT"

Johnston legislative strategy: Michael Johnston, Brenda Smith. Also, the author examined a notebook Johnston kept of his various drafts and strategies.

"OBFUSCATING THE ISSUE . . . FOOLING THE REVIEWERS"

Wrangling over the lift of the charter cap: Merryl Tisch, John King, Joel Klein, Micah Lasher, David Steiner, Craig Smith, Sheldon Silver, Michael Mulgrew.

SCHOOL REFORM: THE MOVIE

Making of *Waiting for Superman*: Lesley Chilcott, Davis Guggenheim, Geoffrey Canada, Randi Weingarten.

"MY BABY IS READING"

Moskowitz had planned for the hearing and her staff had suggested signs for the parents to bring: Jenny Sedlis, Jessica Reid.

Speeches and other aspects of the two co-location hearings: The author attended both and viewed a videotape of the first one.

GOING OVER TO THE OTHER SIDE

Florida Education Association Diane Ravitch speaking fee: Supplied by Florida Education Association spokesman Mark Kudlow.

A "BAFFLING" ROUND ONE

Louisiana preparation of Race to the Top application: Paul Pastorek, Jon Schnur, Sarah Usdin, Walter Isaacson.

Schnur assured his friends that they should not worry: John Schnur, Michael Johnston, Paul Pastorek, Joe Williams, Charles Barone, Tim Daly, Andrew Rotherham, Sarah Usdin, Michael Johnston.

Schnur wasn't sure: Jon Schnur.

States joining the murder boards: Jon Schnur, Andrew Rotherham, Walter Isaacson, Paul Pastorek, Michael Johnston, Charles Barone, Joe Williams.

Klein refusal to participate: Joel Klein, Merryl Tisch, David Steiner, Michael Mulgrew.

Questions and answers at the presentations: The author viewed videotapes and read transcripts made available by the Department of Education.

Identity of the vetters who questioned Rhee and Pastorek: Knowing this is harder than it might seem. Although Secretary Duncan released the names of the vetters, he refused to identify which vetter vetted which applications; nor were they visible on the videotapes or named in the transcripts. However, Rhee said she remembered the name on the nameplate at the hearing of her most persistent questioner, as did Pastorek. Neither vetter, however, would confirm asking the questions Rhee and Pastorek considered to be the most hostile.

TWO WINNERS

Schnur had to talk Pastorek out of dropping out of the Race: Jon Schnur, Paul Pastorek, Michael Johnston.

Reformers were concerned: Tim Daly, Joe Williams, Charles Barone, Whitney Tilson, Jon Schnur, Joel Klein.

BACK ON THE HORSE IN COLORADO

Johnston and Smith discussions: Michael Johnston and Brenda Smith.

BILLIONAIRES TRAPPED IN AN ELEVATOR

Klein meeting with Robin Hood board: Joel Klein, David Saltzman, Geoffrey Canada.

Meeting at Langone's apartment, including elevator scene: Kenneth Langone, Joe Williams, Geoffrey Canada.

Incident with Senator Kevin Parker: Joe Williams, Kevin Parker.

Incident with Assemblyman Camera: Joe Williams, Karim Camara.

Weingarten told friends and associates: Randi Weingarten, three friends who asked not to be named.

New York team knew the equilibrium had shifted: Joel Klein, Micah Lasher, Merryl Tisch.

"HE MET WITH EVERYONE"

Johnston, Smith negotiations: Michael Johnston and Brenda Smith.

A NEW YORK BREAKTHROUGH—OR MIRAGE?

Tisch, King, Mulgrew negotiations: Merryl Tisch, John King, Joel Klein, Michael Mulgrew, a New York State United Teachers official who asked not to be named.

For Klein it seemed too good to be true: Joel Klein.

THE QUIET REVOLUTION

Idea of "Quiet Revolution" speech: Arne Duncan, Peter Cunningham, Heather Higginbottom.

FROM INSIDE BASEBALL TO PUBLIC ACCOUNTABILITY

Background of *Los Angeles Times* series: Jason Song, Jason Felch, Julie Marquis.

"ARNE, HERE'S THE COLUMN YOU'VE BEEN MISSING"

Duncan deliberations with staff over Round Two scoring: Joanne Weiss, Arne Duncan, Peter Cunningham.

Weiss's frustration: Joanne Weiss.

American Enterprise Institute white paper: "Creating Cover and Constructing Capacity"; Patrick McGuinn, "Assessing the Origins, Evolution, and Impact of Race to the Top" (AEI Online, December 2010).

SOARING DREAMS, STREET-LEVEL POLITICS

Formation of Democracy Builders: Seth Andrew.

RHEE REJECTED

Rhee's unannounced decision to leave, and preliminary fund-raising inquiries: Michelle Rhee, Joe Williams, Joel Klein.

Seed money for Rhee's organization goes through DFER website; Joe Williams, Michelle Rhee.

THE "MUJAHIDEEN" AND THE MODERATES

Schnur's pitch: Jon Schnur, two other people who were at the event but asked not to be named.

Klein's reaction as told to a friend: The friend asked not to be named.

Donations to Rhee's organization: Someone who is directly familiar with the donor list.

Tisch and King reactions to Cathleen Black appointment: Merryl Tisch, John King.

Klein story regarding pension benefit: Joel Klein.

PUNCH, COUNTERPUNCH

Moskowitz plan for Upper West Side Success and Klein's perception of it: Eva Moskowitz, Jenny Sedlis, Joel Klein, Joe Williams, an aide to a local elected official who asked not to be named.

Talk among people in the reform network and some on Duncan's staff and in the White House: Joe Williams, Charles Barone, Jon Schnur, Peter Cunningham, Joanne Weiss (two of whom related conversations that had included members of the White House staff).

Duncan's plans for the $1.25 billion in 2011 incentive money: Peter Cunningham, Robert Gordon, Arne Duncan.

A MARATHON, NOT A SPRINT

New York Times article profiling Erin Parker: Trip Gabriel, "Proposed Cuts Strike Teachers as Attacks on Their Value to Society," March 3, 2011.

Milwaukee average total teacher compensation: This is based on a reading of the contract and a calculation of the costs of health insurance, pensions, sick days, and other benefits.

How raising class size by 10 percent would increase average salaries by over $10,000: My estimated cost of all K–12 salaries and benefits for 2010 is $300 billion. This comes from extrapolating up, conservatively, from the 2007 cost of $273 billion, the last data available from the U.S. Department of Education. The figure is likely to be higher than $300 billion for 2010, but this is a conservative, round number. Reducing the number of teachers 10 percent, from 3 million teachers (also an estimate) to 2.7 million, would yield savings of $30 billion, or 10 percent, and $30 billion distributed in additional salaries to 2.7 million teachers yields salary increases of $11,111.

How investing 3 percent of the current education budget would yield $6,000 per teacher: 3 percent of approximately $600 billion is $18 billion. Divided among 3 million teachers, that would be $6,000 per teacher.

Index

About the Author

Steven Brill is the CEO of Press+, which has created a new business model for journalism to flourish online. He has written feature articles for *The New Yorker* (where he wrote about the "Rubber Rooms" that housed teachers accused of incompetence), *The New York Times Magazine*, and *Time*, and has been a columnist for *Newsweek, Esquire,* and *New York.* He teaches journalism at Yale and founded the Yale Journalism Initiative, which recruits and trains journalists. Brill founded and ran *The American Lawyer* magazine, Court TV, and *Brill's Content* magazine. He is the author of *After: How America Confronted The September 12 Era,* and *The Teamsters.* A graduate of Yale College and Yale Law School, he is married with three children and lives in New York.